C000154389

Education in the Asia-Pacifi
Concerns and Prospects

Volume 57

The purpose of this Series is to meet the needs of those interested in an in-depth analysis of current developments in education and schooling in the vast and diverse Asia-Pacific Region. The Series will be invaluable for educational researchers, policy makers and practitioners, who want to better understand the major issues, concerns and prospects regarding educational developments in the Asia-Pacific region.

The Series complements the Handbook of Educational Research in the Asia-Pacific Region, with the elaboration of specific topics, themes and case studies in greater breadth and depth than is possible in the Handbook.

Topics to be covered in the Series include: secondary education reform; reorientation of primary education to achieve education for all; re-engineering education for change; the arts in education; evaluation and assessment; the moral curriculum and values education; technical and vocational education for the world of work; teachers and teaching in society; organisation and management of education; education in rural and remote areas; and, education of the disadvantaged.

Although specifically focusing on major educational innovations for development in the Asia-Pacific region, the Series is directed at an international audience.

The Series Education in the Asia-Pacific Region: Issues, Concerns and Prospects, and the Handbook of Educational Research in the Asia-Pacific Region, are both publications of the Asia-Pacific Educational Research Association.

Those interested in obtaining more information about the Monograph Series, or who wish to explore the possibility of contributing a manuscript, should (in the first instance) contact the publishers.

Please contact Melody Zhang (e-mail: melodymiao.zhang@springer.com) for submitting book proposals for this series.

More information about this series at http://www.springer.com/series/5888

Dat Bao • Thanh Pham
Editors

Transforming Pedagogies Through Engagement with Learners, Teachers and Communities

 Springer

Editors
Dat Bao
Faculty of Education
Monash University
Clayton, Victoria, Australia

Thanh Pham
Faculty of Education
Monash University
Clayton, Victoria, Australia

ISSN 1573-5397   ISSN 2214-9791   (electronic)
Education in the Asia-Pacific Region: Issues, Concerns and Prospects
ISBN 978-981-16-0059-3   ISBN 978-981-16-0057-9   (eBook)
https://doi.org/10.1007/978-981-16-0057-9

This Springer imprint is published by the registered company Springer Nature Singapore Pte Ltd.
The registered company address is: 152 Beach Road, #21-01/04 Gateway East, Singapore 189721, Singapore

Series Editors Introduction

This important book by Dat Bao and Thanh Pham, on *Transforming Pedagogies through Engagement with Learners, Teachers & Communities,* is the latest book to be published in the long-standing Springer Book Series 'Education in the Asia Pacific Region: Issues, Concerns and Prospects'. The first volume in this Springer series was published in 2002, with this edited book by Bao and Pham being the 57th volume to be published to date.

Transforming Pedagogies through Engagement with Learners, Teachers & Communities explores ways of transforming pedagogies. After an introductory overview chapter, the book consists of sixteen chapters, divided into three sections, which contain chapters that examine ways of various transforming pedagogies: through student voice and experience; through teacher beliefs and knowledge; and through community engagement. The chapters explore the various ways in which pedagogies connect with various stakeholders and partners involved in the education enterprise.

The main target audience are classroom teachers and educators involved with conducting professional development courses. The book will also be of interest to researchers and policy makers with a keen interest in exploring, and better understanding, the main ways in which, and the reasons why, pedagogies are currently going through a major period of transformation.

In terms of the Springer Book Series in which this volume is published, the various topics dealt with in the series are wide ranging and varied in coverage, with an emphasis on cutting-edge developments, best practices and education innovations for development. Topics examined in the series include environmental education and education for sustainable development; the interaction between technology and education; the reform of primary, secondary and teacher education; innovative approaches to education assessment; alternative education; most effective ways to achieve quality and highly relevant education for all; active ageing through active learning; case studies of education and schooling systems in various countries in the region; cross country and cross cultural studies of education and schooling; and the sociology of teachers as an occupational group, to mention just a few. More information about the book series is available at http://www.springer.com/series/5888

All volumes in this series aim to meet the interests and priorities of a diverse education audience including researchers, policy makers and practitioners; tertiary students; teachers at all levels within education systems; and members of the public who are interested in better understanding cutting-edge developments in education and schooling in Asia-Pacific.

The main reason why this series has been devoted exclusively to examining various aspects of education and schooling in the Asia-pacific region is that this is a particularly challenging region. It is renowned for its size, diversity and complexity, whether it be geographical, socio-economic, cultural, political or developmental. Education and schooling in countries throughout the region impact on every aspect of people's lives, including employment, labour force considerations, education and training, cultural orientation, and attitudes and values. Asia and the Pacific is home to some 63% of the world's population of 7 billion. Countries with the largest populations (China, 1.4 billion; India, 1.3 billion) and the most rapidly growing megacities are to be found in the region, as are countries with relatively small populations (Bhutan, 755,000; the island of Niue, 1,600).

Levels of economic and sociopolitical development vary widely, with some of the richest countries (such as Japan) and some of the poorest countries on earth (such as Bangladesh). Asia contains the largest number of poor of any region in the world, the incidence of those living below the poverty line remaining as high as 40 percent in some countries in Asia. At the same time, many countries in Asia are experiencing a period of great economic growth and social development. However, inclusive growth remains elusive, as does growth that is sustainable and does not destroy the quality of the environment. The growing prominence of Asian economies and corporations, together with globalisation and technological innovation, are leading to long-term changes in trade, business and labour markets, to the sociology of populations within (and between) countries. There is a rebalancing of power, centred on Asia and the Pacific region, with the Asian Development Bank in Manila declaring that the twenty-first century will be 'the Century of Asia Pacific'.

We know from feedback received from numerous education researchers, policy makers and practitioners, worldwide, that this book series makes a useful contribution to knowledge sharing about cutting-edge developments concerning education and schooling in Asia Pacific.

Any readers of this or other volumes in the series who have an idea for writing or co-writing their own book (or editing/co-editing a book) on any aspect of education and/or schooling, that is relevant to the region, are enthusiastically encouraged to approach the series editors either direct, or through Springer, to publish their own volume in the series, since we are always willing to assist perspective authors shape their manuscripts in ways that make them suitable for publication.

School of Education, RMIT University,   Rupert Maclean
Melbourne, Australia
College of Education, Zhejiang   Lorraine Symaco
University, Hangzhou, China
23 December 2020

Introduction: Exploring Ways of Transforming Pedagogies

Scope of the Book

This book focuses on how pedagogy connects with its stakeholders. It does so for an explicit reason, that is, to utilise the contribution of stakeholders for improving the quality of pedagogy. The discourse on transformation of pedagogy has highlighted three domains that influence the way we teach, namely the broader social context, institutional context, and teaching context (see, for example, Carr & Fraser, 2014). In other words, instruction is seen as being shaped by society, institute, and teachers. The book, however, does not wish to restate this structure but chooses to see the transformation of pedagogy in a slightly different way. It looks at the micro level into the everyday work of individuals who are direct stakeholders of pedagogy, namely students, teachers, and the community who are directly relevant to instructional efforts. The structure of the book will fall into three distinctive sections as a result of the decision to work with the above-mentioned groups.

This introduction tries *not* to summarise what is already presented in the abstract of every chapter or the chapters themselves. Neither does the chapter repeat the wording of any published authors, including the words of the chapter contributors in this book. Instead, it interprets the new angle of each contribution that has not been stated by chapter authors. To do so, this discussion, first of all, justifies the reason why the proposed pedagogy in the book is less common and thus worth reading into. Secondly, this introduction interacts with each chapter with our own comments or observations, as well as connects the chapters to allow different voices to speak to each other in their shared effort to improve pedagogies.

We decided to place pedagogy in the pluralistic form to embrace a variety of traditions and education levels which the authors have touched on, namely early childhood education, secondary education, vocational education, and higher education. We also decided that since this book does not deal particularly with educational content, but with pedagogies, subject matters will vary a great deal, ranging from first and second language education to other instructional content with connection to various curricula, policies, and contexts. Thirteen of the sixteen contributing chapters are comprehensive reports of empirical studies with optimal benefit for pedagogy in mind, while the remaining three chapters are in-depth reviews of significant issues in the field. The ultimate aim of the volume is to collect and showcase a diverse range of efforts in making academic instruction work better.

Target Audience

The book serves readers who are teachers with interest in extended pedagogical practice, students who write theses/dissertations about education in the Asia-Pacific region, and educators who conduct professional development teachers/instructors in the Asia-Pacific region, including teachers of English. Out of 17 chapters in the book, 3 are related to English language teaching (i.e. Chaps. 5, 7, and 14) while the rest are about a wide range of contents, including different types of literacy practice (Chaps. 1, 6, and 16), learning styles (Chap. 2), culture in education (Chaps. 3 and 4), early childhood education (Chap. 8), assessment (Chap. 9), teacher agency and development (Chaps. 10 and 11), science education (Chap. 12), social media and education (Chap. 13), and parenting and education (Chap. 15). Although the chapters touch on various subject contents and are set in various contexts, they unify in many sociocultural, educational, political ways for the shared purpose of enhancing pedagogies.

The Connection Among the Chapters

All the contributing chapters in this book shared three distinctive features. First of all, the authors demonstrate both individualistic and collective concerns in our immediate working environments. Secondly, we all tap into and draw knowledge from student, teacher, and community resources and perspectives. Thirdly, the common purpose of our investigations is to explore possibilities of how stakeholders can inform pedagogy in ways that might have been overlooked before. To reveal such novel angles, contributors of the book have made efforts to engage with participants, and, through empirical research, build conversations with them, listen to their voices, and learn from their every practice.

Logistically, every set of chapters in the book addresses one common theme, which allows the book to fall into three respective thematic parts. In particular, part one, which contains 6 chapters, discusses the process of engaging with student learning. The first four chapters advocate the utilisation of student's individual strengths, specific learning styles, and cultural resources to revise pedagogy. Such resources, in the meanwhile, can also come from specific genres such as art and literature, as well as regional and world knowledge beyond one's own, as suggested in the subsequent two chapters (Chaps. 5 and 6).

Part two, which has 6 chapters, engages with teacher's practical work. It highlights that reflective experiences in a collaborative, systematic, and well-organized manner can inform pedagogy in exciting ways, as recommended in Chaps. 7 and 8. Teacher agency, including a willingness to create changes and the ability to navigate practice in new directions, is promoted in Chaps. 9 and 10. This includes teachers' self-critical stance through questioning their practice, which is the main ideology expressed in Chaps. 11 and 12.

Part three, which includes 4 chapters, treats educational improvement from a community angle. It addresses questions related to space, meaning, challenges, responsibility, and identity. Specifically, the ability to explore new space, construct new meaning, and confronting new challenges is a shared philosophy in Chaps. 13 and 14. Shared responsibilities and role shifts in educational practice, as promoted in Chap. 15, and being critical of the macro picture in education and how it endangers identity in educational practice, as discussed in Chap. 16, represent other ways of transforming pedagogy.

Selection of Contributing Authors

Chapter contributors in the book are of diverse cultural backgrounds, fields of expertise, education sectors, career stages, and even academic publication experiences. We understand that it would be easy to recruit well-established authors so that, with their already advanced writing competence, the book might be subject to less editing effort. In our philosophy, however, socially inclusive education should nurture not only the need of students but also the less-heard voice of real-world practitioners. In other words, we do not wish to transform pedagogy by opting for the easy path of inviting the privileged academic elite while neglecting new, bright scholars with less opportunity to contribute.

For example, the author of Chap. 8 is an early childhood educator who works in a childcare centre. Every day, she helps children play, tidies rooms, cleans toilets, and has very little time for lunch, which she consumes in the backseat of her car during a short break. The life of a university academic is nothing like this at all. However, listening to her real-world experience and humble knowledge, we learned shining ideas which, in our observation, should stay at the same level of brilliance as ideas offered in any academic seminar at a university. In particular, driven by the everyday work via personal reflection and practical trials, she combines concepts that most highly regarded experts in the field have hardly thought of.

For a long time, educational discourse has so proudly advocated socially inclusive pedagogy (see, for example, Gale, Mills & Cross, 2017), yet hardly have scholars ventured into socially inclusive *construction of* pedagogy, which we think is a serious drawback in education. The book, in a small way, is an equitable response to this realisation. With this in mind, we involved contributors who are early-career researchers, school teachers, and doctoral students for their passionate engagement in the real-world industry. These colleagues own, to adopt Zipin's

(2009, p. 324) words, 'funds of pedagogy' and specific ways of accumulating real-world knowledge. They have witnessed critical events which higher-education researchers might not always have access to. In our view, such voices should be brought together with university research without prejudice.

The discussion begins with an overview of how pedagogy needs to evolve further through more diversification of practice in today's highly changeable context. Secondly, we touch on the diversified ways of understanding the concept of engagement as seen by chapter contributors. Thirdly, we present the structure of the book, that is, how chapters are placed together and what they collectively speak for. Fourthly, we emphasise the essence of what each chapter has to offer; and finally, we make comments where appropriate in an attempt to underscore what we feel further attention is necessary in contemplating the volume content.

Scholarly Efforts in Improving Pedagogies

Over the past decades, innovations in teaching and learning practices have increasingly become a strong focus of almost all educational systems in the Asian Pacific region. However, the implementation process of the innovations is far from a linear process not only due to the need to contest one's teaching repertoire but also, more significantly, due to forces at various levels hindering the process. This is because learning is not an independent variable, and thus cannot simply be borrowed and implemented in all contexts. Rather, learning is a complex construct that is shaped and influenced by many factors such as teaching methods, learning tasks, assessment demands, workload, the culture of students. Among these factors, research evidence reveals that understanding the learning practice of students plays an important role in learning reforms (Broadfoot, 2001; Pham, 2014).

An example illustrating the importance of students' learning culture in educational reforms is Confucian heritage cultures. Confucian values have been found in conflict with Western-based pedagogies in various aspects (Pham, 2014). Since such values stay at the inner layer of student mentality, they are not easily altered or removed. Marzano, Zaffron, Zraik, Robbins, and Yoon (1995) argue that the belief and perception of individuals exist in a paradigm and it would be extremely difficult for external forces to break the culture in this paradigm. There is empirical evidence demonstrating that when implementers are forced to change their inherent values, they tend to reject the reforms (Fullan, 1993). Instead of forcing students to alter their learning culture, it would be a wise strategy for reformers to embed local students' learning practices in the reform (Pham, 2014; Phuong-Mai, 2008).

Taking students' learning values into consideration has been well emphasised in teaching and learning renovations in Western institutions. Educational reforms used to be interpreted by many as bringing innovations from the West to the East. However, recently more and more researchers are supportive of the reverse flow that is to bring the East to the West. The internationalisation of education in

Australian higher education has appealed for consideration of this trend. For many years, Australian education has advocated the need for diversifying and internationalising curricula and pedagogies. Nevertheless, many Australian academics continue to overlook 'cultural others' in their classes. The prevailing pedagogic paradigm remains fairly closed, manipulative (as opposed to facilitative), and principally concerned with the transmission of functionally based knowledge, such as the dominance of lectures as the main form of teaching (Pham & Renshaw, 2015). This leaves relatively little space for students to inject their offerings and construct their voices (Barnett, Parrt, & Coate, 2001). Education needs a conversation among different voices to discover cultural perspectives that are absent in traditional academic narratives. There is a need for developing more open-ended forms of pedagogy to ensure that cultural differences are heard and explored.

The long-lasting dominance of Western practices in curricula and teaching practices globally is due to the concept of the North producing theories and the South borrowing (Alatas, 2006). However, more and more researchers have argued against this inferior stereotype by evidencing that non-Western civilisations have a rich arena of philosophical and ethical-sociopolitical thought (e.g. Alatas, 2006; Goody, 2010; Keane, 2009; Singh, 2009). For example, Chinese teaching practices (for example, action education as proposed by Gu, 2003) have attracted curiosity from Western academics due to their significant contribution to the outstanding performance of Asian students on international tests (White Paper, 2012). India is also widely recognised for its rich science, technology, philosophy, literature, art, and critical theories (Kapoor, 2010). Extraordinary Indian intellectuals include Gandhi who produced an ideology founded on peaceful resistance, self-reliant and self-sufficient methods of production to lead a simple life. Sanskrit scholars who initiated mnemocultures emphasise speech and gesture over writing and documentations that constitute Western epistemic forms. To respect these voices, to bring about new knowledge, and to integrate intercultural dimensions into university classrooms, education needs to identify, recognise, and embed non-Western intellectual recourses (including, for example, accumulated artefacts, skills, knowledge, and wisdom) into Western academic conventions (Bradley, Noonan, Nugent, & Scales, 2008; Singh & Shreshtha, 2009).

A means to achieve the above, according to many researchers (e.g. Beck, 2002; Singh, 2009) is to make use of educational assets offered by international students, especially by non-Western students. Non-Western students are educated transnationals (Beck, 2002) with double-knowing capacity—being educated and having access to knowledge from both homeland and host countries. If their intellectual heritages are respected and utilised, they will add new perspectives to Western legacies and broaden Western academic cultures (Singh, 2009). Australia has educated thousands of non-Western students during the last two decades but paid scant attention to their intellectual assets. Ironically, many non-Western students have achieved a better or similar study-performance compared with their Western counterparts both at Australian institutions and on recent international tests (Jerrim, 2014) but their performance has been largely claimed as a result of attentiveness, efforts, task persistence, and eagerness to learn (Pham, 2014) rather than the contribution of their educational values and philosophies where they were nurtured. Integration Asian culture in teaching and learning benefits not only Asian international students but also Australian people. The White policy has strongly called for the integration of Asian culture in Australian curriculum and the new Colombo Plan is trying to send Australian undergraduates to Indo-Pacific countries to learn about Asian culture. Leask (2015) highlight the greater responsibility of teachers to ensure cultural diversity is best explored and effectively unitised in the international classroom.

To embed diverse learning values in teaching and learning, students need to be seen as active and agentic subjects who should be invited to join a variety of communities of practice that provide them with personal resources, learning strategies, and funds of knowledge that they can draw upon in conducting their lives in different formal and informal contexts (Gutierrez & Rogoff, 2003; Moll, Amanti, Neff, & Gonzalez, 1992). From this perspective, (i) *culture* is conceived assets of shared practices, ways of thinking and acting rather than as an inherent set of internal traits and attitudes (Gutierrez, & Rogoff, 2003); (ii) *institutions* are conceived as nested communities of practice that have their established routines, forms of interaction and predictable patterns of relationships and power between members (Wenger, 1998); (iii) *personal resources* are conceived as funds of knowledge and know-how that are appropriated and internalised through engagement with others in shared practices. As such, students should be treated as actors in local contexts and teachers need to understand their experiences and meaning-making processes within the context of their relationships and activities. Educational reforms need to be designed in situ based on a detailed description of the current cultural, institutional, and personal circumstances, and the trailing of alternatives in collaboration with the participants.

To be able to take this position, pedagogies need to be designed as interperspective pedagogies that are resulted from mutual adaptations and what are personal and professional transformative experiences of academics and students. A very common approach that has been applied by researchers globally is to create what is called the third space. This approach has been advocated by educators as the 'middle ground' in order to deal with mismatches and conflicts when 'East meets West' (Gu, Nie, & Yi, 2002). Engeström (1999) claims that when different systems (referred to as Activity Systems) interact with rules underpinned by different traditions and perspectives, various contradictions can be created. To deal with these contradictions, actors in the activity systems are required to understand multiple perspectives and develop solutions to solve the disparities between the two activity systems. Solutions in this situation often entail the generation of new hybrid activities or transformed practices that include elements from both activity systems (Pham, 2016). The third space is where hybridity transformed practices are developed and characterised by alternative points of view, which, in Engeström's (1999) view, affords opportunities for the creation of rich zones of learning.

The Need to Diversify and Enrich Engagement in Education

We would like to argue that one powerful way to improve pedagogy is to focus on engagement with students, teachers, and communities. That engagement is more than just participation but should be an experimental channel of commitment which informs pedagogy, refresh, contextualise, and keep it relevant. In making efforts to enhance pedagogy, one cannot claim in any absolute sense that pedagogy can be best across all contexts. Instead, it is important to note that it is through efforts to bring teaching closer to a target group of learners, tap into teachers' potential and strengths, and connect well with the community, pedagogy finds an opportunity to be relevant and successful.

One such example of relevance can be taken from Chap. 2, which looks at the real need of students' learning repertoire in the Australian educational context. In many Australian higher-education classrooms with a combination of local and international students, it is sometimes observed that while many local students are prone to a verbal discussion, some of their international counterparts remain more reflective. Suppose pedagogy focuses on the former and neglect the latter, the less eloquent students will suffer from their favourite learning style being ignored. While Socratic pedagogy demands the practice of oracy alongside critical thinking and speaking out alongside listening, the reality in the classroom in many cases require to restructure that principle. This means that the proportion between talk and non-talk does not have to be pre-determined but may vary depending on every classroom task and depending on who learners are. While some learning activities require more open sharing of ideas, others might demand more reflective space. If lecturers pay attention to both needs of students, pedagogy has a chance to be more appropriate and thus is improving. This scenario demonstrates how engagement with students might mean in refreshing the quality of pedagogy.

It may be worth clarifying what engagement means, although later on, different authors in their chapters may modify the dynamics of such engagement as it is contingent upon context. Engagement is the involvement of thinking, participation, and well-being. It encompasses the sense of connection between time, effort, and resources to optimise the learning experience (Trowler, 2010). When engagement is effective, individuals (including teachers, students, and community members) can feel a good sense of belonging to the educational climate and become more willing to contribute. This, however, is not a process of technical collaborative nature but comprises how well one behaves towards others, how people enjoy working together, and how one is assisted to cope with learning challenges as well. Drawing on Bloom (1956), such dimensions include behavioural, emotional, and cognitive engagement. Arguably, all of these if well practised would point to the impact of positive rapport, happy collaboration, and learning enrichment.

This book is thus founded upon the spirit of engagement with various populations in a wide range of strategies and through a wide range of topic focuses. The work falls into three major sections, namely enhancing pedagogies through engagement with learners, enhancing pedagogies through working with teachers' beliefs and knowledge, and enhancing pedagogies through engagement with the community. As Fullan (1993) argues, sometimes too much educational hierarchy and the political decision might retain the status quo rather than create change.

In different chapters, the term 'engagement' may or may not be a theme running the discussion. However, methods of engaging people are articulated in a variety of forms. Chapter 1 engages students in an innovative process of re-learning to read. Chapter 2 examines silent, reflective engagement without necessarily using too much speech. Chapter 3 unpacks how internationalised curriculum is about engaging with the global plurality of knowledge sources, including both local and international ways of practice. Chapter 4 analyses the cultural barrier to the academic engagement of North Korean students in the South Korean context and recommends methods to address such complications. Chapter 5 looks at the process of creative writing where students engage themselves with the language, experiment with it, feeling words through different senses, hearing words in different sounds, and convey meanings thanks to different language devices. Chapter 6 explores how Australia's engagement with Asia through the curriculum is sketched out across year levels and learning domains. Due to the location of Australia in the Pacific, there is the need to communicate and engage with the peoples of Asia so that one can effectively live and work in harmony with the region.

In section two, Chap. 7 approaches engagement in practicum activities through observing peer teaching, planning lessons, reflecting on practice, and discussing with mentors. All of these would trigger a series of changes in pre-service teachers' beliefs, including confirmation, realisation, disagreement, elaboration, integration, and even modification of those beliefs. Chapter 8 examines an educator's insights into the integration between heritage language practice and child play, an area that has been largely unexplored in early childhood education research. Utilising field notes and reflection on her daily working experiences, the author frames a different perspective on pedagogy that nurtures heritage language through both linguistic and social lenses and through building trust and bonding with young learners. It shows how knowledge of learners and the understanding of how they learn represents the foundation that would support and strengthen pedagogical practices. Chapter 9 analyses teacher and peer engagement in both formal and informal classroom conversations as a way to provide students with feedback on their work. Such processes help students evaluate their merits and weaknesses so that most effective learning strategies can be worked out for students in their future learning.

In section three, Chap. 10 conceptualises engagement with educational reforms not through leadership and policy as often seen in many reform projects but by highlighting the role and experience of teachers through their voice and agency. Chapter 11 captures teacher engagement and professional development through a form of pedagogical talk known as dialogical pedagogy. Chapter 12 discusses how science teachers engage in an approach known as the construction of representations to describe the scientific phenomenon and to assist students to solve scientific problems. This way of practice enables teachers to improve in their pedagogical practices. Chapter 13 shares language learners' experience of engagement through a full range of functional and formal elements of cultural and linguistic repertoire. Chapter 14 advocates social, affective engagement is service learning, which emphasises the need to connect the academic facility with personal and social development. Chapter 15 promotes the engagement of parents and community residents in the learning process to build mutual trust and cooperation for strengthening educational reform. Finally, Chap. 16 raises the awareness of individual and collective power in individuals and communities for gaining control over their lives.

Another reason for connecting pedagogy with the people who directly receive the impact of teaching, rather than making connecting with education leaders, theorists, or policymakers, is for a sense of equality. Since pedagogical practice serves students, gets carried out by teachers, and affects the community, there is a strong need to acknowledge the role of these populations. With this mind, the book accumulates and constructs students' experience, teachers' wisdom, and community as resources. It also cultivates critical reflection on how all of these endeavours might lead to the improvement of instructional performance. It is believed that in making this commitment, pedagogy has a chance to be broadened in complex ways and with new nuances.

Three Areas of Contribution in This Book

Please note that this section does not summarise the chapters and does not repeat points already made in chapter abstracts. Instead, we expand the understanding of the authors' contributions and position them in perspectives, that is, by bringing out the connection between chapters, into the discourse, and with our appreciative thoughts.

Improving Pedagogies Through Engagement with Student Voice and Experience

Although the current discourse has given a great deal of attention to how pedagogy offers learner engagement (see, for example, Goldspink, Winter, & Foster, 2008), not much has investigated how learner engagement offers feedback to pedagogy. In our observation, many teachers are often too busy focusing on the academic time that they might overlook the need to connect with their students affectively and socially. Arguably, student success is built not only through academic diligence but also through interpersonal dynamics. Because of this, it is important to engage students in all aspects of their learning, such as thoughts, feelings, and behaviours. In other words, to improve ways of teaching requires engaging with students comprehensively as well as helping them develop skills, motivation, and confidence. As Furlong and Christenson (2008) indicates, it is important to pay attention to the psychological connection within the academic environment as a way to support student engagement. This part takes an in-depth look into how effective learning can happen through adaptation to new resources or new combinations of resources. It touches on theoretical and practical issues that are either less commonly explored before or have not been examined from the same angle.

Pedagogy can improve its quality and social inclusivity by making use of Asian students' academic repertoire to improve the learning of these students in the Australian context. The recommendation is drawn from a research effort in which students are guided to utilise their resources in maximising academic reading experiences (Chap. 1). This is an innovative response to the appeal from Australian higher institutions in effectively engaging international students in critical thinking and English literacy. Instead of following the regular learning styles of local counterparts, Asian students might like to consider developing their own way of learning which takes their strengths into account. Arguably, once lecturers understand the strength and resources of international students and can organise for these students to be themselves in the learning process, pedagogy earns more conditions to improve. Such pedagogy is enriched, inclusive, and intelligent as it does not deny students of their academic tradition but respect and maximise everyone's intellectual potential. This contribution of pedagogical perspective is tested through an experiential project in which participants are supported in applying their previously acquired reading strategies learned in their home countries in the Australian educational context. The study and its recommendations open new opportunities for researchers to pursue this area where there is so much more to discover from the inherent learning strengths of international students who come from around the globe. They come to the West with rich learning skills that should be recognised, utilised, and cherished as a part of educational capitals. Chapter 1 connects its proposed philosophy with Chap. 2 which discusses the silent way of learning, with Chap. 3 which recognises the practices of Confucian heritage cultures in the construction of a more globalised pedagogy, and with Chap. 6 which addresses curriculum practice by investigating how Asian resources play a role in the Australian secondary education system.

Chapters 2, 3, and 4 view pedagogy from a cultural perspective and argue that if students' cultures are insufficiently cared about, the quality of teaching and learning will suffer. There is an appeal to educators for not overlooking less verbal students (Chap. 2). To improve pedagogy in university classrooms, one needs to embrace less common introspective learning styles that sometimes get marginalised. Lecturers who misinterpret students' need for silently processing the information as uncooperative will fail to support learning. The discussion highlights the need to recognise the presence of unconventional Australian students who are more reflective than outspoken. The chapter points out the misunderstanding that this group is passive students, analyses the autonomy that these students demonstrate, and proposes a pedagogy that respects and nurtures alternative ways of learning—keeping in mind that talking all the time is not necessarily the best way to learn.

It is important to gain a better understanding of the learning practices of Confucian heritage cultures students to serve the construction of a more globalised pedagogy in Western classrooms (Chap. 3). As Western classroom settings have become increasingly multicultural, pedagogists are faced with the challenge of effectively catering for students with various backgrounds and learning preferences. Reality shows that while Asian students are perceived as being passive and uncritical, Western systems have failed to understand and utilise the resources of these cohorts. Empirical evidence has demonstrated that students from Confucian heritage cultures countries have different learning preferences which are not necessarily seen as passive or uncritical (see, for example, Bao, 2014). The chapter proposes strategies that teachers could employ in supporting marginalised students in culturally diverse classrooms.

Pedagogy can be enhanced through student engagement from a sociocultural, political perspective. That is, teachers need to express empathy towards the suffering of non-mainstream students and make efforts to accommodate their learning (Chap. 4). It does so by identifying the current state of exclusive teaching practice in South Korea, which marginalises North Korean students for their distinctive dialects, accents, interpersonal communication styles, and learning behaviour from their South counterparts. Education in such situations needs to be modified as it perpetuates cultural discrimination and impedes learning. The discussion recommends ways to make pedagogy culturally supportive and provide illustrative samples of how this process can be made achievable. For instance, teachers need to take their sociocultural background into consideration, design and conduct classroom activities which discourage prejudice, look beyond limited historical-political boundaries to build a more humanistic pedagogy, support learning of less privileged students who are asylum seekers, and revise the curriculum which is mindful of education equity in the everyday teaching practice.

The last two chapters of this section look particularly at the use of resources in improving practices in curriculum and pedagogy. A creative pedagogical model, which is proposed by a teacher to promote students' creative learning through literary resources (Chap. 5), stimulates a writing process whereby students not only get to know a range of complex skills but also apply them instantly in producing written output. The model combines literary experimentation with the social sharing of self-initiated stories. Such skills include generating resources, keeping a journal, life observation, reflection on experience, borrowing ideas from literary works, and adapting them, gathering cultural artefacts, among others. All of these abilities are incorporated in a case study that illuminates how students are capable of learning in complex ways and stretching their potential to a new level. The project shows how creative pedagogy by the teacher exerts a powerful impact on student learning by inspiring students to be creative as well. In this experience, pedagogy improves when learning is improved. This is particularly true when the performance of roles becomes diverse: students take on the dual role of learners and writers, while the teacher takes on the dual role of a facilitator of learning and an academic researcher. The chapter shares meaningful implications in the context of creative writing practices of English in Indonesia, which is highly transferrable to other contexts or language programs in which creativity is a strong component.

Students' voices can contribute to curriculum practice. This was made possible through an empirical investigation of how the Australian secondary education system has been teaching about Asia (Chap. 6). Situated in the Asia-Pacific region, the country finds it important to learn about the culture, economics, mindsets, and other aspects of its neighbouring countries, not only to co-exist in harmony but also to build strong cooperation for development. With this ideology in mind, curriculum developers have given Asia Literacy a significant position in the Australian curriculum. Strategically, one way to understand such teaching and learning would be to explore how Australian students, having gone through some schooling in this content, have developed knowledge about and perceive what Asia means to them. Data collection and mixed-methods analysis show that despite initiatives to develop acquaintance and understanding about Asia, progress in the teaching and learning of this priority has been marginal and patchy. It is interesting to be able to find out the gap between theory and practice. To understand educational progress, it is often helpful to see if what we advocate and what we eventually achieve could match. The finding has tremendous implications in pedagogy, especially in the sense that one should be able to compare the outcome with the aim of a program to know how well that program has functioned. Most importantly, the study reveals the operational characteristic of curriculum implementation by gathering students' opinions to speak for educators—rather than educators making assumptions all the time.

Improving Pedagogies Through Engagement with Teacher Belief and Knowledge

This section in the book brings out voices from teachers' beliefs, knowledge, and practices as well as to view teachers' role as pedagogy designers. Our chapter contributors believe that teachers' knowledge, experience, innovation, and real-world adaptive practices all play roles in improving pedagogy, curriculum, and equity when teachers can act as agents in pro-active learning engagement. Scholarly research in Australia has demonstrated that critical reflection on teacher resources, including beliefs, knowledge, and skills, has the power of leading change in schools (Carrington, Deppeler & Moss, 2010). It has been realised, for three decades now, that top-down decisions and practice, such as teacher training, hierarchical management, a policy developed by leaders without consulting teachers, have perpetuated the status quo rather than change (see, for example, Fullan, 1993). We agree with many educators, such as Carrington et al. (2010), that teacher education and professional development programs need to empower teachers in challenging existing problems, critique their teaching world, and reconceptualise how teachers themselves would contribute their ideas for improving pedagogical practices. Specifically, the section presents and analyses many factors in teacher capital that governs everyday engagement with pedagogies and innovations.

The first two of the six chapters in this section look at placement experiences and what university programs can learn from preservice teachers, not just teaching them. A practical framework is recommended to guide teachers in situated practice, which rests on the philosophy that teacher beliefs play a major role in shaping practice. These two dimensions, which were documented during the EAL practicum in Australian secondary schools from a sociocultural perspective, demonstrate how understanding what is going on in teachers' minds and backgrounds can illuminate why teachers practice their profession in the way they do (Chap. 7). After all, pedagogy is a complex area which is formed by a range of sociocultural dimension, including personal ideologies and situated experiences. To be able to document these elements will enable researchers to peel layers of teacher practice and reveal what shapes choices of teaching decisions.

A set of pedagogical principles is proposed which, for the first time, combines elements which have never been combined before in for early childhood education practice: teachers with little knowledge of children's heritage language can become a learner of that language through play and roleplay. The combination of child play, roleplay, and herniate maintenance practice is hardly heard of before and represents a new, exciting area in education. The framework, which shows new ways of engaging with the child, came out of the complex experience of early childhood education as it was documented in work-journal data and personal reflection on it (Chap. 8). To keep such a model alive and successful requires a range of support and real-world negotiation of practice. Such supports are drawn from various stakeholders, including families, school practice, university researchers, and fellow educators. The chapter echoes Dewey's (1938) philosophy of education as a social process in which teachers make a connection with the learning community, active engagement, and responsibility for new meaning-making.

The subsequent two chapters explore the question of teacher agency in improving pedagogy. A classroom case was inspected where formative assessment is implemented with a focus on developing strategies to navigate cultural and structural obstacles (Chap. 9). Based on from empirical research, it is argued although western-based pedagogical practices are often well-received in many Asian classrooms, the success of such pedagogies depends on how local teachers and students are willing and able to navigate such implementation in the local context. This would be similar to a boat being designed for a lake that may not function well in a river. The author identifies several tensions and proposes strategies to ease them out. In the end, the discussion points out that the initiative was effectively implemented thanks to the participating teachers who work hard to cooperate and negotiate their roles in a community. The chapter speaks well to the final chapter in this book by responding to the appeal by Niranjan Casinader and Ayub Sheik for the need to consider local wisdom in curriculum design and pedagogical practice.

By the same token, new pedagogical ideas are proposed through observing the practice of teacher agency in an academic-vocational integration program in the Chinese context. Educational reform is rarely without problems and challenges. In an investigation of educational reform from an all-inclusive perspective, it was found that three years after the Chinese vocational education reform was initiated, educational practices in this area have not been able to reach favourable outcome and the implementation of policy in promoting equity does not seem to be moving ahead very well (Chap. 10). An explanation is provided by pointing out the gap in education research: while many studies focus on school leaders' perspectives in explaining how political and social factors hinder school-level policy implementation, the role and involvement of teachers in this process continue to be neglected. Sadly, the critical voice of teachers is severely marginalised in the everyday activity of negotiating and conceptualising implementation. When the teacher perspective is absent from the discourse of policy for transforming their schools, the overall picture of educational reform risks being untruthful, and the impact of reform suffers. The chapter then addresses this gap by investigating the experience and voice of five teachers in China; and argues for the importance of teacher agency in making a difference.

The remaining two chapters of this section focus on specific tools that are developed to enhance pedagogy. Pedagogical improvement should come from teachers questioning their practice. Such voices of teachers were made audible through an experiential case study where participants not only expressed dissatisfaction with their teaching quality but also took the liberty to create positive change (Chap. 11). In many cases, the enemy of change is a comfortable routine. To transform daily practice from a one-way lecturing mode to a more dialogic approach can represent a challenging task for many teachers in Vietnamese classrooms. Observing how two teachers attempted to adopt a more dialogic approach in reading lessons, the author discovered that when the teachers delegated the authority to the students by asking student-preferred questions and facilitated the discussions with more open questions, classroom interaction witnessed an increase in students' questions that heightened the quality of classroom discussion. Such an improvement in both teacher practice and student performance demonstrates a shift in classroom power. This is particularly true when students are invited to be co-generators of knowledge in the teaching and learning process.

The same theme of teacher change in education can be approached from a different angle, such as through representations as resources to enhance teaching and learning. Little research has explored how the construction of representations can empower teachers to make changes in their pedagogical practices. This gap is responded to by researchers' identification of various models that have been used to support teachers in improving practices (Chap. 12). For instance, one model in science education proves to have a comprehensive impact when it fully explains how internal and external factors work together and influence each other to bring about positive changes in everyday instruction. The key factor that makes this model advanced and different compared to other models is that it emphasises teachers as active learners who enact and reflect during their teaching.

Improving Pedagogies Through Community Engagement

This part discusses how pedagogy and curriculum can be upgraded through educators' engagement with community resources. In other words, we believe in the role of community engagement in informing and improving pedagogy. It is because, through collaboration with the community, education can expand its social dimension and move strongly towards transformation. As Dewey advised as early as 1938, transformation in education 'signifies a society in which every person shall be occupied in something which makes the lives of others better worth living and (...) which breaks down the barriers of distance between them (p. 326). This social view has a great deal of significance when it is applied for pedagogical enhancement. For example, the need for social belonging, mutual responsibility, and attachment to learning peers would be an important factor in effective instruction. One important feature of this section of the book is that the authors view the enhancement of pedagogy as an expansion of practice beyond institutions and into real-world activities. The community in these chapters is highly diverse: they can be within an online space, around an underprivileged neighbourhood, from families, and across different continents. No matter what the setting is, the ability to engage with these communities and understand them can bring a new perspective to pedagogy in particular and education in general.

Online communities with their language use in a social platform can demonstrate how practice can be more innovative, liberating, and spontaneous than routine classroom interaction. Based on the observation of such activities, a proposed pedagogical idea suggests looking at language users and learners' self-resourcefulness and the ability to co-construct new meaning through social interaction (Chap. 13). While linguistic research often divides English into compartments of 'inner', 'outer', and 'expanding' circle variants, the study demonstrates the powerful reality that such distinction can be erased through real evidence. It does so by demonstrating how English and other language resources are utilised by people across different geographic, ethnic, and socio-economic backgrounds. In taking on the freedom to function beyond their traditional boundaries, bloggers construct a society in which members are more open-minded in discussing issues, both in the classroom and online space, not only for the practice of language skills but also for critical awareness of communication in the real world. The chapter offers a pedagogical perspective through a technological means where thoughts are socially shared. Communication becomes vibrant in blogging when everyone can bring their communication repertoires and rich resources into the discussion and where everyone's ability adapts to the diversity of contemporary contexts of communication.

Along the same line of contextualised language education, the pedagogical transformation also comes from confrontation with challenge and the willingness to take it as an opportunity. The next proposed philosophy sounds unusual: when children cannot afford to go to school, highly responsible educators should consider bringing the school to them. The empirical research rethinks pedagogy by reaching out to school-aged children with virtually no access to education and by creating schooling for them outside of the conventional institution (Chap. 14). An experiment was developed in which teachers performed beyond regular teaching but took on the multiple responsibilities of researchers, social workers, and teachers at the same time. Inspired by service-learning ideology, teachers in the study innovated a create model which, instead of making children go to school, brought the school to the children by setting up classes in the local community. Lessons learned from this experience were then utilised to improve the pre-service teacher placement component in a university program. The study demonstrates how a higher-education curriculum can be negotiated by the pre-service teacher themselves rather than implemented in a top-down fashion. The study also expands pedagogical practice by prioritising new experience over current knowledge, students' self-discovery over expert authority, and mutual support over academic skills.

The above idea of multiple-role performance was interpreted differently in Chap. 15 when an innovative research connected parental involvement with peda-gogical practices whereby parents take on the roles of learners, resources, endorsers, and catalysts. Positioned against the discourse that often views parental involvement in childhood education as outsiders of teaching, this is a rare study that offers fresh ideas in education. In particular, the author managed to make visible what should be known as local wisdom in the Japanese context where school reform is characterised by lesson study in which the importance of parental participation in pedagogical practices is accentuated. The chapter is a powerful response to Chap. 16 which highlights the reality that local wisdom is often overrun by imported models of education imported from the superior west.

Sometimes, educational reform can be viewed at the macro level of a curriculum perspective rather than an instructional one. Literacy practice in the Asia-Pacific context follows 'Western' principles by adopting Euro-American concepts of liter-acy. Unfortunately, such models of literacy superficially prepare people to benefit from the globalised economy rather than to develop intellectually. Sadly, while principles of 'Western' education are promoted as academic superior, existing local systems of education are downplayed. While in theory, the multiplicity of literacy is supposed to be promoted around the globe, in reality, the conception of literacy is narrowed down to a Euro-American framework. Highlighting these dilemmas, Chap. 16 challenges how 'Western' notions of capitalism and rationalism have influenced the direction and intentions of global literacy initiatives. It argues that instead of liberating people from socio-economic confinement, educational neo-liberalism contributes to a loss of the cultural identity. Although the discussion does not directly address the question of pedagogy, the implication of the above understanding is valuable in everyday teaching in the sense that it raises awareness for local wisdom to serve education. Pedagogy once imported from a different context, no matter how seemingly superior, needs to be examined and localised to meet the need of the system which it supports. It is thought-provoking to see that both Chaps. 15 and 16 express appreciation for local wisdom, cherish less recognised voices in pedagogy, and appeal for a more community-based practice in education.

Conclusion

Our approach to improving education reflects a constructivist view on pedagogy whereby weighting is devoted to both individuals and communities, with respect for the backgrounds of students, teachers, and society members. We view instruction as both planned and improvisational. We value research efforts and dialogues in which new meanings are explored, articulated, and shared. In doing these, the book opens opportunities for educators to consolidate, modify, challenge, as well as to expand existing beliefs, understandings, and practices. We acknowledge that there is no best practice for everyone. Instead, our advocacy for certain ways of thinking pedagogy is closely connected to the authors' experience in context. What we wish to offer the most in this book is a range of pedagogical elements, perceptions, and ideas for further consideration and interaction so that more opportunities can be co-created to improve student learning. Additionally, the book offers implications for inclusive pedagogy in the sense that it recognises local particularities as well as varying capabilities and circumstances of learners and teachers for expanding our pedagogical thinking. In the end, what we hope to achieve is the opportunity to share our understanding of factors that contribute to the quality of instruction.

Monash University, Melbourne,   Dat Bao
Australia   Thanh Pham

References

Alatas, S. F. (2006). *Alternative discourses in Asian social science: Responses to Eurocentrism.* New Delhi: Sage Publications.

Bao, D. (2014). *Understanding silence and reticence: Ways of participating in second language acquisition.* London: Bloomsbury.

Barnett, R., Parrt, G., & Coate, K. (2001). Conceptualising curriculum change. *Teaching in Higher Education, 6,* 435–449.

Beck, U. (2002). The cosmopolitan society and its enemies. *Theory, Culture & Society, 19*(1–2), 17–44.

Bradley, D., Noonan, P., Nugent, H., & Scales, B. (2008). *Review of Australian higher education: Final report.* Canberra: Australian Government.

Broadfoot, P. (2001). Culture, learning and comparative education. *Comparative Education, 37*(3), 261–266.

Carr, N., & Fraser, K. (2014). Factors that shape pedagogical practices in next generation learning spaces. In K. Fraser (Ed.), *The future of learning and teaching in next generation learning spaces* (pp. 175–198). Bingley, England: Emerald.

Carrington, S., Deppeler, J., & Moss, J. (2010). Cultivating teachers' knowledge and skills for leading change in schools. *Australian Journal of Teacher Education, 35*(1), 1–13.

Dewey, J. (1938) *Experience and education*. New York: Macmillan.

Engeström, Y. (1999). Activity theory and individual and social transformation. Cambridge: Cambridge University Press.

Fullan, M. (1993). *Change forces: Probing the depth of educational reform*. London: Falmer Press.

Furlong, M. J., & Christenson, S. L. (2008). Engaging students at school and with learning: A relevant construct for all students. *Psychology in the Schools, 45*(5), 365–368.

Gale, T., Mills, C., & Cross, R. (2017). Socially inclusive teaching: Belief, design, action as pedagogic work. *Journal of Teacher Education, 68*(3), 345–356.

Goldspink, C., Winter, P., & Foster, M. (2008, September). Student engagement and quality pedagogy. In: *European conference on educational research in Goteborg* (pp. 10–12).

Goody, J. (2010). *The Eurasian miracle*. Cambridge and Malden: Polity Press.

Gu, L. Y. (2003). *Jiaoxue gaige de xingdong yu quanshi [Education reform—Action and interpretation]*. Beijing: People's Education Press.

Gu, L. Y., Nie, B. H., & Yi, L. F. (2002). *Xunzhao zhongjian didai 《尋找中間地帶》 [Searching for the middle ground]*. Shanghai: Shanghai Education Press.

Gutierrez, K. D., & Rogoff, B. (2003). Cultural ways of learning: Individual traits or repertoires of practice. *Educational Researcher, 32*(5), 19–25.

Jerrim, J. (2014). Why do East Asian children perform so well in PISA? An investigation of Western-born children of East Asian descent. *Oxford Review of Education, 41*(3), 310–333.

Kapoor, K. (2010). *The humanities and the social sciences in India*. Prabuddha Bharata. Retrieved from www.advaitaashrama.org.

Keane, J. (2009). *Life and death of democracy*. London & New York: Simon & Schuster.

Leask, B. (2015). *Internationalizing the curriculum*. Milton Park, Abingdon, Oxon, New York: Routledge.

Marzano, R. J., Zaffron, S., Zraik, L., Robbins, S. L., & Yoon, L. (1995). A new paradigm for educational change. *Education, 16*(2), 162–173.

Moll, L., Amanti, C., Neff, D., & Gonzalez, N. (1992). Funds of knowledge for teaching. *Theory into Practice, 2*, 132–141.

Pham, T. (2012). A framework to implement cross-cultural pedagogy: The case of implementing learning reform at Confucian heritage cultures colleges. *Higher Education Review: The International Journal for Policy and Practice in Post School Education, 44*(3), 27–40.

Pham, T. (2016). Student-centredness: exploring the culturally appropriate pedagogical space in Vietnamese higher education classrooms using activity theory. *Australian Journal of Teacher Education, 41*(1), 1–21.

Pham, T. H. T. (2014). *Implementing cross-culture pedagogies: Cooperative learning at Confucian heritage cultures*. Singapore: Springer.

Pham, T., & Pham, L. (2020). Enhancing Asian students' engagement by incorporating Asian intellectual and pedagogical resources in teaching and learning. In S. Hoidn, & M. Klemencic (Eds.), *Handbook of SCL in higher education* (pp. 171–185). London: Routledge.

Pham, T. H. T., & Renshaw, P. D. (2015). Adapting evidence-based pedagogy to local cultural contexts: a design research study of policy borrowing in Vietnam. *Pedagogies: An International Journal, 10*(3), 256–274.

Phuong-Mai, N. (2008*). Culture and cooperation cooperative learning in Asian Confucian heritage cultures: The case of Viet Nam.* Netherlands: IVLOS Institute of Education of Utrecht University.

Singh, M. (2009). Using Chinese in internationalising research education. *Globalisation, Societies & Education, 7*(2), 185–201.

Singh, M., & Shreshtha, M. (2009). International pedagogical structures admittance into the community of scholars via double knowing. In M. Hellstén, & A. Reid (Eds.), *Researching international pedagogies* (pp. 65–82). The Netherlands: Springer.

Trowler, V. (2010). Student engagement literature review. *The Higher Education Academy, 11*(1), 1–15.

Wenger, E. (1998). Communities of practice: Learning, meaning and identity. *Journal of Mathematics Teacher Education, 6*(2), 185–194.

Zipin, L. (2009). Dark funds of knowledge, deep finds of pedagogy: Exploring boundaries between lifeworlds and schools. *Discourse: Studies in Cultural Politics of Education, 30*(3), 317–331.

Contents

Part I Transforming Pedagogies Through Engagement with Student Voice and Experience

1 Engaging Students in Academic Readings at Australian Higher Education: Experience Learned from Confucian Heritage Culture (CHC) Education 3
Thanh Pham and Lam H. Pham

2 Improving Pedagogy in Response to Students' Reflective Learning Needs 17
Dat Bao

3 Developing Effective Global Pedagogies in Western Classrooms: A Need to Understand the Internationalization Process of Confucian Heritage Cultures (CHC) Students 37
Thanh Pham

4 Culturally Supportive Pedagogy: Challenges Faced by North Korean Immigrant Students in South Korea 53
Dat Bao and Giulio Ricci

5 Learners as Story Writers: Creative Writing Practices in English as a Foreign Language Learning in Indonesia 71
Henny Herawati

6 Exploring Attitudes Towards 'Asia Literacy' Among Australian Secondary School Students 89
Gary J Bonar

Part II   Transforming Pedagogies Through Engagement with Teacher Belief and Knowledge

7   **Preservice Teachers' Pedagogical Beliefs and Practices During the EAL Practicum in Australian Secondary Schools**   109
Minh Hue Nguyen

8   **Rethinking Pedagogy for Heritage Language Maintenance in Early Childhood Settings: The Power of Play**   121
Ranran Liu

9   **Implementing Formative Assessment in Vietnamese Classrooms: Strategies to Navigate Cultural and Structural Obstacles**   137
Thanh Pham and Lam H. Pham

10   **Making Sense of Teacher Agency Within a Vocational-Academic Integration Program at a Chinese Vocational High School**   151
Jing Shi and Venesser Fernandes

11   **Teacher Learning Through Dialogue: The Cases of Vietnamese Teachers**   169
Thi Diem Hang Khong

12   **Teacher Change in Science Education: What Could Be Done to Make This Happen?**   189
Lam H. Pham and Russell Tytler

Part III   Transforming Pedagogies Through Community Engagement

13   **Posting Your Thoughts: A Pedagogical Perspective of Blogging** . . .   203
Joseph A. Foley and Marilyn F. Deocampo

14   **Service Learning in a Suburban Community in Vietnam: Pre-Service EFL Teachers as Agents of Change**   217
Nguyen Hoang Tuan and Dat Bao

15   **Parents as Teaching Allies: Some Cases in Japanese Schools**   233
Eisuke Saito

16   **Educational Neoliberalism and the Annexation of Literacy: A Cautionary Tale in the Asia-Pacific Context**   245
Niranjan Casinader and Ayub Sheik

Part I
Transforming Pedagogies Through Engagement with Student Voice and Experience

Chapter 1
Engaging Students in Academic Readings at Australian Higher Education: Experience Learned from Confucian Heritage Culture (CHC) Education

Thanh Pham and Lam H. Pham

Abstract Students' engagement in academic readings has become a concern in Australian classrooms. There has been a strong call for innovative strategies to better engage students in academic readings and improve their understanding of this area. This study deployed a self-study methodology to examine what was offered by international academics and international students to help Australian universities overcome this crisis. Data were collected from the self-reflection of two international academics who have been studying and working in Australia for many years, journals of two international students, and emails of students sent to the first researcher. The findings revealed that the overemphasis on developing 'active learning' in Australian education contributed to demotivating students to undertake academic readings and current pedagogical practices do not help students understand texts deeply. The study found that reading strategies offered from non-Western education such as '*Hoc nhom*' (team reading) and '*Doc so sanh*' (reading to find similarities and differences of the text) could be effective alternatives. It is worthwhile for future research to further pursue this research agenda by empirically examining how these non-Western strategies work in Australian classrooms. More research should be conducted to seek other non-Western reading strategies.

Keywords Literacy · Academic reading · Vietnam · Higher education · Internationalization · Non-Western · Western

T. Pham (✉)
Monash University, Melbourne, VIC, Australia
e-mail: thanh.t.pham@monash.edu

L. H. Pham
Deakin University, Melbourne, VIC, Australia

© Springer Nature Singapore Pte Ltd. 2021
D. Bao, T. Pham (eds.), *Transforming Pedagogies Through Engagement with Learners, Teachers and Communities*, Education in the Asia-Pacific Region: Issues, Concerns and Prospects 57, https://doi.org/10.1007/978-981-16-0057-9_1

1.1 Introduction

During the last two decades, internationalization of education has become a priority in the agenda of almost all Australian universities. However, only little success has been achieved because internationalizing curricula in Australia still aim to infuse some international materials into existing course syllabi (De Vita, 2002). The more important initiative—internationalizing pedagogies by drawing teaching and learning on various global sources of knowledge—has been less successful. Most pedagogical practices are still heavily Eurocentric and colonial, characterized by a narrowly Western ideology (Cross, Mhlanga, & Ojo, 2011). One of the reasons contributing to this is the concept of the global labour division with the North producing theories and South borrowing. This concept has become well recognized amongst Western and non-Western academia (Alatas, 2006). Therefore, the direction of appropriation (from North to South) raises questions about the value given to non-Western intellectual resources.

However, various scholars (e.g. Alatas, 2006; Goody, 2010; Keane, 2009; Pham, 2014) have contested this inferior stereotype by evidencing that non-Western civilisations have a rich arena of philosophical and ethical-sociopolitical thought. Potent examples, just to name a few, are Confucius's teachings with key concepts of memorization, effort attributions, and intrinsic significance which have become key educational values in Asia. Recent Chinese teaching practices (e.g. 'action education' by Gu, 2003) have also attracted curiosity from Western academics due to their significant contribution to the outstanding performance of Asian students on international tests. India is also widely recognized for its rich science, technology, philosophy, literature, art, and critical theories (Kapoor, 2010; Pham & Renshaw, 2015). Extraordinary Indian intellectuals include Gandhi who produced an ideology founded on 'peaceful resistance' and 'self-reliant' and 'self-sufficient' methods of production to have a simple life and Sanskrit scholars who initiated mnemocultures emphasizing speech and gestures over writing and documentation that constitute Western epistemic forms (Rao, 2014).

Therefore, to truly bring about new knowledge and to integrate an international, intercultural, or global dimension into university classrooms, Australian education needs to identify, recognize, and embed non-Western intellectual recourses (e.g. accumulated artefacts, skills, knowledge, ideas, values, lore) into Western academic conventions (Bradley, Noonan, Nugent, & Scales, 2008; Singh & Shreshtha, 2009). A method to do this, according to various researchers (e.g. Beck, 2002; Pham, 2014; Singh, 2009), is to make use of educational assets offered by international students, especially by non-Western students. Non-Western students are 'educated transnationals' (Beck, 2002) and 'double knowing' (Singh, 2009)—being educated and having access to knowledge from both homeland and host countries. If their intellectual heritages are respected, they will add new perspectives to Western legacies and broaden Western academic cultures (Singh, 2009). Australia has educated thousands of non-Western students during the last two decades but paid very scant attention to their intellectual assets. Ironically, many non-Western students have achieved a better or similar study performance compared with their Western counterparts both at Australian institutions and on recent international tests (Jerrim, 2014), but their performance has been largely claimed as a result of attentiveness, efforts, task persistence, and eagerness to learn (Huang, 2014) but not the contribution of their educational values and philosophies where they were nurtured.

Given the context where Western economies and education systems are challenged by standards of literacy, numeracy, general knowledge, and behaviour (Stephen & Keiko, 2014), it is time for Australian education to search for alternatives by identifying relevant non-Western theoretical philosophies and values and exploring possibilities to embed these resources in Western academic cultures. An area that Australian higher education is under great pressure to improve, and non-Western intellectual heritages could offer a solution to achieve this improvement, is to better engage university students in academic readings. Academic readings are essential to academic success and to intellectual growth as they require sustained focused attention, working with the powers of memory and imagination. Gee (2008) claims that academic readings are part of a disciplinary 'Discourse' (that is, socially recognized ways of behaving, interacting, valuing, thinking, speaking, as well as reading and writing). Students could only obtain knowledge in their discipline if they engaged in academic readings in that discipline. This is because academic disciplinary readings help them learn the central concepts and ideas that shape the disciplinary field (Gee, 2008). Chou (2011) claims that the ability to read academic texts is considered one of the most important skills that university students need to acquire.

Unfortunately, academic readings have become an increasing area of concern in Australian universities. Spencer (2012) claims that the frequent failure of university students to 'do the reading' is widely reported in the relevant literature and anecdotally amongst lecturers. There is an alarmingly low rate of pre-reading and preparation that students undertake prior to coming to class. This is accompanied by the similarly low rate of participation in online discussion forums pertaining to the pre-class readings. In a sample of 2422 first-year students across nine Australian universities, James, Krause, and Jennings (2010) found that the students' self-reported preparedness for the class was declining: 58% of the students 'sometimes' and only 13% 'frequently' come to class without completing readings or assignments. Similarly, Hobson (2004) reported that on any given day, 70% of the students had not done the set preparatory readings. Although little has been known about the direct correlation between reading preparation and academic performance, research has found that those high-achieving students were more likely to come to class having completed the required readings (Spencer, 2012).

It is also equally important to know that Australian university students' reading comprehension has become a major concern (Fujimoto, Hagel, Turner, Kattiyapornpong, & Zutshi, 2011). Bharuthram and Clarence (2012) claim that the ability to read relevant texts critically and analyse, synthesize, and evaluate knowledge is a common requirement at the university level. Unfortunately, these days it is very common to hear academics complaining about university students' poor understanding of academic readings. They tend to only stop at the superficial level of understanding but do not engage in reading analytically. Fujimoto et al. (2011) clarified that students often cannot distinguish between important and unimportant ideas and fail to recognize how multiple perspectives differ. The ability to read well is no longer something that university academics take for granted in their students (Cabral, 2008). To better engage students at Australian universities in academic readings and improve their understanding, it is time to examine if there are pedagogical alternatives. This chapter investigates these alternatives by looking into what international academics and students could offer based on their experience and from their home education.

The research is guided by two following questions:

1. What are the perceptions of international students and academics towards engaging students in academic readings at Australian universities?
2. What are the possible reading strategies offered by non-Western education that could help enhance Australian university students' academic reading capacity?

1.2 Methodology

1.2.1 Background of the Study

In 2014 the first researcher became a lecturer in Education. She was teaching in two main programmes including the Bachelor of Education and the Master of Teaching. These two programmes had various areas including early childhood, primary or secondary education—or even a combination of these. The units chosen for the research were two foundation units in these two programmes. The units were similar in their nature as they both aimed to build a theoretical foundation for students, so readings were a strong component with which students needed to be engaged to achieve good marks. The Bachelor of Education unit had a complied textbook that had 24 chapters; so each week, students were asked to prepare two chapters. The Master of Teaching unit did not have a textbook but used relevant journal articles for each weekly topic. A list of weekly readings was added in the Unit Guide that was published for students at the beginning of the semester. The unit's delivery modes included a 1-hour lecture and a 2-hour tutorial each week. To ensure all students had a similar learning experience, the chief examiners of the two units took a primary role in designing and determining what should be presented in lectures and tutorials. The two units used the same format: The lectures presented the main ideas of the chapters but also incorporated additional information and examples, whereas tutorials were designed mainly for students to discuss case studies and problems they encountered in real life and on their practicum. The first researcher worked as a unit coordinator who delivered some of the lectures. She was also in charge of one out of seven tutorials.

During her teaching in the units, the poor engagement of students in academic readings was one of her biggest concerns. Very few students in each tutorial did some reading before coming to class. She was disappointed to read assignments that presented key concepts wrongly and were poorly referenced and cited. She was, therefore, continuously looking for strategies to improve the situation and keen on seeking strategies offered by international academics and students. This was because she was always impressed by international students' reading preparation in her tutorials. Although these students did not always complete each week's readings, they at least did some reading. This was evident by their active participation in answering questions in lectures and tutorials. Also, although these students, like their Western counterparts, focused their attention on the assessment and final grades, they expected their teachers to focus the additional reading materials in areas relating to their general learning and assessment. The literature also reported that in learning, Asian students are taught to read not only what reading is for, like a university course, but also beyond the course (Lee, 1996). Jerrim (2014) has recently emphasized the important influence of reading on students' academic outcomes when claiming that one of the reasons contributing to East Asian students' academic success was that they see reading as part of their common home cultural traditions. This background motivated the first researcher to conduct an inquiry to examine techniques that could engage international students in academic readings. When marking assignments, the first researcher was also impressed by many assignments written by international students. These students demonstrated their deep understanding of difficult English texts. She was, therefore, curious to know if international students had any special technique in reading, so that they could obtain such a deep level of understanding.

1.2.2   Research Methodology

This research utilized a self-study methodology (Loughran, 2004). The self-study was used in order to learn about ourselves and our programme and, ultimately, to seek improvement of graduate teacher education through reflection and self-inquiry (Conway, Palmer, Edgar, & Hansen, 2014). Self-study tends to be interpreted as a means to present private and personal stories, as the label might suggest. However, Loughran and Russell (2006) noted that using the label self-study is not the same as rigorously applying a self-study methodology. Rather, self-study relies on interaction with other people who can listen actively and constructively and their ideas and perspectives that could help the researcher acquire better insights into his or her personal teaching. Various researchers have agreed that the incorporation of alternative perspectives and the seeking of data outside of the self do improve the rigour and reliability of self-study research.

This study used four data sources. The first was the first researcher's journals that were conducted during two semesters of 2016. She wrote self-study journals to document how her students coped with readings in each tutorial and especially techniques that international students utilized to work with academic readings. She also documented her thoughts (personal growth, feedback about the curriculum, etc.). The second data source was journals of two international students, one Chinese and one Indian, who were completing their Master of Teaching programme. They were invited to journal main events like problems and suggestions that they had about academic readings in their programme. They both had been college teachers in China and India for some years. The students enrolled in the programme because they wanted to obtain a degree to find a teaching job and then apply for permanent residency in Australia. At the time of the study, they were in the last semester of their programme. There was no consistent format, and each participant chose to write about what worked for him or her. The first researcher's journal was 4000 words and the students produced from 1000 words to 2000 words.

The third data source was three conversation sessions between the first researcher and the second researcher. The second researcher participated in the research as a mentor who was invited to give the first researcher advice when she dealt with her students' reading engagement. The second researcher had an international cultural background, completing his schooling and university degrees in Vietnam, then working as a lecturer in Vietnam for 5 years before coming to Australia to complete his Ph.D. in pharmacy and then a second Ph.D. in education. He also worked as a research fellow and a sessional teaching staff at Australian universities. He had an excellent academic record as he won several awards in literacy (for his poem composing and literacy analysis) at the national level in his schools and university in Vietnam. Such a background made him an excellent mentor who could provide the first researcher valuable advice on how to engage her students in academic readings. The last data source was emails of students sent to the first researcher to reflect on how they were engaged with readings. The first researcher received ethics approval to use these emails as data for the research because they were relevant to the purpose of this research.

1.2.3 Analysis and Trustworthiness

All journals were collected in word documents. Conversation sessions were transcribed by a research assistant. Then, the first researcher completed the first round of coding and shared her scheme with the second researcher. Both the researchers participated in coding the data and continuously cross-checked the codes until the inter-rater agreement was 100%. A deductive approach was applied to analyse the data. The analysing process moved from a more general level to a more specific one. The two broad categories 'the poor incorporation of readings in tutorials' and 'alternative reading strategies' were first established. Then, the data were disentangled into segments (this can be a word, a single sentence or a paragraph), so that annotations and codes could be attached to them.

1.3   Results

The findings revealed two main issues (two main categories) that contributed to the disengagement and superficial understanding of students in academic readings. The first was the poor incorporation of readings in tutorials. The second was ineffective strategies that failed to engage students in a deep understanding of the academic readings.

1.3.1   The Poor Incorporation of Readings in Tutorials

Tutorials were organized in a manner that strongly required students to participate in group discussions. Common discussion topics were case studies in short video clips, hot events on the media, and issues students came across on their practicum. The topics were presented by either tutors or students, and then students worked in small groups to discuss and then groups shared their outcomes. Although this format was effective in terms of involving all students in group discussion and forced each of them to be 'active' in thinking and bringing their real-life experience into discussions, it demotivated students in doing readings in various ways. Below were notes documented in journals of the first researcher and the two international students.

Today's topic was the learning environment. Group discussions were informative because students discussed lots of useful tips that could help them with class management. However, very few students referred to strategies in this week's readings. (The first researcher's journal documented in April 2016)

The piece of information about using colours to decorate classrooms shown in the video clip was interesting and useful. Many students shared how their classrooms on practicum were coloured. However, no one mentioned the rule of using six colours at maximum presented in the textbook. It was clear that they did not read this week's chapters. (The first researcher's journal documented in May 2016)

One student commented on the Moodle site that she liked all activities in this week but became a bit dissatisfied at the end of the tutorial when a concrete answer was not given, so she did not know what she should do if she was in a similar situation. It seemed that the student was looking for tutors to use information from the textbook as a final answer. (The first researcher's journal documented in August 2016)

We were asked to prepare readings but we did not have much chance to discuss readings in class. Workshops required lots of discussion but ideas raised and presented were not based on any concrete source but mainly came from students' personal points of view. There was not enough extrinsic motivation ... When I did my university study in China, my teacher always went through key readings to ensure that everyone understood 'key concepts' first. Then, when students worked in small discussions, they were asked to relate their points to 'key concepts' in academic readings as much as possible by showing how their ideas were similar or different. This way forced everyone to prepare readings before coming to class. (The first student's journal)

I understand Australian education emphasizes critical and active learning, so students have to be active in thinking and doing. Personal points of view are highly appreciated here. However, sometimes I felt lost because I did not know what was right and what was wrong because we did not often have a conclusion based on some concrete source. Many students came to class without preparation of the week's readings but still were very confident because they had more than enough real experience to share in small groups. (The second student's journal)

In conversations with the second researcher, the first researcher shared a concern about her students' poor engagement of academic readings. The second researcher advised that to make students read, they need to have a reason to read. When readings are not incorporated in in-class tasks, only those who have intrinsic motivation do readings. Unfortunately, there are not many such students. If students are asked to use what they obtain from readings to support their ideas in a group discussion—a kind of extrinsic motivation, they will certainly do much more readings. The second researcher further explained he believes instinct and extrinsic motivations are not separated but intertwined somehow. If students are given extrinsic motivation first, they are more likely to develop their intrinsic motivation; so tutorials' activities should be designed in a manner that could give students motivation to read.

1.3.2   Alternative Strategies

The students' journals and conversations with the second researcher also revealed that lectures and tutorials did not prompt students effectively to help them achieve a deep understanding of academic readings. Below was evidence.

It was very disappointing to read these assignments. Students saw Piaget and Vygotsky supporting constructivism, so assumed they shared similar research ideas but did not read further to see how they are different. They mixed up Piagetian and Vygotskian perspectives at several places in their writing. (The first researcher's journal documented in August 2016)

At the end of the semester, I got a collection of readings each of which was about a research perspective or a researcher's insights. It would be useful if we had worked more on comparing and contrasting these perspectives so that we could know the limitations and advantages of each perspective. I found it interesting that Australian education emphasizes critical thinking but we were not asked to work on readings critically. 'Critical' does not mean 'criticize the readings' but 'knowing strengths and weaknesses of various perspectives'. (The first student's journal)

We learned designing lesson sequences but we did not see good sequences in workshop and lecture activities. Hardly we got activities that required a connection of readings across workshops and lectures. We used mind mapping to summarize key ideas of what we read but within one lesson only, so the whole picture of readings in a semester was not seen. (The second student's journal)

After reading the first researcher's concerns and the above notes of the two students as well as reviewing the reading load that the students were coping with in the two units, the second researcher suggested that there was too much material, so what the students were probably having trouble with was in distinguishing interesting anecdotes used as illustrations from important concepts and ideas. To enable every student to obtain what is presented in readings better, he suggested the application of '*hoc nhom*' (small reciprocal reading group). The strategy is that at the beginning of the semester, each tutorial is divided into small reading groups that continue for the whole semester. Students in each group divide each week's readings into different parts, and each group member works on one part then presents the key ideas to the whole group. This helps all group members spend less time on readings but still obtain key concepts of all readings. He had often used this strategy in his teaching at Vietnamese universities and found the strategy effective in helping students deal with a large number of readings.

To engage students in deep readings more effectively, he suggested that the idea of using a strategy called '*doc so sanh*'. Different from other methods that aim to guide students to obtain the gist of the readings, this method emphasizes the drawing out of similarities and differences amongst various objectives and things. The second researcher shared that understanding the key concepts of reading does not mean having a deep understanding yet. Deep understanding only comes when the reader sees how various perspectives are similar or different. This strategy requires students to continuously link what they are reading to what they have read. This strategy is similar to what is called 'mind-mapping'—a common information processing practice widely used in Western classrooms (McInerney & McInerney, 1994). However, '*doc so sanh*' does not capture the connections of main ideas within a reading but across readings. This practice enables students to remember important ideas well and also understand them in-depth. This strategy could also enable students to produce critical writing because they could bring multiple perspectives into their discussions—an area with which students at Australian universities are often struggling.

The first researcher then brought these strategies to her teaching in the second half of the semester. The qualitative data of the large survey at the end of the semester reported positive feedback from the students about these strategies. The students recognized them as 'rich and comprehensive' and 'very informative'. They perceived every lesson live, experiential, and rich in multiple perspectives. Students commented on the first researcher's teaching: 'The lectures encourage us to really think about how I was taught and how should I teach after four years' education; It welcomes international students as their cultural knowledge are being valued; The intertwined relationships between contextual factors (culture, ethnicity, geographical differences, policies, governmental regulations) and educational agenda', and '[The lecturer] made information presented was stimulating and challenging'.

1.4   Discussion

The findings presented in this chapter revealed two main aspects that should be taken into consideration in teaching at Australian higher education. These are the critical ability of international students and alternative reading comprehension strategies deployed in Confucian heritage culture classrooms. Regarding international students' critical ability, various studies (e.g. Hellmundt, 2003; Pham & Renshaw, 2013; Singh, 2009) claim that academic research on non-Western international students in Western universities often takes a deficit view that international students do not have the critical ability because they do not have opportunities to develop these higher-order academic skills in their home countries. What was reported in the international students' journals in this research demonstrated that international students had very critical thinking because they had the ability to see how teaching and learning should be designed so that students could obtain a deep understanding of what they learned. They also saw the type of pedagogies that could enable them to understand teaching and learning from multiple perspectives. These abilities are, as Haigh (2009) and O'Connor and Zeichner (2011) claimed, essential qualities of today's teacher education when they work in today's interconnected, interdependent world. Cervetti, Pardales, and Damico (2001) also confirm that this ability is called 'critical reading' which requires readers to ask questions and probe texts: to be active in their reading by making meaning as they read rather than passively absorbing information, and this is essentially important in higher education. The students showed that they did not think reading should only be about making sense of the contents but about persuading, arguing, or justifying—a higher-order thinking capacity (McLaughlin & DeVoogd, 2004).

The critical ability shown by the international students in this study has led to a need to understand 'critical ability' properly. There has not been, so far, any universal agreement on criteria utilized to define 'deep/critical' and 'surface/rote' learning. Jin and Cortazzi (2006) point out that these terms are often interpreted differently, depending on the expectations of the 'culture of learning' into which one has been socialized. Recently the idea using Vygotskian notions of language as the tool for thought has become very popular, especially in the Western world. In Western classrooms, talks and verbal participation are seen as the pathway to a critical questioning approach, and learner-centred pedagogies are designed to encourage students to 'learn by participating, through talking and active involvement' (Jin & Cortazzi, 2006, p. 6). This explains why Western academics have an implicit and explicit preference for these activities and expect that their students, including both local and international, to actively engage in these practices. If students are not verbally participatory, they are very likely to be seen as 'problematic'. Consequently, it is now common to see many Western institutions compulsorily requiring students to actively participate in class discussions, tutorials, and online forums by allocating a portion of their marks to these activities.

This view of 'effective' learning contrasts with the 'more cognitive-centered, learning–listening approach' that is favoured by Chinese educators (Jin & Cortazzi,

1998, p. 744). Within this tradition, being 'active' suggests 'cognitive involvement, lesson preparation, reflection, and review, thinking, memorisation, and self-study' (Cortazzi & Jin, 1996, p. 71). Therefore, claims that Chinese classrooms may indeed appear relatively static in comparison to those of the anglophone West, but just because the students operate in a receptive mode, this does not imply that they are any less engaged. Conversely, just because students in anglophone Western class-rooms are seen to be verbally participatory, this does not necessarily guarantee that learning is taking place. For instance, in their study, Volet and Kee (1993) reported that Confucian Heritage Cultures students found it astonishing and culturally inap-propriate when Australian students interrupted someone who was talking to make a point or asking very simple questions but they could just keep quiet and find out from their friends later. As such, it appears that each specific learning context has its own explicit and tacit rules to define what should be called 'deep' learning and what should be called 'rote' learning. Teachers need to take cautious steps before making judgements on what accounts for 'good learning'. Holliday (2005) has sent a message to warn teachers: one should not automatically assume that 'good lessons' are those in which students are 'lively' and 'orally 'active' (p. 81). The international students participating in this research and many others in the first researcher's classes were generally less verbally active than their Western counterparts. However, they demonstrated a high critical capacity in thinking. Their ideas are worthwhile for Australian higher education to take into consideration if it wishes to improve students' current literacy capacity.

Second, the findings in this research also revealed that Asian education has produced interesting reading strategies that are worthwhile being further examined and brought into Australian higher education. The first strategy is the need to help students understand the 'key concept' of each reading before freeing them to work independently or in small groups. This idea is originated from an important concept in Asian teacher education which advocates that teachers must be trained and expected to identify for students at least three elements of a curriculum topic: the knowledge point (zhishidian) [知識點], the key point (zhongdian) [重點], and the difficult point (nan dian) [難點] (Gu, 2003). Subsequently, Gu (2003) notes that Asian teachers tend to explicitly name the concepts that students will need to learn, specify the key aspects of the concepts related to the topic, and identify the aspects that students are likely to find most difficult. In this research, both the students and the second researcher believe tutorials need to be organized in a manner that could enable students to understand 'key concepts' and bring them into an in-class discussion, and then students could compare and contrast their points of view with these 'key concepts'.

The second strategy, as suggested by the second researcher, was 'doc so sanh' which does not focus on key ideas of any perspective but emphasizes the analysis of similarities and differences of various perspectives. This strategy requires both academics and students to develop first logical thinking and then critical thinking because they need to continuously relate what they are reading to their prior reading and then draw out how they are related to each other. When learning about infor-mation processing strategies, students in Western classrooms are often introduced to a wide range of strategies like chunking information, repetition, concept mapping, summaries, and mnemonics (McInerney & McInerney, 1994). '*Doc so sanh*' is different from these strategies in terms of requiring students to logically connect what they have read not within a single reading but amongst various readings and not within a week but across many weeks. Vietnamese students are familiar with this '*Doc so sanh*' strategy which might be because an important component of teaching literacy in Vietnamese education is to teach students the capacity to compare and contrast subjects and objects. They then carry and apply this skill in what they read—a practice that the first researcher rarely had in her studying and working experiences in Australia.

1.5   Conclusion

This research was the first attempt to examine what non-Western education could offer to enhance Australian students' literacy capacity. This research was innovative in utilizing a novel approach to intercultural education because intercultural practices currently reported in the literature largely relate to the introduction of Western theories and pedagogies into the non-Western context, but not the reverse. By introducing non-Western intellectual assets into the Western academy, this research contributes to the interruption of the privileging English-only pedagogies and Euro-American theories that have been utilized as universal knowledge and practices. Future research will further this agenda by bringing non-Western reading strategies like '*hoc nhom*' and '*doc so sanh*' into Australian classrooms to examine their effectiveness.

References

Alatas, S. F. (2006). *Alternative discourses in Asian social science: Responses to Eurocentrism.* New Delhi: Sage Publications.

Beck, U. (2002). The cosmopolitan society and its enemies. *Theory, Culture & Society, 19*(1–2), 17–44.

Bharuthram, S., & Clarence, S. (2012). Teaching academic reading as a disciplinary knowledge practice in higher education. *South African Journal of Higher Education, 29*(2), 42–55.

Bradley, D., Noonan, P., Nugent, H., & Scales, B. (2008). *Review of Australian higher education: Final report.* Canberra: Australian Government.

Cabral, A. (2008). Reading and writing in higher education: A Portuguese case study. *The Reading Matrix, 8*(1), 64–77.

Cervetti, G., Pardales, M., Damico, S. (2001). A tale of differences: Comparing the traditions, perspectives, and educational goals of critical reading and critical literacy. *Reading Online, 4*(9). Retrieved January 20, 2018, from http://www.readingonline.org/articles/art_index.asp? HREF=/articles/cervetti/index

Chou, I. C. (2011). Understanding on-screen reading behaviours in academic contexts: A case study of five graduate English-as-a-second-language students. *Computer-Assisted Language Learning, 25*(5), 1–23.

Conway, C., Palmer, C., Edgar, S., & Hansen, E. (2014). Learning to teach graduate students: A self-study by students and a faculty member. *Applications of Research in Music Education, 34* (2), 54–60.

Cortazzi, M., & Jin, L. (1996). Cultures of learning: Language classrooms in China. In H. Coleman (Ed.), *Society and the language classroom* (pp. 169–206). Cambridge: Cambridge University Press.

Cross, M., Mhlanga, E., & Ojo, E. (2011). Emerging concept of internationalisation in south African higher education: Conversations on local and global exposure at the University of the Witwatersrand (Wits). *Journal of Studies in International Education, 15*(1), 75–92.

De Vita, G. (2002). Does assessed multicultural group work really pull UK students' average down? *Assessment and Evaluation in Higher Education, 27*(2), 153–161.

Fujimoto, Y., Hagel, P., Turner, P., Kattiyapornpong, U., & Zutshi, A. (2011). Helping university students to 'read' scholarly journal articles: The benefits of a structured and collaborative approach. *Journal of University Teaching & Learning Practice, 8*(3). Retrieved January 10, 2019, from https://ro.uow.edu.au/cgi/viewcontent.cgi?article=1193&context=jutlp

Gee, J. P. (2008). *Social linguistics and literacies: Ideology in discourses*. Oxford: Routledge.

Goody, J. (2010). *The Eurasian miracle*. Cambridge and Malden: Polity Press.

Gu, L. Y. (2003). *Jiaoxue gaige de xingdong yu quanshi* [*Education reform—action and interpretation*]. Beijing: People's Education Press.

Haigh, M. (2009). Fostering cross-cultural empathy with non-western curricular structures. *Journal of Studies in International Education, 13*(2), 271–284.

Hellmundt, S. (2003). *Research briefing the internationalisation of the tertiary curriculum: Linking intercultural communication theory with teaching and learning practices*. Retrieved January 10, 2018, from http://www.heacademy

Hobson, E. (2004). *Getting students to read: Fourteen tips*. Retrieved February 10, 2018, from http://www.theideacenter.org/sites/default/files/Idea_Paper_40.pdf

Holliday, A. R. (2005). *The struggle to teach English as an international language*. Oxford: Oxford University Press.

Huang, Q. (2014). *The hybrid tiger: Secrets of the extraordinary success of Asian-American kids*. Amherst, NY: Prometheus Books.

James, R., Krause, K., & Jennings, C. (2010). *The first-year experience in Australian universities: Findings from 1994 to 2009*. Retrieved February 10, 2017, from http://www.cshe.unimelb.edu.au/research/experience/docs/FYE_Report_1994_to_2009.pdf

Jerrim, J. (2014). *Why do East Asian children perform so well in PISA? An investigation of Western-born children of East Asian descent*. Department of Quantitative Social Science. Working Paper No. 14–16

Jin, L. X., & Cortazzi, M. (1998). The culture the learner brings: A bridge or a barrier? In M. Byram & M. Fleming (Eds.), *Language learning in intercultural perspective: Approaches through drama and ethnography* (pp. 98–118). Cambridge: Cambridge University Press.

Jin, L., & Cortazzi, M. (2006). Changing practices in Chinese cultures of learning. *Language, Culture and Curriculum, 19*(1), 5–20. https://doi.org/10.1080/07908310608668751

Kapoor, K. (2010). The humanities and the social sciences in India. *Prabuddha Bharata*. Retrieved February 10, 2018, from www.advaitaashrama.org

Keane, J. (2009). *Life and death of democracy*. London & New York: Simon & Schuster.

Lee, W. O. (1996). The cultural context for Chinese learners: Conceptions of learning in the Confucian tradition. In D. A. Watkins & J. B. Biggs (Eds.), *The Chinese learner: Cultural, psychological and contextual influences* (pp. 25–41). Hong Kong/Melbourne: Comparative Education Research Centre, The University of Hong Kong/Australian Council for Educational Research.

Loughran, J. J. (2004). A history and context of self-study of teaching and teacher education practices. In J. J. Loughran, M. L. Hamilton, V. K. LaBoskey, & T. Russell (Eds.), *International handbook of self-study of teaching and teacher education practices* (pp. 7–30). Dordrecht: Kluwer Academic.

Loughran, L., & Russell, T. (2006). Narrative accounts of self-study. *Studying Teacher Education, 2*(1), 1–3.

McInerney, D. M., & McInerney, V. (1994). *Educational psychology: Constructing learning.* Sydney: Hal.

McLaughlin, M., & DeVoogd, G. (2004). Critical literacy as comprehension: Expanding reader response. *Journal of Adolescent and Adult Literacy, 48*(1), 52–62.

O'Connor, K., & Zeichner, K. (2011). Preparing US teachers for critical global education. *Globalisation, Societies and Education, 9*(3–4), 521–536.

Pham, T. (2014). *Implementing cross-culture pedagogies: Cooperative learning at Confucian heritage cultures.* Singapore: Springer.

Pham, T., & Renshaw, P. D. (2013). How to enable Asian teachers to empower students to adopt student-centred learning. *Australian Journal of Teacher Education, 38*(11), 65–85.

Pham, T., & Renshaw, P. D. (2015). Formative assessment in Confucian heritage cultures classrooms: Activity theory analysis of tensions, contradictions and hybrid practices. *Assessment & Evaluation in Higher Education., 40*, 45. https://doi.org/10.1080/02602938.2014.886325

Rao, V. (2014). *Cultures of memory in South Asia: Orality, literacy and the problem of inheritance.* New Delhi: Springer.

Singh, M. (2009). Using Chinese in internationalising research education. *Globalisation, Societies & Education, 7*(2), 185–201.

Singh, M., & Shreshtha, M. (2009). International pedagogical structures admittance into the community of scholars via double knowing. In M. Hellstén & A. Reid (Eds.), *Researching international pedagogies* (pp. 65–82). The Netherlands: Springer.

Spencer, L. (2012). *Motivating law students to 'do the reading' before class: Appropriate extrinsic and intrinsic.* Retrieved from http://www.austlii.edu.au/au/journals/JlALawTA/2012/16.pdf

Stephen, B., & Keiko, Y. (2014). A tale of two councils. *International Journal of Training Research, 9*(3), 218–233.

Volet, S., & Kee, P. (1993). *Studying in Singapore—Studying in Australia: A student perspective.* Perth: Murdoch University.

Chapter 2
Improving Pedagogy in Response to Students' Reflective Learning Needs

Dat Bao

Abstract Reflective students who are pro-active in thought processing in the classroom often do not receive the same level of positive appraisal from teachers. Many educators have been conditioned by universal norms to believe that to talk profusely during class time means to engage while to remain frequently quiet tends to denote a lack of engagement. The chapter challenges this positioning and argues that teachers who neglect introverted students or treat them all as a low-engagement community risk perpetuating exclusivity in pedagogy. The discussion unpacks the dynamics of productive mental processing and points to the need of revamping pedagogical practices in ways which not only acknowledge students' need to learn contemplatively but also provide equitable assistance to the learning process. With education offered in this way, both highly articulate students and their reflective counterparts can benefit from a compassionate and inclusive pedagogy that does not diminish any individuals as peripheral.

Keywords Reflection · Silence · Talk · Engagement · Silent learning · Mental processing · Inclusive pedagogy

2.1 Introduction

The chapter advocates a better understanding of students' reflective learning behaviour and, based on this, proposes a pedagogy that responds to that knowledge. The concept of reflective students in this discussion refers to those who are pro-actively thoughtful in the learning process and may or may not feel the need to speak much during classroom processes. The fact that these students tend to keep quiet does not necessarily mean they are not learning as enthusiastically as many of their peers.

D. Bao (✉)
Monash University, Melbourne, VIC, Australia
e-mail: dat.bao@monash.edu

© Springer Nature Singapore Pte Ltd. 2021
D. Bao, T. Pham (eds.), *Transforming Pedagogies Through Engagement with Learners, Teachers and Communities*, Education in the Asia-Pacific Region: Issues, Concerns and Prospects 57, https://doi.org/10.1007/978-981-16-0057-9_2

Instead, they do process information as much as those who regularly participate in classroom discussions.

Educators and scholars' views on silent students, especially students of East Asian background, are sometimes exaggerated by too much attention being paid to students' national background and traditional beliefs as the outright source of influence (Han, 2003; Kennedy, 2002; Li, 2003; Matthews, 2001; Moon, 2011; Tamai & Lee, 2002). The serious problem of such a view comes from an excessive interest in students' static, original culture rather than the complex dynamics of classroom factors that govern silent behaviour. To assume silence primarily as the product of inherited values is to treat silence out of context and regard students as passive, powerless, and dependent individuals. To do so also means denying the reality that international students who come to study in Western countries are constantly exposed to different ways of thinking, learning, and behaving and have been making efforts to adapt to new academic settings.

Based on this realisation, there is a need to rethink the learning nature of quiet students in the classroom. This is because holding on to cultural background to explain the present-day classroom behaviour would risk disempowering students' autonomy and undermining individuals' resourcefulness. Education research has shown that during their silence, many students share contribution space with others (Bao, 2014). They care about the quality of verbal contribution, consider others' viewpoints, save class time by whispering to peers, perform mental processing, attentively listen, and connect with others in their thoughts.

2.2 Discourse on the Topic

2.2.1 The Need to Rethink Students' Silent Behaviour

Misperception about the silent mode of learning does not uniquely apply to students of Asian backgrounds. Anglo-Western students are also subject to misunderstanding if they are prone to silent learning behaviour. In a discussion on how silence serves as a learning strategy in a middle school classroom in the United States, Hall (2007) reports how silence was connected to students' learning disabilities and underperformance. In Hall's report, some American students who mainly employed silence as a way of learning to read had to go against the natural talking norm and suffered from being misunderstood as passive learners. While recognising the learning value of silence to some extent, the report highlights silent American students as those with weaker abilities than others: they struggle and hold on to silence as if holding on to a crutch.

Bao's (2014) empirical research at Monash University also denotes how many Australian students experience proactive silence within themselves in a culture of learning different from the highly verbal interaction styles expected in many Australian universities. In particular, they weigh silence as a significant processing tool. Some of them employ silence in ways that may be unknown to the teacher, such as cognitive thinking and intellectual engagement. This experience seems distant to some of the Anglo educational discourse which tends to treat classroom silence as a foreign behaviour.

Silent processing has exciting and flexible dynamics. Students' experiences with silent learning in many cases are filled with multiple cognitive, affective, and socio-cultural functions. It is interesting to note that not all members of a culture display behaviour commonly recognised of that culture, as in the case of many Anglo-Australian students who genuinely prefer the silent learning mode despite their international counterparts' belief that Australians only enjoy talking. In today's globalised context where learning styles are frequently exchanged, it is becoming harder to assume certain cultural groups would statically prefer certain learning modes. No matter how useful talk and silence may be, there will be moments when each of these behaviours may become awkward. In the everyday classroom, many teachers have experienced instants when they desperately want their students to speak up; as well as moments when they desperately want their students to 'shut up'.

Silence can be unpredictable in its quality. It can be purposeful or aimless, planned or impulsive, relaxed or strained, sophisticated or superficial, self-directed or other-oriented. The quality of silence is as important as the quality of talk. Silence is of high quality when it is well-timed, leaves necessary space for others to speak, has a communicative intention, serves mental processing, and helps to prepare for further interaction. On the contrary, its quality can be low if silence happens due to absent-mindedness or undesirable emotions such as fear, shyness or dissatisfaction. Observation and common-sense show that we all make conscious efforts to move in and out of silence in various needs to modify how we communicate. It is through efforts to break the silent routine or to refrain from a chatting desire that students' experiences become enriched, new skills are piloted and their comfort zone is challenged. Overall, both talk and silence have 'merits and demerits' in students' learning (Agyekum, 2002, p. 49). While silence allows space for reflection on talk, talk helps one to test the outcome of silence; in this way, one mode functions effectively thanks to the other.

2.2.2 Silence as a Mode of Communication

Silence and talk represent two modes of communication that exist in everyone's repertoire and which one is to be used in what context should be the matter of personal choice rather than of lack of ability. According to Dolya (2010), both internalised monologue and thinking aloud form the basic speech structures of human thoughts. Which mode to resort to, however, is dependent upon one's sociocultural experience. Because of this, the success or failure of language learning cannot be understood by looking at one single phenomenon and giving it one simplified interpretation. Instead, one needs to consider many social, cultural, political, historical, and economic forces where learning takes place. Every student, whether consciously or subconsciously, is bound by these factors which constantly play their roles in the educational process. Classroom preference and acceptance towards learning styles are examples of these forces. Many silent students feel intimidated when sensing how eloquent peers tend to hold themselves above others. Open-minded pedagogy could be a tool for social inclusion because verbal involvement has been used to exclude classroom members who are not prone to spontaneous verbal discourse. Educational processes will be most meaningful when the teacher is aware of how talk and silence, respectively or collectively, can help students learn effectively as well as overcome learning challenges.

When complex ideas cannot be put into words, some participants put them in a silent space where people do not judge. In doing so, they assume the right to make choices of how to most comfortably learn. This individual capacity to self-regulate classroom performance is often considered as student agency (Duff, 2012; Wright, 2012) assuming supreme ways of teaching and learning, then imposing them on students without consulting them would amount to the act of erasing such agency. Students should have the right and responsibility to resist what is unsuited without having to feel that this act denotes passivity. Passivity is often defined as the routine of rejecting new ideas being offered. However, in many cases if the new way is irrelevant to students' needs, not accepting it could mean that students are proactively taking control of their development. Agency as defined and understood by Pavlenko and Lantoff (2000, p. 169) is the foundation on which 'ultimate attainment' in learning is built. Forcing students to reflect silently when they wish to speak or making them verbally participate when they need quiet reflection would cause damage to their learning system.

Having said that, one also needs to be cautious about the belief that all kinds of silence can represent students' internal dialogues. In some cases, there is even the need to silence the internal voice to make learning more effective. One example of this would be student development of speed reading, whereby the act of thinking in words may represent intrusive thoughts that slow down the reading process. Sometimes, there is the need to view silence and talk with less focus on them as separate internal and external domains but as integrated, cohesive abilities without a clear-cut boundary in between. Silence can be seen as the beginning of talk and a portion of talk, so that to think and to talk might not be fundamentally different. As Ridgway (2009, p. 49) observes, 'thinking in a language provides practice which is arguably as good as speaking it. Processes as important as automatisation continue to operate and one's proficiency continues to develop'.

It remains a matter of managing one's resources depending on specific needs and situations. Learning involves the process of controlling talk as well as controlling the mind. In many cases, practising thoughts in the mind can be more challenging than practising talk, as inaccurate talk can get corrected by others while inaccurate thoughts are often left unnoticed. Silence can be the longest or the shortest distance between two people, and so can talk. Both dimensions may reach out to others or may turn away from others. Since talk and silence share surprisingly similar features, the dichotomy between them should be re-evaluated, so that these two domains do not have to expel one another but work collaboratively for mutual merits.

2.2.3 The Need for Silence Literacy Acquisition

The understanding that effective silence is not inherent but needs to be learned (Wardhaugh, 1992) and acquired (Agyekum, 2002) has been occasionally mentioned in scholarly discourse. To refrain from words when the situation requires quietness is an important ability in the development of socialising, acculturative, and communicative competences. The skill to construct eloquent silence would be a valuable addition to the ability for articulation, both of which would constitute what Haskins (2010, p. 1) refers to as 'human wholeness' rather than single-sided development. Such a prerequisite is evident in the studies when participants express aspiration for high-quality silence, which refers to its appropriate timing and moderate nature, to be considered as a condition for collaborative learning in the classroom.

It is important to respect a thoughtful balance between talk and silence as necessary behaviour for working effectively with peers. My interview with both Australian and international students (Bao, 2014) reveals that an ideal classmate to pair with is someone who can share a valuable idea and refrains from speaking when there is nothing meaningful to say—rather than someone who talks persistently to fill in the gap. Besides, students' untimely silence during verbal discussion can send out the message that the pedagogy or content needs adjustment to become more inspiring. Silence does not come from individual students but is governed by factors in lesson content as well as in teacher and peer behaviour.

In many cases, when the desire to express one's view is not well-timed, that is, when classroom discussion has not provided the right gap for the right contribution, one might consider restraining that desire for a moment. Such delay does not mean that communication is lacking but may imply that the person knows how to communicate. Blurting out words any time one wishes to do so is not always the best policy. To share meaningful ideas requires preparation to ensure that the message is fully well-versed. If sociocultural competence is perceived as part of communication ability, knowing when and how to keep silent is a socialisation acquisition process alongside language acquisition (Agyekum, 2002; Wardhaugh, 1992). Teachers need to be socioculturally and pedagogically sensitive to facilitate this process rather than ignore or frown on the absence of words as a lack of cooperation. It is the ability to mediate speech and silence in students' competence, rather than to produce talkative interlocutors who act the same in all contexts, that can represent productive learning and appropriate pedagogy.

To achieve the above abilities would require teachers' pedagogical competence to embrace some acquisition of silence literacy, because verbal and silent skills function together in many real-world social settings. Silence, like talk, should not be employed in the same way all the time, especially in cross-cultural contexts where members of various cultures hold different sociopragmatic values. Even within the same culture, ways of talking and behaving in silence need to be adjusted to reflect the communicative intention and social dominance between interlocutors. It is commonly acknowledged that without relevant sociocultural understanding, students would not be able to vary their message to achieve nuances of meaning (Harlow, 1990; Leech, 1983; Thomas, 1983). For this reason, only learning how to speak would make interactive skills incomplete, but a thoughtful communicator also needs to learn to refrain from speech in a timely manner to show interpersonal understanding and maintain a good relationship. To develop such ability entails both learning in the classroom and observing social interaction. From a pedagogical viewpoint, being made to talk when one feels more comfortable with silent thinking would be detrimental to learning (Chalmers & Volet, 1997; Moust, Schmidt, De Volder, Belien, & De Grave, 1987; Remedios, Clark, & Hawthorne, 2008; Wilson, 2004). Besides, being able to select one's favourite learning mode and to control how to learn is more important than simply following the teacher's instruction (Armstrong, 2012).

In everyone's communication repertoire, silence and verbalisation may happen in subconscious combinations, and as interaction proceeds, one person's talk may overlap with another person's silence, making it hard to notice whose silence is currently playing what role. It is only when talk ceases that silence becomes more obvious. Talk, as Picard (1952) emphasises, is a virtue when a good explanation saves misunderstanding. Likewise, silence is a virtue when a good pause saves superfluous abuse of meaning. In many cases, silence takes over when language reaches the limit of its expressive capacity. When words fail, it is not the emptiness that is left behind but sometimes an imperative space is proposed to build further understanding. In this case, silence does not represent the loss of words but the replacement of words by a more expressive means of message delivery.

Silence as situated within the students' home country and silence as recontextualised in an overseas academic institution can be practised differently. Research shows that Japanese students in Australia simply do not practise silence in the same way as they would in their classrooms in Japan (Morikawa, 2013). Instead, many students internalise the need to modify their behaviour as demanded by new learning situations. Such socio-educational adjustment suggests that the nature of silence is dynamic and unsettled rather than static and largely reliant on home culture. Many international students in Australia have made efforts to adopt new learning and communicative styles which may be distant from their pre-existing behaviour. The difficulty, however, arises when they have to debate with eloquent Australian native users of English. The language barrier, local knowledge, and academic culture make it hard to contribute much, resulting in what sometimes gets misjudged as a static representation of Confucian behaviour. Many East Asian students in Australia have been resistant to this identifier as an insult to their learning dynamics and individual intelligence. Silence is subject to a great degree of repositioning, negotiation, and reconstruction as students shift their academic settings. As Cortazzi and Jin (2002) emphasise, culture of learning, which refers to a student's practice, expectation, and interpretation, does not have an inert nature but is constantly changing based on changes in both home education and host education. It has been widely acknowledged that students' educational beliefs, values, and learning styles can become highly modifiable as the exposure to and interaction with international cultures increases (Li, 2010; Ryan & Louie, 2007; Shi, 2006; Zhao & Liu, 2008).

2.2.4 Silence in Writing Practice

Talk and silence both have a close relationship with the written word. Not unlike talk which needs related skills such as attentive listening and relevant gestures, silent thinking might need to be supported by tools to make learning happen, and one such closely related tool would be writing. The main reason for connecting silence with writing is because the cognitive processing function of silence allows it to go well with the need for recording thoughts to keep or use them. As Elbow (1985, p. 299) emphasises, to 'write is to rehearse mental events inside our heads before putting them down'. According to Moffett (1982), education serves to direct the mind, and it is the teacher's job to help students expand their inner speech rather than restrict or neglect it.

Although a great deal of research has been conducted into the relationship between speech and writing, not many studies have investigated the relationship between silence and writing. Regarding the question of whether students write better when they are talking or when they keep silent, many studies have pointed to the direction where it is talk that improves writing (Hubert, 2011; Rozin, Bressman, & Taft, 1974; Zhu, 2007). Despite this, many projects have only compared well-organised talk with the mere absence of talk—rather than well-organised talk and well-organised silence. This is a worthwhile gap in current research which deserves serious attention to further our understanding of the role silence plays in an academic setting.

2.3 Methodology

The chapter provides a pedagogical discussion as a follow-up on a series of empirical research projects by Bao (2014) with over 100 students from Australia, China, Japan, Korea, and Vietnam who study in Australian universities. These projects were conducted for 3 years, that is, during 2011 and 2013, and their outcomes were published in a book titled *Understanding Silence and Reticence* (Bao, 2014). The studies rest upon a phenomenological qualitative case study design, with open-ended in-depth interviews as the main source of data. The focus was on how students employ the silent learning mode in their academic study, which includes issues such as strengths, challenges, self-management of learning, peer preferences, learning conditions, and influential factors.

Although all the studies shared the same design, they were replicated with five different target groups and produced five different sets of findings. Such a variety powerfully demonstrated the fact silence as a learning choice is not at all simple: individuals, based on their personality and interaction with their learning contexts, exhibited various ways of employing silence to serve learning. Due to the scope of this chapter, I shall not present all the findings from the above projects. However, I would like to share three most helpful insights from them, which are often overlooked by educators, and which I would like to utilise to propose the pedagogy for this discussion.

The main reason for following up in the above-mentioned projects in developing this chapter comes the need to apply knowledge about reflective learning, or productive silence, to enhancing pedagogy. Drawing from my research-based understanding of how students have employed silence to learn, such as processing information and rehearsing verbalisation in the mind, I would like to propose several strategies for teachers to help students maximise their reflective learning potential. Such strategies, as later will be presented in some detail, include being attentive to students' reflection time and space, refraining from encouraging untimely participation, considering task-related factors that might require silent thinking, among other kinds of support that silence-inclusive pedagogy should be able to provide. In a word, the focus of this chapter is about how pedagogy can benefit from knowledge about students' silent mode of learning, which was discovered from my previous empirical studies.

2.4 Research Findings

The following discoveries came from my multiple research projects as mentioned above. These selected findings point to students' awareness of silence as an autonomous choice, a learning foundation, and an affective domain. These ideas are presented to serve as the basis for the pedagogical discussion which is the major theme of this chapter.

2.4.1 Autonomous Choice

Firstly, silence in many cases represents a conscious choice rather than inherent passivity. Many students express the need to work in silence when learning content seems cognitively demanding. When this need is felt, reflective students find highly verbal peers' premature participation fairly unpleasant as it interferes with their mental processing space. For reflective students, collaborative learning is not just about incessantly talking with each other, which at times might become a form of abuse, but is also about being verbally moderate and respectful of peers' learning space. Some Anglo-Australian students resent the fact that their natural silent learning behaviour is often treated as going against the talking norm, and thus, they suffer from being misunderstood as passive learners. This realisation also reflects Hall's (2007) observation of how silent American students are perceived as less competent learners.

2.4.2 Learning Foundation

Secondly, silence if well observed, guided, and managed can become a powerful foundation of learning on which many processing tools are exercised including, for example, connecting knowledge, critical thinking of target content, comparing and contrasting views, gathering resources, talking in the mind and taking notes of one's thoughts. A well-utilised silence time can play the role of transferring ideas from internal processing to external output, which is likely to be a high-quality contribution to classroom learning after students have processed an issue of shared interest. It is revealed by participants that the practice of inner speech generates useful resources for the selective presentation of good ideas. As Rogers (1969) observes, students' internal processing skills, which are often overlooked, should be recognised as having their creditability.

2.4.3 Affective Domain

Thirdly, silence itself is perceived as affect, that is, being characterised by learner emotions which influence learning mood and inspiration. For example, students who enjoy a reflective process but are pressured to verbally participate would feel mentally disturbed and lose interest in the learning activity to the extent that they might give up making the best effort possible. This understanding responds well to Bloom's (1956) taxonomy which embraces three dimensions constituting effective learning, namely cognition, psychomotor, and affect. Arguably, some students use silence mainly for self-learning, that is, mostly learning in quietness; while others eventually make use of silence for social learning, that is, speaking out the ideas that they have process quietly in the mind. Being able to observe and respect both of these tendencies would maintain a helpful social balance and a healthy peer relationship.

2.5 Main Discussion

This discussion unpacks the findings presented above to show the process of how silent reflection is selected by students as their natural learning inclination and ways in which such reflection functions. The section then touches on how classroom verbal participation and silent learning work together, both of which represent a well-balanced foundation for learning. The relationship between talk and silence, in a political sense, also perpetuates classroom hierarchy and, in many cases, throw classroom power off balance. Based on all these ideas, pedagogy will be revisited with the usefulness of silent processing in mind; and finally, a concrete pedagogical model is recommended to help teachers consider task design that respects and nurtures such students' silent learning space.

2.5.1 Silent Reflection as a Learning Choice

There is a need to recognise both mental processing and verbal interaction as the two dimensions of academic learning. However, the practice of such mode is subject to contextual factors. For instance, as international students move to a different culture of learning, their social practice is subject to institutional control, and oppressive acts are likely to take place if there is no facilitating agent to mediate this process. Students may wish to adapt, and the institution should provide thoughtful support. Classrooms in contemporary times in pursuit of diversity in social, cultural, and academic ways need to look at education from both pedagogical and learning perspectives and recognise this tension: while silence makes teaching difficult for teachers, low acceptance of silence makes learning difficult for students.

Silence exists in every student's repertoire and negating it, neglecting it, or not finding ways to utilise it would amount to a waste of learning resources. Many students employ silence in classroom learning whether the teacher is aware of such practice or not; some attempt to turn silence into speech production; others withdraw into themselves after realising that their teacher cares more about verbal participation than organised reflection. Arguably, students need concrete classroom processes to strengthen their mental processing ability rather than merely receiving the teacher's sympathy. Along this line, it is important to be aware that the proactive use of silence can support the production of high-quality speech. Teachers with this understanding are likely to allow room for mental rehearsal to reach its optimum.

Mental rehearsal provides conditions for self-directed learning which can be either connected to or independent from teaching. Pedagogically recognised silence can liberate students from the constraint of having to produce the impulsive, low-quality participation. Silence needs to be managed with an acute awareness of why, how, when, and how long one needs it to support their learning, and when the verbal mode of learning should take over. Obligatory talk can be frustrating when students are required to publicise their half-baked thoughts when they are unprepared to do so. Silence training should be organised to include reflectivity, concentration, outcome, and avoidance of idle, unproductive moments—the same way as talk that needs to be directed to enhance learning rather than become a mere social time in the classroom. The structure of learning will fundamentally change when this knowledge is applied so that students can employ both silence and talk as learning tools in conscious, informed ways.

Suppose every student in the classroom takes every single opportunity to speak out, which might be considered odd and the person could be disliked by the rest of the class for being too talkative. Rather than saying everything that crosses their mind, students might consider selecting only the chances when they have something worthwhile to say. The rest of their time not spent on speaking can be invested in cognitive thinking and building inspiration for further discussion. Some students can think and talk effectively at the same time; others may find it hard to combine spontaneous talk and cognitive thinking.

2.5.2 Silence and Talk as a Foundation of Learning

According to Yang's (1994) social orientation theory, for a society to be culturally healthy, its members should be involved in the practice of reciprocity, shared responsibility, solidarity, and belonging. To apply these principles in educational settings, students should talk or keep silent not only to serve their learning but also to benefit the learning of the community. Doing so is to make shared norms productive, build interpersonal acceptance, and work towards the welfare of the group. Words are not to be thrown into the air and become lost, but they are meant to be a useful substance of learning for others. Classroom time is too limited and valuable to be wasted upon the careless word from the casual mind. If everyone learns to be a considerate partner, every minute of learning will be more efficiently spent; the shared learning environment, instead of being filled with social talk, will be enriched with worthwhile thoughts, good-quality contribution, and well-deserved attention.

Silence, like talk, should not be used by students in the same way permanently, but the skills in employing the internal space in fact must improve. When a speaker becomes increasingly eloquent, he or she might spend less time on internal rehearsal—not because the person has stopped rehearsing, but because many years of experience in rehearsing communication skills have made that person so skilful that the rehearsal step happens almost as fast as not happening at all. The same phenomenon occurs when someone practises marksmanship. At first, the person aims his or her gun towards the target, which takes a moment. Over time as practice increases, the aiming takes less and less time until 1 day, the marksman simply raises the gun and shoots almost without preparation. This, however, does not mean that aiming does not take place but simply suggests that the aiming act has become such a gift that the viewer's eye cannot detect it anymore—although it always happens every time the shot is exercised.

Using silence, likewise, should become a gift developed over the years so that it is used in the least time possible. In many cases, although reflection continues to take place, it precedes and merges so well with speech that the listener can hardly notice it. A speaker who, over many years of practising internal and external speech, still holds on to long silent pauses might not be considered as an effective communicator. Although, in classroom settings, where the teacher allows time for silence to operate as a learning tool, students should eventually reach the point where they employ silent rehearsal skilfully enough to avoid unreasonable delays in real-world communication. While silence can be a thoughtful tool for learning, it should not become a permanent habit of communicating.

2.5.3   The Silence–Talk Hierarchy

Classroom hierarchy among peers has its complex dynamics. Affectively speaking, peers in the same classroom might exert influence over one another's learning behaviour. In a four-year course I have taught at Monash University, most students happened to be Anglo-white except two. During class discussion, these two students felt so inhibited by their eloquent Anglo peers that they could not participate much. Despite my efforts to involve these two by connecting discussion with their cultural resources, they simply lost interest in verbal interaction altogether. Halfway through the semester, they dropped out of the course. It was not so much the cultural factors but the different histories of educational behaviour that drew a line between the two modes of participation, in the end making these students give up their sense of belonging in the class community. This anecdote shows how classroom hierarchy was subconsciously established not necessarily through pedagogy. As a lecturer who supports both the silent and verbal modes of learning, I held little power to reshape the culture of participation in this class, which reflects important values of Australian higher education concerning the broader outspoken, democratic society.

In many cases, students' history of and experience with classroom dynamics tend to position students on an unequal socio-political footing. To reform this position requires constructing new rules of classroom participation by moderating between talking space and silent space, so that the talkative student can withdraw into reflection and leave room for the reflective student to attempt speaking out more. When it comes to modifying students' learning behaviour and expanding their learning mode, breaking silence to promote talk in some students would be just as important as reducing talk to promote silence in some others. This might be a real challenge, however, if the majority of class members are prone to one dominant learning mode. Changing the participation style of a large group of students could be a more demanding task for the teacher than changing that of a few individuals.

Power hierarchy in the classroom is reinforced through teachers' attitudes towards silence and talk, as well as teachers' preferences for certain interaction dynamics, both of which play a role in confirming the dominant structure of values in classroom practice and making students feel included in or excluded from the learning process. Discourse in education indicates that students' sociocultural identity is constituted by age, gender, social class, and racial background, each of which plays a part in how students participate and are received by the teacher. Likewise, students who are underprivileged for choosing to learn in the silent mode may become victims of classroom hierarchy and inequality. This can make verbal students develop more positive emotions towards the learning process than those who are more silent. Such favouritism not only reduces learning enthusiasm but also affects formative assessment processes and may influence students' future in undesirable ways.

Teachers' verbal performance also plays a role in asserting power. Many teachers have an inherent tendency to be repetitive in classroom talk. For example, one might reiterate certain items during lectures and discussions for emphasis or filling time during the thinking process. Classroom power is never balanced: when students are busy thinking, they do not normally talk; but teachers seem to assume the authority to think aloud without being criticised. Because of this, instruction is sometimes rephrased and repeated to the extent of becoming redundant in the teaching process.

Silence has been recognised in the projects as a site of disempowerment, which according to the participants is a major issue that needs to be addressed. Treating silence and talk as equal learning tools therefore would contribute to the creation of equality, justice, and inclusivity in the educational setting. Unfortunately, students are not inherently in the position of power to challenge the dominant ideology of what constitutes good learning. It is also important to notice that classroom behaviour is not always controlled by the teacher but can be shaped by the dominant culture of a class. In my observation, class members who talk eloquently not only seem to assert more authority than quiet counterparts but also hold patronising perception towards their silent peers. This attitude can be sensed by quiet students, some of whom easily become intimidated and withdraw further into themselves. Others try harder to speak out hopefully to mend their public image but at the same time internalise classroom as a struggle site where they cannot remain themselves but must behave according to social convention. This situation could become worse if the teacher tends to favour speech over silence and somehow develops low perception towards silent students' ability.

2.6 Embracing Silence in Pedagogy

Drawn from the above-mentioned understanding, it would be helpful for pedagogy to acknowledge silence as a natural part of the learning process. This, however, does not mean that teachers should leave silent students on their own to develop any strategies that might work with them. Doing that would mean giving up helping students to learn. Silence should be made productive through guidance rather than be treated with another kind of silence. Respecting silence through neglect implies that the teacher is only responsible for classroom learning when students agree to speak; otherwise, they are left on their own.

Pedagogical response to student silence also needs to be positioned in a broader social context. As educators stress the importance of developing real-world communication competences, which involves the ability to initiate and manipulate conversations, it is essential to challenge students' capability to move beyond their comfort zone of behaviour. Suppose the value of silence is over-cherished in the classroom, the reflective student who later steps out into the world might experience difficulty in coping with the complex reality of human interaction in which not everybody can respect silence as much as the kind-hearted teacher. Education needs to create challenges and push learning beyond where it is, and this should happen in a well-intended and well-informed pedagogical manner without undermining students' ability to learn. As the globalised world is becoming more tolerant towards a culturally diverse climate, education needs to be more tolerant towards academically diverse styles.

Some of these insights agree with the current discourse on silence and disempowerment. Teachers' negative perceptions of silence and reluctance in inviting reticent students to participate can marginalise them from classroom events (Ellwood & Nakane, 2009; Granger, 2013). When students sense that the teacher does not have confidence in their ability and contribution, they will feel 'powerless', 'alienated' (Morita, 2004, p. 589), and tend to withdraw not only from participation but also from the desire to cooperate and learn. In a word, student reticence can be constituted by the perception, attitude, and behaviour of peers, teachers, and the reticent students themselves. In other words, classroom behaviour has an interpersonal nature, since how one group perceives others may have an impact on how others act. If the views of this group could be mediated to become more tolerant, accepting, and accommodating towards others' styles, learning effectiveness would be enhanced.

For the above reasons, teachers may consider making their role less dominant to create a more desirable power balance. Classroom discussion if not well handled, can be a site of the silencing of others (Leander, 2002) as teacher talk and frequent nomination of eloquent students might expel less verbal students from their optimum learning practice. As equal members of the classroom society, everyone has the right and responsibility to avoid this form of subjugation from happening as it might cause damage not only to optimal learning conditions but also to a positive classroom relationship. This scenario should be seen beyond a participation problem among students to be recognised as a pedagogical issue in practice.

Teachers need to build awareness in appropriate pedagogy to meet the changing needs and preferences of their students. This can be made possible by observing students' reactions, emotions, and learning readiness to modify teaching. It might be helpful to develop the habit of observing non-verbal expressions from students, treating them as feedback signs of connection with the teacher, and lesson content. In many cases, pedagogical adaptation can be made by the teacher not only based on talk but also based on observation of student silence. Arguably, to be able to read students' non-verbal behaviour in the classroom, teachers must be good at using non-verbal behaviour themselves.

Effective classroom management requires the teacher to see how this picture makes sense to balance talk and silence in a way that both modes obtain their deserving places in the learning process. Letting talkative students talk too much and silent students remain silent too long may not be an ideal policy because that kind of permission simply maintains the status quo. Such an attitude will not require any skills from the teacher, nor will it help students improve what they are not good at. As a teacher, it might be helpful to advise students not only to maximise the potential of their favourite learning styles but also to stretch beyond their regular learning habits whenever necessary.

For teachers to be able to detect the nature of silence, organise it, and provide a strategic response to it would be taking one giant step towards more effective pedagogy. Working in educational settings on an everyday basis without being equipped with a good understanding of and some experience in interpreting silence might get teachers to become dramatically deskilled because that could mean having little or no control over students until they choose to engage in talking. The lack of this ability and the bias against silence could bring disaster because every time students decide to switch to the silent learning mode, which means the teacher might get cut off from communication with them. For the above reason, teachers must be able to negotiate classroom participation structures and ensure that every learning style has a place to operate without forcing students to restrain themselves and without giving the impression of any formulaic learning model as being supreme.

2.7 A Proposed Pedagogical Framework

Silence can shift its perspectives and become noisy, depending on the question of whose experience we are talking about. While the term 'silence' indicates someone's muteness as viewed by others, inside her mind the silent person may not perceive herself as silent at all as she can hear the articulation of her voice. In this way, what outsiders perceive as 'silence' would be perceived by the insider as a form of thinking engagement. Inspired by this change in standpoints, I would like to propose a practical model for teachers to construct tasks which assist a reflective learning experience. The model is named as 'RADAR', which stands for Review—Aim—Direction—Assessment—Reflection. To perform each of these steps requires the teacher to answer many questions which will take the class through a silent engagement activity. In the end, students will have gathered ideas and language to share with peers, and the options for this sharing could be in written, verbal, or reading aloud form. This method can be applied to both task design and teaching practice.

Review—Are students willing to perform a classroom activity in some degree of silence?—Can the teacher think of a task that is cognitively demanding and affectively engaging enough to require some silent processing and reflection?

Aim—What is the aim of the activity? What skills does the activity teach? How much silent time should students spend on the task? Can they also talk if they like?

Direction—What role does silence play? In particular, what do students need to process and reflect on? What linguistic, cultural, and experiential resources do students need to perform this activity? Can they obtain such resources by themselves or do they need teacher assistance? What should the teacher do to guide students through the task?

Assessment—How does the teacher judge if student silence is being used productively? What should be done when the silent time ends? What outcome will be produced? How should the outcome be evaluated? Who will evaluate the task, the teacher or students?

Reflection—What do students learn from the experience? What does the teacher learn from the experience? What are some learning and teaching difficulties? What evidence demonstrates the success of the activity? How do students feel? What should be done differently next time?

2.8   Implications for Teacher Professional Development

Teachers are often trained to work with talk, such as organising discussion, raising questions, and responding to ideas. Since it is uncommon for teacher development programs to explore the use of silence, it often becomes confusing when many teachers encounter this phenomenon in the everyday educational setting and silence easily becomes a hindrance to pedagogy. For this reason, development programs should develop teacher sensitivities for timely talk or silent reflection in response to the changing needs and classroom conditions. As a tool for both learning and communication, silence should be cognitively useful and socially authentic, that is, functioning well in the academic classroom and making sense in the broader social context.

Silence requires adaptation practice as one moves to a new cultural setting and communicates with members of that culture. If students are comfortable with a culture where either silence or talk is dominant, there may be the need to adapt and adjust beyond that norm. Mutual adaptation will ease the challenge of differences and contribute to more sensible cultures of learning and a productive learning environment. This attitude goes well with Hinkel's (2006, p. 110) review of current pedagogical trends in which he highlights the need for 'situationally relevant pedagogy', a direction which is deemed more important than the development of any single method. Flexibility and sensitivity towards context have become important qualities besides knowledge about learning.

The challenging part of this practice may come from the fact that not all students will need silence in the same activity and not all of those who are prone to silence would use it in the same way. Some may process comprehension of learning content in silence; others may formulate inner dialogues. In many cases, one activity might need to fall into multiple sub-tasks, so that students can opt for a silent option, a verbal option, or a combined option. Being able to self-select how to learn will reflect the true meaning of student-centredness as advocated by Edwards (2001, p.37), which emphasises that students should be 'able to learn what is relevant for them in ways that are appropriate' rather than be forced to speak out at any cost because the teacher believes they should. That would be considered as oppression, not student-centredness.

To employ silence as a way of learning and a tool to prepare for thoughtful classroom discussion, students must be aware of how they have engaged in silence so far and what is required to fill in the gap between desirable and undesirable silence. The task of scrutinising and self-regulating the use of silence for learning requires both awareness and actions. According to many psychologists, no successful self-regulation of behaviour can take place without awareness of what is going on. 'You cannot change a given behaviour in the desired direction if you are oblivious to the way you act and if you don't even know how you should behave' (Morin & Everett, 1990, p. 352).

2.9 Conclusion

I would like to take this opportunity to recommend three themes for future research into the silent mode of learning. The reason for the recommendation is that our understanding of silent learning on a deeper level would benefit the quality of future pedagogy. They include teachers' and students' comparative perspectives on silence, personal factors influencing silence, looking beyond the classroom and into online silence. First of all, it would be useful to conduct comparative research on teacher and student perspectives on silence. There has been a growing awareness that students' view of the classroom process frequently often differs from teachers' view. Many empirical studies have discovered the divergence between teacher and student perceptions towards classroom process (Barkhuizen, 1998; McDonough, 2002; Nunan, 1988; Spratt, 1999; Williams & Burden, 1997), which is related to what Holliday (1994, p. 7) explains: 'all teachers are outsiders to the cultures of their students'.

Secondly, personal factors influencing silence represent another worthwhile area for scholarly investigation. Silence may vary from person to person depending on factors such as age, gender, disposition, and social class. Empirical research shows that some students who are more mature than others tend to keep quiet for fear of appearing less competent than younger peers (Bao, 2014). Regarding social class, it is noticed that the middle-class Anglo-white students in Britain and North America are more prone to a high degree of verbalisation while other social groups tend to be more tolerant towards silence (Brantlinger, 1993; Jaworski & Sachdev, 2004; Milroy, 1981). As far as gender is concerned, some scholars observed that in many contexts, male students seem to be more verbal than their female counterparts (see, for example, Schmidt, Zaleski, Shumow, Ochoa-Angrino, & Hamidova, 2011). My experiences teaching education in an Australian university setting, however, indicate a different tendency in which male students seem less verbal. These observations may not be absolute in all situations but vary across national, social, and academic sub-cultures. Arguably, how such personal factors influence the use of silence represents interesting areas for further research.

Thirdly, silence research can expand beyond face-to-face classroom settings into virtual learning space. Today's changing globalised contexts may prompt the need to research silence beyond a face-to-face learning mode, that is, online silence. Nowadays as words such as 'interaction' and 'chat' are placed in Google search, their meanings often take on a digital connotation. Likewise, the concept of 'silence' has altered its meaning as the nature of communication in the digital age constantly changes. As much as the concepts of social presence and social interaction have been modified (Gunawardena et al., 2001; Leh, 2001), silence can also refer to the state of being quiet from writing rather than from talking (Zembylas & Vrasidas, 2007). When someone is not making written comments during the engagement with online discussion, the person is considered as keeping quiet. Silence in this sense indicates a social and psychological distance between humans, that is, the lack of attentiveness, engagement, responsiveness, and participation. The need to understand the nature of and reasons for such types of silence should be studied alongside the need to improve online learning and communication.

The outcome from the above investigation would serve to enhance the quality to classroom activities which take silence into consideration. Classroom tasks should involve productive use of silence, with a clear rationale related to why, how, and how long to practice silence, as well as arrangement for following up on tasks and assessing student performance. The implementation of such tasks may go through reflection and theorisation that would benefit intellectuality. Scholars and educators should also consider cross-cultural understandings of silence share ways to consider silence in pedagogy, develop frameworks for silent engagement in task design, develop approaches to interpret, and assess silence as ways of learning.

References

Agyekum, K. (2002). The communicative role of silence in Akan. *Pragmatics, 12*(1), 31–51.

Armstrong, J. S. (2012). Natural learning in higher education. In N. M. Seel (Ed.), *Encyclopedia of the sciences of learning* (pp. 2426–2433). New York: Springer.

Bao, D. (2014). *Understanding silence and reticence: Nonverbal participation in second language acquisition*. London: Bloomsbury.

Barkhuizen, G. P. (1998). Discovering learners' perceptions of ESL classroom teaching/learning activities in a south African context. *TESOL Quarterly, 32*(1), 85–108.

Bloom, B. S. (1956). *Taxonomy of educational objective, handbook I: The cognitive domain*. New York: David McKay.

Brantlinger, E. A. (1993). *The politics of social classes in secondary school: Views of affluent and impoverished youth*. New York: Teachers College, Columbia University.

Chalmers, D., & Volet, S. (1997). Common misconceptions about students from Southeast-Asia studying in Australia. *Higher Education Research and Development, 16*(1), 87–98.

Cortazzi, M., & Jin, L. (2002). Communication for learning across cultures. In R. Harris & D. McNamara (Eds.), *Overseas students in higher education: Issues in teaching and learning* (3rd ed.). New York: Routledge.

Dolya, G. (2010). *Vygotsky in action in the early years: The 'key to learning' curriculum*. London: Routledge.

Duff, P. (2012). Second language socialization. In A. Duranti, E. Ochs, & B. Schieffelin (Eds.), *Handbook of language socialization* (pp. 564–586). New York: Blackwell Publishing.

Edwards, R. (2001). Meeting individual learner needs: Power, subject, subjection. In C. Paechter, M. Preedy, D. Scott, & J. Soler (Eds.), *Knowledge, power and learning* (pp. 37–46). London: Sage Publications.

Elbow, P. (1985). The shifting relationship between speech and writing. *College Composition and Communication, 36*(3), 283–303.

Ellwood, C., & Nakane, I. (2009). Privileging of speech in EAP and mainstream university classrooms: A critical evaluation of participation. *TESOL Quarterly, 43*(2), 203–230.

Granger, C. A. (2013). Silence and participation in the language classroom. In C. A. Chapelle (Ed.), *The encyclopedia of applied linguistics* (pp. 1–4). Oxford: Blackwell Publishing.

Gunawardena, C. N., Nolla, A. C., Wilson, P. L., Lopez Islas, J. R., Ramirez-Angel, N., & Megchun-Alpizar, R. M. (2001). A cross-cultural study of group processes and development in online conferences. *Distance Education: An International Journal, 22*(1), 85–121.

Hall, L. A. (2007). Understanding the silence: Struggling readers discuss decisions about reading expository texts. *Journal of Educational Research, 100*(3), 132–141.

Han, S. A. (2003). *Do South Korean adult learners like native English speaking teachers more than Korean teachers of English?* Paper presented at the AARE conference in Auckland, New Zealand, November 30.

Harlow, L. (1990). Do they mean what they say?: Sociopragmatic competence and second language learner. *The Modern Language Journal, 74*, 328–351.

Haskins, C. (2010). Integrating silence practices into the classroom. E value of quiet. *ENCOUNTER: Education for Meaning and Social Justice, 23*(3), 1–6.

Hinkel, E. (2006). Current perspectives on teaching the four skills. *TESOL Quarterly, 40*(1), 109–131.

Holliday, A. (1994). *Appropriate methodology and social context.* Cambridge: Cambridge University Press.

Hubert, M. (2011). The speaking-writing connection: Integrating dialogue into a foreign language writing course. *Electronic Journal of Foreign Language Teaching, 8*(2), 170–183.

Jaworski, A., & Sachdev, I. (2004). Teachers' beliefs about students' talk and silence: Constructing academic success and failure through metapragmatic comments. In A. Jaworski, N. Coupland, & D. Galasinki (Eds.), *Metalanguage: Social and ideological perspectives* (pp. 227–244). Berlin: Mouton de Gruyter.

Kennedy, P. (2002). Learning culture and learning styles: Myth-understanding about adult (Hong Kong) Chinese learners. *International Journal of Lifelong Education, 21*(5), 430–445.

Leander, K. M. (2002). Silencing in classroom interaction: Producing and relating social spaces. *Discourse Processes, 34*(2), 193–235.

Leech, G. (1983). *Principles of pragmatics.* London: Longman.

Leh, A. S. C. (2001). Computer-mediated communication and social presence in a distance learning environment. *International Journal of Educational Telecommunications, 7*, 109–128.

Li, J. (2003). The core of Confucian learning. *American Psychologist*, February, 146–7.

Li, J. G. (2010). 大学英语课堂学生沉默行为的原因分析及其相关对策 [An analysis of the reasons for learner silence in college English classrooms and some relevant solutions]. *Journal of Huaihua University, 29*(10), 152–3.

Matthews, B. (2001). The relationship between values and learning. *International Education Journal, 2*(4), 223–232.

McDonough, J. (2002). The teacher as language learner: Worlds of difference? *ELT Journal, 56*(4), 404–411.

Milroy, J. (1981). *Regional accents of English: Belfast.* Belfast: Blackstaff.

Moffett, J. (1982). Writing, inner speech, and meditation. *College English, 44*(3), 231–246.

Moon, S. (2011). Expectation and reality: Korean sojourner families in the UK. *Language and Education, 25*(2), 163–176.

Morikawa, S. (2013), *Japanese university students' perception of studying at an Australian university.* Unpublished Master's thesis. Melbourne: Monash University.

Morin, A., & Everett, J. (1990). Inner speech as a mediator of self-awareness, self-consciousness, and self-knowledge: A hypothesis. *New Ideas in Psychology, 8*(3), 337–356.

Morita, N. (2004). Negotiating participation and identity in second language academic communities. *TESOL Quarterly, 38*(4), 573–603.

Moust, J., Schmidt, H., De Volder, M., Belien, J., & De Grave, W. (1987). Effects of verbal participation in small group discussion. In J. Richardson & W. Eysenck (Eds.), *Student learning: Research in education and cognitive psychology* (pp. 147–154). Milton Keynes: Open University Press.

Nunan, D. (1988). *The learner-centred curriculum.* Cambridge: Cambridge University Press.

Pavlenko, A., & Lantoff, J. P. (2000). Second language learning as participation and the (re)construction of selves. In J. P. Lanto (Ed.), *Sociocultural theory and second language learning* (pp. 155–177). New York: Oxford University Press.

Picard, M. (1952). *The world of silence.* S. Godman (Trans.). Chicago: Henry Regnery.

Remedios, L., Clark, D., & Hawthorne, L. (2008). The silent participant in small group collaborative learning contexts. *Active Learning in Higher Education, 9*(3), 201–216.

Ridgway, A. J. (2009). The inner voice. *The International Journal of English Studies, 9*(2), 45.

Rogers, C. (1969). *Freedom to learn: A view of what education might become* (1st ed.). Columbus, OH: Charles Merrill.

Rozin, P., Bressman, B., & Taft, M. (1974). Do children understand the basic relationship between speech and writing? The Mow-motorcycle Testa. *Journal of Reading Behaviour, 6*, 327–334.

Ryan, J., & Louie, K. (2007). False dichotomy? "Western" and "Confucian" concepts of scholarship and learning. *Education Philosophy and Theory, 39*(4), 404–417.

Schmidt, J. A., Zaleski, D. J., Shumow, L., Ochoa-Angrino, S., & Hamidova, N. (2011). 'What are they really doing? A descriptive analysis of science teachers' instructional practices and verbal interaction with students', *Science-in-the-moment*. Northern Illinois University. Retrieved October 4, 2013, from http://scienceinthemoment.cedu.niu.edu/scienceinthemoment/reports/SchmidtZaleskiShumowOchoaHamidova2011gender.pdf

Shi, L. (2006). The successors to Confucianism or a new generation? A questionnaire study on Chinese students' culture of learning English. *Language, Culture and Curriculum, 19*(1), 122–147.

Spratt, M. (1999). How good are we at knowing what learners like? *System, 27*(2), 141–155.

Tamai, K., & Lee, J. (2002). Confucianism as cultural constraint: A comparison of Confucian values of Japanese and Korean university students. *International Education Journal, 3*(5), 33–49.

Thomas, J. (1983). Cross-cultural pragmatic failure. *Applied Linguistics, 4*(2), 91–112.

Wardhaugh, R. (1992). *An introduction to sociolinguistics* (2nd ed.). Oxford: Blackwell.

Williams, M., & Burden, R. L. (1997). *Psychology for language teachers—A social constructivist approach*. Cambridge: Cambridge University Press.

Wilson, J. L. (2004). *Talking beyond the text: Identifying and fostering critical talk in a middle-school classroom*. Unpublished PhD dissertation. University of Missouri, Columbia.

Wright, L. (2012). *Second language learner and social agency*. Bristol: Multilingual Matters.

Yang, K. S. (1994). Chinese social orientation: A social interactional approach. In K. S. Yang & A. B. Yeu (Eds.), *The psychological behaviour of the Chinese* (pp. 82–142). Taipei: Kuei-Kuan. (in Chinese).

Zembylas, M., & Vrasidas, C. (2007). Listening for silence in text-based, online encounters. *Distant Education, 28*(1), 5–24.

Zhao, E. & Liu, L. (2008). *China's generation Y: Understanding the workforce*. Proceedings of the ICMIT 2008 4th IEEE International Conference on Management of Innovation and Technology (pp. 612–616). Singapore: The National University of Singapore.

Zhu, X. H. (2007). What do we know about the relationship between speaking and writing in college-level ESL students? *US-China Foreign Language, 5*(3), 31–40.

Chapter 3
Developing Effective Global Pedagogies in Western Classrooms: A Need to Understand the Internationalization Process of Confucian Heritage Cultures (CHC) Students

Thanh Pham

Abstract To support international students better, Australian institutions have called for the internationalization of the curriculum. Internationalization is defined as the integration of international or inter-cultural dimensions into the teaching, research, and service functions of higher education institutions. However, the process of internationalizing curricula at Australian institutions has been found to achieve minimal success due to conflicting understandings and arguments about how international, especially CHC, students learn. This study aimed to systematically and critically review and discuss CHC learners' practices from various perspectives. The study reported common stereotypes about CHC learners as well as myths that are not often discussed in the Western literature about CHC learners. Insights discussed in the study would help Western educators and researchers achieve a deeper understanding of CHC learners, so that they can implement more effective pedagogies in teaching CHC learners.

Keywords Confucian heritage cultures · Asia · Pedagogies · Australia · Internationalization · Higher education

3.1 Introduction

Australia's international education activities have become an important sector contributing to the country's economy. International students account for more than 20% of tertiary education students—the highest proportion of international students in all OECD countries. The majority of these international students are from Asian

T. Pham (✉)
Monash University, Melbourne, VIC, Australia
e-mail: thanh.t.pham@monash.edu

© Springer Nature Singapore Pte Ltd. 2021
D. Bao, T. Pham (eds.), *Transforming Pedagogies Through Engagement with Learners, Teachers and Communities*, Education in the Asia-Pacific Region: Issues, Concerns and Prospects 57, https://doi.org/10.1007/978-981-16-0057-9_3

countries; thus, there has been great interest in examining the learning practices of Asian students at Australian universities. One of the methods that many Australian institutions are implementing to become closer to and to learn from Asia as well as to attract more Asian students is internationalizing their curriculum. Knight (1997) claims that this is also one of the ways that many institutions worldwide are implementing to respond to the impact of globalization. In essence, internationalizing curriculum is defined as a process of integrating international or inter-cultural dimensions into the teaching, research, and service functions of higher education institutions (Harman, 2002). This means that content does not arise from a single cultural base but engages with the global plurality in terms of sources of knowledge (Webb, 2005, p. 110). For this meaning, the success in internationalizing curriculum at Australian institutions very much depends on how academics understand international students so that they can integrate this knowledge into their syllabus and teaching. Unfortunately, there are still many misunderstandings about the learning practices of CHC students. Characteristic learning attributes and identities assigned to CHC learners are often described on an evaluative continuum. At one end are constructions that see CHC learners as being obedient to authority, passive, dependent, surface/rote learners prone to plagiarism, lacking in critical thinking, and adopting inadequate learning strategies (Hammond & Gao, 2002). At the other end of the continuum, many researchers believe that Chinese learners have positive attributes as valuing active and reflective thinking, open-mindedness, and a spirit of inquiry (e.g. Biggs, 1996a, 1996b; Cheng, 2000). These extreme perspectives have created a real puzzle that has placed Western academics in a situation where they do not know how to work with Asian students effectively and appropriately. Consequently, Western academics, to a large extent, still set and use their own rules and expectations which provide subjective criteria for evaluating what are appropriate learning behaviours and methods of instruction in Australia's learning environment (Volet, 1999). This is why Webb (2005) claims that in reality, it is rare to see any real examination of the appropriateness of conventional Western pedagogical approaches to contemporary, more globalized and culturally interdependent contexts for both domestic and international students. What most Western institutions are doing is merely provide 'add-ons' such as the inclusion of international examples to their syllabus. Unfortunately, researchers have warned that any reform that only solves problems at the superficial level would not have long-term effects (Elmore, 1996; Fullan, 2000). This is why Webb further proposes that internationalization must move beyond such superficial approaches.

To clarify how CHC learners' learning should be understood correctly as well as to make some contribution to the process of internationalizing curriculum at Western institutions, this chapter aims to provide a review of research on CHC learners' learning practices and critically discuss how researchers from different discourses have argued over the relationship between culture and learning practices and how learning practices of CHC learners are transformed at Western institutions. It is hoped that these discussions will provide Western academics with better insights, so that they can then develop effective and appropriate pedagogical practices to work with CHC students. It is noted that this chapter focuses on discussing the learning of students coming from CHC countries (e.g. Vietnam, China, Malaysia, Hong Kong, Japan, Korea, Singapore, and Taiwan) but not from all Asian countries. The authors acknowledge that Asia is a broad term that covers a range of nations among which many do not inherit or are influenced by Confucian cultures (e.g. Thailand, India). Therefore, when the relationship between Confucian culture and students' learning is investigated, it should be within CHC countries but not within all Asian countries. Regarding structure, this chapter consists of three main parts. Part I provides an overall view of how CHC learners' learning has been understood and characterized across times. The second part discusses theoretical perspectives that underpin different views on CHC learners' learning, and the final part discusses the implications for educational practice.

3.2 Various Perspectives About CHC Students' Learning Approaches

3.2.1 CHC Learners and Rote/Surface Learning

CHC learners' approaches to learning started to attract the attention of researchers in the late 1980s and early 1990s. During this early period, most researchers, relying heavily on personal experiences and anecdotes, argued that CHC learners exhibit a lack of learner autonomy requiring step-by-step guidance and support; are uncritical consumers of information presented in the textbook or lectures; display reticence in class, and tutorials; prefer a reproductive approach to learning; and rely on a limited range of learning strategies, especially rote memorization (Ballard, 1996; Tsui, 1996). CHC students often receive knowledge from teachers as a truth rather than trying to think independently, challenge the teacher's knowledge, and draw their conclusions (Ruby & Ladd, 1999). To teach these learners, teaching is described as filling the 'empty-vessel' model, with the teacher as the 'full-vessel' pouring his/her knowledge into the 'empty-vessels', his/her students (Allen & Spada, 1982, p. 191). Such beliefs have been so prevalent and entrenched that even CHC students themselves have often internalized these descriptions and accept the image of themselves as lacking in initiative, being socially inept and boringly bookish (Ryan & Louie, 2006). These learning attributes contrast the image of teaching and learning practices at Western educational institutions where the ideal student is seen as inquiring, questioning, and self-reliant (Renshaw, 1999). This indicates that CHC learners must encounter many difficulties when studying in a Western environment.

However, it has been shown that international students achieve similar rates of academic success as domestic students in their higher education studies in Australia (DEST, 2004), and many CHC learners have been found to outperform their Western counterparts on international comparisons of student achievement. For instance, Jessen (2012) reported that mean scores for reading, mathematics, and science on PISA assessments of students from Shanghai, Korea, Hong Kong, and Singapore were consistently higher than those of students coming from Australia, the USA, UK, and Europe. An important note is that PISA assesses meta-cognitive content knowledge and problem-solving abilities. These skills are not conducive to rote learning (Jessen, 2012). Therefore, if CHC students only deploy a rote approach to learning in preparation for PISA assessment, they should achieve lower scores. This paradox has driven many researchers from a range of theoretical perspectives (e.g. Biggs, 1996a, 1996b; Cheng, 2000; Watkins & Biggs, 2001) to start reconstructing the stereotyped views on CHC learners, questioning if CHC students only learn by rote (as a mindless machine), they certainly cannot obtain so many impressive academic achievements both at Western institutions and on international tests. This doubtfulness initiated the birth of the second phase of research that aimed to seek evidence, demonstrating that CHC learners are not simply rote and surface learners.

3.2.2   CHC Learners and Deep Learning

The most well-known representative of this perspective is John Biggs (1989, 1990, 1991, 1992, 1993, 1994, 1996a, 1996b) who mainly draws on Confucian heritage discourse arguing that it is not accurate when researchers use Confucian teachings as the underpinning theory to argue that CHC learners are rote and surface learners. This is because Confucius saw himself as a deep learner and encouraged deep teaching and learning (Biggs, 1996a, 1996b). The evidence Biggs utilized to protect his argument was that Confucius was keen on delighting his students in leading their better disciples to enlightenment through a process of questions and answers (Ryan & Louie, 2006). This is an interesting discovery that researchers in the literature have rarely mentioned and accepted. Based on this inference, later Watkins and Biggs wrote several papers aiming to dispel Western misconceptions. They collected empirical evidence to reveal that Chinese learners did value active and reflective thinking, open-mindedness, and a spirit of inquiry and engage in autonomous, problem-solving activities; Chinese societies did value an exploratory and reflective approach to learning; and Chinese teachers did not rely exclusively upon the transmission mode of delivery; engage in autonomous, problem-solving activities. They explained that Western researchers and educators did not see these positive aspects of 'Confucian heritage' education because the process of absorbing and digesting knowledge of CHC learners differs from that of their Western counterparts and Westerners were not aware of this differentiation.

Specifically, Biggs (1993) claims that the 'memorized learning' that Western researchers and educators often label Chinese learners should be called 'repetitive learning'. This practice is only used once the material has been understood to recall accurate information during exams. Repetition here actually helps students increase their attention to the details of the text and deepen their understanding. It is therefore suggested that CHC students do not simply rote learn unprocessed information, but attempt first to understand the new information in a systematic, step-by-step manner and, once each part of the task is understood, memorize the 'deeply processed information' as repetition (Biggs, 1991, p. 21). Later, Watkins (1996) conducted a study in a Hong Kong school to investigate further explanations of CHC learners' learning process. He claimed that the learning process of CHC learners was divided into three clear-cut stages which the students seem to reach and pass through. First, students at primary and junior levels tended to achieve learning through total rote learning as a reproduction of everything. However, when students reached secondary school, under the pressure of workload they needed to be selective about what they had to memorize as their mind only allowed them to memorize important information in each subject. It was the process of selecting what to memorize that made the learner understand the materials. Thus, at this stage, the students achieved learning through reproduction with understanding. Finally, when reaching university, students continued using memorization as a means to understand, and their memorizing capacity was enhanced by understanding the material. It could, therefore, be argued that such students are well versed in the skills of memorization and rote learning as well as comprehension and understanding when they commence their tertiary education. They are very adaptable and can use a range of learning methods depending on the situation. This may enable CHC students to succeed academically more than local students in Western institutions.

In summary, this perspective aims to defend that when facing an academic task, Western and CHC learners have the same primary goal of trying to reach understanding, but CHC students use memorization, rehearsal, and repetition as a means to achieve this goal in a special way—a concept which Westerners find difficult to understand. Although the use of repetition and memorization strategies by Western learners has been found to indicate a surface approach to learning, the use of these same strategies by CHC learners does not necessarily indicate that they are adopting a surface approach (Chalmers & Volet, 1997; Renshaw & Volet, 1995). The process of learning applied by CHC students may not be common in Western education but it is not necessarily an incorrect approach, nor is it useless considering the advantages of discipline and foundation accrued. CHC learners are strategic, knowing how to use their abilities and skills correctly at the right times. This explains why they are well evidenced to outperform their Western counterparts in certain areas such as science and mathematics. Analyses of the cultural and educational processes of countries such as Singapore, Hong Kong, and Japan are being used to critique the practices in the West and to argue for reforms to teaching methods in Western countries (Renshaw, 1999; Stevenson & Stigler, 1996).

3.3   How to Understand CHC Students' Learning
        Accurately

The discussion above has shown that there exists a dilemma about CHC learners' learning. Any judgement made to argue one approach is more useful, valid, and accurate than the other does not sound sufficiently satisfactory and convincing because researchers on both ends have provided rich evidence to protect their views. To unpack this puzzle, it is proposed that researchers and educators must revert to examining the foundational theories underpinning these arguments and critically evaluate how effective and valid these theories are in today's globalization discourse. Besides, to understand the learning practices adopted by CHC students correctly, the criteria that are utilized to classify the types of learning must be investigated. If these criteria are not universally agreed, learning characteristics assigned to CHC learners' learning based on Western values and by Westerners become questionable and culturally inappropriate in the CHC context.

3.3.1   The Historical Perspective and CHC Learners'
          Learning

Ryan and Louie (2006) claim that to interpret contemporary Chinese education and its participants, too often researchers adopt a historical perspective and see cultural values as discrete, homogenous, and unchanging. Hofstede (1991) is probably the most popular protagonist representing this view. Hofstede bases much of his work on the characteristics which differentiate national cultures and presents geographical maps that present a world divided into cultural bubbles (Holliday, 1999). His cultural differentiation theory has influenced and shaped many other researchers' works which draw distinctions between 'Chinese' and 'Western cultures of learning' (Jin & Cortazzi, 1998, 2006), or between the 'Confucian' and the 'Socratic traditions' (Tweed & Lehman, 2002). Holliday (1999, 2005) claims that when researchers label a set of particular characteristics to describe people from a certain region(s), they deploy a 'large culture' approach that assumes that 'a culture' behaves like a single-minded person with a specific, exclusive personality (p. 5). Within this discourse, CHC learners are referred to as a homogeneous group embodying the values, identities, and behaviours of a shared culture which is 'Confucian culture'. Clark and Gieve (2006) highlight another characteristic of the historical discourse which views that cultures are determined by a historical heritage rather than emerging through history and thus dynamically evolving.

Researchers who have evaluated the two contrasting sets of attributes assigned to CHC learners discussed above fall into this trap. They believe that CHC learners' learning practices have their genesis in and are determined by cultural traditions left behind from the old times. They use teachings of historical sages as a theoretical foundation underpinning their evaluations and judgements. For instance, those researchers who label CHC learners as passive and rote learners have often used the Confucian tradition that instructs teachers as knowledge masters and learners need to respect, obey and receive knowledge transformed from the teacher (Confucius, 1947) as evidence to protect their argument. In contrast, those researchers who see CHC learners as deep learners have proposed the idea that Confucius did emphasize deep learning and led his students through the dialectical process of questions and more questions (e.g. John Biggs as aforementioned) to provide evidence for their conclusion.

Since historical sages are often philosophers who represent a large community (e.g. Confucius is known as the representative of CHC countries; Socrates represents many Western nations), researchers supporting the historical perspective then tend to generalize that learning attributes shaped and influenced by teachings of these historical figures are similar among all participants who share the same national or ethnic cultures. If they find, for instance, Chinese students in Australia competitive, they then mask Chinese learners everywhere (both in China and in other CHC countries) as competitive learners. If they find Chinese culture values friendship, they will not hesitate to conclude that CHC learners worldwide appreciate friendship above competition, explaining why CHC people have such a saying as 'Friendship First, Competition Later'. Finally, as explained above, researchers underpinned by the historical perspective argue that student learning is determined by cultural values that are 'fixed' rather than emerging through history. They then assume that CHC learners carry fixed learning characteristics that do not change across times and in different situated contexts.

3.4 Alternative Discourses and CHC Learners' Learning

Arguments and conclusions underpinned by the historical perspective have been challenged by interpretations based on critical sociology, with theoretical contributions from cultural studies and post-structuralist discourse theory (Kubota, 2001, 2002, 2004; Kumaravadivelu, 2003; Norton & Toohey, 2004; Pennycook, 1998; Spack, 1997). Researchers supporting these critical discourses argue for the idea that there are no distinctions between cultures because cultures have 'blurred boundaries', to 'flow, change, intermingle, cut across and through one another' (Holliday, Hyde, & Kullman, 2004, p. 4). There should not be any particular attribute (s) labelled to any individual or community because cultural flows have, at different degrees, influenced every single person in all societies. Individuals are now belonging to 'a complex multiplicity of cultures both within and across societies and their identities are moderated by the membership of the various cultures' (p. 5). These researchers, therefore, claim that cultural heritages cannot be the only determinant of teaching and learning preferences and experiences. More accurately, one's learning patterns and paths are more likely to result from and built on both personal factors, i.e., their educational and family backgrounds and goals and motivation for learning as well as external factors with which they come into contact, i.e., their instructors and friends both inside and outside the school and social activities they are involved in. This view is becoming increasingly popular and widely accepted because there is now a large corpus of research evidencing that CHC learners have changed their learning strategies, skills, and habits in a new learning environment where they faced new requirements of academic programs and came into contact with people with different cultural backgrounds.

Key studies reporting such findings include a study conducted by Volet and Renshaw in 1996 who found that the requirements of academic programs at Australian institutions influenced their Chinese student sample to change their learning practices. The students did become more independent and have stronger responsibility for their study at the end of the course as a result of program requirements. Later, Gieve and Clark (2005) announced similar findings showing that Chinese students learned and adopted new learning habits and skills, i.e., how to prepare assignments, how to operate in learning groups, and how to work on their own, as a response to their programs at British institutions. In another study, Volet and Kee (1993) reported that Asian students tend to be more reserved than Australian counterparts when it comes to participation in group discussions. The authors, however, noted that this characteristic was not the true nature of Asian students but as a result of the educational contexts in Asian countries that did not strongly encourage students to participate in class discussions (e.g. this activity was only organized in some disciplines, never assessed and not strongly encouraged by teachers). This argument became highly valid when later in a study that examined the actual tutorial participation levels of Australian and Singaporean students at an Australian university conducted by Renshaw and Volet (1995), the authors found an interesting point that the overall levels of participation of the two groups were not significantly different, but they were within the group of local students. Based on these findings, Volet (1999) concluded that new studying requirements can influence CHC students to change their learning practices dramatically in compliance with rules and norms in the new system.

Having argued that not essential cultural heritages but social factors have a strong impact on students' learning, post-structuralist researchers also question the concept of 'large' culture widely adopted by those who follow the historical perspective. This is because CHC learners are well surrounded by students who vary in family backgrounds, goals of learning, and degrees of commitment to study as well as are educated in various socio-cultural contexts where their instructors and fellow friends may give them different degrees of support and instruction. Therefore, each CHC leaner in different contexts or different CHC learners in the same context may be situated to deploy various forms of learning depending on other individuals' appreciation and acceptance in their contexts. Ryan and Louie (2006), for instance, provided an example to argue against the universal generalization made by Lee (1996) who claims that 'Asian students are not only diligent, but they also have high achievement motivation. Invariably they have high regard for education' (p. 3). Based on their teaching experience, Ryan and Louie explained that they have seen many Asian students do indeed have high regard for education but many others do not. Tang and Biggs (1996) also advised researchers to be cautious when concluding or generalizing that the test-oriented culture of CHC educational institutions has trained all CHC learners to become 'experts' in identifying assessment demands. It is true that after years of repeated practice of test-taking throughout their schooling, CHC learners have become skilful with exams. However, these identification skills varied among students from Hong Kong and Singapore, among students studying different disciplines and among students who are trained by different teachers.

In summary, all of the aforementioned arguments have warned that the powerful role of the learning context and question the adequacy of the construct of CHC learners as a homogeneous group. Whatever the approaches to learning adopted by CHC learners, rote or deep, surface or critical, they are more likely to be the result of influences that various factors in their educational contexts make on them than of cultural heritage left behind by their historical sages and ancestors. For instance, Pierson (1996) pointed out that Chinese Hong Kong students become passive rote learners who want to be told what to do, show little initiative, and accordingly have difficulty dealing with autonomy because they study with teachers who decide what is correct and little room is given for the students to exercise personal initiative in the context of the traditional Chinese learning culture. Furthermore, Clark and Gieve (2006) warn that researchers and educators should not make any generalization about CHC learners because such generalizations hide as much as they reveal and, in reducing individuals to inadequately understood group characteristics, approach racial stereotyping. The extent to which CHC learners are shared across locations (e.g. countries, regions, districts), social status (e.g. family background, financial situation), and especially schooling (e.g. teachers, friends, requirements of academic programs) cannot be taken for granted.

All of this evidence has conceptualized that when CHC learners move into a new situated context, they are heavily influenced by both cultural dimensions, i.e., the sets of beliefs, value systems, assumptions, and social expectations that prevail and are shared by participants in that context as well as physical contact, namely the support of and relationship with instructors and friends. Therefore, fixed attributes labelled to Chinese learners are highly questionable. Clark and Gieve (2006) have pointed out a range of such approaches that provide opportunities to address many aspects that the historical perspective has ignored or undervalued but have now been recognized and widely accepted as influential factors determining one's learning practices. These new perspectives are post-structuralist, critical pedagogy, anthropological, and cultural studies discourses. These discourses are now beginning to be recognized to be well suited to small culture ways of thinking (Breen, 2001; Norton & Toohey, 2004), emphasise the concepts of identity (Norton, 1997; Toohey, 2000), agency (Lantolf, 2000; Lantolf & Pavlenko, 2001), investment (Norton-Pierce, 1995), accommodation, resistance and non-participation (McKay & Wong, 1996; Nichols, 2003; Norton, 2001), colonial and post-colonial discourse (Pennycook, 1998; Phillipson, 1992), voice and empowerment (Canagarajah, 1999; Giroux, 1992; Spack, 1997), critical multiculturalism (Kubota, 1999), and peripheral participation (Lave & Wenger, 1991).

3.5 How 'Active' and 'Passive' Learning Is Defined

There has not been, so far, any universal agreement on criteria utilized to define 'deep/critical' and 'surface/rote' learning. Jin and Cortazzi (1995) point out that these terms are often interpreted differently, depending on the expectations of the 'culture of learning' into which one has been socialized. Recently the idea using Vygotskian notions of language as the tool for thought has become very popular, especially in the Western world. In Western classrooms talk or verbal participation is seen as the pathway to a critical questioning approach (Ryan & Louie, 2006), and learner-centred pedagogies are defined to aim to encourage students to 'learn by participating, through talking and active involvement' (Jin & Cortazzi, 1995, p. 6). This explains why Western academics have an implicit and explicit preference for these activities and expect that their students including both local and international to actively engage in these practices. If students are not verbally participatory, they are very likely to be seen as problematic. Consequently, it is now common to see many Western institutions compulsorily requiring students to actively participate in class discussions, tutorials, and online forums by allocating a portion of their marks to these activities (although the amusing side of this policy is that it does not always require the quality and appropriateness of such 'active participation' to be taken into account).

This view of 'effective' learning contrasts with the 'more cognitive-centred, learning–listening approach' that is favoured by Chinese educators (Jin & Cortazzi, 1998, p. 744). Within this tradition, being 'active' suggests 'cognitive involvement, lesson preparation, reflection and review, thinking, memorisation and self-study' (Cortazzi & Jin, 1996, p. 71). Therefore, Littlewood (2000) claims that Chinese classrooms may indeed appear relatively static in comparison to those of the anglophone West, but just because the students operate in a receptive mode, this does not imply that they are any less engaged. Conversely, just because students in anglophone Western classrooms are seen to be verbally participatory, this does not necessarily guarantee that learning is taking place. For instance, in their study, Volet and Kee (1993) reported that CHC students found it astonishing and culturally inappropriate when Australian students interrupted someone who was talking to make a point or ask very simple questions when they should just keep quiet and find out from friends later.

As such, it appears that each specific learning context has its own explicit and tacit rules to define what should be called 'deep' learning and what should be called 'rote' learning. Teachers need to take cautious steps before making judgements on what accounts for 'good learning'. Holliday (2005) has sent a message warning teachers that "one should not automatically assume that 'good lessons' are those in which students are 'lively' and 'orally 'active'" (p. 81).

3.6 Conclusion

The discussions provided in this chapter aim to draw the attention of educators and researchers to the following points. First, there has been rich evidence demonstrating that both a 'deficit' and 'surplus' view of Confucian education is inadequate to evaluate CHC learners' learning accurately. Therefore, instead of taking either one of the extreme perspectives, teachers need to be sensitive to the diversity and complexity of approaches to study among students across cultures and within a culture. When teachers operate in classrooms on stereotypes and generalizations, they may adopt ineffective teaching approaches leading to negative impacts on their students. Furthermore, Ryan (2000, 2005) claims that when teachers do not have critical views but simply accept stereotypes and generalization, they would face difficulties and confusion when responding to the increasing globalization and internationalization of the curriculum and their pedagogy. These cautions need to be taken among students within a culture as well.

Second, teachers need to be aware that learning is not a predetermined concept but evolves in situated contexts. This point of view would accord with Accommodation Theory, which focuses on how aspects of social context, rather than cultural heritage, affect individual behaviours. Therefore, to develop and deploy effective teaching and pedagogical practices, Renshaw (1999) claims that teachers need to consider the interplay of a wide range of actors including pedagogical factors (assessment tasks, curriculum content, and teaching practices), the students' level of initial background knowledge, their level of interest and enthusiasm of the subject, and their appraisal of the relevance of the subject to their long-term goals. However, Volet (1999) notes that it is unsatisfactory to adapt the host educational context to suit individual [cultural] differences. This is because it not only would be practically unrealistic to cater to all styles of learning but also because it would involve using individual learning styles as the criteria for deciding on appropriate methods of instruction. The only valid approach is to teach in a way that maximizes effective learning by all students, local and international alike. The question now is how to develop such teaching methods. Boekaerts (1997) and Salomon and Perkins (1998) have helped answer this question by claiming that regardless of their cultural-educational backgrounds, all students need to be provided with opportunities to learn how to cognitively, motivationally, and emotionally self-scaffold their learning for independent as well as interdependent modes of participation. Regarding theoretical perspectives and instructions that researchers and educators should utilize to achieve these goals, Volet (1999) points out that the principles of learning applied in Communities of Learners settings (Brown, 1994; Cognition and Technology Group at Vanderbilt, 1994), self-regulated learning programs (Boekaerts, 1997), and process-oriented instruction (De Corte, 1996; De Jong, 1995; Vermunt, 1994; Volet, 1995) provide a sound basis for designing powerful learning environments in an international, multicultural perspective. In summary, as expressed in Kostogriz's words (2005)*, educators now need to 'work out the shifts from how best to *teach*, to how best to *learn*. Without this shift, current approaches to pedagogy will probably perpetuate the hegemony of one system of cultural practice over another, and lose opportunities for the development of new knowledge through the critical falsifying of the known' (p. 3).

Third, international education should not be seen as a problem but an opportunity to enrich the understanding of both Western academics and CHC learners. For Western academics, CHC learners are outsiders or 'others' who come and bring a 'surplus of vision' (Bakhtin, 1990). Therefore, international students have given local academics 'proximity' to act as anthropologists to learn about their cultural practices (Ryan & Louie, 2006), so that they could understand how the normative assumptions underpinning their teaching practices can be problematic for international students or indeed for other groups of local students as well (Ryan, 2000). For CHC learners, the topic that has attracted lots of educational debate is whether these students should and could keep their identity while studying in the Western learning context. Gieve and Clark (2005) claim that from the monolithic perspective, Chinese students are seen to lose their identity (i.e., a loss of linguistic identity, a loss of the 'inner voice', and a loss of their first language) when coming into contact with Western attitudes and practices. A conceptualization of identity which accepted fluid and multiple identities, however, would allow for students taking on the attitudes and practices of different social and cultural groups simultaneously, contingently, instrumentally, and flexibly. They might still feel themselves to be very much Chinese and not acknowledge any contradiction between 'being Chinese' and following 'Western' learning practices.

Fourth, as discussed elsewhere in this chapter, the concepts of 'active' and 'passive' are built on criteria that are based on different Western and CHC cultural values. Therefore, Western academics should be more considerate and inclusive when setting up assessment criteria. What decides 'good learners' should be based on the quality of their work, i.e., the quality of assignments, the quality of what they say, the quality of what they voice on online forums, but not on the quantitative of their actions, i.e., the number of their questions in the class, the number of their posts on online forums. Unfortunately, assessment criteria at Western institutions now seem very quantitative-oriented. Therefore, CHC learners are disadvantaged because the language barrier significantly hinders them from participating in discussions verbally. Therefore, they are perceived as a 'reduced other' who contrast with the 'enlightened self' of the native English-speaking Westerner (Holliday, 2005, p. 82). Such deficit understanding and evaluation have certainly made a negative impact on the mentality and motivation of CHC students at Australian institutions.

Fifth, discussions provided in this chapter also send a message that researchers need to be critical when evaluating research findings. Any research on CHC students' learning conducted in a country beyond CHC countries may result in questionable findings. This is because obstacles such as the pressure of studying in a second language, being surrounded by unfamiliar friends, coping with personal life pressures, and so on may hinder CHC learners from expressing their true personalities. CHC learners may perform less actively than local students due to the language barrier but not by expressing opinions. Consequently, results obtained from such research should not be utilized to generalize CHC learners in their home countries.

Finally, the chapter draws the attention of researchers and educators to the issue of utilizing appropriate research methodologies if they wish to investigate how to maximize students' learning. As discussed throughout this chapter, learning should be seen as a factor in a complexity in which it has a close connection with and is influenced by many other dynamic factors. Therefore, an effective research methodology would be the one that creates opportunities for all of these factors to emerge and to be adjusted to support each other so that the best learning outcomes can be brought about. For this purpose, design-based research and activity theory appear to be effective methods because they give researchers the opportunities to question the effectiveness of those teaching and learning practices that have been seen as 'norms' and 'standard' practices and adjust to make them culturally appropriate in a different situated context. These methodologies also create opportunities for hidden factors and marginalized voices to be seen and heard. It is these 'ignored' factors and voices that may then turn out to be influential elements, making significant contributions to constructing effective teaching and learning.

References

Allen, W., & Spada, N. (1982). A materials writing project in China. *Language Learning and Communication, 1*(2), 187–196.

Bakhtin, M. (1990). *Art and answerability*. Austin, TX: University of Texas Press.

Ballard, B. (1996). Through language to learning: Preparing overseas students for study in Western universities. In H. Coleman (Ed.), *Society and the language classroom* (pp. 20–35). Cambridge: Cambridge University Press.

Biggs, J. B. (1989). Approaches to the enhancement of tertiary teaching. *Higher Education Research and Development, 8*(1), 7–25.

Biggs, J. B. (1990). Effects of language medium of instruction on approaches to learning. *Educational Research Journal (Hong Kong), 5*, 18–28.

Biggs, J. B. (1991). Approaches to learning in secondary and tertiary students in Hong Kong: Some comparative studies. *Educational Research Journal, 6*, 27–39.

Biggs, J. B. (1992). Why and how do Hong Kong students learn? Using the learning and study process questionnaires. *Education Paper 14*. Faculty of Education, University of Hong Kong.

Biggs, J. B. (1993). What do inventories of students' learning processes really measure? A theoretical review and clarification. *British Journal of Educational Psychology, 63*(1), 3–19.

Biggs, J. B. (1994). What are effective schools? Lessons from east and west. *Australian Educational Researcher, 21*(1), 19–39.

Biggs, J. B. (1996a). Western misconceptions of the Confucian-heritage learning culture. In D. A. Watkins & J. B. Biggs (Eds.), *The Chinese learner: Cultural, psychological, and contextual influences* (pp. 45–67). Hong Kong: CERC and ACER.

Biggs, J. (1996b). Western misperceptions of the Confucian heritage learning culture. In D. Watson & J. Biggs (Eds.), *The Chinese learner: Cultural, psychological and contextual influences* (pp. 45–67). Hong Kong: Comparative Education Research Centre and Melbourne, The Australian Council for Educational Research Ltd..

Boekaerts, M. (1997). Self-regulated learning: A new concept embraced by researchers, policy makers, educator, teachers and students. *Learning and Instruction, 7*(161), 186.

Breen, M. (2001). *Learner contributions to language learning*. Harlow: Pearson Education.

Brown, A. L. (1994). The advancement of learning. *Educational Researcher, 23*(8), 4–12.

Canagarajah, S. (1999). *Resisting linguistic imperialism*. Oxford: Oxford University Press.

Chalmers, D., & Volet, S. E. (1997). South-east Asian students learning in Australia. *Higher Education Research & Development, 16*(1), 87–98.

Cheng, X. (2000). Asian students' reticence revisited. *System, 28,* 435–446.

Clark, R., & Gieve, S. N. (2006). On the discursive construction of 'the Chinese learner'. *Language, Culture and Curriculum, 19*(1), 54–73.

Cognition and Technology Group at Vanderbilt. (1994). From visual word problems to learning communities: Changing conceptions of cognitive research. In K. McGilly (Ed.), *Classroom lessons: Integrating cognitive theory and classroom practice* (pp. 157–200). Cambridge, MA: MIT Press/Bradford.

Confucius. (1947). The wisdom of Confucius. In S. Commins & R. N. Linscott (Eds.), *Man and man: The social philosophers* (pp. 323–258). New York: Random House.

Cortazzi, M., & Jin, L. (1996). Cultures of learning: Language classrooms in China. In H. Coleman (Ed.), *Society and the language classroom* (pp. 169–206). Cambridge: Cambridge University Press.

De Corte, E. (1996). Instructional psychology: Overview. In E. De Corte & F. E. Weinert (Eds.), *International encyclopedia of developmental and instructional psychology* (pp. 33–43). Oxford: UK: Elsevier Science Ltd.

De Jong, F. P. C. M. (1995). Process-oriented instruction: Some considerations. *European Journal of Psychology of Education, 10,* 317–324.

Department of Education, Science and Training (2004). *International higher education students: How do they differ from other education students?* Strategic Analysis and Evaluation Group Research Note No. 2. Retrieved February 20, 2019, from http://www.dest.gov.au/research/publications/research_notes/2.htm

Elmore, R. (1996). Getting to scale with good educational practice. *Harvard Educational Review, 66*(1), 1–26.

Fullan, M. (2000). The three stories of education reform. *Phi Delta Kappan, 81*(8), 581–584.

Gieve, S., & Clark, R. (2005). The Chinese approach to learning: Cultural trait or situated response? The case of a self-directed learning programme. *System, 33*(2005), 261–276.

Giroux, H. (1992). Resisting difference: Cultural studies and the discourse of critical pedagogy. In L. Grossberg, C. Nelson, & P. Treichler (Eds.), *Cultural Studies* (pp. 199–212). New York: Routledge.

Hammond, S., & Gao, H. (2002). Pan Gu's paradigm: Chinese education's return to holistic communication in learning. In X. Lu, W. Jia, & R. Heisey (Eds.), *Chinese communication studies: Contexts and comparisons* (pp. 227–244). Westport, CT: Ablex.

Harman, G. (2002). *Internationalization of the higher education sector: Draft annotated bibliography and report on literature review.* Canberra: Department of Education, Science and Training.

Hofstede, G. (1991). *Cultures and organisations: Software of the mind.* Maidenhead: McGraw-Hill.

Holliday, A. R. (1999). Small cultures. *Applied Linguistics, 20*(2), 237–264.

Holliday, A. R. (2005). *The struggle to teach English as an international language.* Oxford: Oxford University Press.

Holliday, A., Hyde, M., & Kullman, J. (2004). *Inter-cultural communication: An advanced resource book.* London: Routledge.

Jessen, B. (2012). Catching up: Learning from the best school systems in East Asia. Grattan institute report. Retrieved March 20, 2019, from http://grattan.edu.au/publications/reports/post/catching-up-learning-from-the-best-school-systems-in-east-asia/

Jin, L., & Cortazzi, M. (1995). A cultural synergy model for academic language use. In P. Bruthiaux, T. Boswood, & B. Du-Babcock (Eds.), *Explorations in English for professional communication* (pp. 20–35). Hong Kong: University of Hong Kong.

Jin, L., & Cortazzi, M. (1998). Dimensions of dialogue: Large classes in China. *International Journal of Educational Research, 29,* 739–761.

Jin, L., & Cortazzi, M. (2006). Changing practices in Chinese cultures of learning. *Language, Culture and Curriculum, 19*(1), 5–20.

Knight, J. (1997). Internationalization of higher education: A conceptual framework. In J. Knight & H. deWit (Eds.), *Internationalization of higher education in Asia Pacific countries* (pp. 5–19). Amsterdam: European Association for International Education.

Kubota, R. (1999). Japanese culture constructed by discourses: Implications for applied linguistics. *TESOL Quarterly, 33*(1), 9–35.

Kubota, R. (2001). Discursive construction of the images of US classrooms. *TESOL Quarterly, 35* (1), 9–38.

Kubota, R. (2002). The author responds: (un)ravelling racism in a nice field like TESOL. *TESOL Quarterly, 36*(1), 84–92.

Kubota, R. (2004). Critical multiculturalism and second language education. In B. Norton & K. Toohey (Eds.), *Critical pedagogies and language learning* (pp. 30–52). Cambridge: Cambridge University Press.

Kumaravadivelu, B. (2003). Problematizing cultural stereotypes in TESOL. *TESOL Quarterly, 37* (4), 709–719.

Lantolf, J. P. (Ed.). (2000). *Sociocultural theory and second language learning*. Oxford: Oxford University Press.

Lantolf, J., & Pavlenko, A. (2001). (S)econd (l)anguage (a)ctivity theory: Understanding second language learners as people. In M. Breen (Ed.), *Learner contributions to language learning* (pp. 141–158). Harlow: Longman.

Lave, J., & Wenger, E. (1991). *Situated learning. Legitimate peripheral participation*. Cambridge: Cambridge University Press.

Lee, W. O. (1996). The cultural context for Chinese learners: Conceptions of learning in the Confucian tradition. In D. Watkins & J. Biggs (Eds.), *The Chinese learner: Cultural, psychological and contextual influences* (pp. 25–41). Hong Kong: Comparative Education Research Centre and Melbourne.

Littlewood, W. (2000). Do Asian students really want to listen and obey? *ELT Journal, 5*(1), 31–36.

McKay, S., & Wong, S. (1996). Multiple discourses, multiple identities: Investment and agency in second-language learning among Chinese adolescent immigrant students. *Harvard Educational Review, 66*(3), 577–608.

Nichols, S. (2003). They just won't critique anything: The 'problem' of international students in the Western academy. In J. E. Satterthwaite, E. Atkinson, & K. Gale (Eds.), *Discourse, power and resistance* (pp. 135–148). Stoke on Trent: Trentham.

Norton, B. (1997). Language, identity and the ownership of English. *TESOL Quarterly, 31*(3), 409–429.

Norton, B. (2001). Non-participation, imagined communities and the language classroom. In M. P. Breen (Ed.), *Learner contributions to language learning* (pp. 159–171). Harlow: Pearson Education.

Norton, B., & Toohey, K. (Eds.). (2004). *Critical pedagogies and language learning*. Cambridge: Cambridge University Press.

Norton-Pierce, B. (1995). Social identity, investment, and language learning. *TESOL Quarterly, 29* (1), 9–31.

Pennycook, A. (1998). *English and the discourses of colonialism*. London: Routledge.

Phillipson, R. (1992). *Linguistic imperialism*. Oxford: Oxford University Press.

Pierson, H. D. (1996). Learner culture and learner autonomy in the Hong Kong Chinese context. In R. Pemberton, E. S. L. Li, W. W. F. Or, & H. D. Pierson (Eds.), *Taking control: Autonomy in language learning* (pp. 49–58). Hong Kong: Hong Kong University Press.

Renshaw, P. (1999). Learning and culture: Representations of the Chinese learner at Australian universities. In L. Jie (Ed.), *Education of Chinese: The global prospect of national cultural tradition* (pp. 48–71). Nanjing: Nanjing Normal University Press.

Renshaw, P. D., & Volet, S. E. (1995). South east Asian students at Australian universities: A reappraisal of their tutorial participation and approaches to study. *Australian Educational Researcher, 22*(2), 85–106.

Ruby, R., & Ladd, P. (1999). Learning styles and adjustment issues of international students. *Journal of Education for Business, 7*(6), 363–379.

Ryan, J. (2000). *A guide to teaching international students*. Oxford: Oxford Centre for Staff and Learning Development.

Ryan, J. (2005). Improving teaching and learning practices for international students: Implications for curriculum, pedagogy and assessment. In J. Carroll & J. Ryan (Eds.), *Teaching international students: Improving learning for all* (pp. 92–100). London: Routledge Falmer.

Ryan, J., & Louie, K. (2006). False dichotomy? 'Western' and 'Confucian' concepts of scholarship and learning. *Educational Philosophy and Theory, 39*(4), 404–417.

Salomon, G., & Perkins, D. (1998). Individual and social aspects of learning. In P. D. Pearson & A. Iran-Nejad (Eds.), *Review of research in education* (pp. 1–24). Washington: AERA.

Spack, R. (1997). The rhetorical construction of multilingual students. *TESOL Quarterly, 31*(4), 765–774.

Stevenson, H., & Stigler, J. (1996). *The learning gap: Why our schools are failing and what we learn from Japanese and Chinese education*. New York: Summit Books.

Tang, C., & Biggs, J. B. (1996). How Hong Kong students cope with assessment. In D. Watkins & J. Biggs (Eds.), *The Chinese learner: Cultural, psychological and contextual influences* (pp. 159–182). Hong Kong: CERC: The University of Hong Kong/ACER.

Toohey, K. (2000). *Learning English in schools: Identity, social relations, and classroom practice*. Clevedon: Multilingual Matters.

Tsui, A. (1996). Reticence and anxiety in second language learning. In K. Bailey & D. Nunan (Eds.), *Voices from the language classroom* (pp. 145–167). Cambridge: Cambridge University Press.

Tweed, R. G., & Lehman, D. (2002). Learning considered within a cultural context: Confucian and Socratic approaches. *American Psychologist, 57*(2), 89–99.

Vermunt, J. D. H. M. (1994). Design principles of process-oriented instruction. In F. P. C. M. de Jong & B. H. A. M. Van Hout-Wolters (Eds.), *Process-oriented instruction and learning from text* (pp. 15–26). Amsterdam: VU University Press.

Volet, S. E. (1995). Process-oriented instruction: A discussion. *European Journal of Psychology of Education, 10*, 449–459.

Volet, S. E. (1999). Learning across cultures: Appropriateness of knowledge transfer. *International Journal of Educational Research, 31*(7), 625–643.

Volet, S. E., & Kee, J. P. P. (1993). *Studying in Singapore and studying in Australia: A student perspective*. Occasional paper no 1: Murdoch University Teaching Excellence Committee, Murdoch.

Volet, S. E., & Renshaw, P. D. (1996). Chinese students at an Australian university: Adaptability and continuity. In D. Watkins & J. Biggs (Eds.), *The Chinese learner: Cultural, psychological and contextual influences* (pp. 205–220). Hong Kong: CERC: The University of Hong Kong/ ACER.

Watkins, D. (1996). Hong Kong secondary school learners: A developmental perspective. In D. Watkins & J. Biggs (Eds.), *The Chinese learner: Cultural, psychological, and contextual influences*. Hong Kong: Centre for Comparative Research in Education/Camberwell, Victoria: Australian Council for Educational Research.

Watkins, D. A., & Biggs, J. B. (2001). The paradox of the Chinese learner and beyond. In D. A. Watkins & J. B. Biggs (Eds.), *Teaching the Chinese learner: Psychological and pedagogical perspectives* (pp. 3–26). Hong Kong: CERC.

Webb, G. (2005). Internationalisation of the curriculum: An institutional approach. In J. Carroll & J. Ryan (Eds.), *Teaching international students: Improving learning for all* (pp. 109–118). London: Routledge Falmer.

Chapter 4
Culturally Supportive Pedagogy: Challenges Faced by North Korean Immigrant Students in South Korea

Dat Bao and Giulio Ricci

Abstract This chapter identifies and presents a range of factors that impedes North Korean students' learning and social adaptation in the South Korean educational system. Such factors include differences in learning approaches, social experiences, behaviour, mindset, language use, among others. All of these lead to low acceptance by the host towards the immigrant both in schools and in everyday communication. Attempting to stretch beyond painting a bleak picture of cultural mismatch, this chapter argues that while it seems impossible to restructure the thinking of a society overnight, small changes can take place in the everyday classroom learning through culturally sensitive activities. Such activities need to help students demonstrate respect, build social understanding, reduce communication mismatch, break social stereotypes, avoid discrimination, develop supportive principles, tolerate differences, and nurture a healthy sense of belonging. All of these are to be considered for the practice of a more inclusive, empathetic, and culturally sensitive pedagogy, which teachers would need not only to help students learn but also to strengthen teachers' professional development.

Keywords Culturally sensitive pedagogy · Empathy · Adjustment · Inclusivity · Social stereotypes

4.1 Introduction

This chapter analyses many factors that cause difficulties in North Korean students' academic learning and social adaptation in the South Korean educational system. This is due to the differences in political systems, language varieties, sociocultural values, and lifestyles since the establishment of two separate governments and the Korean Armistice Agreement that brought about a complete cessation of hostilities

D. Bao · G. Ricci (✉)
Monash University, Melbourne, VIC, Australia

© Springer Nature Singapore Pte Ltd. 2021
D. Bao, T. Pham (eds.), *Transforming Pedagogies Through Engagement with Learners, Teachers and Communities*, Education in the Asia-Pacific Region: Issues, Concerns and Prospects 57, https://doi.org/10.1007/978-981-16-0057-9_4

of the Korean War at P'anmunjŏm on 27 July 1953. Those problems, which occur in learning approaches, social experiences, behaviour, mindset, language use, among others, create challenges not only to North Korean students' adaptation but also to the host's ability to accept Northern immigrants both in schools and in everyday communication and broader society. As such, historically, humans have created subjective judgement between societies with discrimination occurring, when people treat others less favourably, simply because they are different from them in some way. Such processes are damaging to the learning mind as it diminishes their sense of self-empowerment, and ultimately, a phenomenon that is known as oppression, which in education minimises students' talent and contribution and right to learn in a safe conducive environment and not go through inequitable experiences.

The chapter contends that while it is hard to restructure the thinking of a society overnight, small changes can take place in every classroom. We advocate a socio-culturally supportive pedagogy in which effective teaching needs to avoid all forms of discrimination. We selected South Korea as the context of our discussion because this setting represents one of the sites of very competitive and intense educational, ideological conflict of our time. The chapter begins by presenting the relevant discourse on North Korean migrant students' struggle and adjustment in the South Korean educational context. Secondly, a brief overview of the methodology is provided to explain how the chapter is constructed. Thirdly, the main discussion comes in with a range of issues confronting North Korean students in context. While analysing such situations, we also highlight teaching approaches that do not cater to North Korean refugee students in South Korean schools by failing to recognise their vastly different backgrounds. Fourthly, based on this understanding, we appeal for classroom instruction to be conducted regarding the local identity, ethnicity, and socio-cultural norms of the students. Fifthly, we then build on this knowledge to suggest a set of principles to support the process of North Korean students' adaptation in the South Korean educational context. Finally, an example lesson is proposed to illustrate how the above support can be made achievable.

4.2 Discourse on the Topic

4.2.1 The Need to Foster Inclusivity

Over the past decades, students in many countries have become increasingly diverse as a result of globalisation and migration. This global context has promoted educators to increasingly recognise the need for cultural inclusivity in education (Chang, Pak, & Sleeter, 2018). Coming from various cultural backgrounds, immigrant students build new experiences when sharing the same classroom. This development requires teachers who work in such a context to take on the new responsibility to make use of cultural diversity at school as the foundation of learning. Unlike Australia which is a migration-friendly country where cultural diversity has become a fundamental concept in education that shaped many learning values, South Korea's educational system is yet to develop programs and curriculum content that cater to immigrants from a different context (see, for example, Lee, 2014). Arguably, schools are meaningful sites of socialisation through which children learn not only to accept differences but also to construct a sense of belonging (Walton et al., 2014).

4.2.2 Challenges Faced by North Korean Students in the South

North Korean refugee students acknowledge difficulties in adapting to the South Korean educational system and to the broader society. There were 26,483 North Korean refugees living in South Korea and as of March 2014, approximately 40% of them being children and young adults, aged between 10 and 30 years. A survey by the Korean Educational Development Institute (KEDI) (Ministry of Education, 2013) showed that out of 429 elementary and middle school North Korean refugee students, 10.7% reported being discriminated against or socially ostracised solely because they arrived from North Korea. Moreover, 54% of them reported not letting their South Korean peers know they originated from North Korea, particularly if given the chance to transfer to a dissimilar school and experts affirmed teachers who interacted with North Korean refugee students, most were not equipped nor trained to address their educational requirements (Kim & Lee, 2013). Thus, employing South Korean teachers with their unique teaching background (Akiba, LeTendre, & Scribner, 2007) to teach North Korean immigrants would be difficult as they have little or no knowledge of relevant teaching approaches. Below are key challenges as experienced by North Korean students:

- Little or no opportunity to learn English, particularly the underprivileged.
- Male students were more comfortable being the focus of attention while female students were more comfortable being passive and reserved.
- All suffered from culture shock.
- Most had difficulties to adapt to a new setting.
- Despite the same language and sharing the same Korean origin of approximately 7000 years, there was a vast cultural gap between the two countries, particularly as the South is global, and the North, is insular (Akiba et al., 2007).
- North Korean students speaking sounding different and foreign, and incredibly difficult to be understood.
- Often encountered misunderstanding, as they looked South Korean on the outside.
- Shifting from a life where they were indoctrinated with political propaganda to life in a democratic nation that requires daily effort.
- Given little time to prepare for tests; and, therefore extremely stressed as their results determined their future.
- Having difficulty 'keeping up' and understanding the context in education and social space.

- North Korean students were more comfortable with non-participative, passive, teacher-centred learning; requiring various motivating techniques to make lessons enjoyable and encouraging.
- Requiring empathy, particularly as they also dislike speaking and prefer grammar rule lessons (West, 2010).

4.2.3   Empirical Efforts to Investigate Student Adjustment in Korea

Some research studies have elaborated on the difficulties among North Koreans who migrated to South Korea in adjusting during their transitional and settling phase, and how this would later have repercussions on their daily life and education (Ahn, 2010; Chung, Chung, & Yang, 2004; Kum, Kwon, Lee, & Lee, 2003; Kwon, Lee, Kim, Kim, & Jung, 2008). Findings have demonstrated that North Korean refugee students are provided minimal forms of support and protection on their arrival (Chung, 2008). Thus, they face many challenges in their transitional period before settlement (Ministry of Unification, 2012). Although there has been a mutual agreement between Koreans residing in North and South Korea that to suit the current economic and political global market, the fundamental system needs to meet daily requirements as a tool for promotion and opportunities, and according to Song (2011), Park (2009), Chung et al. (2004), and Kum et al. (2003), the South Korean education system does not seem to have adequate nor systematic strategies in facilitating the learning adaptation of North Korean refugee students. Instead, the dominance of cultural and educational ideologies of South Korea represents a cultural barrier to the academic engagement of North Korean students.

It is realised that this situation has a long way to go before improvement could become a reality. Much of the dilemma stems from prejudices and the lack of communication and context between Koreas living on each side of the demilitarised zone (DMZ) border barrier that divides the Korean Peninsula roughly in half and was created by agreement between by the United Nations Command in 1953 (Lee, 2012). Although the majority of North Korean refugees are still content going to South Korea and starting a new life (Haggard & Noland, 2010), they publicise variants of what Castles (2002) refers to as 'differential exclusion', in which citizenship in the nation-state for North Koreans does not confer membership in civil society. After they depart from North Korea and arrival in South Korea, most refugees have a multifaceted array of challenges to contend with, including in education (Jeon et al., 2005; Withnall, 2013). And according to Hornberger and McKey (2010), such difficulties include:

- Lack of interaction with South Koreans
- Low acceptance and high exclusion from various social events
- Difficulty understanding the context of their class lessons

- Miscommunication with teachers due to unlearned psychological and discourse variations between the North and South Korea
- Poor physical and mental health
- The need to cope with newfound freedom and choice of subjects at school
- Inability to communicate and express oneself freely
- Frustration and powerlessness due to uncertainty about who to speak to in times of trouble
- Limited awareness of the new social stereotypes and trends encountered in South Korea

4.3   Methodology

The main content shaping this chapter is founded upon the analysis of academic and public discourse rather than from empirical research. Part of the discourse comes from empirical studies mainly drawn from public discourse such as the media and available official documents from South Korea. Some of the empirical research literature is written in the Korean language, which makes it hard to synthesise a complete picture of all research efforts (see, for example, Park, 2018). Because of this, we have performed the best we could by analytical reading into what is accessible, employing a range of skills such as collation, connecting, comparing, contrasting, as well as observing and commenting in the sense critical review and analysis. By and large, this chapter is primarily based on academic published works, media resources, official documents, and text-based analysis as the method of building the case. We do acknowledge the limitation of not being able to tap into the everyday voice of North Korean migrant students in the current South Korean education system. Being academics based in an Australian institute with an interest in educational equity and inclusivity, at the moment we do not have the conditions to be in the South Korean context to conduct empirical studies on this topic.

4.4   Main Discussion

This section presents the relevant discourse on North Korean migrant students' struggle and adjustment in the South Korean educational context. In particular, the discussion portrays and analyses three types of challenges confronting North Korean students in context, which include educational, interpersonal, and psychological dimensions of the challenge. After that, a set of recommendations will be provided in the subsequent section.

4.4.1 Challenges in Primary Education in South Korea

As a primary concern for most Korean students as it determines their future and social status (Chung, 2008; Chung et al., 2004; Jeon, Yu, Eom, & Kim, 2009; Kwon et al., 2008; Lee, 2003), a substantial number of North Korean refugee students have difficulty attending schools in South Korea (Ahn, 2010; Chung et al., 2004; Yang & Bae, 2010). Some, unfortunately, even decide to drop out of the education system (Park, 2008) due to the age differences with their classmates (Yang & Bae, 2010) and difficulty in catching up with the loss of earlier schooling previously in North Korea (Ahn, 2010; Chung, 2008; Chung et al., 2004; Han, Yoon, Lee, Kim, & Lee, 2009; Kwon et al., 2008; Lee, 2003; Yang & Bae, 2010). Subsequently, there are not only obstacles in the educational system between their two countries (Chung et al., 2004) but also differences in exposure to foreign languages, including English (Kum et al., 2003).

To reduce the impact of the culture shock and to assist with adjusting to their new school environment in South Korea, specific schools are being created by various religious denominations. These schools also try to overcome situations where the pedagogical approaches fail to consider the element that North Korean refugee students in South Korean schools have originated from a vastly different setting (Alptekin, 1984, pp. 14–20). Alptekin expands that teaching should take place regarding the local identity, ethnicity, and socio-cultural norms of the students in class or else there is the creation of bicultural people or conflict of identity (Medgyes, 1999). Besides, many local schools in South Korea perceive the situation as futile as there is a strong belief that both learning systems are vastly different. Moreover, South Korean teachers with their unique teaching background (Akiba et al., 2007) have little or no knowledge of other teaching approaches than what they have always been used to (Chang, 2010).

4.4.2 Challenges in Interpersonal Communication

North Korean students enter into a new environment where they need to re-accommodate themselves to cope with conflicting sociocultural experiences with their southern peers. Lardner, Adams, and Yeats (2004) share some cultural traits found as typical in South Korea. For example, when it comes to socialising, South Koreans tend to involve those of similar backgrounds and attitudes rather than those too different from them. Despite the same ancestry, North Koreans are treated differently in South Korea and are, therefore, not fully accepted by the wider South Korean society. The two groups no longer have a similar mindset, identity, and lifestyle has been very much divided by the Korean War (Moreland & Beach, 2004). Adler, Rosenfeld, Towne, and Procter (1998) explain that in intercultural communications in South Korea, it requires different groups of people to exchange messages in a manner that is influenced by their different cultural perceptions and symbol systems, and several conditions are necessary to have successful communi-cations and relationships. In other words, people would usually try to be the 'same' as others, as being different means to hinder a relationship. For North Korean refugee students, however, such adaptation seems much more demanding besides sorting out cultural differences, they also have to cope with their sense of confusion, anxiety, and stress (Beebe, Beebe, & Ivy, 2004).

Yum (1987a) maintains that North Korean students follow a highly regimented and subservient behaviour, whereas the South Korean students participate within a more constructive criticism and open discussion style class and are therefore more communicative, while North Korean students are less able to communicate by freely expressing themselves (Kim, 2003, p. 441). Furthermore, Yum (1987a) highlights South Koreans learning to use *nun-chi,* a deeply rooted and unique metacognitive approach, and form of communications that assist them throughout their lives (Yum, 1987b, p. 80). North Koreans attending schools in South Korea are unable to do this easily as they are unable to 'tune-into' the current South Korean 'sixth sense' psyche. Yum explains that this is a skill or an ability to understand what is going on in a situation without speaking, and being able to read between the lines, hear between the sound, and to competently tune in. Failure in doing so is generally considered inferior by South Koreans, and therefore, discriminated and marginalised, particularly in their competitive lifestyle (Kim, 2003). Besides, many have difficulties tuning into the South Korean Christian communities, which accounted for a significant proportion of South Korean society (Chung et al., 2004; Jeon & Cho, 2003; Jeon et al., 2010; Yoo, 2005).

4.4.3   Challenges in Well-bBeing and Development

The research shows refugees around the world experience challenges with their health when trying to adjust to their new host country (Bronstein & Montgomery, 2011; Fazel, Reed, Panter-Brick, & Stein, 2012; Rousseau, Drapeau, & Rahimi, 2003; Weine, 2011). In this context, North Korean refugees have extreme difficulty adjusting to South Korea and dealing with stress following their defection from North Korea. Common ailments included depression, anxiety disorders, and post-traumatic stress disorder (PTSD), while others are seen to exhibit behavioural problems (Ahn, 2010; Han et al., 2010; Kwon et al., 2008). Many also demonstrate feelings of inferiority due to their poor health conditions (Choi, Choi, & Kang, 2006; Han et al., 2010; Yang & Bae, 2010). Therefore, North Korean refugees have higher rates of failure compared to South Koreans (Jeon et al., 2009; Lee, 2003) because their adjustment process is more prone to difficulty (Jeon et al., 2009; Noland et al., 2006). In many cases, North Koreans experience confusion while adjusting to South Korean meaning although they are supposed to be speaking the same language (Hornberger & McKey, 2010). Consequently, much of the ability for North Korean refugee students to perform well in South Korean schools depends on their well-being. It is therefore crucial that South Korean education decision-makers promote positive social and health outcomes. Potential benefits for them and the wider South Korean society include:

- Improved ways to engage student learning
- Enriched social and emotional competence
- Fewer emotional and behavioural challenges
- Greater capacity for problem-solving and resilience
- Reduced incidence of mental illness (Jeon, 2000; Lan'kov, 2006a, 2006b).

It is important to identify those students that require additional support for their well-being and link them with support mechanisms, for example, tutor services, mentors and develop and implement broader community, organisational, school strategies that support well-being as this would ensure they are not being marginalised nor left behind (Jeon, 2000), and no longer be categorised as 'saeteomin', 새터민, new settlers. This would attract less negative attention because of their maladjustment to schools, and emotional distance or isolation (Kim & Jang, 2007). Failure to do this would mean failure to adequately adjust to a society with different social structures, values, expectations, political systems, beliefs, and practices (Lan'kov, 2006a).

4.5   Implications

This section proposes several principles for educators to assist North Korean students in coping with their learning difficulty. In doing so, we also highlight teaching approaches that do not cater to North Korean refugee students in South Korean schools by failing to recognise their vastly different backgrounds. Our recommendation also includes a practical lesson idea to support students' learning adaptation, a suggestion to give curriculum content a stronger focus on learning skills and, finally, the need to build a supportive learning environment. Through all these concrete recommendations, we appeal for classroom instruction to be conducted with reference to the local identity, ethnicity, and socio-cultural norms of the students.

4.5.1   Proposed Insights for Coping with a Learning Difficulty

In light of the challenges that North Korean refugee students experience in South Korea, many education decision-makers encourage change in the classroom culture (Alfred, 2005). There is the need to address their physical and mental challenges and overcome the conflict of identity and the cultural barriers that are fundamental to both their personal and academic performance and development. One important way to achieve this is by implementing measures to form a support community that addresses the needs of these students (Walker, 1999). Failure to do so would handicap the refugees to reach their academic goals (Erichsen, 2009), and they would suffer from not existing within a larger societal context, in which they interact with others of a different race, ethnicity, social status, religion, and ideology (Leary, 1983, pp. 39–41). In this light, we would like to make some practical recommendations:

- Decorate and equip the classrooms with images, artefacts, books, posters, and other materials that reflect diversity, that is, different ways of revealing the world.
- Organise projects and activities that allow both North and South Korean students to contribute with their specific knowledge and understanding. Some examples would be co-designing a diversity poster, joining sports teams, painting the staircase together, etc.
- Display in school corridors images and quotes that encourage harmony, cooperation, inclusive knowledge, various backgrounds, and that discourage bullying or discrimination.
- Involve supportive teachers, administrators, guest speakers (including writers, actors, and celebrities) so that students become aware that a healthy, safe, diverse environment is being co-constructed by the whole school and anyone who wishes to stay outside of this ideal would feel they are being left behind the development.
- In the classroom, teach students about the origin, nature, and negative effect of bias on their personal development. Make efforts to advocate language that is unbiased, inclusive, and non-divisive. For example, 'Okay, all good boys and girls in this class. . .', 'This task is great for all kinds of Koreans who care about learning', etc.
- Create discussions that address key concerns in society, analyse the value of social differences, promote equity, and acknowledge all kinds of contributions. If tension and discomfort occur in the classroom, do the best to recognise it and organise the time for reflection either in verbal discussion or in writing.
- Keep parents informed and involved, so that they can suggest ways to make their children's learning more collaborative and productive.
- Do not tolerate discriminative behaviour by avoiding it or by keeping silent. Turn it into an opportunity for a class discussion, a story sharing session, a reading lesson, or an essay topic. If a student gets humiliated, invite other class members to put themselves in the student's shoes, and share how they would feel. Share stories of great people in history who got discriminated against and who have become successful in what they believe in.

By and large, socioculturally sensitive education in South Korea requires employing strategies and approaches that facilitate fairness and inclusivity. Son (2009) and Noh (2009) argued that North Koreans should be included in the South Korean education system and not dislocated in South Korean society. Besides, dislocated North Koreans should be 'compensated for their maladjustment', for example, group homes that are dwelling facilities with peer group tutoring. The merits would have a decrease in the social and cultural gap caused by fundamentally different systems of education (Ko, 2013). Ko placed a strong emphasis on the linguistic adaptation process of students as they were in trouble with their acquisition because they lacked a basic educational foundation. Therefore, the one method to help overcome this challenge is helping them to adapt to the South Korean society (Altbach & Knight, 2007; Bhatia, 2006; Cho, 2009; Kim & Lee, 2010; McKay, 2002; McKay, 2003; West, 2010). Essentially, having an education system that combines all students within a fair and balanced teaching approach, and using an appropriate inclusive South Korean curriculum (Phelan, Macfarlane, & Pinson, 2011) would be the best solution (West, 2010). Such a system would demonstrate empathy by being sensitive to students' needs, motivating them accordingly, and providing encouragement when required. This is because there are often substantial gaps in some students' education including English proficiency, as they have been deprived of suitable learning activities to achieve communicative competence (Canagarajah, 1999; Chang, Haggard, & Noland, 2009; Miller, 2003). Hence, more sympathy should be shown towards North Korean refugee students who are trying to adjust and settle in South Korean society (Chung et al., 2004) to overcome continued stigma. For example, Heavenly Dream School (?늘꿈학교) and Yeomyung School (여명학교) provided North Korean refugee students with advice on how they should behave in South Korea (Ahn, 2012; Lee, 2012), which would also help them shift their ideological misunderstanding in South Korea (Yoo, 2005).

4.5.2   A Lesson Idea to Support Students' Learning Adaptation

It would be impossible to make amendments to the broad sociocultural, historical, and educational context. However, as teachers, we have the right and responsibility to influence pedagogical practices within the everyday classroom to make students' learning experience less traumatising and the most pleasurable learning experience possible. Therefore, to serve as an illustrating example, we would like to propose a lesson plan, which aims at helping students engage with cultural adaptation. The objectives are to inspire students to explore their peers' dissimilar backgrounds and share experiences with peers whom they did not have a history of socialising with. The main task is to encourage students to communicate with one another by finding classmates who have had the experiences as listed in an activity sheet. This handout might list out occurrences such as find someone who has travelled to a different place before and learned a new way of behaving or thinking, have coped with a challenging situation that required personal effort and specific skills, can make handicraft and can teach a peer how to do it, and so on. This exchange provides opportunities for all students to learn more about peers' profiles to hopefully improve the extent of social engagement as well as class involvement. In this procedure, students first of all use worksheets to walk around and ask questions to peers. Secondly, they collect answers by writing them down in the worksheet until it is fairly complete. Thirdly, they come back to their seats and continue with the follow-up discussion as guided by the teacher, who then invites everyone to share their findings as well as expand the content further. Moreover, some of the key highlights in the lesson include teacher encouragement of socialisation and students expressing the information about peers that impressed them or that aroused their interest. The task should create an enjoyable and mutually accepting environment for everyone, as well as teacher feedback and peer feedback where possible. In the end, the lesson plan also recommends a few optional steps if time allows, which invite students to write their own question list, visit another class to share the same activity, and explore peers' profiles somewhat further for deeper socialisation.

We would argue, therefore, that this lesson would work well in an integrated unit comprising such areas as social development, communication, and cultural awareness because the lesson contains a rich range of those elements that engage students in social, linguistic, communicative, and intercultural skills, and to a degree well-connected together. By and large, this plan encourages acceptance of diversity, well-organised support for culturally different profiles, open-ended or student-generated content, and creative ways of tasks that make students feel comfortable, active, amused, and intrigued in the learning process.

The lesson plan aims to produce four positive qualities, which are helpful support, increased participation, sharing deep information, and an accepting classroom climate. First of all, it supports peer learning engagement, with some emphasis upon what Topping (2005), advocates as equal-opportunity involvement in peer learning and engagement of all members of the educational community without exception. In the plan, students are given the freedom to discuss and share their own experiences and background, which creates a rich learning community for everyone. Secondly, it creates high participation. According to Jordan, Schwartz, and McGhie-Richmond (2009), effective teaching involves student participation based on thoughtful time control and classroom management skills. The lesson plan achieves this by providing reasonable time, space, and clear instruction for students to exchange ideas within a good amount of talk time. Thirdly, the lesson helps the teacher and students discover new information from each other. A positive relationship between students and teachers is an important factor that boosts learning motivation (Alder, 2000). The teacher should show a genuine interest in student talk by asking whether any response from classmates seems most surprising and by further pursuing new information from such sharing moments. Fourthly, the lesson offers an accepting classroom climate. While cultural diversity represents an important resource for education in Australia, like the United Kingdom, and some European countries (Schachner, Noack, Van de Vijver, & Eckstein, 2016), many schools are often ill-prepared for the optimal use of such content but tend to be overwhelmed by the intake of large student populations. The lesson attempts to make up for this by paying some attention to the intercultural adjustment processes by creating a welcoming environment for all children with some degree of respect and understanding.

The lesson implies some positive principles including accepting differences, supporting diverse learners, the view of learning as a socio-constructive process, and creative ways of teaching. To ensure productive engagement, it is important that teachers understand the target group in terms of abilities and learning styles and not just cultural diversity. Knowing who your students are, as a group and as individuals, is an important part of good teaching, which requires the teacher to have a specific understanding of students. The reason for the need to know about learners' heredity, experiences, perspectives, backgrounds, talents, interests, and capacities is to ensure the teacher can cater for a learner-centred approach (Brown, 2003) as well as to apply knowledge in a relevant manner to learners' needs (Alder, 2000). Therefore, our recommendation, based on the above, would be for students' sociocultural background to be taken into consideration. This could mean the above aspects of the student profile, together with any other characteristics that might distinguish students from the mainstream by social class, ethnicity, and communication styles. Teachers should also consider students' cultural differences in the lesson plan, such as habits, customs, and taboos. For example, teachers need to avoid children touching on words or topics which may raise controversies, such as famine, political conflict, and stereotypes.

4.5.3 Giving Curriculum Content a Stronger Focus on Learning Skills

Materials need to engage students in more understanding and critical thinking rather than just an exchange of facts. Although the selected lesson claims learning engagement, the content of the activity mainly focuses on factual information, such as finding someone who has visited an island in the Pacific or who can say 10 names of animals in English, and so on. Research has demonstrated that engaging students in the learning process involves the increase of attention and focus, motivating students to practice higher-level critical thinking skills and promotion of meaningful learning experiences (Furlong & Christenson, 2008). It might also be helpful to create some additional questions on the list so that besides finding who has certain abilities, students can also ask peers more deeply into the experience such as how they learned certain skills, where and when they did so, why they need such ability and the occasions in which they use it. These can be optional ideas that students can choose from to suit each specific context. As Brown (2003) indicates, teachers' knowledge of students' characteristics also allows instructional practices that foster critical thinking and problem-solving. Besides, evaluation of learning can happen if the teacher can observe to detect where in the learning process students encounter difficulties, what types, and how they work to overcome them. Some examples of such incidents include the need for seeking help, explaining things, having a good relationship with others, and so on. This requires teachers to provide opportunities for children to choose the level on which they engage with lessons. It is important to be aware that students with specific learning difficulties need more attention as it is often difficult to remedy those within a mainstream classroom through normal teaching methods (Yuen, Westwood, & Wong, 2005).

4.5.4   Building a Supportive Learning Environment

Our final suggestion would be to develop effective caring and nurturing procedures for managing student behaviour and creating a classroom environment that is open, safe, and supportive, and free for individual self-expression. In many cases, difficulties arise because the learning conditions are restricting rather than helpful for everyone. Some students can learn well in many situations, but others might need more empathetic encouragement. A good teaching environment must allow everyone with various needs to be catered for. Each student must feel comfortable sharing unpopular perspectives and beliefs, even when they conflict with the teacher (Evans, Avery, & Pederson, 1999). Furthermore, learning would be made easier with regular feedback to promote improvement. The importance of realistic expectations, the provision of specific feedback, and clear communication are important factors for effective teaching (Alder, 2000). Therefore, much education research has demonstrated that in every inclusive classroom, effective teaching skills should be effective for all types of students including those with special needs or, in this case, cultural adaptation needs (Jordan et al., 2009). Besides, the classroom should be a place that welcomes a nice balance of ethnic composition, including both immigrant and local students with all possible diversity in capabilities and needs (Schachner et al., 2016). Eventually, a successful inclusive lesson must be one that does not discriminate, that taps into diverse needs, and that supports a wide range of learning difficulties, all of which should be conducted with care and in an innovative manner, so that learning can always be fresh and inspiring for everyone.

4.6   Conclusion

This chapter has created space and opportunity to discuss how the allocation of power in the dominant and marginalised subordinate group of Korean people created social stratification and tensions in schools. It has suggested ideas for teachers to assist the learning of North Korean refugee students who are disadvantaged and placed in a vulnerable predicament and situation. Hopefully, teachers can contribute to allowing fair opportunities that should be given as a sign of recognition, acceptance, and assimilation in the classroom in South Korea.

Although some schools in South Korea are sensitive to cultural diversity, few have been able to understand the various issues concerning education and assimilation of some groups of Koreans coming to South Korea such as North Korean refugee students (Kim, 2001). The challenges North Koreans experience when learning English in South Korea is well documented in the literature. Hart (2000), discusses how refugee students experience feeling isolated in South Korea and attribute this to South Koreans not accepting them and at times, ostracising them. It is against and within these areas of contestation that this study is located.

In identifying challenges North Koreans experience within South Korea's education, this chapter has attempted to question or challenge the political and ideological interests at work in education decision-making in the hope to frame cultural reform agendas, rather than analyse from an ethnographic approach, as clearly, North Korean refugee students are one of the underrepresented Korean groups in South Korea's population having a substantial degree of difficulty in learning in classrooms, and with English acquisition (Lan'kov, 2006a). Finally, this research topic presents the realness of their experiences and highlights the fact that this mindset of existing power relations and social arrangement sustains them in a space with a limited opportunity such as the allocation of power being dominant and marginalising a subordinate group of Korean people that creates social stratification and tensions occurring in schools and beyond (Bourdieu, 1977; Haggard & Noland, 2010; Holliday, 2005).

It remains a complex endeavour to attempt grasping the historical, sociocultural, and educational relationship between members of the two differing societies. The challenge was to develop a methodology that allowed scholars to examine how the private challenges are connected to public issues and to respond to these challenges. These responses included narratives and writing of stories of experiences defined by meaning, voice, reflexivity, presence, and representation. There is a social justice agenda to inquire and address issues of inequality and injustice in particular social moments and places. The main and basic question in this chapter was how people gave and continue to give meaning to their lives and perform and explain these meanings in their lives. Moreover, there is also the pressing demand to show how the successful practices of critical, interpretative, and qualitative research can help change the world in positive ways.

References

Adler, R. B., Rosenfeld, L. B., Towne, N., & Procter, R. F. (1998). *Interplay, The process of interpersonal communications* (7th ed.). New York: Harcourt Brace College Publishers.

Ahn, K. S. (2010). A study on the plan for supporting adolescents defecting from North Korean for their adjustment in South Korea society. *Adolescent Studies, 17*, 25–45.

Ahn, H. N. (2012). Starting hope Gongbubang for North Korean adolescents. GunpoNews. Retrieved November 7, 2013, from http://gunpo.newsk.com/bbs/bbs.asp?exe=view&group_name=332&idx_num=19741

Akiba, M., LeTendre, G. K., & Scribner, J. P. (2007). Teacher quality, opportunity gap, and national achievement in 46 countries. *Educational Researcher, 36*(7), 369–387.

Alder, N. (2000). Teaching diverse students. *Multicultural Perspectives, 2*(2), 28–31.

Alfred, M. V. (2005). Overlooked in academe: What do we know about immigrant students in adult and higher education? *New Horizons in Adult and Continuing Education 19*(1). (Electronic Journal).

Alptekin, M. (1984). The question of culture: EFL teaching in non-English-speaking countries. *ELT Journal, 38*(1), 14–20.

Altbach, P. G., & Knight, J. (2007). The internationalization of higher education: Motivations and realities. *Journal of Studies in International Education, 11*(3–4), 290–305.

Beebe, S. A., Beebe, S. J., & Ivy, D. K. (2004). *Communication, principles for a lifetime.* New York: Pearson Publishers.

Bhatia, T. K. (2006). Super-heroes to super languages: American popular culture through south Asian language comics. *World Englishes, 25*(2), 279–298.

Bourdieu, P. (1977). *Outline of a theory of practice.* Cambridge: Cambridge University Press.

Bronstein, I., & Montgomery, P. (2011). Psychological distress in refugee children: A systematic review. *Clinical Child and Family Psychology Review, 14*, 44–56.

Brown, K. L. (2003). From teacher-centred to learner-centred curriculum: Improving learning in diverse classrooms. *Education, 124*(1), 49.

Canagarajah, A. (1999). *Resisting linguistic imperialism in English teaching.* Oxford: Oxford University Press.

Castles, S. (2002). Migration and community formation under conditions of globalisation. *International Migration Review, 36*(4), 1143–1168.

Chang, L. T. (2010). *Factory girls: Voices from the heart of modern China.* London: Picador Publishers.

Chang, Y., Haggard, S., & Noland, M. (2009). Exit polls: Refugee assessments of North Korea's transition. *Journal of Comparative Economics, 37*(1), 144–150.

Chang, H., Pak, S. Y., & Sleeter, C. E. (2018). Multicultural education: Using our past to build our future. *International Journal of Multicultural Education, 20*(1), 1–4.

Cho, E. S. (2009). The effect of religion on adaptation to south Korean society: A study based on student defectors from North Korea. *Korean Journal for Christian Studies, 63*(2009), 245–259, Christian Institute of South Korea: Korea Christian Theology Publications.

Choi, M. S., Choi, T. S., & Kang, J. H. (2006). Psychological characteristics of children and adolescents escaped from North Korea and seeing a counselling strategy. *Korean Journal of Play Therapy, 9*, 23–34.

Chung, B. H. (2008). Between defector and migrant: Identities and strategies of north Koreans in South Korea. *Korean Studies, 32*(1), 1–27.

Chung, J. K., Chung, B. H., & Yang, K. M. (2004). Adjustment of North Korean refugee youths in South Korean schools. *Unification Issues Studies, 11*, 209–239.

Erichsen, E. A. (2009). *Reinventing selves: International students' conceptions of self and learning for transformation.* Ph.D. dissertation, University of Wyoming, Laramie.

Evans, R. W., Avery, P. G., & Pederson, P. V. (1999). Taboo topics: Cultural restraint on teaching social issues. *The Social Studies, 90*(5), 218–224.

Fazel, M., Reed, R., Panter-Brick, C., & Stein, A. (2012). Mental health of displaced and refugee children resettled in high-income countries: Risk and protective factors. *The Lancet, 379*, 266–282. Retrieved from http://ewha.ac.kr

Furlong, M. J., & Christenson, S. L. (2008). Engaging students at school and with learning: A relevant construct for all students. *Psychology in the Schools, 45*(5), 365–368.

Haggard, S., & Noland, M. (2010). *Political attitudes under repression: Evidence from North Korean refugees.* US: East-West Centre Publishers.

Han, M. K., Lee, H. K., Kim, Y. Y., Chae, J. M., Kim, Y. N., Kim, I. H., et al. (2010). *Longitudinal study on North Korean adolescent defectors' education.* Jincheon-gun: Educational Korean Educational Development Institute.

Han, M. K., Yoon, J. H., Lee, H. K., Kim, I. H., & Lee, K. H. (2009). *Research on North Korean defectors educational situation and analysis.* Jincheon-gun: Educational Korean Educational Development Institute.

Hart, D. (2000). Proclaiming identity, claiming the past: National identity and modernity in north and South Korean education. *Asian Perspective, 24*(3), 135–158.

Holliday, A. (2005). *The struggle to teach English as an international language.* Oxford: Oxford University Press.

Hornberger, N. H., & McKey, S. L. (2010). *Sociolinguistics and language education.* Toronto: Multilingual Matters Publishers.

Jeon, W. T. (2000). Issues and problems of adaptation of North Korean defectors to South Korean society: An in-depth interview study with 32 defectors. *Yonsei Medical Journal, 41*(3), 362–371.

Jeon, W. T., & Cho, Y. A. (2003). Religious experiences of North Korean defectors in South Korea and the role of churches for Korean unification. *Unification Studies, 7,* 105–128.

Jeon, W., Hong, C., Lee, C., Kim, D. K., Han, M., & Min, S. (2005). Correlation between traumatic events and posttraumatic stress disorder among north Korean defectors in South Korea. *Journal of Traumatic Stress, 18*(2), 147–154.

Jeon, W. T., Yu, S. E., Eom, J. S., & Kim, H. J. (2009). 7-year follow up study of society adaptation of North Korean defectors: With focus given to education and life. *Unification Studies, 13,* 127–157.

Jordan, A., Schwartz, E., & McGhie-Richmond, D. (2009). Preparing teachers for inclusive classrooms. *Teaching and Teacher Education, 25*(4), 535–542.

Kim, H. Y. (2001). *Philosophy of masters.* Baton Rouge: Andrew Jackson College Press.

Kim, Y. (2003). Intercultural personhood: An integration of eastern and Western perspectives. In L. A. Samovar & R. E. Porter (Eds.), *Intercultural communication* (pp. 436–448). Belmont: Wadsworth/ Thomson Learning.

Kim, J. U., & Jang, D. I. (2007). Aliens among brothers? The status and perception of North Korean refugees in South Korea. *Asian Perspective, 31*(2), 5–22.

Kim, S., & Lee, J. H. (2010). Private tutoring and demand for education in South Korea. *Economic Development and Cultural Change, 58*(2), 259–296.

Kim, M., & Lee, D. (2013). Adaptation of North Korean adolescent refugees to South Korean society: A review of literature. *Journal of Rehabilitation Psychology, 20*(1), 39–64.

Ko, G. H. (2013). *A study on linguistic adaptation process of North Korean refugee adolescents.* (Thesis (MA)), Sookmyung Women's University, Education of Korean Language and Literature.

Kum, M. J., Kwon, H. S., Lee, J. Y., & Lee, H. S. (2003). *Development of adolescent counselling programs in preparation of unification II.* Korea Youth Counselling Institute.

Kwon, Y. J., Lee, S.O., Kim, Y. K., Kim, S. Y., Jung, U. H. (2008). *Suggestions for changes in educational legislation for new settlers adolescents.* Ministry of Unification.

Lan'kov, A. N. (2006a). Bitter taste of paradise: North Korean refugees in South Korea. *Journal of East Asian Studies, 6*(1), 105–137.

Lan'kov, A. N. (2006b). The natural death of North Korean Stalinism. *Asia Policy, 1*(1), 95–121.

Lardner, R., Adams, H. B., & Yeats, W. B. (2004). First impression and interpersonal attraction. In H. T. Reis & C. E. Rusbult (Eds.), *Key readings in social psychology, close relationship* (pp. 75–77). New York: Psychology Press.

Leary, M. R. (1983). *Understanding social anxiety: Social, personality, and clinical perspectives.* London: Sage Publications.

Lee, G. (2003). The political philosophy of Juche. *Stanford Journal of East Asian Affairs, 3,* 105–112. Retrieved from http://www.stanford.edu/group/sjeaa/journal3/korea1.pdf

Lee, J. H. (2012). *Inchon youth red cross opens firefly Gongbubang.* Kihoilbo. Retrieved June 18, from http://www.kihoilbo.co.kr/news/articleView.html?idno=468969.

Lee, M. W. (2014). A participatory EFL curriculum for the marginalized: The case of North Korean refugee students in South Korea. *System, 47,* 1–11.

McKay, S. L. (2002). *Teaching English as an international language: Rethinking goals and perspectives.* New York: OUP.

McKay, S. L. (2003). Toward an appropriate EIL pedagogy: Re-examining common ELT assumptions. *International Journal of Applied Linguistics, 13*(1), 1–22.

Medgyes, P. (1999). *The non-native teacher.* London: Macmillan Publishers.

Miller, J. (2003). *Audible difference: ESL and social identity in schools.* Clevedon: Multilingual Matters Publishers.

Ministry of Education (2013). *2013 North Korean refugee student statistics.* Ministry of Education.

Ministry of Unification (2012). *Eight refugees were admitted in 1993*. Retrieved from Act on Protection and Resettlement Support for the Residents Who Escaped from North Korea (1997). 북한이탈주민의 **보호 및** 정착지원에관한 **법률** [시행 1997.7.14] [**법률 제5259호**, 1997.1.13, 제정] http://law.go.kr/main.html

Moreland, R. L., & Beach, S. R. (2004). Exposure effects in the classroom: The development of affinity among students. In H. T. Reis & C. E. Rusbult (Eds.), *Key readings in social psychology, close relationship* (pp. 89–96). New York: Psychology Press.

Noh, Y. H. (2009). *Programs for North Korean refugees adjusting to life in Universities: Focus on group home system and peer tutoring in dormitories.* (Thesis MA), Myongji University, Seoul, South Korea, Myongji University Graduate School bukhanhakgwa, 2009. 2. Document Number: (325.21 22).

Noland, M., Haggard, S., Chang, Y., Kurlantzick, J., Lan'kov, A. & Mason, J. (2006). The North Korean refugee crisis: Human rights and international response. *Korea Yearbook 2006.*

Park, Y. S. (2008). Study on the characteristics of social support and social adjustment of North Korean refugee adolescents in South Korea. *Youth Culture Forum, 19*, 79–117.

Park, J. K. (2009). 'English fever' in South Korea: Its history and symptoms. *English Today, 97*(1), 50–57.

Park, H. (2018). Research trend in North Korean migrant student education. *Korean Association for Learner-Centred Curriculum and Instruction, 18*(24), 641–663.

Phelan, L., Macfarlane, S., & Pinson, J. (2011). Supporting successful learning for refugee students: The classroom connect project. *Issues in Educational Research, 213*, 310–329. University of New England, Catholic Education Office, Sydney.

Rousseau, C., Drapeau, A., & Rahimi, S. (2003). The complexity of trauma response: A 4-year follow-up of adolescent Cambodian refugees. *Child Abuse & Neglect, 27*, 1277–1290.

Schachner, M. K., Noack, P., Van de Vijver, F. J., & Eckstein, K. (2016). Cultural diversity, climate and psychological adjustment at school—Equality and inclusion versus cultural pluralism. *Child Development, 87*(4), 1175–1191.

Son, J. J. (2009). The importance of patience in English teaching and learning. 영어영문학연구, *35*(3), 319–338.

Song, J. J. (2011). English as an official language in South Korea: Global English or social malady? *Language Problems and Language Planning, 35*(1), 35–55.

Topping, K. J. (2005). Trends in peer learning. *Educational Psychology, 25*(6), 631–645.

Walker, V. S. (1999). Culture and commitment challenges for the future training of education researchers. In E. C. Lagemann & L. S. Shulman (Eds.), *Issues in education research*. San Francisco: Jossey-Bass.

Walton, J., Priest, N., Kowal, E., White, F., Brickwood, K., Fox, B., et al. (2014). Talking culture? Egalitarianism, color-blindness and racism in Australian elementary schools. *Teaching and Teacher Education, 39*, 112–122.

Weine, S. M. (2011). Developing preventive mental health interventions for refugee families in resettlement. *Family Process, 50*, 410–430.

West, D. A. (2010). Teaching English to North Korean refugees in South Korea: An interview with Karen Choi. *North Korean Review, 6*(1), 108–119.

Withnall, A. (2013). South Korean defectors flee to North Korea 'in search of better life'—but end up in detention for up to 45 months. *The Independent*. Retrieved from http://www.independent.co.uk/news/world/asia/south-korean-defectors-flee-to-north-korea-in-search-of-better-life%2D%2Dbut-end-up-in-detention-for-up-to-45-months-8909299.html

Yang, Y. E., & Bae, I. (2010). A study on the adaptation process of North Korean immigrant youth discontinuing formal education. *Korean Journal of Social Welfare Studies, 41*, 189–224.

Yoo, M. B. (2005). Adjustment of North Korean refugee adolescents in South Korea and the task of Christian education. In *Bible & Theology* (Vol. 37, pp. 297–318). Korea: Evangelical Theological Society Korea.

Yuen, M., Westwood, P., & Wong, G. (2005). Meeting the needs of students with specific learning difficulties in the mainstream education system: Data from primary school teachers in Hong Kong. *International Journal of Special Education, 20*(1), 67–76.

Yum, J. (1987a). The Korean philosophy and communication. In D. L. Kincaid (Ed.), *Communication theory: Eastern and Western perspectives*. San Diego: Academic Press.

Yum, J. (1987b). The practice of uye-ri in interpersonal relationships. In D. L. Kincaid (Ed.), *Communication theory: Eastern and Western perspectives*. San Diego: Academic Press.

Chapter 5
Learners as Story Writers: Creative Writing Practices in English as a Foreign Language Learning in Indonesia

Henny Herawati

Abstract This research project aimed to investigate creative writing practices in English as a foreign language (EFL) learning in Indonesia, focusing on students' capacities in using their resources to write stories in English. This qualitative case study involved two Indonesian students taking a Creative Writing subject as participants. The data were collected from semi-structured one-on-one interviews, guided journals, and samples of students' writings. The study revealed notable findings. First, there were two capacities that the two Indonesian students demonstrated, namely inciting inspirations and synthesising. To induce inspirations, the students did three practices, i.e. observing surroundings, drawing inspirations from experiences, and getting ideas from others' creative works (i.e. novels, movies, songs, photos). These practices might not be unique techniques, yet, they allowed snapshots of local, cultural facets (e.g. incidents, values, issues, beliefs, norms) to emerge in the students' writings. Second, synthesising has been identified as a valuable capacity employed by the two students to develop and write stories in English. This capacity to synthesise information, ideas, skills, and knowledge from different sources may enhance creativity in writing. Third, this study found that the students' capacities and practices of writing stories corresponded to the stages of learning in Dewantara's 3N (*Niteni-Nirokake-Nambahi*) learning principles.

Keywords Creativity · Creative writing · Inciting inspiration · Synthesising · Dewantara's 3N Learning concept

H. Herawati (✉)
Sanata Dharma University, Yogyakarta, Indonesia
e-mail: henny@usd.ac.id

© Springer Nature Singapore Pte Ltd. 2021
D. Bao, T. Pham (eds.), *Transforming Pedagogies Through Engagement with Learners, Teachers and Communities*, Education in the Asia-Pacific Region: Issues, Concerns and Prospects 57, https://doi.org/10.1007/978-981-16-0057-9_5

5.1   Introduction

Creativity, with its multi-faceted attributes, has been valued and has drawn a wide research interest in diverse fields such as arts, literature, business, psychology, and education (Amabile, 2012; Collard & Looney, 2014; Feist, Reiter-Palmon, & Kaufman, 2017; Grigorenko & Tan, 2008; Jones, 2016; Runco, 2004; Tin, 2016; Xerri & Vassallo, 2016). It has also been studied in its relations with language learning, including in English as a second or foreign language (ESL/EFL) context (Disney, 2014; Harper, 2016; Pennington, 2016; Tin, 2016; Zhao, 2015). Among those studies is Tin's (2016, p. 436) which highlights the issue of how creativity can contribute to the development of 'rich, complex second-language patterns' produced by learners. She also asserts that 'recent work in complex/dynamic theory and emergentism has transformed our view of language from a "communicative" to a "creative" view' (Tin, 2016, p. 436). Hence, language is not a mere means of communication, but also a tool for creating new ideas and meanings.

Despite some sceptical views on the viability of non-native learners of English to write creative writings in English, there has been a growing interest to foster creativity in writing by encouraging students to write different kinds of creative texts, such as story or poetry. In Indonesia, the interest in creative writing in English is also expanding. Yet, studies investigating issues around the areas, especially on the practices and capacities of Indonesian students to write short stories in English, are few. With an underlying view that learners are potential writers who have unique cultural-intellectual resources, it is important to investigate how they use these resources when writing stories in English. As a part of a larger study investigating EFL creative writing practices in Indonesia, this chapter focuses on the students' capacities, in particular in using their cultural-intellectual resources to write stories in English.

5.2   Creativity Process

As an expression of creativity, the making of creative writing takes on the process of producing creativity in general. Among the literature in creativity discussing its production process is Amabile's componential theory of creativity (1996). Amabile (1996, 2012) argues that creativity needs a confluence of four components: domain-relevant skills, creativity-relevant skills (character traits and cognitive styles), motivation, and social environment. The discussion in this chapter, however, centres around the *domain-relevant skills*. This component includes one's knowledge, expertise, skills, intelligence, and talent (Amabile, 1996). When producing a creative product or idea, one uses his/her domain-relevant skills. The knowledge, intelligence, and skills used are not only those related to a particular creativity field but also those of other areas that can be used in the production of creativity. It is, hence, possible to use cross-domain skills when performing creativity in a particular domain.

Included as well in the domain-relevant skills are one's cultural-intellectual resources. Adapting Handa's (2013, p.31) definition of '(non-Western) knowledge', cultural-intellectual resources in this study are understood as 'knowledge, abilities, skills, values, and perspectives' that emerged 'due to one's intellectual heritage and bilingual skills'. These are resources or 'raw materials' that one can draw in the process of producing a creative product. A person's cultural background, values, and ideologies, which are most likely influenced by the society he/she lives in, may become resources that one can retrieve and become lenses that one uses to interpret a particular experience (Lubart & Georgsdottir, 2004; Kwang, 2001; Runco, 2004). All of the aforementioned domain-relevant skills can be learned and developed through formal learning in school, or an informal one, such as through experience or observation.

Regarding the process to produce creativity, Boden (2004) asserts that an original and novel idea or artefact can be created by blending, exploring, or transforming. In the context of creative writing, which is an expression of creativity in language, Bakhtin explicates with the term heteroglossia that originality in the context of language creativity is gained when one can make a language one's own by synthesising words and 'when the speaker populates it with his intentions, his own accent, when he appropriates the word, adapting it to his own semantic and expressive intention' (Bakhtin, 1981, p. 294).

In the Indonesian literature about the creativity process, Munandar (2009) explicates that the process of '*kreativitas*'—the Indonesian word for creativity—involves making new combinations based on data, information, and other available components as well as previously existed products. Likewise, Supriadi (1994) affirms that to produce creativity, one makes new combinations of existing objects or ideas to give birth to a new thing.

In the context of learning in Indonesia, one perspective about the creativity process is contained in Dewantara's 3N (*Niteni-Nirokake-Nambahi (Jv.)* = observing-imitating-adding/developing) concept. In the 3N concept, which is one of the basic principles of learning in Indonesia (Suroso, 2011), a learner's initial step of learning is to observe closely (*niteni*) and identify the characteristics, the procedures, the reality, and the meaning of an object by using his/her senses. Then, he/she can imitate or *nirokake* (Jv.), followed with *nambahi* (Javanese) which means adding or developing. *Nirokake* and *Nambahi* are done as the application stages after *Niteni*. There is a process of creation or innovation in the third stage, which highlights the importance of not merely copying or imitating what already exists but adding, improving, developing, or modifying to produce something new (Suroso, 2011).

5.3   Creative Writing in ESL/EFL Pedagogy

Creative writing is a form of creative expression involving language in a written form. It is defined as any writing that expresses thoughts, feelings, and emotions imaginatively and poetically and has an aesthetic purpose, instead of merely for conveying information or for other practical purposes (Maley, 2009). Creative writing also refers to the act of writing imaginatively and artistically, drawing from one's 'imagination' and 'intellect', using one's 'personal and cultural knowledge' (Harper, 2016, p. 498). Whereas the writing process can be inspired by intuition, observation, imagination, and personal memories (Maley, 2009).

Studies have indicated the benefits that language learners can get from creative writing practice. First, it develops the students' language mastery as it requires learners to play with the language to create a new, unique, and personal meaning (Maley, 2009; Maley & Kiss, 2018; McLoughlin, 2008; Smith, 2013; Tin, 2013). As they write, students engage themselves with the language, experiment with it, use words with different senses and sounds, and convey meanings with different language devices. Creative writing encourages learners to explore, manipulate, and take risks with the language and when doing so, learners develop their 'grammar, vocabulary, phonology, and discourse' (Maley, 2009). McLoughlin (2008) and Maley (2009) further highlight the importance of play in creative writing and affirm that students should be given the freedom to take the prompt and to make their writings appealing, original, and their own. Besides, creative writing encourages a higher language competence as students develop the ability to use metaphorical language in their writings.

Furthermore, creative writing develops students' affective aspects in the use of language, such as in expressing feelings, emotions, and intuitions. It focuses on the right side of the brain which is the centre of 'feelings, physical sensations, intuition, and musicality' (Maley, 2009, p.1). Besides, creative writing in EFL/ESL context is humanising as it encourages the attainment of self-esteem, self-confidence, and self-empowerment in using the target language (Hanauer, 2010, 2014; Iida, 2013; Maley, 2009; Zhao, 2014, 2015). The feat of producing a piece of artistic writing in a foreign language can build the students' confidence (Maley, 2009).

In Indonesia, up to date, few studies have been conducted to investigate the EFL creative writing practices. Among others is a study involving Indonesian university students by Tin (2011) which revealed that creative writing tasks with high formal constraints (acrostics) could create opportunities for creative language use and stimulate the use of complex language compared to tasks with looser formal constraints (similes). Some conference papers also present Indonesian teachers' practices of exploring and incorporating local literature and folklore (Susanti & Trisusana, 2014), local traditional song (Sukraini, 2014), the local language, names, settings, and cultural issues (Herawati, 2014; Lestari, 2014; Rakhmawati, 2014) in their creative writing subject. Yet, little has been known about the Indonesian students' capacities and practices of creative writing in English.

Scholars including Tay (2014) emphasise that creative writing does not happen in a 'cultural vacuum', and writers, in whatever language they write, cannot elude from representing their self-images in their writings (Ivanic & Camps, 2001; Zhao, 2014). Similarly, Chin (2014) asserts that L2 creative writing is 'a social construct' and that 'it is deeply rooted in sociocultural beliefs, values, language, and thought systems' (p. 122). Hence, when writing, students use their unique cultural backgrounds, values, personal experiences, and knowledge as resources and lenses to express their feelings, thoughts, and imagination. However, we still know very little about how students use their cultural and intellectual resources in developing their writing. This research aimed to gain more insights into this area. It aimed to answer the following question:

How did Indonesian students utilise their cultural-intellectual resources to write short stories in English?

5.4 Methodology

This study was a qualitative case study conducted under the constructivist paradigm. It explored in-depth how two Indonesian students practiced creative writing in English. This research valued the subjectivity of each student participant who brought about their idiosyncratic creative writing practices.

5.4.1 Research Site

The research was conducted at a university in Central Java Province, Indonesia. The selection of the university was based on the following three criteria: first, it had an English Department that offered Creative Writing class for at least 5 years, either as a compulsory or as an elective subject; second, the English Department in the university was accredited 'A' by the National Accreditation Board for Higher Education in Indonesia, thus confirming its good quality; and third, the Creative Writing class was offered at the time the data was collected.

5.4.2 Research Participants

This study is a part of a larger study involving 11 Indonesian undergraduate students and four teachers as participants. However, this chapter reports and discusses the practices of two students only. These two student participants who were selected using a purposeful sampling strategy will henceforth be addressed as Tika and Sella. These students were at their third year and taking a creative writing subject focusing on fiction writing when this study was conducted. The two students were taking this subject as they opted to take the creative writing major.

Both Tika and Sella were selected as they had interest and passion in writing short stories and poems and had practised writing them even before taking the Creative Writing subject, in Indonesian language or English or both. Tika began to write stories since primary school and poetry since high school. She had a blog where she shared her poems, travel writings, and reflective notes, some in Indonesian, others in English. Sella was also passionate about writing stories, poems, and songs, mostly in English. Sella had a blog where she shared her short stories and an Instagram to share her poems.

5.4.3   Data Collection Methods

The data collection methods were interview, i.e. semi-structured one-on-one interviews, and documents, i.e. guided journals and samples of students' writings. The interviews were conducted with one person at a time, and in Indonesian, English, or a mixture of the two languages, depending on the participants' preferences. In the audio-recorded interviews, the students were inquired about their experiences when writing short stories in English, particularly regarding their ways of inciting ideas and their story writing process. Hence, the interviews were done around the middle of the semester, after the students submitting two story writing assignments. While in the guided journal, students were requested to write a weekly entry about anything related to their writing practice, including their thoughts, feelings, and experiences related to their creative writing practices that week. The journals were collected twice, i.e. first, before the interview to enable exploration of what the students wrote in the journals, and after the semester was over. Samples of students' writings were also collected to tap how the students utilise their cultural resources in their short stories.

5.4.4   Data Analysis

The interviews were transcribed, and because they were conducted in two languages—Indonesian language and/or English—some parts needed to be translated into English. The focus of the analysis was on identifying how the two students utilised their resources to practise creativity in writing stories. However, within the scope of this chapter, only two themes are reported as they emerged as important practices in the cases of the two students. The researcher then coded all data and continuously rechecked and cross-checked the codes across different methods. The analysing process began with two broad categories 'inspiration generating strategies' and 'capacity to develop ideas into stories'. Then, the process moved to a more specific one and codes could be labelled to them. Under these two categories, the codes that referred to the same phenomenon were grouped as a theme.

5.5   Findings

This section presents the findings on the two students' creative writing practices, i.e. first, how these students gathered inspirations at the initial writing stage, and second, what capacity students utilised to develop the ideas into short stories in English. The data indicated two significant capacities demonstrated by the two students, namely inciting inspirations and synthesising. The following sections expound each capacity.

5.5.1   Inciting Inspirations

This study found three recurrent practices are done by the two students to generate ideas for the stories, namely (1) observing surroundings, (2) drawing from experience, and (3) getting inspired by others' creative works.

5.5.1.1   Observing Surroundings

Both Tika and Sella mentioned that they were keen on observing people, objects, and nature around them. These students observed their surroundings not only when they were inside the creative writing classroom or when they had writing assignments but also when they were outside the classroom, in their daily life. When working on a class assignment, Sella preferred to go out of the class once in a while to get inspirations, where she could see trees and people doing their chores. She stated in her journal that 'it would be nice to have a little field trip and then write based on what we see' (Sella, journal). Even when not working on assignments, she enjoyed watching people in her daily life. She asserted that people and nature inspired her the most.

> People's behaviour, their reactions to certain situations. I also have a lot of interest in nature, so I write a lot of things that are connected to nature. People and nature are the things that inspire me the most. (Sella, interview)

Similarly, in the focus group discussion, Tika revealed what she liked to do when going home on a public minibus.

> *Aku suka ngamatin orang, nguping percakapan mereka trus dibikin cerita.* (Tika, interview)

> I like observing people, eavesdropping, then make it into a story. (Tika, interview)

Tika was fond of watching people in a public minibus or on the street while waiting for the bus and eavesdropping bits of their conversations. Then, she would imagine and build a story around them.

Both Sella and Tika also shared what happened in their minds when observing the surrounding people, object, or nature and how the observations incited inspirations for their stories and poems. While Tika liked to eavesdrop conversations and imagined a story framing the conversations, Sella liked to play 'what if' in her mind.

> I usually just observe an object and think what if. What if this comes, what if that object becomes this, what if something happens to that. Just thinking about what if. (Sella, interview)

When watching objects around her, Tika also let her imagination transform an ordinary object into an out of the ordinary object. She said:

> Sometimes when I look at my surrounding, like when I see something like a chair. Sometimes I think why don't I write about a chair. Maybe a magic chair. (Tika, interview)

While Sella, when watching people around her, liked to capture people's expressions on the street in her mind and recalled this image when writing a story. Watching people's behaviour, such as their reactions to particular situations, and observing nature was what inspired her most. Sella said:

> Sometimes people have these expressions, on a bike, on the street. Sometimes they have weird expressions, and those expressions can be used in the story. (Sella, interview)

Observing people close to her upon returning from living abroad also made Sella aware of the gender inequality issue experienced by her female relatives from her mother's side. She sensed the injustice due to the restrictions on what these Javanese women were allowed to do.

> Like how and what you are supposed to do things because of your gender. It makes me think of a way to go past those boundaries. That is why there are some stories … my stories … I make the girl would have to act a certain way, and if she doesn't act accordingly, she will be outcasted from the rest of the crowd. (Sella, interview)

Driven by her concern about what she believed as an inequality, she raised this gender inequality issue experienced by Javanese women in her family in her stories.

5.5.1.2   Drawing from One's Own or Other's Experiences

Besides observing surroundings, students also drew from their own or others' experiences for inspiration. Sella mentioned that her stories and poems were often derived from her experiences of living in four different countries. She stated in the interview that she enjoyed moving from one place to another because she learned different cultures, different languages, got new friends and new experiences. She said that her experiences enabled her to describe different places and people in different countries more easily. Sella wrote in her journal that she often drew on her experiences when writing.

> In the exercise, I used a situation I was in. I love to travel, and one of the places I have travelled to was Holland. I was there for the winter season and I was drinking a cup of cocoa near a fireplace with the rest of the family. It was my first time seeing snow. It became a memory I remember vividly. (Sella, journal)

Sella also explicated that she based the ghost character in her story entitled 'Devil child of the lake' on the girl ghost that she saw on a street near her house many years back. The apparition of the little girl dressing in white who suddenly vanished before her eyes was still vivid in her mind. Therefore, when she wanted to write a mysterious, ghostly story, she developed a character from this ghost figure.

Likewise, when asked to share what inspired her to write 'Trap'—the story she submitted for the horror story class project—Tika told her childhood experience of being mysteriously locked and trapped inside the school toilet for a few minutes before the toilet door suddenly opened by itself. According to the local belief, the toilet was haunted and this scary incident imprinted in her memory. This petrifying experience inspired her to write a story about a girl ghost dwelling in the school toilet, luring a new female student to go to the toilet where the ghost would kill her and made her a ghost. This ghost would lure another newly arrived female student in school, and the same incident would repeat again and again.

5.5.1.3   Getting Inspired by Others' Creative Works

In addition to the previously discussed practices, the two students also gather inspirations and ideas from others' creative works, such as novels, songs, movies, and photos. Sella said that she loved reading since little and liked 'to imagine stuff' from the books and 'those imaginations give [her] ideas'. Among the many books she liked were R.L Stine's novels. She revealed that Stine's novels had enchanted her and made her want to write thrillers. She had been practicing on it, including when writing stories for the Creative Writing class.

With a different genre preference, Tika shared the same enjoyment in reading since young like Sella. She said that she started reading novels, mostly teen litera-ture, since junior high school. She liked reading novels by Indonesian writers, such as Ilana Tan and Dee Lestari, and the Indonesian translation of foreign writers' novels. Tika shared her experience that to be able to write a story of a particular genre, she had to read stories of that genre; not only to learn about the story plot but also to familiarise herself with the diction used in a particular genre. In her journal, Tika also wrote that she borrowed Sherlock Holmes novels and liked reading mystery and detective stories by Indonesian writers, too. Reading these books inspired her to write stories of this genre.

> . . . I've read an Indonesian novel, tells about a teenager who can solve the mystery. It mixes with a thriller. The writer is Lexie Xu, it's a teenlit, but I love her books, all her books. That's why I want to write a horror story and mystery. (Tika, journal)

Tika also found watching movies inspiring, as she said below.

Dulu suka nonton film ... Paranormal Activity judulnya dan kayaknya kok bagus nih, soalnya orang-orang biasa bikin horror itu yang ada hantunya secara nyata. Jarang yang bikin hantunya yang nggak kasat mata gitu. Cuma suara atau benda gerak sendiri. Jadi kayaknya bagus kalau dibikin cerita gitu. (Tika, interview)

[I used to watch films ... the title was Paranormal Activity and I thought it was really good because people usually make horror [movies] that show real ghosts. It's very rare that the ghosts were invisible like that. Like the voice or moving objects. So, I think it's good to write stories like that.] (Tika, interview)

For Sella, movies were useful when she had a gap in her experience, such as when she had to write a love story. She admitted that she found it difficult to describe the character's feelings and to come up with an appealing plot because she did not have the experience of falling in love and did not have a boyfriend. To fill this gap, she watched some love story movies to help her develop the idea for the story and describe a romantic atmosphere. She revealed in her journal 'for making the setting for the romantic part, I use my imaginations from watching so many romantic comedy movies' (Sella, journal).

Besides movies, both Tika and Sella also mentioned song lyrics and photos as sources of inspiration, but they used them in different ways. For Tika, song lyrics could be used 'to fish' idea, because they told stories (Tika, interview). Similarly, Sella mentioned that she got inspiration also from songs, because 'songs representing certain situations' (Sella, journal). Sella, who was creatively prolific, also played musical instruments and wrote songs. Oftentimes, she got an inspiration for a story or poem when randomly played her guitar. Playing guitar or keyboard helped her in her writing as it sparked ideas as well as made her relaxed when writing. Sella also liked taking pictures, and she frequently got inspired by the pictures. She said that 'there are pictures that can become stories' (Sella, interview).

5.6   Synthesising

Both students also demonstrate the capacity to synthesise by combining information from different sources or combining already existed ideas with new ones. Sella liked to watch nature and people around her and combined her observation with a 'what if' play in her mind, such as 'what if this comes, what if that object becomes this, what if something happens to that. Just thinking what if'. She exemplified what she did as follow.

[...] I really liked going on the roof looking up at the sky, and I could stay there for hours. I once stayed there until night, and I could still remember how beautiful the night sky was. It was so full of stars, and the moon was gleaming its bright silver light. I thought about how some people say that the people who die become stars. I imagined what if they were really looking down on us? How would they describe this place? Quiet or boring? Would they like the place here? (Sella, interview)

Another experience Sella shared in her journal was when she was in a coffee shop alone. She looked around and no one was there. Then, her mind imagined 'what if the furniture come to life? As they do, would some of them fly around? Will there be more people coming in and out of the coffee shop? Or maybe the chairs will be serving me my snacks?' (Sella, journal). Sella combined her observations of surroundings and imagination prompted by 'what if' play in her mind.

In her short story entitled 'Devil child of the lake', Sella created the ghost character based on the image of the girl ghost she saw when she was little. She revealed the way she developed the story as follows:

> I was fascinated with lakes, and because at that time I wanted to write a horror story, I searched for the most haunted lakes in certain areas. I found out about the Great Lakes and was instantly in love with the myth it had. So, I thought what if I incorporate the myth and my experience of being able to see the ghost when I was a child? Then the story was written. About the exorcism part, I remembered watching a movie of it with my friends at home, so I added part of that to the story, and most of it is just my imagination. (Sella, interview)

To write the story, Sella developed the ghost character from the child ghost she saw a long time ago. She also did research on myths about lakes around the world and recalled the lake she visited when abroad to describe the setting. She added the idea of exorcism from a movie she watched. In conclusion, Sella combined her memory of ghostly experience, a little research on lakes around the world, an idea from a movie she watched and weaved them with her imagination.

The other student, Tika, was inspired by her terrifying childhood experience in the schools' toilet. She developed her story 'Trap' by combining her memory on the incident, particularly the setting—the toilet in her school—and creating the ghost character as well as the story plot based on her imagination and a horror movie she watched about a family haunted house (Tika, interview). By combining personal experience, imagination, and ideas from a movie, Tika created a story that she could call her own.

Besides, Tika also blended stories already existed with her own imagination or experience. She said:

> And sometimes when I read books and when I think the idea is good, why don't I make similar to this but change a little. [. . .] Sometimes from songs. Because actually it's a story. So, I think I can make like a fan fiction for my idol. (Tika, interview)

By adding or changing some parts, Tika also created her stories based on the stories in the books she read, from song lyrics which she considered as a kind of story, and from stories she heard from other people. She described the process of writing 'The Hawk', the fable she wrote as one of the class assignments, as follows:

> At first, I don't know what to write. Then, I remember in the church, the priest says about the hawk that it has to let the feather and the other to make a change. So, I think it is good to make it as a story. And I make the moral first [pause] that we have to let go to make it better. [. . .] First, I make the moral. And I searched on the internet about the hawk. I read that the hawk is like that. (Tika, interview)

Tika developed the fable 'The Hawk' based on the story of a hawk mentioned in a priest's sermon in a church service she went to. She then decided on the moral lesson that she wanted to convey in her fable and browsed for more information about a hawk on the internet to help her create the story.

5.7   Discussion

Piirto (2011) points out that creative people often get inspirations from novel surroundings, such as when travelling to a new place. The present study found that the two Indonesian students did not only gather inspirations from the new environments, such as when travelling, but mostly from their everyday, ordinary surroundings. In addition to the observations purposefully done to incite ideas for stories, they also developed a habitual practice of observing people's expressions, behaviours, things, and nature with writer's eyes and imagination. When the students observed their surroundings, they collected information and knowledge in an informal way, i.e. by watching and noting down, in their notebook or in their memory, incidences, people's expressions, nature's beauty, and whatever it was they found interesting. These may both generate story ideas and provide images they could retrieve when writing stories.

Besides, as also pointed out by scholars (Hanauer, 2014; Mansoor, 2013; Piirto, 2004; Runco, 2006; Sui, 2015) that reflecting on one's own experiences can enhance one's creativity, both Tika and Sella recollected and reflected on their experiences to incite ideas for stories. Both of them often drew fragments of their experiences to generate the storylines. A study that involved Indonesian students and teachers evaluating poems written by a group of Indonesian students concludes that poems that contained 'reality, truthfulness, and personal values' were considered most creative (Tin, Manara, & Ragawanti, 2010). It is possible that for Indonesians, stories or poems that depict realities and convey values are more favourable. This reason might also influence the students' preferred strategies to get ideas by observing surroundings and drawing from one's or others' experiences as these practices enabled them to capture realities and personal values. The abilities to develop ideas out of mundane things from observing surroundings and to reflect on their daily life experiences to get inspiration seem to be important capacities for the two Indonesian students in this study.

Watching, listening, and reading others' creative work are also ways of learning or getting ideas from others to produce one's creative work (Mansoor, 2013; Piirto, 2011; Sui, 2015). Even though they did different practices and they had different preferences of the genres, both Sella and Tika were often inspired by the novels they read, movies they watched, and songs they listened to.

For Sella, reading historical, autobiographical, and thriller books inspired her to write novels of those genres and incited her imagination. Whereas watching movies was useful for her to fill the gaps in her experiences. When she needed to get ideas about a particular incident, moment, or feeling that she had not experienced herself yet, she would retrieve it from the movies she watched. Since Sella also wrote song lyrics, she found it inspiring to listen to songs composed by others. For Tika, books, movies, and songs were means to get ideas and, more importantly, to learn about the ways to write stories in particular genres, such as horror, mystery, and detective stories that she was interested in. For both students, their being bilinguals gave them advantages as they also read Indonesian novels to get inspiration. Tika, especially, mentioned that she got inspirations on the story plot from novels in the Indonesian language, whereas from reading novels in English, she learned from the writers' word choices and expressions commonly used in stories of particular genres (Tika, interview, journal).

The students' story writing process indicated stages comparable to the stages of learning suggested by one of the Indonesian educational philosophers, Ki Hadjar Dewantara. In Dewantara's 3N learning concept, the initial stage of learning is called *Niteni,* in which students observe closely, and identify the details using their senses (Suroso, 2011). When examined from the perspective of this learning concept, the stage when Sella and Tika observed surroundings, and when they learned from others' creative works can be identified as the *Niteni* stage. Tika, who was still struggling when writing in English, also learned to develop her writing skills by using the expressions or words she found in the books she read. This stage, according to Dewantara's learning concept, is the *Nirokake* (imitating) stage. As told by Tika, she read closely novels of the horror genre, not only to generate ideas for her own story, but also to identify vocabularies commonly used to create a ghastly atmosphere and ways to describe the creepy setting (Tika, interview).

In the process of writing stories, students retrieved the information needed to write from their observations and experiences and relived it by using their mental imagery. Mental imagery, which is included in Amabile's concept of special talents, is the ability to retrieve any visual, auditory, or kinaesthetic images (Amabile, 1996; Piirto, 2004). Both Sella and Tika also developed this mental imagery capacity when reliving the images they have observed or experienced when writing. Sella, who had a strong mental imagery ability, stored most of the images in her memory. Whereas Tika developed a strategy using a diary to help her recall and visualise the images.

Furthermore, both Tika and Sella showed the capacity to produce a short story by synthesising different components. As highlighted by Munandar (2009) and Supriadi (1994), the keywords in the idea of *kreativitas*—the Indonesian word for creativity—are making new combinations from existing objects or ideas to produce a new artefact or idea. Besides, *Nambahi,* which is the third principle, highlights the importance of developing, adding, combining, and modifying what already exists. These actions are parts of the creating and innovating process. When writing their stories, both Tika and Sella developed, added, and synthesised their observations, experiences, imaginations, knowledge in different domains, and whatever they learned from others' creative work (e.g. movies, songs) to create their own short stories.

Another practice that one of the students did was creating a story based on an already existing story. Tika expanded the story about a hawk that she learned from the priest in a church service by developing the plot based on her imagination and enriching the descriptions based on her small research on the internet about hawks. This practice of adding new components to what already exists is the *Nambahi* stage, which is the most important stage of learning in Ki Hadjar Dewantara's 3N philosophy of education. One's openness to experience and how one makes meaning of that experience and observation are equally important in enhancing one's creative process. As Runco also points out, 'the key mechanism in personal creativity is the capacity to produce an original interpretation of experience' (2006, p. 101). There-fore, the production of creativity also depends on the ability of the creator to interpret and express his/her experience.

5.8   Conclusion

This study aimed at exploring the students' capacities to retrieve and employ their cultural-intellectual resources when writing stories in English. In conclusion, there are three key findings of this study. First, there are two capacities that the two Indonesian EFL students demonstrated to write stories in English, namely inciting inspirations and synthesising. To induce inspirations, the students did three prac-tices, namely observing surroundings, drawing inspirations from experiences, and getting ideas from others' creative works (i.e. novels, movies, songs, photos). These practices may not be distinctive practices, yet, they permit glimpses of local, cultural facets, such as incidents, values, issues, beliefs, and norms, to emerge in the students' short stories.

Second, synthesising has been identified as a valuable capacity employed by the two students to develop and write stories in English. This capacity to synthesise information, ideas, skills, and knowledge they learned formally and informally from different sources may enhance creativity in writing. Being bilinguals also benefited the two students as they could use their mother tongue(s)—Indonesian (and a regional language)—such as to gather ideas and to brainstorm or draft the stories.

Third, the students' capacities and practices of writing stories in English reflect the stages of learning in Dewantara's 3N (*Niteni-Nirokake-Nambahi*). When observ-ing surroundings, watching, or reading others' creative work, students are at the first stage of learning, namely *Niteni*. Then, on the next step, the students meshed and blended the information, imagination, and the intellectual, cultural knowledge they learned formally at school as well as informally from their personal experiences and the society's values and norms, to develop their own short stories. These practices show both the second and third learning principles of Ki Hadjar Dewantara's 3N learning concept, namely *Nirokake* (imitating) and *Nambahi* (adding, developing, combining, modifying). The essence of creative writing is at the last stage—*Nambahi*—that indicates the nature of creative production done by the students.

The Indonesian students have the potentials and their idiosyncratic resources that can be utilised to produce creative writings in English that are crafted to present their unique selves. Understanding the students' EFL creative writing capacities and practices will assist teachers to create opportunities and environments that can further enhance the students' EFL creative writing skills.

References

Amabile, T. (1996). *Creativity in context*. Oxford: Westview Press.

Amabile, T. (2012). *Componential theory of creativity*. A working paper. Boston: Harvard Business School.

Bakhtin, M. M. (1981). The dialogic imagination. In Michael Holquist (ed.). Caryl Emerson and Michael Holquist (trans.). *Four essays*. Austin: The University of Texas Press.

Boden, M. A. (2004). *The creative mind: Myths and mechanisms*. London: Routledge.

Chin, G. V. S. (2014). Co-constructing a community of creative writers: Exploring L2 identity formations through Bruneian playwriting. In S. Zyngier & J. Gavins (Series Eds.) & D. Disney (Vol. Ed.), *Linguistic approaches to literature (LAL). Exploring second language creative writing. Beyond babel* (pp. 119–138). Philadelphia, PA: John Benjamins.

Collard, P., & Looney, J. (2014). Nurturing creativity in education. *European Journal of Education, 49*(3), 348–364. https://doi.org/10.1111/ejed.12090

Disney, D. (2014). "Is this how it's supposed to work?": Poetry as a radical technology in L2 creative writing classrooms. In D. Disney (Ed.), *Exploring second language creative writing. Beyond babel* (pp. 41–56). Amsterdam: John Benjamins Publishing Company.

Feist, G. J., Reiter-Palmon, R., & Kaufman, J. C. (Eds.). (2017). *The Cambridge handbook of creativity and personality research*. New York: Cambridge University Press.

Grigorenko, E. L., & Tan, M. (2008). Teaching creativity as a demand-led competency. In O. S. Tan, D. M. McInerney, A. D. Liem, & A. Tan (Eds.), *What the west can learn from the east. Asian perspectives on the psychology of learning and motivation* (pp. 11–29). Information Age Pub: Charlotte, NC.

Hanauer, D. I. (2010). Poetry as research: Exploring second language poetry writing. In *Linguistic approaches to literature* (Vol. 9). Philadelphia, PA: John Benjamins.

Hanauer, D. I. (2014). Appreciating the beauty of second language poetry writing. In S. Zyngier & J. Gavins (Series Ed.) & D. Disney (Vol. Ed.), *Linguistic approaches to literature (LAL). Exploring second language creative writing. Beyond babel.* (pp. 11–22). Philadelphia, PA: John Benjamins.

Handa, N. (2013). *Engaging non-Western international students' intellectual agency in the internationalisation of Australian teacher education: a case study of possibilities for transnational knowledge exchange*. Ph.D. Thesis, University of Western Sydney.

Harper, G. (2016). Teaching creative writing. In R. H. Jones (Ed.), *The Routledge handbook of language and creativity* (pp. 498–512). New York: Routledge.

Herawati, H. (2014). Voicing local culture through creative writing. In The State University of Surabaya (Ed). *The role of local wisdom in shaping identity*. Paper presented at Asia creative writing conference, 21–22 March 2014 (pp. 213–225). Surabaya: Unesa University Press.

Iida, A. (2013). Critical review of literary reading and writing in a second language. *The Journal of Literature in Language Teaching, 2*(May), 5–11.

Ivanic, R., & Camps, D. (2001). I am how I sound. Voice as self-representation in L2 writing. *Journal of Second Language Writing, 10*(2001), 3–33. issn: 1060-3743.

Jones, R. H. (2016). Creativity and discourse analysis. In R. H. Jones (Ed.), *The Routledge handbook of language and creativity* (pp. 61–77). New York: Routledge.

Kwang, N. A. (2001). *Why Asians are less creative than Westerners*. Singapore: Prentice Hall. Pearson Education Asia.

Lestari, I. P. (2014). Local language in global communication. In The State University of Surabaya (Ed). *The role of local wisdom in shaping identity*. Paper presented at Asia creative writing conference, 21–22 March 2014 (pp. 145–153). Surabaya: Unesa University Press.

Lubart, T. I., & Georgsdottir, A. (2004). Creativity: Developmental and cross-cultural issues. In S. Lau, A. N. N. Hui, & G. Y. C. Ng (Eds.), *Creativity: When East meets West* (pp. 23–54). Singapore: World Scientific.

Maley, A. (2009). *Creative writing for language learners (and teachers)*. Retrieved January 8, 2016, from https://www.teachingenglish.org.uk/article/creative-writing-language-learners-teachers?page=1

Maley, A., & Kiss, T. (2018). *Creativity and English language teaching: From inspiration to implementation*. London: Palgrave Macmillan.

Mansoor, A. (2013). The recipe for novelty: Using bilingualism and indigenous literary genres in an advanced level L2 creative writing context in Pakistan. *New Writing, 10*(1), 52–66. https://doi.org/10.1080/14790726.2012.742550

McLoughlin, N. (2008). Creating an integrated model for teaching creative writing: One approach. In G. Harper & J. Kroll (Eds.), *Creative writing studies: Practice, research, and pedagogy*. Toronto: Multilingual Matters, Ltd..

Munandar, S. C. U. (2009). *Pengembangan kreativitas anak berbakat*. Jakarta: PT Rineka Cipta dan Dep. Pendidikan dan Kebudayaan.

Pennington, M. C. (2016). Creativity in composition. In R. H. Jones (Ed.), *The Routledge handbook of language and creativity* (pp. 483–497). New York: Routledge.

Piirto, J. (2004). *Understanding creativity*. Scottsdale: Great Potential Press.

Piirto, J. (2011). Creativity for the 21st-century skills. In *How to embed creativity into the curriculum*. Rotterdam: Sense Publishers.

Rakhmawati, D. E. N. (2014). Representing local values through cultural places in EFL creative writing class. In The State University of Surabaya (Ed). *The role of local wisdom in shaping identity*. Paper presented at Asia creative writing conference, 21–22 March 2014 (pp. 226–236). Surabaya: Unesa University Press.

Runco, M. (2004). Personal creativity and culture. In S. Lau, A. N. N. Hui, & G. Y. C. Ng (Eds.), *Creativity: When East meets West* (pp. 9–21). Singapore: World Scientific.

Runco, M. A. (2006). Reasoning and personal creativity. In J. C. Kaufman & J. Baer (Eds.), *Creativity and reason in cognitive development*. New York: Cambridge University Press.

Smith, C. (2013). Creative writing as an important tool in second language acquisition and practice. *The Journal of Literature in Language Teaching, 2*(2013), 12–18.

Sui, G. (2015). Bilingual creativity: University–level poetry writing workshops in English in China. *English Today, 31*(3), 40–45. https://doi.org/10.1017/s0266078415000243

Sukraini, N. W. (2014). Let traditional Dayak music inspire your short stories. In The State University of Surabaya (Ed). *The role of local wisdom in shaping identity*. Paper presented at Asia creative writing conference, 21–22 March 2014 (pp. 483–396). Surabaya: Unesa University Press.

Supriadi, D. (1994). *Kreativitas, Kebudayaan & Perkembangan Iptek*. Bandung: Alfabeta.

Suroso. (2011). Pemikiran Ki Hadjar Dewantara tentang belajar dan pembelajaran. *Scholaria, 1*(1), 46–72.

Susanti, A., & Trisusana. A. (2014). Folklore for teaching short story writing. In The State University of Surabaya (Ed). *The role of local wisdom in shaping identity*. Paper presented at Asia creative writing conference, 21–22 March 2014 (pp. 307–315). Surabaya: Unesa University Press.

Tay, E. (2014). Curriculum as cultural critique: Creative writing pedagogy in Hong Kong. In D. Disney (Ed.), *Exploring second language creative writing. Beyond babel* (pp. 103–118). John Benjamins: Philadelphia, PA.

Tin, T. B. (2011). Language creativity and co-emergence of form and meaning in creative writing tasks. *Applied Linguistics, 32*(2), 215–235. https://doi.org/10.1093/applin/amq050

Tin, T. B. (2013). Towards creativity in ELT: The need to say something new. *ELT Journal, 67*(4), 385. https://doi.org/10.1093/elt/cct022

Tin, T. B. (2016). Creativity in second-language learning. In R. H. Jones (Ed.), *The Routledge handbook of language and creativity* (pp. 433–451). New York: Routledge.

Tin, T. B., Manara, C., & Ragawanti, D. T. (2010). Views on creativity from an Indonesian perspective. *ELT Journal, 64*(1), 75–84. https://doi.org/10.1093/elt/ccp022

Xerri, D., & Vassallo, O. (Eds.). (2016). *Creativity in English language teaching*. Floriana: ELT Council.

Zhao, Y. (2014). L2 creative writers' identities: Their cognitive writing processes and sense of empowerment. *New Writing, 11*(3), 452–466. https://doi.org/10.1080/14790726.2014.956124

Zhao, Y. (2015). Second language creative writers: Identities and writing processes. In D. Singleton (Series Ed.), *Second language acquisition*. Bristol: Multilingual Matters.

Chapter 6
Exploring Attitudes Towards 'Asia Literacy' Among Australian Secondary School Students

Gary J Bonar

Abstract Australia's national curriculum includes explicit learning of the diverse countries, cultures, and peoples of Asia as a cross-curriculum priority. Despite this and previous initiatives to develop what has been called 'Asia literacy', recent evidence suggests that progress in the teaching and learning of this priority has been marginal and patchy. Based on the premise that current student attitudes to this learning are largely unknown, this chapter presents a subset of findings from a broader study of Australian secondary students' attitudes towards Asia-related learning. This quantitative component of a mixed-method study utilises a 2002 survey instrument in order to explore the attitudes of Year 8 students in 2002 with respect to responses of Year 7 and 8 cohorts in this current study. The findings indicate that although levels of the most positive attitudes were lower, the proportion of students who were generally interested in Asia-related learning had increased significantly. The overall level of negative attitudes remained similar to those found in the 2002 study, with boys expressing fewer of the very positive attitudes and more of the negative attitudes. Finally, in terms of context of learning, students in 2002 and 2015 have the view that their learning about Asia within the school context has barely changed, despite this 13-year period being characterised by an increased interest and enactment of policies that have sought to promote studies of Asia in schools. This suggests the need to further investigate the drivers and motivators for student attitudes towards Asia-related learning and reassess current approaches accordingly.

Keywords Asia literacy · Asia-related learning · Asia capability · Studies of Asia · Student voice

G. J. Bonar (✉)
Monash University, Melbourne, VIC, Australia
e-mail: gary.bonar@monash.edu

© Springer Nature Singapore Pte Ltd. 2021
D. Bao, T. Pham (eds.), *Transforming Pedagogies Through Engagement with Learners, Teachers and Communities*, Education in the Asia-Pacific Region: Issues, Concerns and Prospects 57, https://doi.org/10.1007/978-981-16-0057-9_6

6.1   Introduction

The term 'Asia literacy' is the most recent expression used to convey an emphasis on increasing the knowledge and understanding among Australian school students of the diverse countries and cultures of Asia, a process which has experienced periods of prioritisation and marginalisation in the education system for over 40 years (Asia Education Foundation, 2014a; Auchmuty, 1970). The topic came to prominence in a 1970 government report into Asian languages and Asian studies in Australia, which noted that 'there is at present an inadequate treatment of Asia, as an obligatory element, in social studies and other courses at secondary level' (Auchmuty, 1970, p. 89). In the national curriculum (known as the Australian Curriculum), the cross-curriculum priority of *Asia and Australia's engagement with Asia* elevates its importance again with its presence in the curriculum sketched out across year levels and learning domains (ACARA, 2014a). However, despite numerous state and federal governments publicly stressing the importance of increasing knowledge about Asia in Australian society, the educational outcomes achieved to date have significantly failed to match policy objectives. Learning of Asian languages has been in decline for over a decade, and there is limited diffusion of Asia-related studies in the content taught in Australian schools (Asia Education Foundation, 2012b; Lindsey, 2011; Wilkinson & Milgate, 2009a). Among the multiple and complex factors that have led to this outcome, it has been argued that a major reason has been an insufficient focus on driving 'change through building demand… among students, their parents and school leaders' (Asia Education Foundation, 2012b, p. 2). Building this demand, however, is problematic as there is a lack of detailed and systematic knowledge of current students' attitudes and understandings of the Asia literacy concept. This research, as a part of a broader study, seeks to reduce this knowledge gap.

6.2   Defining Asia Literacy

Just as the term 'Asia' eludes straightforward definitions (see Mackerras (1995) for more than 50 contestable definitions identified in existing literature), Asia literacy is also a term that is often contested, reformulated, and problematic to define. Nevertheless, over the past 25 years, it has become more prominently used in political, educational, economic, and cultural discussions in Australia (FitzGerald, Boomer, Lo Bianco, & McKay, 1988; Henderson, 2003; Henderson, Allan, & Mallan, 2013). In the 2008 overarching policy statement for schooling in Australia, known as the Melbourne Declaration, the term was defined as the capacity 'to relate to and communicate across cultures, especially the cultures and countries of Asia' (MCEETYA, 2008, p. 9), a definition which appears again in the government White Paper on Australia in the Asian Century (Australia in the Asian Century Task Force, 2011). Prior to and following on from this declaration, efforts to work towards this goal have been manifest in numerous language policies and targeted programs (Asia Education Foundation, 2012b; Lo Bianco & Aliani, 2013). The Australian Curriculum (AC) describes Asia literacy as teaching and learning that provides students with a knowledge of 'Asian societies, cultures, beliefs and environments, and the connections between the peoples of Asia, Australia, and the rest of the world', and 'the skills to communicate and engage with the peoples of Asia so they can effectively live, work and learn in the region' (ACARA, 2014a). Intercultural Understanding, one of the seven General Capabilities in the AC, echoes the principles of Asia literacy as it 'promotes recognition, communication and engagement with the different countries and cultures within Asia' (ACARA, 2014b, p. 3).

6.3 Asia Literacy Rationale and Critiques

Calls to increase Asia literacy are commonly premised on the growing economic and cultural importance of countries in the Asian region and the parallel growth of an Asian-related presence within Australia. This change in the demographics of the Australian population, both permanent and transient, is evident in an increasing number of people originating from Asian countries (Australian Bureau of Statistics, 2012, 2013). Proponents of Asia literacy argue that if these trends continue, then current and future students are more likely to have opportunities and face challenges that will require the knowledge and skills that are at the core of the concept of Asia literacy.

Despite the consensus on its importance, there is divergence among its advocates on the deeper rationale and aims of the concept. Successive governments on both sides have consistently promoted the need for Asia literacy in largely reductionist, economic terms where the primary objective is to secure Australia's future trade and industry (Abbott, 2014; Australia in the Asian Century Task Department of Foreign Affairs and Trade, 2013; Australia in the Asian Century Task Force, 2011; Rudd, 1994). Business and industry groups have also endorsed the concept from this instrumentalist viewpoint (Australia Industry Group & Asialink, 2011; Business Alliance for Asia Literacy, 2009; Love, Kamener, von Oertzen, & Minifie, 2012). Framing the promotion of Asia literacy in these narrow terms has been criticised as 'a neo-colonial project which aspires to understand the object of Australia's economic desires' (Singh, 1995, p. 9), and this has led to a 'dominance of an economic rationale that is seemingly impossible to resist' (Salter, 2013, p. 3). This discourse is also criticised as reducing the complex nature of intercultural understanding down to the problematic constructs of *us* and *them* and perpetuating the 'dualism between Australians and their Asian others' (Rizvi, 2012, p. 74). To counter this narrow focus, these critics argue for a more self-reflexive approach that places greater emphasis on developing 'cultural relations that transcend instrumentalism' (Rizvi, 2012, p. 78).

If becoming 'Asia literate' is an actual possibility (it has been noted by Williamson-Fien (1994) that achieving 'semi-literacy' might be a more realistic goal), then this implies that there is a body of knowledge about which one is literate in. At one level, it is possible to critique this concept of Asia literacy by focusing on the possible meanings of 'literacy' and how the word suggests that a person can be considered 'Asia literate' once a certain level of knowledge of Asian cultures, histories, geography, societies, and even languages have been 'mastered'. This approach has been taken by Heryanto when he labels Asia literacy as a dangerous metaphor that harks back to 'Euro-American centricism', and 'unequivocally articulates the notation of Asia as a fixed text for reading' (2015, pp. 171–172). Lo Bianco makes a similar critique when he writes that the notion of 'Asia' has been presented in curricula as merely a 'text to be read or a task to be undertaken' (2014, p. 64).

This notion of Asia as a fixed text to be read can be further explored by considering the dominant modes of viewing Asia that are prevalent within Australian society. According to Pan (2015), the three modes of viewing Asia; namely, 'absence of Asia', 'Asia as threat', and 'Asia as opportunity' have conditioned not only how 'Asia' is imagined within the Australian national consciousness, but by implication, how Australians then construct what it means to be literate about the imagined 'Asia'. The contention is that although there are significant structural, material, and financial issues that have hampered previous efforts to raise levels of knowledge of Asia at the educational level, attempts to address these problems will always struggle to succeed unless the underlying fundamental assumptions are brought to the fore. For Pan, the priority should be to first critically examine the existing 'prior knowledge about Asia and how such knowledge or preunderstanding has come about' (2015, p. 198).

6.4 Research on Student Understandings and Attitudes Towards Asia Literacy

Currently little is known about what Australian students think or understand what Asia literacy is and its relevance to them. There are no comparable large-scale, longitudinal surveys similar to the ones that have been carried out in New Zealand by the Asia New Zealand Foundation (Colmar Brunton, 2013, 2017). Most of the existing data available on what students know and think about Asia and Asia-related studies are derived from the uptake of Asian languages and the presence of Asia-related content in other subjects (Sturak & Naughten, 2010; Wilkinson & Milgate, 2009a). An increase or decrease in these numbers is then considered as an indicator of actual student knowledge of, and attitudes to, the region. This lack of knowledge has led to calls to explore further the experiences of students regarding their learning, in particular regarding the study of Asian languages and Asia literacy. Scarino (2014) argues that 'we also need evidence from students and their actual experiences of learning... The[ir] experiences are the voice that speaks the need for change and create a deeper understanding of the need for change' (p. 303). Lo Bianco and Aliani (2013) also found in their study on student perspectives on language study that, when consulted, 'students are active in forming opinion and in speaking back to the part of the policy implementation they encounter' (p. 121).

The most comprehensive research to explore student attitudes carried out to date was a national study in 2002, which looked at the attitudes and understandings of Australian primary and secondary students of Asia (Griffin, Woods, Dulhunty, & Coates, 2002). Surveys of more than 7000 Year 5 and Year 8 students revealed that while the growth and development of knowledge of Asia was considered to be generally good, there was not a similar growth and development in attitudes towards studying about Asia. The results of that 2002 survey are discussed in more detail below with respect to the data from this 2015 study.

6.5   Methodology

The data presented here is a subset of findings from a larger study of students' attitudes towards Asia literacy. The broader study follows a case study approach, obtaining both quantitative data and rich descriptions from students at different year levels to provide an extensive picture of student attitudes in relation to Asia literacy at different stages in their schooling. The data presented here focus on one component of this mixed-method study, namely the utilisation of a survey tool originally deployed in a 2002 national study on student understandings and attitudes towards Asia. As the 2002 study is the only detailed research into students' attitudes to studies of Asia, it was judged useful to replicate that component of their data collection to compare responses 13 years on. For that reason, the original theoretical framework and survey details of the 2002 study have been maintained for consistency.

6.5.1   Schools and Participants

Both schools were single-sex, non-government secondary schools (Years 7–12) in the east-southeast of Melbourne, Victoria. Wattle College (pseudonyms used) is an all-boys school while Banksia College is all-girls. In the year of data collection (2015), both schools had approximately 1000 students enrolled. Table 6.1 provides some more details on each school.

The Index of Community Socio-Educational Advantage (ICSEA) is a scale developed by the Australian Curriculum, Assessment and Reporting Authority (ACARA) based on four criteria: geographical location, parents' occupation, parents' education, and proportion of indigenous students. The scale is used to compare similar schools based on the level of educational advantage or disadvantage that

Table 6.1 Profiles of schools in 2015 study

	Wattle College	Banksia College
Location	Metropolitan: East/South east of Melbourne, VIC	Metropolitan: East/South east of Melbourne, VIC
Sector	Non-government	Non-government
Year levels and type	7–12 single-sex male	7–12 single-sex female
Enrolments (2014)	1046	956
ICSEA[a] value (avg. 1000)	999	1072
LBOTE[b]	3%	15%
Attendance rate	94%	91%
Languages offered	Japanese & Italian	Chinese & French
Indigenous	1%	0%

Source: www.myschool.com.au (2014)
[a]Index of Community Socio-Educational Advantage
[b]Language Background Other Than English

Table 6.2 Demographic data of the 2002 and 2015 student cohorts

	2002 Study Year 8 n = 3779		2015 Study Year 7 & 8 n = 90[a]	
Questions	Yes	No	Yes	No
1. Were either of your parents born in Asia?	13%	87%	7%	93%
2. Were you born in Asia?	5%	95%	4%	96%
3. Do you speak an Asian language at home?	10%	90%	6%	94%
4. Have you ever visited an Asian country?	23%	77%	32%	68%
5. Have you ever lived in Asia for more than 6 months?	6%	94%	4%	96%

[a]Comprised of 48 boys and 42 girls

students bring to their academic studies (ACARA, 2013). The median score for ICSEA is 1000. Both of these two schools have an ICSEA score very close to this benchmark, indicating cohorts with 'average' levels of socioeconomic status. The schools both offer an Asian language, but limited Asia-related learning across the curriculum. This is a characteristic common in many other Australian secondary schools (AEF, 2012a; AEF, 2014b; Wilkinson & Milgate, 2009b).

6.5.2 Cohort Demographics

Though the 2015 study had a narrower focus than the 2002 national one, there are some parallels in the demographic data collected between the two studies that permit some comparisons. Along with gender and year level, the demographic data collected in both studies were limited to the information shown in Table 6.2.

The higher numbers for the parent(s) born in Asia (Q1) and Asian language spoken at home (Q3) are consistent with the sample size used in 2002, which more closely reflected the broader population demographics. The two schools in the 2015 study have students from a less diverse language and cultural background. The higher percentage of students who have visited an Asian country in 2015 compared to 2002 (Q5) may be due to a combination of a more general trend within the broader population of increased travel within the Asian region (Australian Bureau of Statistics, 2016) and possibly greater opportunities to travel abroad that students in these two schools may experience.

6.6 Survey Results and Discussion

6.6.1 Attitudes Comparison

To provide a theoretical framework for analysis of student attitudes, the authors of the 2002 study developed a scale (Table 6.3) based on the affective domain in the taxonomy of educational objectives constructed by Krathwohl, Bloom, and Masia (1964). The sixth level in the taxonomy of *Characterisation*, which involves a thorough change of behaviour and a tendency to steer the behaviour of others, was not addressed in the attitude survey and excluded by the researchers.

The students in the 2002 study responded with either 'agree' or 'disagree' to 23 attitude items which were grouped to align with the five levels of attitude. As Fig. 6.1 shows, although the data indicated a greater proportion of students at levels 4 and 5, Year 8 students had fewer positive attitudes (down 10%) and more negative attitudes (up 10%) compared to Year 5 students. When differentiated by gender, the

Table 6.3 Description of attitude levels with taxonomy of affective domains (Griffin et al., 2002, p. 32)

Level	Description of attitude levels	Corresponding taxonomy of affective domain levels
5	Keen to learn about Asia and develop relationships, personal involvement, and commitment to learn	Organisation
4	Can see benefits; has a positive approach to learning about Asia, personal involvement and caring approach emerged	Valuing
3	Recognises possible benefits linked to learning about Asia, and the importance of Asia as well as the possible difference related to a lack of involvement	Responding
2	Personal response to Asia as an entity, willingness to receive information and to participate in basic activities related to Asia	Receiving
1	Negative reaction and avoidance of Asia culture and people	Avoidance

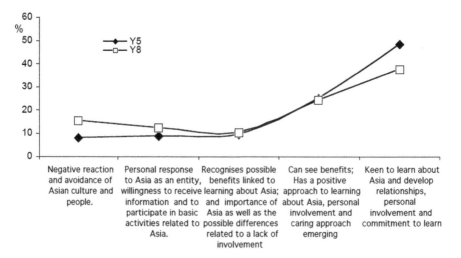

Fig. 6.1 Distribution of Year 5 and 8 students' levels of attitude towards learning about Asia (Griffin et al., 2002, p. 3 [Use permitted under the Creative Commons Attribution License CC BY 4.0])

boys at both year levels tended to have more negative attitudes than the girls, though reasons for this were not discussed.

6.6.1.1 Evaluating the 2015 and 2002 Survey Results

To evaluate the attitudes of the 2015 cohort against those of the 2002 Year 8 cohort shown above in Fig. 6.1, the proportion of agreement with each statement within the five attitudinal levels is shown in the tables below.

6.6.2   Avoidance

The lowest level of *Avoidance* indicates a negative reaction to learning about Asia and general avoidance of Asian cultures and peoples. As was the case in 2002, the boys also tended to hold more of these indifferent and negative views compared to the girls (Table 6.4).

The different language learning experiences of the boys and girls appear to have influenced their responses to the third and fourth statements. The boys learn Japanese, and only 8% agreed that Australia has nothing to learn from Japan. The girls, who learn Chinese in Year 7, were less positive in response to statement 3, though they still rated China above Japan in terms of a source of learning for Australia. This suggests that the negative responses to this statement could be based more on a lack of knowledge rather than a negative evaluation of the country. With respect to the

Table 6.4 Percentage of affirmative responses to avoidance level statements

Statements	Affirmative responses	
	Girls	Boys
1. Asian cultures are a problem for Australia	10%	19%
2. I try and avoid Asian people or customs	2%	13%
3. Australia has nothing to learn from countries like China	14%	17%
4. Australia has nothing to learn from countries like Japan	17%	8%
5. I have called kids names because of their Asian background	0%	2%

Table 6.5 Percentage of affirmative responses to receiving level statements

Statements	Affirmative responses	
	Girls	Boys
1. I would like to visit a country in Asia	69%	67%
2. I do NOT need to learn about Asia	29%	29%
3. People from countries of Asia contribute little to the world	21%	35%

Othering of Asia and Pan's three dominant modes of viewing Asia (Pan, 2015), there is some evidence to suggest that the 'Asia as threat' narrative is still influential, with nearly one-fifth of boys and 10% of girls regarding Asia cultures as problematic for Australia. It is unclear if this refers to Asian cultures within or outside of Australia. Though the proportion is not large, there is an average of approximately 15% of students who see little for Australia to learn from countries like Japan and China. This could be reflective of the 'absence of Asia' view in which Australians either do not recognise the external or internal presence of Asia or when they do, it is disregarded as being of little relevance. With respect to these views, the fact that approximately 80% or more of students disagreed with these statements suggests that those views of Asia are less entrenched in this generation. Though there are variations in agreement to statements within this level of *Avoidance*, overall these responses from the 2015 cohort broadly align with those of the 2002 cohort.

6.6.3   Receiving

The next affective level of *Receiving* describes a personal response to Asia and some willingness to learn about it. Three statements were allocated to this level, as shown in Table 6.5.

Compared to the 2002 results, the proportion of students that responded positively to these statements is higher. Over two-thirds of the students expressed a desire to visit an Asian country, which appears far higher than it was in 2002. As noted in the demographic question data (Table 6.2), more of the 2015 cohort has experienced travel to Asia. This response may therefore be an indication of not only these students wanting to travel to Asia again, but also other students, possibly influenced by their peers, expressing a desire to visit an Asian country. Despite this strong intention to travel, nearly a third of all students saw no need to learn about Asia. Looking more closely at the correlation between these two responses, nearly 70% of the students who said they do not need to learn about Asia also said they would not like to visit an Asian country. This suggests that there is still a strong sense that learning about Asia is tethered to the narrative of an external Asia, 'out there', which can be either explored or ignored depending on imagined future travel in the region. This is also consistent with the 'absence of Asia' mode of viewing in which the 'Asia' within Australian borders is still invisible or easily ignored by Australians.

Though the relatively high level of agreement (35% of boys and 21% of girls) to the final statement regarding the perceived minimal contribution of Asian countries to the world appears higher than in 2002, the statement seems to raise more questions than answers. If taken on its face value, it does suggest that the 'absence of Asia' perspective is still influential in how these students see the contribution from the Asia region to the world. However, to comprehend this response fully, it would require an understanding of what students are considering when they imagined what the form and nature of contributions could be. Domains such as music, cinema, cuisine, sport, art, and fashion are just a few of the areas of interest for students, and a very general statement like this provides an insufficient context in which to gauge the response.

6.6.4   Responding

A student at the level of *Responding* sees potential benefits to learning about Asia, and this echoes the frequently emphasised instrumental value of learning about Asia. The proportion of students who responded positively to the four statements at this affective level seems to be greater than was the case in 2002 (Table 6.6).

The responses to statements two and four, which range from nearly two-thirds to three-quarters of students responding that learning about Asia is not only a good thing but will be beneficial in their future life, indicate an expression of the intrinsic and utility value attached to these statements. This may also align with the 'Asia as opportunity' view, though in this case the personal importance that these two statements imply may indicate a deeper meaning to the idea of 'opportunity'; one which goes beyond the transactional nature of how that mode of viewing Asia has

Table 6.6 Percentage of affirmative responses to responding level statements

Statements	Affirmative responses	
	Girls	Boys
1. Asian cultures of are no interest to me	31%	35%
2. Learning about Asia will help me later in life	62%	73%
3. I avoid Asian festivals	24%	19%
4. Learning about Asia is a good thing	60%	79%

often figured in the Australian view of Asia. Of note for this category, the boys appear to be more positive in their attitudes to both the present value of learning about Asia and for imagined future scenarios than the cohort of boys were 2002. The experience of learning Japanese may have introduced previously unknown present and future opportunities for these boys. Only some of the boys in the 2002 study would have been learning an Asian language, and this may account for their fewer positive responses to these statements.

6.6.5 *Valuing*

The affective level of *Valuing* adds a degree of personal involvement and an emerging caring approach to the previous level of *Responding*. The responses to these six statements appear generally more positive than those reported in 2002, as shown in Fig. 5.6 (Table 6.7).

The comparison between responses from boys and girls is more complex, with shifts in responses that tend to balance out to an overall similar level of attitude. It is also noticeable that the predominantly instrumentalist language used in some of these statements has a strong resemblance to the language used in many recent rationales for promoting Asia literacy. This also aligns with the 'Asia as opportunity' mode of view, though when looking at the set of responses, there may be more depth to this view than just 'opportunity'. Nearly two-thirds of students consider learning about Asia as valuable, though the meaning that students place on the word 'valuable' is open to interpretation. As approximately half of the students also expressed enjoyment about Asia-related learning, this may suggest that the value they recognise is not only the instrumental value but also the intrinsic worth of that learning. This set of responses also serves to counter the idea that Asia is absent from the outlook of the majority of these students, though this may only apply to the view of Asia existing exclusively outside of Australia.

Table 6.7 Percentage of affirmative responses to valuing level statements

Statements	Affirmative responses	
	Girls	Boys
1. It would be better if Australia had closer relations with Asian countries	60%	42%
2. It is important that Australians know lots about Asia	57%	48%
3. I enjoy learning things about Asia	45%	58%
4. Learning about Asia is valuable	60%	63%
5. Thai people have weird religions	31%	33%
6. Studying things about Asia is important	57%	58%

6.6.6   Organisation

Agreement with these statements at the *Organisation* level would place a student at the most positive end of the 2002 modified affective domain scale. Not only do positive responses to these statements indicate students who are keen to learn about Asia, but they also regard this as a personal commitment that may go beyond the utilitarian motivation (Table 6.8).

The responses from the 2015 cohort suggest fewer students being classified at this affective level when viewed against the responses in the 2002 survey. The lower levels of positive attitudes among boys that was apparent in 2002 are also evident in these responses. Though very few students expressed a wish to live in an Asian country (6% of boys and 10% of girls), the young age of the students (12–14 years old) would have a strong influence on these responses. It is possible that the view of 'Asia as threat' has had some influence on this attitude. This is less the idea of Asia as a direct threat to Australia, but more common representation of Asia in Australian mass media as a place of civil unrest, catastrophic natural disasters, and endemic poverty (Jakubowicz & Seneviratne, 1996).

6.6.7   Summary of 2002 and 2015 Attitudes of Years 7/8

While noting that direct comparisons between the 2002 and 2015 data sets were not possible due to cohort variances and different data analysis procedures, some general points can be made. At the first level of *Avoidance*, both cohorts seem to have similar response levels, with the boys in both 2002 and 2015 slightly more representative at this level of negative reaction to learning about Asia than the girls. At the next level of *Receiving*, the students in 2015 seemed to be more inclined to agree with these statements than those in 2002, with little apparent difference between boys and girls.

The level of *Responding* captures some of the utility value in Asia-related learning, and the 2015 cohort appeared to identify considerably more with the statements at this affective domain level than those students in 2002. The boys in the 2015 cohort expressed more positive responses to most of these level 3 statements than the girls, suggesting a greater degree of alignment with this utility aspect of Asia-related learning.

Table 6.8 Percentage of affirmative responses to organisation level statements

Statements	Affirmative responses	
	Girls	Boys
1. Countries of Asia are my favourite	14%	10%
2. I would like to live in a country in Asia	10%	6%
3. Reading books about Asia is fun	21%	21%
4. I would like people from Asia to visit my home	33%	25%
5. Learning about Asia is fun	48%	56%

The pattern in responses to statements at the fourth level of *Valuing* also suggests more students in 2015 aligning with the more personal involvement that this affective domain signifies. The statements at this level express a combination of attainment, intrinsic, and utility value, and this may explain why the majority of students were able to identify with and respond positively to most of these statements. The responses to statements at the fifth level of *Organisation* shows a reversal in numbers with the 2002 cohort tending to identify more with this level than the students in 2015. The 2002 study reported more girls than boys at the level of *Organisation*, and though this was also the case for the 2015 cohort, this difference seemed less noticeable.

6.6.8   Context of Learning

In the 2002 study, an additional survey instrument was used to assess how much students learnt about Asia at school and outside of school. In response to the question 'How much have you learnt about Asia through each of the following things?', 15 items for each group (total 30) were rated by students as *lots, some things, not very much*, or *nothing*. In the 2002 study, these four responses were combined into two; 'learn' and 'not learn' and the percentage scores obtained are listed in Table 6.9 along with the 2015 study results.

Most noticeable is the almost identical results for how students self-assess the amount they learn about Asia at school. At 22% in 2002 and 23% in 2015, the results suggest that this new generation of students do not perceive any difference in the amount or quality of Asia-related curriculum within their daily school lives.

The evaluation for what is perceived to be learnt outside of school has declined for this 2015 cohort. The reasons for this are unclear at this stage; however, other components of this mixed-method study provide avenues to explore this further. In focus group interviews carried out with students at diverse year levels, one topic of discussion has been the widespread use of social media and mobile technology. Though these devices offer opportunities to access an almost unlimited variety of material and resources, they also enable students to exclusively focus on their immediate interests. While the 2002 cohort would have been viewing mostly mainstream print, TV, and radio media with the Asia-related content that was standard for those mediums, students today can completely bypass these channels of communication and create a much narrow and filtered source of information. This may be one reason why the 2015 students self-assessed 'not learn outside school' at over 10% higher than in 2002. Unless they are actively seeking this Asia-related information, then it may not be as present in their customised daily media stream.

Table 6.9 Context for learning about Asia—2002 and 2015 totals

	Learn at school				Not learn at school				Learn outside school				Not learn outside school		
2002 study	Total 22%				Total 78%				Total 29%				Total 71%		
2015 study	Lots	Some	Total		Little	Nothing	Total		Lots	Some	Total		Little	Nothing	Total
	6%	17%	23%		23%	54%	77%		4%	13%	18%		20%	60%	82%

6.7 Conclusion

As one component of a larger study, this chapter has reported on the attitudes of Year 7 and 8 students towards Asia-related learning in light of data from a 2002 cohort of Year 8 students. The research revealed three key findings. Firstly, although levels of the most positive attitudes were lower, the proportion of students who had generally more positive attitudes to Asia and learning about Asia increased significantly. This was particularly evident in the high levels of agreement with statements that accentuated the personal benefits of learning about Asia. Secondly, the overall level of negative attitudes remained similar to those found in the 2002 study. Also, as was seen in 2002, boys continued to express fewer of the very positive attitudes and more of the negative attitudes. Finally, in terms of the context of learning, students in 2002 and 2015 have the view that their learning about Asia within the school context has barely changed, despite these 13 years being characterised by increased interest and enactment of policies that have sought to promote studies of Asia in schools. Of concern is that the 2015 cohort perceive their learning about Asia outside of school as considerably lower than those in 2002. While there are limitations to this survey instrument, it can provide useful data for teachers and schools to gain some insights into their students' attitudes to the studies of Asia and how students rate the amount they learn about Asia in and outside of school.

References

Abbott, T. (2014). *Address to the Asia society*. Retrieved from http://www.pm.gov.au/media/2014-03-25/address-asia-society-canberra

ACARA. (2013). *Guide to understanding index of community socio-educational advantage (ICSEA values)*. Australian Curriculum, Assessment and Reporting Authority. Retrieved from http://www.acara.edu.au/verve/_resources/Guide_to_understanding_2013_ICSEA_values.pdf

ACARA. (2014a). *Australian curriculum: Cross-curriculum priorities*. Retrieved from http://www.acara.edu.au/curriculum/cross_curriculum_priorities.html

ACARA. (2014b). *Intercultural understanding—General capabilities*. Retrieved from http://www.australiancurriculum.edu.au/GeneralCapabilities/Pdf/Intercultural-understanding

Asia Education Foundation. (2012a). *Building demand for Asia literacy in Australian schools: Literature review*. Retrieved from http://www.asiaeducation.edu.au/docs/default-source/what-works-pdf/literature_review.pdf?sfvrsn=2

Asia Education Foundation. (2012b). *Building demand for Asia literacy: What works report*. Parkville: The University of Melbourne—Asia Education Foundation.

Asia Education Foundation. (2014a). *Australian curriculum review: Asia education foundation submission*. Asia Education Foundation.

Asia Education Foundation. (2014b). *Australian curriculum review: Asia education foundation submission*. Retrieved from http://www.asiaeducation.edu.au/research-and-policy/australian-curriculum-review/aef-submission

Auchmuty, J. J. (1970). *Report by the commonwealth advisory committee on the teaching of Asian languages and cultures in Australia*. Canberra: Govt. Printer.

Australia in the Asian Century Task Force. (2011). *Australia in the Asian century*. Canberra: Australia in the Asian Century Task Force.

Australia Industry Group & Asialink. (2011). *Engaging Asia: Getting it right for Australian business*. Parkville: Univeristy of Melbourne.

Australian Bureau of Statistics. (2012, 16th April). *Reflecting a Nation: Stories from the 2011 census, 2012–2013*. Retrieved from http://www.abs.gov.au/ausstats/abs@.nsf/Lookup/2071. 0main+features902012-2013

Australian Bureau of Statistics. (2013, 24th April). The 'average' Australian. Retrieved from http:// abs.gov.au/AUSSTATS/abs@.nsf/Lookup/4102.0Main+Features30April+2013#back3

Australian Bureau of Statistics. (2016). *Overseas arrivals and departures, Australia, 2016*. Retrieved from http://www.abs.gov.au/ausstats/abs@.nsf/products/ 961B6B53B87C130ACA2574030010BD05

Brunton, C. (2013). *Asia aware: Students' survey research results*. Retrieved from http://www. asianz.org.nz/reports/wp-content/uploads/2013/05/Asia_Aware_Students_Survey_May_2013. pdf

Brunton, C. (2017). *Losing momentum: School leavers' Asia engagement*. Retrieved from http:// www.asianz.org.nz/reports/wp-content/uploads/2017/07/987_ANZF_SchoolLeaversReport_ WEB_v2.pdf

Business Alliance for Asia Literacy. (2009). Statement of the business alliance for Asia literacy. EQ Australia, Winter, 1.

Department of Foreign Affairs and Trade. (2013). *Julie bishop sworn in as minister for foreign affairs*. Retrieved from http://foreignminister.gov.au/releases/Pages/2013/jb_mr_130918.aspx? ministerid=4

FitzGerald, S., Boomer, G., Lo Bianco, J., & McKay, E. M. (1988). *Towards an Asia-literate society*. Parkville: Asian Studies Association of Australia.

Griffin, P., Woods, K., Dulhunty, M., & Coates, H. (2002). *Australian students' knowledge and understanding of Asia*. Canberra: Commonwealth of Australia.

Henderson, D. (2003). Meeting the national interest through Asia literacy—An overview of the major stages and debates. *Asian Studies Review, 27*(1), 23–53.

Henderson, D., Allan, C., & Mallan, K. M. (2013). Towards Asia literacy: The Australian curriculum and Asian-Australian children's literature. *Curriculum Perspectives, 33*(1), 42–51.

Heryanto, A. (2015). Asia literacy: A deeply problematic metaphor. In C. Johnson, V. C. Mackie, & T. Morris-Suzuki (Eds.), *The social sciences in the Asian century* (pp. 171–189). Acton: ANU Press.

Jakubowicz, A., & Seneviratne, K. (1996). *Making multicultural Australia: Ethnic conflict and the Australian media*. Sydney: University of Technology, Australian Centre for Independent Journalism.

Krathwohl, D. R., Bloom, B. S., & Masia, B. B. (1964). *Taxonomy of educational objectives—the classification of educational goals: Handbook II: Affective domain*. London: Longmans.

Lindsey, T. (2011). Australia's Asia literacy wipe-out. Retrieved from http://www.lowyinterpreter. org/post/2011/11/04/Australias-Asia-literacy-wipe-out.aspx

Lo Bianco, J. (2014). Asia and anglosphere: Public symbolism and language policy in Australia. In N. Murray & A. Scarino (Eds.), *Dynamic ecologies* (pp. 59–73). Dordrecht: Springer.

Lo Bianco, J., & Aliani, R. (2013). *Language planning and student experiences: Intention, rhetoric and implementation*. Bristol: Multilingual Matters.

Love, R., Kamener, L., von Oertzen, T., & Minifie, J. (2012). *Imagining Australia in the Asian century: How Australian businesses are capturing the Asian opportunity*. Sydney: The Boston Consulting Group. Retrieved from http://www.bostonconsulting.com.au/documents/ file115487.pdf

Mackerras, C. (Ed.). (1995). *East and Southeast Asia: A multidisciplinary survey*. Boulder, CO: Lynne Rienner Publishers.

MCEETYA. (2008). *Melbourne declaration on educational goals for young Australians*. Melbourne: Ministerial Council on Education, Employment, Training and Youth Affairs. Retrieved from http://www.mceetya.edu.au/verve/_resources/National_Declaration_on_the_Educational_ Goals_for_Young_Australians.pdf

Pan, C. (2015). Australia's self-identity and three modes of imaging Asia: A critical perspective on Asia literacy. In C. Halse (Ed.), *Asia literate schooling in the Asian century* (pp. 197–210). Abingdon: Routledge.

Rizvi, F. (2012). Engaging the Asian century. *ACCESS: Critical Perspectives on Communication, Cultural & Policy Studies, 31*(1), 73.

Rudd, K. M. (1994). *Asian languages and Australia's economic future: A report prepared for the Council of Australian Governments on a proposed national Asian languages/studies strategy for Australian schools.* Brisbane: Queensland Govt. Printer.

Salter, P. (2013). The problem in policy: Representations of Asia literacy in Australian education for the Asian century. *Asian Studies Review, 37*(1), 3–23. https://doi.org/10.1080/10357823.2012.760530

Scarino, A. (2014). Situating the challenges in current languages education policy in Australia—Unlearning monolingualism. *International Journal of Multilingualism, 11*(3), 289–306. https://doi.org/10.1080/14790718.2014.921176

Singh, M. G. (1995). *Translating studies of Asia: A curriculum statement for negotiation in Australian schools.* Belconnen: Australian Curriculum Studies Association.

Sturak, K., & Naughten, Z. (2010). *The current state of Chinese, Indonesian, Japanese and Korean language education in Australian schools four languages, four stories.* Carlton South: Asia Education Foundation.

Wilkinson, J., & Milgate, G. (2009a). *Studies of Asia in year 12.* Melbourne: Asia Education Foundation & Australian Council for Educational Research.

Wilkinson, J., & Milgate, G. (2009b). *Studies of Asia in year 12.* Melbourne. Retrieved from http://www.asiaeducation.edu.au/docs/default-source/Research-reports/studiesofasia_year12_file_2.pdf

Williamson-Fien, J. (1994). Facing the tiger: The problematics of Asian studies education. *Discourse, 15*(1), 75–87.

Part II
Transforming Pedagogies Through Engagement with Teacher Belief and Knowledge

Chapter 7
Preservice Teachers' Pedagogical Beliefs and Practices During the EAL Practicum in Australian Secondary Schools

Minh Hue Nguyen

Abstract Although teacher beliefs are well-researched in the second language teacher education field, most studies used survey methods to identify teachers' beliefs rather than examining the relationship between beliefs and instructional practice. Recently, research on second language teaching placement has focused on how the realities of the placement shape the development of preservice teachers' beliefs. However, how preservice teachers' prior beliefs influence their professional learning during the practicum remains underexplored. Given the widely acknowledged importance of teacher beliefs in the work of language teachers, this gap needs to be filled. Underpinned by a sociocultural perspective on teacher learning and drawing primarily on data from interviews, the qualitative case study reported in this chapter investigated the pedagogical beliefs that three preservice English as an additional language (EAL) teachers had during their school-based placements in Australia and how these influenced their professional learning during the placement. The study found that beliefs related to language teaching and learning played an influential role in shaping the preservice teachers' professional experiences, and the influence manifested differently across the three participants due to the interface between their beliefs and other personal and contextual factors. The findings offer implications for supporting preservice EAL teachers in effectively socialising into the profession.

Keywords Second language · Teaching practicum · Teacher beliefs · Sociocultural theory

M. H. Nguyen (✉)
Faculty of Education, Monash University, Melbourne, Australia
e-mail: minh.hue.nguyen@monash.edu

© Springer Nature Singapore Pte Ltd. 2021
D. Bao, T. Pham (eds.), *Transforming Pedagogies Through Engagement with Learners, Teachers and Communities*, Education in the Asia-Pacific Region: Issues, Concerns and Prospects 57, https://doi.org/10.1007/978-981-16-0057-9_7

7.1 Introduction

There has been a paradigm shift in second language teacher education (SLTE) to a sociocultural perspective on language teacher professional learning (Johnson, 2009). This view has been grounded in the work of Vygotsky (1978) and later developed by other scholars (e.g. Engeström, 1987; Johnson, 2009; Leontiev, 1981). Sociocultural perspective views learning as a mediated activity situated in sociocultural contexts and practices and teachers as learners of teaching, whose personal histories play an influential role in shaping their learning. On entering teacher education, PSTs generally have years of schooling experiences and have therefore formed numerous beliefs relevant to teaching and learning (Nguyen, 2019). Teacher beliefs are personal ideologies (Verloop, Van Driel, & Meijer, 2001) or cognitive structures (Wallace & Priestley, 2011), which can shape and be shaped by teacher practices and experiences (Borg, 2003). As learning is influenced by the values, including beliefs that have emerged from personal histories (Vygotsky, 1978), understanding teacher beliefs are of paramount importance in understanding teacher learning. Yet, the current discourses around teacher beliefs lack a focus on how these shape teacher learning during the TESOL practicum. In an attempt to address this gap, the current chapter reports on a qualitative case study that explored the relationship between beliefs and practices of three preservice teachers (PSTs) of English as an additional language (EAL) during their teaching placements in secondary schools in Victoria, Australia. Drawing on a sociocultural perspective on SLTE and interview data from a larger project on EAL PSTs' professional learning during the placement, it identified the EAL PSTs' pedagogical beliefs and how their learning of EAL teaching was shaped by the beliefs in conjunction with other sociocultural factors inherent in the professional experience context.

In the following section, a review of the current discourse on the topic of TESOL teachers' beliefs and practice is presented, together with an identification of research gaps and research questions guiding this study. This is followed by the methodology of the study and the main discussion of findings yielded in relation to the research questions. Next, the chapter presents implications for TESOL teacher education pedagogy based on the findings and concludes with a highlight of the main ideas and a recommendation for future research.

7.2 Discourse on the Topic

Teacher beliefs are well-researched in the TESOL field. However, the existing studies mostly identify and describe teachers' beliefs rather than understanding the relationship between beliefs and classroom practices (Mak, 2011). TESOL researchers have recently begun to examine the dialectic relation between these two issues (Farrell & Tomenson-Filion, 2014). Some have focused on the issue among experienced TESOL teachers (Farrell & Ives, 2014; Farrell &

Tomenson-Filion, 2014), while greater attention is given to that among PSTs, especially in relation to the practicum.

Of the studies on PSTs' beliefs in the TESOL practicum, the consensus is that pedagogical beliefs change due to the influence of the multidimensional practicum experience (e.g. Mak, 2011; Ng, Nicholas, & Williams, 2010; Yuan & Lee, 2014). For example, in Mak (2011), a PST's belief in teacher-fronted teaching was challenged by the students' underperformance, which motivated her to experiment with Communicative Language Teaching (CLT). An increase in students' motivation made her believe in the motivating effect of CLT, and she further refined her belief over the practicum. Likewise, Yuan and Lee (2014) found that PSTs' engagement in practicum activities including observing the mentors' teaching, lesson planning, reflecting on practice, and discussing with the mentors triggered a series of changes in their beliefs including confirmation, realisation, disagreement, elaboration, integration, and modification of beliefs. Similarly, Ng et al. (2010) found that PSTs changed from believing in teacher-centred approach to believing in student-centred approach. Tang, Lee, and Chun (2012) indicate that before the practicum EAL PSTs held diverse beliefs regarding the theoretical orientations of EAL teaching. However, they reconceptualised these during the practicum and eventually followed a similar teaching approach because of the influence of the classroom realities such as students' characteristics, limited class time, inflexible school schedules, and their perceived self-management skills. This is supported by Le (2014), who found that preservice EFL teachers' belief about the use of English in EFL classrooms was challenged by the reality of learners' low proficiency level.

The above literature on preservice TESOL teachers' beliefs in the practicum provides useful insights into how the realities of the TESOL practicum shape the development of PSTs' beliefs. However, it does not adequately deal with how PSTs' beliefs influence their professional learning. This aspect of the dialectic relation, from a sociocultural perspective on SLTE (Johnson, 2009), is a key question in understanding PSTs' learning. This chapter ties together the major themes aforementioned and investigates the following questions:

1. What pedagogical beliefs do PSTs have that influence their professional learning during the EAL practicum?
2. In what ways do PSTs' pedagogical beliefs shape their professional learning?

7.3 Methodology

To investigate the questions above, the study used a qualitative case study design. Following ethics approvals, voluntary written informed consent and purposive sampling, the study involved three international PSTs who were enrolled in a postgraduate entry EAL preservice program at Greystone University in Melbourne, Australia. Frank, a Singaporean in his early 30s, entered the program with rich and varied professional experiences, a Bachelor of Business Management, and several vocational certificates. Kate, a British national in her late 20s, had a rich language learning experience, a Bachelor of the Japanese language, and some experience as an EAL aide before attending the program. While Frank and Kate consider themselves native speakers of English, Maria, also in her late 20s, is an EAL speaker from Russia with about 20 years of English language learning experience. She had a Bachelor of Teaching (History) from a Russian university.

The preservice program consisted of coursework and two rounds of EAL practicum lasting 5 weeks in total. The data reported in this chapter were collected during the second practicum lasting 2 weeks. The three PSTs were placed in three different secondary schools in Melbourne during data collection. Frank was placed to teach EAL in a mainstream secondary school, while Kate taught intensive EAL classes an English language centre for newly arrived EAL students. Maria taught EAL classes alongside mainstream English classes in an elite private school. Each of the PSTs was mentored by an experienced EAL teacher from their host school/centre.

Each PST participated in three interviews at three stages: pre-practicum, during-practicum, and post-practicum. The last two interviews were conducted based on the PST-nominated lesson recordings, lesson plans, and teaching materials. Data were first transcribed and then analysed using qualitative content analysis, which enabled the study to conduct a holistic and comprehensive analysis of the complex socio-cultural experience to understand how PSTs' beliefs functioned in it. A code is assigned to the end of each data excerpt to indicate the source of data. For example, F.IN.1, F.IN.2, and F.IN.3 refer to Frank's first, second, and third interviews, respectively. Ellipses in data are indicated through the use of [. . .].

In this research, I did not have any personal and professional relationships with the participants, nor was I involved in the SLTE program and its placement units under research. In this sense, I considered myself an outsider in relation to the research context and participants. However, I was also an insider in some sense because I am an EAL speaker, having lectured and researched in SLTE for over 10 years both in Australia and overseas. Through my years of education and professional experience in EAL teacher education, I had developed an insider perspective, which allowed me to interact with the participants in ways that helped to elicit useful and relevant data and interpret the data using this perspective.

7.4 Main Discussion

The three participants hold a common broad belief that EAL teaching should be learner-centred, which allows for plenty of group work and other interactive activities, but they expressed it in slightly different ways. While Frank believed that language learning should be fun and social, for Kate it should involve a lot of visuals and diverse interactive activities, and Maria strongly believed in CLT. The beliefs also manifested differently between the participants due to the interaction between the beliefs and the participants' different personal histories and practicum contexts in shaping their practices.

7.4.1 Language Learning Should be Fun and Social

A belief that language learning should be fun and social was explicitly expressed by Frank. For example, he said:

> I think [language] learning should be fun, and you know I think if it is not fun, nobody will want to be in class. Students have to be there, so I've got something that is a bit more entertaining and a bit more light-hearted so that they can enjoy it; so that they will remember it better. (F.IN.1)

This belief about language learning originated in his personal experience as a games tester and influenced his choice of educational games as tools to make EAL learning fun and entertaining. Data from lesson recordings and teaching artefacts confirmed that throughout the 2-week practicum, Frank used many games, some of which are shown below:

> I've been using *Royal Story Cubes*. I've been using *Once upon a Time*, *Fairy Tales*, and [...] I will be using *Taboo*. (F.IN.2)

Frank also believed that EAL students needed to learn EAL for both academic and social purposes. In Frank's words, 'They should be there to learn why and how to do things in their daily life rather than just for academic purposes' (F.IN.1). He added that incorporating social elements into the classroom would make the academic side of EAL learning more engaging and productive for the students:

> If a person goes into learning a language because they want to communicate with somebody, or you know, 'How do I ask this Japanese girl out? I don't know Japanese,' so they might want to learn Japanese for the specific purpose of that. But most of the students that come in from overseas, they are forced to learn English simply because all the texts are in English and all the teachers speak English. That's, to me, that's not a good way to learn. [...] But if you teach children how to communicate with somebody else for purposes of leisure or [...] interest, you know, then the learning of the language becomes more meaningful. (F.IN.1)

In this extract, Frank emphasised the importance of creating conditions where learners have intrinsic motivation to engage in meaningful social interaction and learn the language, which is potentially a core motivator of the teaching and learning process (Dörnyei, 1994). Frank's belief that learning should be fun and social seemed to be strengthened by his understanding of the challenges of engaging EAL students, who came from overseas and are 'forced to learn English' (F.IN.1).

Frank's teaching was strongly influenced by this belief and characterised by a range of social activities targeting EAL learning. For example:

> I've brought the social into the classroom. They played games. They got together in groups a lot. They read out aloud to each other. So it's a very social kind of thing. (F.IN.3)

It appeared that Frank organised activities for students to participate actively in social exchanges and navigate away from traditional learning activities where the students would be passive recipients of knowledge. Following is an example of such an activity:

I've also gotten them to plan and prepare a party that they want to do on Friday. I said, 'OK, we need to find out who I need to ask and what we're allowed to bring.' And so I gave them the task to go and find everything out and they came back to me yesterday and said, 'OK, we found all the information. This is who we're supposed to ask; here's what we can bring.' I said, 'OK, so now you need to decide who's going to bring what food, what drinks, what we're going to do.' So [...] I've let them carry on by themselves to discuss and tell each other what they want to bring and encourage their friends to bring something. (F.IN.2)

Here, Frank made the teaching and learning of EAL fun, social, and engaging by assigning real-life tasks that required collaborative information gathering, social interaction, and negotiation of responsibilities. Through these activities, the students had various opportunities for communicating in English, a real social purpose, and high motivation for real-life communication, which closely reflects Frank's belief above.

7.4.2   Language Teaching Should Involve Lots of Visuals and Diverse Activities

Also advocating learner-centredness, Kate expressed a belief in the importance of incorporating a range of visuals and interactive activities into EAL teaching. She believes that 'use of lots of visuals, use of games, use of lots of group work, jointly constructing texts' (K.IN.1) are the most important aspects of EAL teaching. An interview shows that her belief in the benefits of visuals was reinforced by her previous practicum experiences where she realised that she needed to use visuals more often, especially in teaching abstract concepts. On the other hand, Kate's belief about the use of varied activities appears to be shaped by her university coursework, which introduced many teaching and learning activities that she could later resort to:

I've compiled all the notes from my EAL lectures and my LOTE lectures, my second language pedagogy lectures, [...] and I had that list in the back of my folder and I would always refer to it when I was planning the lessons. (K.IN.2)

As illustrated above, through the teacher education program, Kate had developed a repertoire of teaching activities, which made it easy for her to refer to and choose from during her practicum. Her belief in the importance of varied activities also played an influential role in motivating her to compile those activities for easy reference.

Kate's belief relating to diverse activities was also reinforced by her school mentor's support for experimental learning, as she recounted, 'My mentor said, you know, you should take risks now because this is the time when you can take risks; you've got someone else in the room' (K.IN.2). This is in marked contrast with the mentoring approach reported in an Australian study (Nguyen, 2014, 2017) and studies in Asia (Farrell, 2008; Nguyen, 2010; Trent, 2013). The mentor's support, together with Kate's past practicum and coursework experience mentioned above, allowed the belief to exert a strong influence on Kate's learning. Analysis of the interviews, supported by lesson recordings and teaching artefacts, showed that throughout the 2-week practicum, Kate used many interactive activities, such as *Running Dictation*, *Hot Potato*, *Group Story Writing*, *Subject*, and *Predicate Interactive Quiz*, and *Text Annotation*. The belief motivated her to actively engage in finding and using a variety of teaching resources to enrich EAL learning. For example, in the activity called *Hot Potato*, a large group brainstorming activity as part of a writing lesson, Kate used many visuals to stimulate interaction:

> When we did the *Hot Potato* activity, which was where they all do a giant group brainstorm on large paper in lots of different colours and we were able to put that up. That's writing but with the visuals and the colours and the size and we were able to put around the classroom. (K.IN.3)

7.4.3 CLT Is Ideal

Although existing pedagogical beliefs appeared to exert a strong influence on Frank and Kate's EAL teaching practices, this was not the case for Maria. Before the practicum, Maria also reported a strong belief that EAL teaching should engage students in communicative activities. When asked to describe her ideal EAL classroom, Maria said:

> Communicative classroom ideally. I think it's just a combination of different activities like student-oriented, teacher-directed, or like teacher and students working together. I think you can introduce a lot of different ways of communicative in an ideal classroom. (M.IN.1)

Although this belief did not change in the course of the practicum, it had little influence on her professional practice due to the strong influence of contextual factors. For instance, Maria's belief mentioned above contradicted the mentor's teacher-centred teaching style. Maria recalled:

> I felt that it is too many teacher-centred lessons. While I like students to do a bit of [guessing] and independent thinking, she would just tell the answer, wouldn't make students think. [...] and I just had to give up all my sort of ideas and themes that I wanted to do and to adjust to my mentor teacher because I needed to get a good report. (M.IN.2)

As a result of this contradiction, although Maria wanted to experiment with CLT, she was unable to teach the way she believed teaching should be. Despite this, the belief shaped her development of a strong identity as a communicative teacher as opposed to the teacher-centred approach she saw and had to follow during the practicum. After the practicum, she noted:

> I'm just building upon what I stand on and I stand for, and I definitely would get more interactive learning [...]. I just can't see the point of the old traditional way of studying where students are sitting and writing down. [...] And for me as a teacher I need to see engagement to feel that I'm doing a good job. (M.IN.3)

The analysis revealed Maria's crises, which can be seen through the contradictions between her preferred teaching style and that of her mentor and between her belief in CLT and her practice of teacher-centredness. Meijer (2011) suggests that such crises are needed in teachers' professional learning. In this study, through her critical experiences, Maria developed a greater commitment to persevering with CLT in her future teaching.

7.5 Implications

The new insights gained from the systematic examination of pedagogical beliefs in relation to personal and contextual factors offer some implications for TESOL education pedagogy within the Australian context and the wider Asia-Pacific region. Due to the limited number of cases and the specific contextual features involved in the research settings, readers are encouraged to use these implications with careful examination of how much the participant profiles and context are relevant to the readers' contexts.

Firstly, the findings suggest that PSTs draw on belief systems emerging from multiple resources such as personal schooling and employment experiences, interactions with others, and self-research (Pridham, Deed, & Cox, 2013). Therefore, the study recommends that TESOL education adopt a transformative approach to teacher learning (Brandt, 2006) to capitalise on PSTs' existing values. Following this transformative approach, PSTs should be encouraged to reflect on and make their pedagogical beliefs explicit and examine how these beliefs shape and are shaped by their professional learning during teacher education. Teacher education curriculum and pedagogy should create an opportunity to develop PSTs' ability to reflect on principles of practice, especially their assumptions, beliefs, and conceptions of teaching (Farrell, 2015).

Secondly, teacher educators, especially mentor teachers, would benefit from an enhanced understanding of PSTs' existing beliefs about EAL teaching and learning. They could use their knowledge of PSTs' pedagogical beliefs to guide their teacher education pedagogy and mentoring approach in ways that leverage the values PSTs bring into their professional learning and transform PSTs' beliefs in productive ways through teacher education. This approach is more likely to create a greater depth of learning for both PSTs and teacher educators, which is supported empirically by this study and past research (Hudson, 2013) and underpinned conceptually by the learning community model of professional experience advocated in Australia (Le Cornu, 2010).

7.6 Conclusion

This chapter set out to examine (1) the types of pedagogical beliefs that the three preservice EAL teachers had that were influential in their professional experiences and (2) how these contributed to shaping their professional experiences. Regarding the first question, the study identified a generally common broad belief about EAL teaching among the participants, that is, EAL teaching should be learner-centred and interactive. In relation to the second question, this broadly shared belief was manifested differently in each case, with Frank focusing on making EAL learning resemble fun social activities, Kate using a wide range of visuals and activity types, and Maria not being able to implement her ideal teaching approach at all. The manifestation of the broad belief in the form of different pedagogical strategies was found to be influenced by other personal and contextual factors within each placement context. Although most of past research on teacher beliefs claim that teacher beliefs change as a result of their participation in the social practices and contexts of teaching (e.g. Mak, 2011; Ng et al., 2010; Yuan & Lee, 2014), in this study I do not claim any modified beliefs. However, I argue that the PSTs' pedagogical beliefs interfaced with other sociocultural factors and shaped the participants' practices and identity.

According to Vygotsky (1978), the key to understanding human higher mental functioning is to trace its origins, but this is yet to be adequately explored in the TESOL literature. The sociocultural framework enabled this study to gain insights that have not before been documented in the literature on TESOL teachers' beliefs and practices. The study has systematically taken into account PSTs' personal histories that contribute to refining their beliefs and the interaction between beliefs and other sociocultural factors in shaping their practices. The research goes beyond a mere description of beliefs and practices which is often the case in early SLTE research (Cross, 2010) and takes an explanatory approach to the issues. As such, it responds to and promotes the call for a theoretical framework that is broad enough to unify thinking, practice, and context (Cross, 2010).

Learner-centredness was found to be preferable among the PSTs in this study. What is new in the research is that both personal and contextual dimensions were considered in understanding beliefs and practices relating to learner-centredness. Similar to studies in Asia (e.g. Pham, 2016; Tsui & Wong, 2009), in this study contextual knowledge informed the PSTs' thinking and practices regarding learner-centredness. However, although located in the Asia-Pacific region, the Australian TESOL context is unique in comparison with Asian countries in that English is the primary language in Australia while in Asia it is mostly only spoken inside the classroom or in some cases as an additional language. Australia shares with Asian countries many learner factors because most of its EAL students come from Asia (Department of Education and Training, 2018), but Asian students in Australia learn EAL in a distinctive immersion mode where they are 'forced' to use English. Within the Australian context itself, EAL students have diverse cultural, linguistic, and educational backgrounds, and schools vary in their EAL provision mode. In this study, the PSTs' beliefs interfaced with features of their distinctive EAL contexts in shaping their practices, which explains the different manifestations of beliefs and practices across the participants. The findings support Tsui and Wong's (2009) argument that teaching ideologies must be integrated both with the local cultural traditions and with the teachers' situated experience to maximise efficacy. Similarly, the research cases support the argument that SLTE research must account for the diverse contexts and personal backgrounds of teachers in understanding why they do what they do. Such research has the capacity to overcome the descriptive nature of earlier research and bring the field forward.

Finally, a limitation of this study is that it involved only three cases of PSTs, who shared a similar pathway into the postgraduate entry preservice teacher education program. That is, all the three PSTs had a first degree related to their teaching method and some level of professional experience before entering the teacher education program. They were also all international students who had diverse educational and professional experiences in both Australia and overseas. As argued previously, teachers formed beliefs about teaching and learning through their prior learning and professional experiences. Therefore, the pedagogical beliefs demonstrated by the participants in this study might be different from domestic Australian students and those entering teacher education straight after leaving secondary school. I would recommend that further research involve participants with more diverse backgrounds to examine how such diversity might impact on their pedagogical beliefs and how PSTs function in their contexts in relation to these beliefs. Such research would yield rich insights that could inform teacher education pedagogy for the increasingly diverse population of EAL PSTs in Australia and similar contexts (Nguyen, 2019).

References

Borg, S. (2003). Teacher cognition in language teaching: A review of research on what teachers think, know, believe, and do. *Language Teaching, 36*, 81–109. https://doi.org/10.1017/S0261444803001903.

Brandt, C. (2006). Allowing for practice: A critical issue in TESOL teacher preparation. *ELT Journal, 60*(4), 355–364. https://doi.org/10.1093/elt/ccl026.

Cross, R. (2010). Language teaching as sociocultural activity: Rethinking language teacher practice. *The Modern Language Journal, 94*(iii), 434–452. https://doi.org/10.1111/j.1540-4781.2010.01058.x.

Department of Education and Training. (2018). *English as an additional language in Victorian government schools 2018*. Melbourne: Department of Education and Training.

Dörnyei, Z. (1994). Motivation and motivating in the foreign language classroom. *The Modern Language Journal, 78*(3), 273–284. https://doi.org/10.1111/j.1540-4781.1994.tb02042.x.

Engeström, Y. (1987). *Learning by expanding: An activity-theoretical approach to developmental research*. Retrieved 2 February 2014, from http://lchc.ucsd.edu/MCA/Paper/Engestrom/expanding/toc.htm

Farrell, T. S. C. (2008). 'Here's the book, go teach the class': ELT practicum support. *RELC Journal, 39*(2), 226–241. https://doi.org/10.1177/0033688208092186.

Farrell, T. S. C. (2015). *Promoting teacher reflection in second language education: A framework for TESOL professionals*. New York: Routledge.

Farrell, T. S. C., & Ives, J. (2014). Exploring teacher beliefs and classroom practices through reflective practice: A case study. *Language Teaching Research., 19*, 594. https://doi.org/10.1177/1362168814541722.

Farrell, T. S. C., & Tomenson-Filion, B. (2014). Teacher beliefs and classroom practice: A case study of an ESL teacher in Canada. In S. B. Said & L. J. Zhang (Eds.), *Language teachers and teaching: Global perspectives, local initiatives* (pp. 169–184). New York: Routledge.

Hudson, P. (2013). Mentoring as professional development: 'Growth for both' mentor and mentee. *Professional Development in Education, 39*(5), 771–783. https://doi.org/10.1080/19415257.2012.749415.

Johnson, K. E. (2009). *Second language teacher education: A sociocultural perspective.* New York: Routledge.

Le Cornu, R. (2010). Changing roles, relationships and responsibilities in changing times. *Asia-Pacific Journal of Teacher Education, 38*(3), 195–206. https://doi.org/10.1080/1359866x.2010.493298.

Le, V. C. (2014). Great expectations: The TESOL practicum as a professional learning experience. *TESOL Journal, 5*(2), 199–224. https://doi.org/10.1002/tesj.103.

Leontiev, A. N. (1981). *Problems of the development of the mind.* Moscow: Progress.

Mak, S. H. (2011). Tensions between conflicting beliefs of an EFL teacher in teaching practice. *RELC Journal, 42*(1), 53–67. https://doi.org/10.1177/0033688210390266.

Meijer, P. C. (2011). The role of crisis in the development of student teachers' professional identity. In A. Lauriala, R. Rajala, H. Ruokamo, & O. Ylitapio-Mäntylä (Eds.), *Navigating in educational contexts: Identities and cultures in dialogue* (pp. 41–54). Boston: Sense Publishers.

Ng, W., Nicholas, H., & Williams, A. (2010). School experience influences on pre-service teachers' evolving beliefs about effective teaching. *Teaching and Teacher Education, 26*(2), 278–289. https://doi.org/10.1016/j.tate.2009.03.010.

Nguyen, H. T. M. (2010). *Peer mentoring: Practicum practices of pre-service EFL teachers in Vietnam.* (Unpublished doctoral dessertation), The University of Queensland, Brisbane.

Nguyen, M. H. (2014). Preservice EAL teaching as emotional experiences: Practicum experience in an Australian secondary school. *Australian Journal of Teacher Education, 39*(8), 4. https://doi.org/10.14221/ajte.2014v39n8.5.

Nguyen, M. H. (2017). Negotiating contradictions in developing teacher identity during the EAL practicum in Australia. *Asia-Pacific Journal of Teacher Education, 45*(4), 399–415. https://doi.org/10.1080/1359866X.2017.1295132.

Nguyen, M. H. (2019). *English language teacher education: A sociocultural perspective on preservice teachers' learning in the professional experience.* Singapore: Springer Nature. https://doi.org/10.1007/978-981-13-9761-5.

Pham, T. (2016). Student-centredness: Exploring the culturally appropriate pedagogical space in Vietnamese higher education classrooms using activity theory. *Australian Journal of Teacher Education, 41*(1), 1–21.

Pridham, B. A., Deed, C., & Cox, P. (2013). Workplace-based practicum: Enabling expansive practices. *Australian Journal of Teacher Education, 38*(4), n4. https://doi.org/10.14221/ajte.2013v38n4.7.

Tang, E. L.-Y., Lee, J. C.-K., & Chun, C. K.-W. (2012). Development of teaching beliefs and the focus of change in the process of pre-service ESL teacher education. *Australian Journal of Teacher Education, 37*(5), 90–107. https://doi.org/10.14221/ajte.2012v37n5.8.

Trent, J. (2013). From learner to teacher: Practice, language, and identity in a teaching practicum. *Asia-Pacific Journal of Teacher Education, 41*(4), 426–440. https://doi.org/10.1080/1359866X.2013.838621.

Tsui, A., & Wong, L. J. (2009). In search of a third space: Teacher development in mainland China. In K. K. Chan & N. Rao (Eds.), *Revisiting the Chinese learner: Changing contexts, changing education* (pp. 281–313). Dordrecht: Springer.

Verloop, N., Van Driel, J., & Meijer, P. (2001). Teacher knowledge and the knowledge base of teaching. *International Journal of Educational Research, 35*(5), 441–461. https://doi.org/10.1016/S0883-0355(02)00003-4.

Vygotsky, L. S. (1978). *Mind in society: The development of higher psychological processes.* Masachusetts: Harvard University Press.

Wallace, C. S., & Priestley, M. (2011). Teacher beliefs and the mediation of curriculum innovation in Scotland: A sociocultural perspective on professional development and change. *Journal of Curriculum Studies, 43*(3), 357–381. https://doi.org/10.1080/00220272.2011.563447.

Yuan, R., & Lee, I. (2014). Pre-service teachers' changing beliefs in the teaching practicum: Three cases in an EFL context. *System, 44*, 1–12. https://doi.org/10.1016/j.system.2014.02.002.

Chapter 8
Rethinking Pedagogy for Heritage Language Maintenance in Early Childhood Settings: The Power of Play

Ranran Liu

Abstract The chapter is a reflective discussion of an educator who has made efforts to incorporate heritage language practice in child play in the real-world everyday setting of early childhood education. This combination between heritage language and child play has hardly been explored before in the relevant discourse. As children in Australia possess diverse cultural and linguistic backgrounds, their heritage language (HL) should be cherished as a way of respect for their cultural diversity and identity. Despite this, as much of the current discourse indicates, many children risk losing their HL especially when they study in the mainstream English-spoken education context. This issue deserves scholarly attention from the early childhood level. Although a large body of literature has investigated this area, most of it tends to focus on family settings or school–family collaboration, with much less devoted to the early childhood context as relating to educators' pedagogy or from an educator's perspective. In response to this gap in the field, the chapter explores the author's reflective experiences, as an early childhood educator, with how she has learned to foster children's heritage language practice.

Keywords Heritage language (HL) · Play · Educator · Early childhood education

8.1 Introduction

A recent research census has provided highpoints for rich cultural and linguistic diversity in Australia. According to ABS (2017), Australians come from 200 counties and speak over 300 different languages at home. However, a study by Oriyama (2012) showed that it is fairly common for immigrant families to lose out on their heritage language (HL), especially among young children who are studying in the mainstream English-spoken educational settings. Thus, HL

R. Liu (✉)
Western Sydney University, Sydney, Australia

© Springer Nature Singapore Pte Ltd. 2021
D. Bao, T. Pham (eds.), *Transforming Pedagogies Through Engagement with Learners, Teachers and Communities*, Education in the Asia-Pacific Region: Issues, Concerns and Prospects 57, https://doi.org/10.1007/978-981-16-0057-9_8

maintenance as a rising issue has drawn increased attention not only from immigrant parents but also from the community and the nation. Nevertheless, while many scholars (Budiyana, 2017; Hu, Torr, & Whiteman, 2014; Li, 2012) have researched on how parents support children's HL learning in the home environment, not much has been explored regarding how support could happen in school contexts. Moreover, when it comes to maintaining HL, this topic has hardly been investigated in early childhood settings, especially with reference to child play. Since play-based pedagogy has been widely utilised in the Australian early childhood context, it is important not to neglect the power of play. In a word, this chapter argues for the need to experiment with the idea of connecting play with the preservation of HL.

Arguably, bilingual children in Australia enjoy a unique advantage in their cognitive, linguistic, cultural, and educational development. As thoughtfully highlighted in the current discourse, children of bilingual communication facilities tend to surpass monolingual children in many cognitive processing skills (Qi, 2011). The first language often brings benefits to second language development rather than impedes it. For example, scholars have maintained that early oral language competence in the heritage language can facilitate later reading efficiency in English (Bialystok & Martin, 2004).

The significant impact of early childhood education on children's HL has been acknowledged by scholars and researchers. As a large body of research signifies, early childhood education experiences often contribute to the development of children's literacy and language skills in their heritage language (Tagoilelagi-LeotaGlynn, McNaughton, MacDonald, & Farry, 2005). This is a necessity because, as shown by Oriyama's (2012) study, it is common among immigrant families to lose out on their heritage language (HL), especially among young children who will need to catch up with the mainstream English-spoken educational settings. Based on the above understanding of the discourse as well as my own experience as an educator, I have come up with this question that lays the foundation for my research pursuit: In what ways can I, as an early childhood educator, foster children's heritage language?

8.2 Discourse on the Topic

8.2.1 Heritage Language in Early Childhood Settings

Children's diverse cultural background and the need for first language development have been recognised in early childhood settings. The necessity of encouraging and supporting children's HL has been written down in the national Early Years Learning Framework. According to DEEWR (2009), children feel a sense of belonging when their language and communication styles are respected.

However, the role of formal educational institutions in HL development has been neglected, and minimal literature has touched on pedagogical teaching and learning of HL in early childhood educational settings. Although the role of educators in promoting HL is essential, most scholars when dealing with HL development tend to restrict such responsibility within the home. In particular, many narrowly argue that since HL is primarily spoken and acquired at home, it is parents who should take critical responsibility to children's language learning (Li, 2012; Park & Sarkar, 2007). Surprisingly, research on multilingual children's experience reflects this narrow understanding of who should take this role. For example, in a study by Melo-Pfeifer (2015), the researcher who gathered drawings from children with a migrant background about their language biography again indicates that home is the ideal place for HL development. In these pictures, school is not shown as an optimal place for them to learn HL.

8.2.2   The Role of Child Play in Heritage Language Learning

Play-based learning has been widely implemented in Australian early childhood education. With regard to the use of this approach in enhancing children's heritage language, a study by Charalambous and Yerosimou (2015) points out that drama, owing to its playful nature, creates an effective space for children to practice language safely through which the level of self-confidence and attitude toward language learning has been raised. Due to the drama project they employed, the children involved became keener to speak their HL language at home and enjoyed learning the language even when making mistakes. Not only did the children activated HL use in school, but they also continue to cherish it further in their family setting.

As far as the value of child play is concerned, a large body of literature generally highlights the role of play in language learning rather than dealing specifically with the relationship between play and HL itself. For example, scholars such as Björk-Willén (2007), Björk-Willén and Cromdal (2009), and Cromdal (2001) all emphasise the benefits of peer play in children's language development in general without any specific reference to the child's mother tongue. One incident described by Björk-Willén and Cromdal (2009) is about two 4-year-old children role-playing teacher and student. Child A who acted as 'teacher' picked a paper animal and asked 'what is this?' and child B who acted as 'student' needed to answer the question. Then the activity is repeated by child A picking another animal. Through such interaction, the two children were provided with multiple opportunities to practice their pronunciation. These role-play can be seen as peer tutoring activities, which benefits both children as tutor and tutee. One the one hand, children's learning motivation would be enhanced by acting as the role of teachers. If a child acts like a teacher, he/she would take on the teacher's characteristics, including status, authority, self-perception, and attitudes, which then affects achievement (Nevi, 1983). On the other hand, Slavin (1996) states that when children explain things to each other, they can relate the concepts in their minds to other knowledge that they know, which makes new cognitive connections, and hence enhances memory and learning.

8.2.3   Educators' Role in Play and Its Effect on Children's HL Development

As discussed above, the importance of play in children's HL development has been identified and emphasised. We also know that in early childhood education, play is a professional tool utilised by educators to engage children in activities as a way of working towards certain curricular goals, and in that process, educators play a crucial role in managing how children get involved in these play activities. Taken together, there is a great deal of potential for educators' role to play in children's HL improvement, especially through play experience.

To make that possible, educators need to develop an acute awareness of play as an important tool in HL development. Teachers' beliefs, along with professional identity, influence their practices and greatly impact student's perceptions as well (Kagan & Dillon, 2009; Wu, Palmer, & Field, 2011). However, due to educators' various cultural backgrounds, the levels of commitment towards how much play can motivate learning might differ. For example, research by Kagan and Dillon (2009) argue that influenced by Confucian philosophy, some Chinese teachers who believe in the transmission of knowledge expect their students to be attentive listeners. Whether this view is reliable or not, some educators might believe more or less in the value of play than others. Arguably, the more convinced an educator feels about the positive impact of play, the more likely they will put the effort into making play a worthwhile experience for children, and vice versa. In other words, educators' performance and awareness do play a role in the quality of children's learning experience.

To take this argument further, educators' guidance is needed to produce a positive impact on children's language development through play experience as having been acknowledged. Although in joint play, adults' instructions have effective functions in children's language development (Li, 2012), the discourse on specific instructions for educators to help children's HL improvement is currently unavailable. In real practice settings, due to children's multiplicity linguistic backgrounds, educators struggle to meet every students' language needs (Kagan & Dillon, 2009) and thus can hardly help everyone to develop HL. To resolve this issue requires specific and thoughtful measures, which we presently do not have. More research and experiment, therefore, should be conducted to address this situation. In the meanwhile, there is a need to impart the value of keeping HL and the fact that bilingualism is an important linguistic accomplishment. Although it is hard to provide specific educational classrooms for all HL learners, promoting children's HL can still be achieved by educators' differentiated instructions in play activities, which, according to Kagan and Dillon (2009), would allow learners to progress at their own pace towards higher levels of proficiency.

8.2.4 The Role of Play in Building a Trustful Relationship and Language Practice

The discourse has highlighted the significant role of the teacher–child relationship in influencing children's social and emotional development. As Parlakian and Seibel (2002) note: 'through a relationship with important adults in their lives, children develop mental health, or social-emotional wellness, which includes that ability to form satisfying connections with others, play, communicate, learn and experience the full spectrum of human emotions' (p.1).

With regard to people from different cultural backgrounds, individuals from the same home countries tend to form trustful relationships easily as they share similar cultural norms and feelings. The mothers in a study conducted by Kim (2011) believed that a mainstream educational setting could not offer social and emotional support for their children. They had to seek support from their cultural community. However, the barriers among people from different backgrounds, especially between educators and children, could be broke through shared play experience. When teachers as co-player participate in children's play, they model roles and provide ideas to enhance play and support children's growth (Jones & Reynolds, 1992). In play activities, teachers as mediators support children's interactions and language practice. These aspects of trust, later on, became useful in the scenarios which I have experienced in my professional practice, especially exhibited through my opportunity in building the bond with children during playtime. The complexity of such bonding was demonstrated not only in behaviour but also in talk.

8.2.5 Methodology

I conducted a self-reflective project using a qualitative self-study approach to form the case. Based on my own professional experience, the study did not involve the recruitment of research participants for it. Instead, data for the study was drawn from the researcher's reflective working diary from a specific early childhood centre that has been recorded outside of working time and space. The case was constructed from self-reflection on my practice as an early childhood educator who attempted to seek ways of fostering every child's HL from various cultural backgrounds, which will be discussed in connection with child play.

I have been working in a special bilingual early childhood centre for 1 year, where all the children and educators possess a bilingual cultural background. This is a distinctive feature of the centre, which is different from my previous working experience in native English-spoken children-dominated centres. With this understanding in mind, I would like to use my personal working dairy which recorded my experience and reflection in this specific context. As well acknowledged in the relevant discourse, it is important that teachers critically reflect on their practice and strive to make sense of their teaching and participate consciously and creatively in their growth and development (Zeichner, 1999). The bilingual early childhood centre is located in the Southern suburb of Melbourne, established by an experienced kindergarten teacher originally from Korea. It employs educators mostly from the same cultural background to accommodate Korean immigrant families who wish to improve their children's bilingual ability. Besides, it is noticed that the Chinese community is the largest constitution in the district. As part of such a residential populace in this area, children of Chinese background make up the second major group of attendees. In addition to these two groups, children of other cultural backgrounds who attend this centre are relatively diverse, including Indian, Japanese, and South Arabian.

The philosophy of the centre is to encourage children to speak the language they feel most comfortable with, either home language or English. Influenced by this, educators of diverse cultural and linguistic backgrounds are recruited to meet children's various needs. Being a member of this very community has motivated me, as a bilingual educator, to innovate ways of helping children better their bilingualism in a play-based setting.

8.2.6   Presentation of Data from Work Journal

8.2.6.1   Learning from the Child

My data shows that learning from children can be a powerful way of motivating their heritage language. The majority of children at the early childhood centre came from a Korean background; some of them spoke limited English. At the beginning of my working journey in this centre, as an educator who does not speak their language, I felt anxious about how to communicate and build relationships with the children. To reduce my anxiety and ensure a positive approach to children learning, I made a conscious effort to involve myself in drama play, which is a common activity employed at the centre. It was through drama play that I could utilise different forms of expression to communicate with children, including gestures, facial expressions, and body movement. In one of those scenarios, we performed roles during a 'café shop' activity in the kitchen corner. I would act as a customer who made an order, then the children 'cooked' and served me at a small table. In our world, the game can be flexible and creative: even when I ordered a pizza, they might serve me a cup of coffee instead. But that did not matter because the essence of such experience, in my understanding, is about building a positive relationship and bonding through play. I shall now demonstrate this awareness in the next accounts of play incidents.

One day, during play, I asked a girl, Anna (pseudonym), how to say 'how much' in Korean, which is her HL. I then repeated the words in Korean after her. In response, she approved with a nod and a big smile. Inspired by this incident, I gained confidence in asking her to teach me more words in her HL. As my interest in Korean was shown, Anna began to feel comfortable in teaching me additional

Korean words and expect me to mimic them. Interestingly, this social interaction is not without emotion. For example, at times she even made fun of my pronunciation if I made a silly mistake. In this way, our relationship seemed to become closer to those playing and imitation moments.

This helped me to realise that I could apply this method to other children who come from a different cultural background to provide a chance for a minor group of children to practice their HL language in this centre as well. I was very happy to discover a new pedagogical approach as a way of motivating every child to practice their HL in a formal early childhood setting. As I engaged in this practice in my work, I would keep a record of and reflect on interactions that had happened each day in my private diary.

On another occasion, I asked a girl who speaks Japanese at home to teach me some Japanese words as arising from the drama we were performing together. She was always happy to teach me her HL words. Over time, the girl became more comfortable in teaching me more. Even when I didn't ask, sometimes she would initiatively tell me 'this is...in Japanese' with a big smile on her face. One time, I asked her 'how to say biscuit in Japanese'. She replied with 'biscuit', which left me wondering why she repeated the English word and whether she understood my question. Later on, I learned from her mother that 'biscuit' in Japanese is the same as in English. Reflecting on this incident, I realised that it may not matter how accurate the language exchange is; instead what seems to count more would be the opportunity for children to practice their HL in a safe, trustful environment.

Encouraged by the above positive incidents, I continued to engage in play activities with other children. I decided to stretch my experience by applying the same method to children with different linguistic backgrounds. As it turned out, most of them enjoyed teaching me their HL, and thus, the frequency of speaking HL with me has increased dramatically.

8.2.6.2   A Barrier to Language Maintenance

As the data show, learning language from the child is not always easy but, in many cases, might experience complexity. I would like to demonstrate how the boundary between the child's mother tongue and English can become a barrier to fostering children's heritage language maintenance, which was what I recorded as critical incidents in my diary. By this boundary, I mean that sometimes the child makes a distinction in language roles, such as the mother tongue is to be used with family members, while English is used with outsiders of the family. On one occasion, when I was playing with Roy (pseudonym), a Saudi Arabian boy, and I asked him to tell me some words in his HL. However, he deniably said 'I don't know', though I was aware of his HL fluency.

With curiosity and desire for learning, I went through my diary entries to hopefully find out the reasons why my teaching strategy did not seem to work as I expected. I noticed that the same method employed with different children has produced different responses. Over some time, I discovered that an influential factor would be how much the child has his/her HL speaking peers in the same social environment. As evident, Anna, the Korean girl, was surrounded by Korean speaking friends, thus for her, it is natural to use HL with both peers and educators; while Roy, the Arabian boy, was the only child of his background at the centre so he felt less comfortable in sharing his HL.

For some time, I would have thought this is a consistent factor that works well in explaining the degree of HL openness in every child. However, upon studying various incidents again, it struck me that the Japanese girl was the only child of her background at the centre without any other Japanese-speaking peers. Yet, unlike Roy, she was more willing to share her HL with me. This kept me wondering what other elements must have come into play in the process of engagement with child play. I was then driven to think further about other potential social, cultural factors. I asked myself: What else would help consolidate the bond with children and help them open up to me more?

I then revisited my reflection and examine the same event, especially my involvement with Roy. I noticed that one time, I made a second attempt to learn HL from Roy and encouraged him: 'you are my teacher now! I want to learn from you!' However, he continued to refuse me, this time explaining that he would speak his HL with daddy only. Although I continued to fail in learning his HL, I was given a clue about why this is happening. Roy's response showed me how children might set a cultural boundary due to the lack of shared language. This seems to be a case of language-culture dynamic where we can note how the language barrier might affect cultural behaviour.

This incident raises another question in my thinking: I wonder if it would be the case that most children would set a language boundary due to the language alone. There might be other factors such as appearance, manner, and gestures, all of which are hard to be separated within the same communication setting. Although I can witness most of these constructs, I might not be able to jump to a conclusion at this point by explicitly identifying and providing all relevant pieces of evidence. However, as a researcher, I feel that I have the responsibility to consider the dynamic of language and culture in the same scenario. It is hard to single out one factor, such as peer background, and employ it as the only way to understand how HL is shared.

8.2.6.3 Play as a Space for Crossing Language Boundary

When I was pursuing my master's degree at Monash University, I had the opportunity to study many national documents including the Early Years Learning Framework and National Quality Standard. These documents helped me become aware of how important they are as guidance for my practice. Every time I was lost in teaching, I would refer to the documents for advice. According to the Australian Children's Education and Care Quality Authority (2018), children could develop a sense of security, well-being, and belonging from a responsive and meaningful relationship. Challenged by the language barrier, I struggled to create an interactive bonding with children and made effort to bridge the language gap by involving myself in their play. We shared the same imaginative situation where we created our ways of communicating and crossing each other's language boundaries. On such occasions, I noticed children sometimes subconsciously speak their HL to me as they naturally grew less aware of our communication obstacle. It is such play that magically allowed me to build a 'language free' environment. In the process of playing, whenever I showed a high amount of interest in children's HL and attempted to learn, I realised children would respond to me more openly and with less hesitation.

Such moments were encouraging as they convinced me that bonding can be developed through a combination of, or an alternation between, language and play. I then made further efforts in putting this understanding into practice. For instance, instead of approaching a child and directly asking him/her to teach me some words of their HL, I utilised the approach in a play context as children felt more comfortable, and their learning is easily inspired during play.

I would like to elaborate further on Roy's case and try to understand how play as space can negotiate language differences. Since Roy and I shared one common language, which is English, we had no trouble understanding each other. This scenario did not provide the opportunity for us to resort to the use of his HL. As discussed before, Roy had never had a chance to practice HL in the centre, which somehow shaped his perception of the difference between 'home (heritage) language' and 'mainstream society language'. For him, Arabian is a language to be used with family members, whereas English is more of the social tool among educators and peers.

Arguably, it is through constructing further positive play experience with Roy that the boundary was becoming blurred and the distance between us was becoming closer. At first, when I showed interest in his HL, he was not responsive. However, when I made more effort in finding his interest, based on which I found more opportunities to be involved in his play. After I warmed up with him a few times, he became more open to me. I applied my method and encouraged him to teach me some words in his HL again. Although he still did not respond to my request, he told me the reason that he felt uncomfortable speaking HL with me instead of moving away or being reserved. So far, I had not gained his complete trust and had not found myself the opportunity to learn HL from him yet. However, I develop the positive feeling that he would remove the boundary for me one day after more frequency of shared play and will treat me as an insider. This would be the case if I continue to show that not only his family but educators in the centre also value his HL.

By way of concluding, learning from children, language boundary, and play are major areas that shape my understanding of how HL is nurtured and shared through my engagement in play with the child. It is important to be aware of how those factors contribute to the complex dynamic of language, culture, and bonding through play.

8.2.7 Main Discussion

8.2.7.1 Child Roleplay as a 'Teacher'

This section proposes a pedagogical approach to foster children's HL practice. In the current discourse, the significant role of educators in children's heritage language development cannot be more emphasised. According to DEEWR (2009), early childhood professionals need to provide opportunities for children to practice either first language or additional language. However, practical pedagogies that can be applied in real early childhood settings for educators have not been discussed. Most scholars focused on strategies that can be used at home for parents to foster children's HL (Li, 2012; Park & Sarkar, 2007). In addressing this gap, I have sought a relevant pedagogical approach to motivate children's HL practice through my experiences

The approach contributes to early childhood educators' awareness in showing respect to language diversity. It also opens more opportunities for children to practice their HL in early childhood settings. In applying this approach, educators might wish to involve themselves in children's play, whereby children could be encouraged to share their HL use with educators. Among the few articles that discussed teachers' dual role, one bilingual research study conducted by Dubiner, Deeb, and Schwartz (2018) has touched on how adults as a model of linguistic behaviour could learn from children. In this research, a teacher named Yoav asked L1-Arabic-speaking children to correct his pronunciation or to translate from Hebrew into Arabic. The teacher's double role as a teacher and a learner allows children to realise the 'lack of knowledge as a natural corollary of language acquisition processes' (p. 246). While the study by Dubiner et al. (2018) encourages children's language practice as *co-learners*, my study discovers children as *role-players*, whereby the children and I performed role reversal by children acting as teachers to show me their HL. Their learning interest was stimulated by the fact that they initiatively *taught* me their HL even without being asked. In addition, in the process of showing me their HL, they could connect two languages that conveyed the same meaning and which gave them an opportunity to practice both languages at the same time. Meanwhile, children like to correct my pronunciation every time I repeated after them. It is through this process that they are able to reinforce the language.

I would like to recommend that future researchers extend such practice by considering the need to build a partnership with the family in applying the above-mentioned approach. Families, who are a crucial influence on children's learning, would be able to provide valuable information about their children's strengths, ability, interests, and challenges (DEEWR, 2009). Such support can help educators to build knowledge of what and how much the children have learned their HL before using the approach. Additionally, most immigrant parents hold positive attitudes towards their children's HL maintenance since a high level of proficiency in HL would help foster cultural identity, ensure a wider future economic prospect, and equip them with more opportunities to communicate with their grandparents (Park & Sarkar, 2007). Having said this, I have learned from parents that in actual practice, some children mainly speak English at home, and thus their HL is not well developed. This situation makes it less possible for educators to utilise the approach. To address this dilemma, I would like to propose well-managed cooperation with parents to share responsibility in HL maintenance. If parents become more aware of the need to help children learn their HL at home first, educators can get informed of what children have practiced at home and help them reinforce that through the approach under discussion.

8.2.7.2 Bonding with Children as Pedagogy

I would like to stress the importance of building a trustful relationship with children for supporting their HL practice. At the beginning of my working journey, I had decided to work on a relationship with children before focusing on improving their other skills and development. According to Pianta (1999), the teacher-child relationship has been recognised as an important contributor to children's achievement. A positive relationship between teachers and children would produce a great impact on children's higher levels of academic competence (Pianta & Nimetz, 1991). This awareness resonates Vygotsky's sociocultural theory, which emphasises the great influence of the social environment in children's development. My bonding with children at the centre has paved the way for children's willingness to teach me their HL. In this situation, as an educator, I have provided more opportunities for children to use their HL with me. Even though sometimes they made fun of my pronunciation and laughed at me, their language learning enthusiasm had been increased dramatically.

The discourse has highlighted how adults' instructions produce a positive impact on children's language development (Li, 2012). However, this could not be achieved without an encouraging relationship. As discussed in the second finding, children tend to set language boundaries against educators who fail to build security and trust. To achieve such a foundation, adults' engagement with children would help them develop a sense of belonging, cultural understandings, as well as language and communication skills (O'Connor & McCartney, 2007). My experience is a case in point where my effort to build a safe environment and trust with Anna and Roy has laid a foundation for the children to open up to me and teach me their HL's.

Nurturing a positive relationship with children is a good start for encouraging their HL. Roy's case provides useful insights into how educators can work with children of less dominant background in various early childhood centres in Australia. Since many centres are dominated by English-speaking children, children of other linguistic backgrounds as minor groups have few opportunities to speak their HL and they might feel less comfortable speaking HL. Through this project, I have learned that educators can improve the engagement with the child through building a relationship in play and providing opportunities for HL practice. According to DEEWR (2009), children who experienced positive relationships are able to construct a positive image of themselves and behave as secure, significant, respected individuals.

8.2.7.3 The Power of Play in HL Pedagogy

As a post-graduate who undertook professional education and practice in the Australian context, I believe in the power of play in educators' teaching and children's learning. Teachers' beliefs produce a great impact on teaching practices (Kagan & Dillon, 2009; Wu et al., 2011). When I confronted challenges to teaching and building a relationship with children, I sought solutions by involving myself in children's play. During this process, I accumulated knowledge about children's personalities, interests, and needs, all of which equipped me with more appropriate teaching pedagogy. According to DEEWR (2009), integrating learning and play involves active engagement with children, sustained shared conversations, and intentional teaching. This ideology could be implemented in drama play where children and I actively interacted with each other, sustained conversation, and shared the same imaginative world. In my working experience, a positive bonding with children has been built through frequent drama play.

The importance of play could not be more emphasised. Play represents space for crossing boundaries in both language and culture with the child. It is through such space dynamic that the pressure caused by the language barrier is removed for children to freely express themselves in a safe environment. My finding consolidates an insight by Charalambous and Yerosimou (2015) who emphasise the role of drama in supporting freedom of expression in the child. When children threw themselves into play, a more engaging language environment is created. In play, the need for collaborative social interaction with others provides the chance to use language in thought processes as well as demonstrate linguistic knowledge and skills (Li, 2013).

On an additional note, educators need to develop knowledge about the dynamic of play, so that they can provide well-contextualised instruction to enhance children's HL learning. 'Guided play and learning occur when adults are involved in children's play and learning, following children's interests and responding to spontaneous learning opportunities as they arise' (DEEWR, 2009, p. 13). In play, educators could experiment with my recommended pedagogical approach for fostering children's HL practice.

8.3   Conclusion

In this chapter, I have employed field notes and reflect on my experiences to bring out the process of how HL is fostered through the combination of linguistic and social factors, which are represented by language and play put together. In the heart of the discussion, I have discovered the important significance of trust-building in a complex process that requires constant engagement and positive effort in bonding with the child. Such a process also involves the understanding of language cultural dynamics. For instance, the fact that I valued children's HL and insist upon learning it has convinced children that it is safe to share the language with me. Such a response from the child also eases out the cultural and linguistic differences between us.

I also discovered that the rule of HL sharing in many cases is contingent upon the distance felt by the child towards the educator. The shorter the distance, the more open the child tends to be, and vice versa. Sometimes the cultural distance maybe wide, it can be shortened through social relationships. As Cummins (1984) maintains, children have a strong need to belong to a group, and when they feel that friends, teachers, and the wider society around them do not accept their language and culture, they will try to hide it.

According to Berry and Forgasz (2018), self-study researchers' insights and understanding could be taken up and transformed by others through making pubic their story. As demonstrated through the project, HL sharing practices require a complex process of playful engagement and thoughtful effort. In my diary entries, especially during the early days of my professional experience at this centre, I found a similar response from the Korean children: they communicated with me with less openness and hardly spoke to me in their HL. It was because I was new to the centre and I could neither understand them nor say any Korean words. Such awareness together with my experience with the Saudi-Arabian boy suggests that the distance between children and me seems to represent a range of factors including the language barrier, familiarity, cultural difference, my ability to connect with children, my engagement with the child, and his/her sense of belonging that I could help develop.

The above experiences with all their challenges have guided me in understanding and unpacking the complex significance of the boundary between the child and the educator. What troubled my thinking as an educator, to begin with, had been my inability to see the bonding process and all its influential factors. Over time and with experience, I gradually was able to detect and identify the above factors. I became acutely aware that if a child wishes to communicate his/her need to the educator, it is perhaps natural and understandable that their first port of call will be someone who can understand and care about them and, ideally, is willing to speak their HL. All of these aspects of my experience with the child, in my view, has helped me identify the nature of my relationship with children and showed me the importance of nurturing that process. Arguably, in these scenarios, the nature of how language and culture come into play exhibits a complex nature that can only be understood through both experiences and the effort to reflect on them.

As an early childhood educator, I have explored ways to engage with children's HL in play contexts, which has allowed me to propose a pedagogical approach characterised by a responsive relationship with children. The strength of this approach is that it provides additional opportunities for children to practice their HL in a formal early childhood setting, that is, by incorporating HL roleplay through child play. The purpose of such practice is not simply for proficiency or competence, because, in my case, many children have already developed proficient HL skills.

Instead, it takes on the significance of respecting children's rights and cultural heritage in their everyday educational context outside of family life. In other words, the proposed pedagogy allows the educator to share responsibility with parents in HL maintenance, which at the moment is an underexplored theme in early childhood education. As I explored and analysed my experience, I can see through myself that educators have the power to foster all children's HL speaking despite language barrier. It is, additionally, important to realise that there are still minor groups of children who never seem to have the opportunity to use their HL in the centre, which represents another exciting area for research.

References

Australian Bureau of Statistics. (2017). *Clayton south (state suburb)*. Retrieved from http://quickstats.censusdata.abs.gov.au/census_services/getproduct/census/2016/quickstat/SSC20567

Australian Children's Education and Care Quality Authority. (2018). *National quality framework*. Retrieved from https://www.acecqa.gov.au

Berry, A., & Forgasz, R. (2018). Disseminating secret-story-knowledge through the self-study of teacher education practices. *Studying Teacher Education, 14*(3), 235–245.

Bialystok, E., & Martin, M. M. (2004). Attention and inhibition in bilingual children: Evidence from the dimensional change card sort task. *Developmental Science, 7*, 325–339.

Björk-Willén, P. (2007). Participation in multilingual preschool play: Shadowing and crossing as interactional resources. *Journal of Pragmatics, 39*(12), 2133–2158.

Björk-Willén, P., & Cromdal, J. (2009). When education seeps into 'free play': How preschool children accomplish multilingual education. *Journal of Pragmatics, 41*(8), 1493–1518.

Budiyana, Y. E. (2017). Students' parents' attitudes toward Chinese heritage language maintenance. *Theory and Practice in Language Studies, 7*(3), 195–200.

Charalambous, C., & Yerosimou, M. (2015). Drama, music and media in heritage language learning. *Journal of Education Culture and Society, 2*, 370–381.

Cromdal, J. (2001). Can I be with?: Negotiating play entry in a bilingual school. *Journal of Pragmatics, 33*(4), 515–543.

Cummins, J. (1984). *Bilingualism and special education: Issues in assessment and pedagogy* (Vol. 6). Milton Park: Taylor & Francis Group.

Department of Education, Employment and Workplace Relation. (2009). *Belonging, being & becoming: The early years learning framework for Australia*. Retrieved from https://docs.education.gov.au/system/files/doc/other/belonging_being_and_becoming_the_early_years_learning_framework_for_australia.pdf

Dubiner, D., Deeb, I., & Schwartz, M. (2018). 'We are creating a reality': Teacher agency in early bilingual education. *Language, Culture and Curriculum, 31*(3), 255–271.

Hu, J., Torr, J., & Whiteman, P. (2014). Australian Chinese parents' language attitudes and practices relating to their children's bilingual development prior to school. *Journal of Early Childhood Research, 12*(2), 139–153.

Kagan, O., & Dillon, K. (2009). The professional development of teachers of heritage language learners: A matrix. *Bridging Contexts, Making Connections* (pp. 155–175).

Jones, E., & Reynolds, G. (1992). *The play's the thing: Teachers' roles in children's play*. Teachers College Press.

Kim, J. (2011). Korean immigrant mothers' perspectives: The meanings of a Korean heritage language school for their children's American early schooling experiences. *Early Childhood Education Journal, 39*(2), 133–141.

Li, L. (2012). How do immigrant parents support preschoolers' bilingual heritage language development in a role-play context? *Australasian Journal of Early Childhood, 37*(1), 142.

Li, L. (2013). Children's collective imagination in play: A preschooler's bilingual heritage language development. In *Children's play and development* (pp. 107–126). Dordrecht: Springer.

Melo-Pfeifer, S. (2015). Multilingual awareness and heritage language education: children's multimodal representations of their multilingualism. *Language Awareness, 24*(3), 197–215.

Nevi, C. N. (1983). Cross-age tutoring: Why does it help tutors? *The Reading Teacher, 36*(9), 892–898.

O'Connor, E., & McCartney, K. (2007). Examining teacher–child relationships and achievement as part of an ecological model of development. *American Educational Research Journal, 44*(2), 340–369.

Oriyama, K. (2012). What role can community contact play in heritage language literacy development? Japanese–English bilingual children in Sydney. *Journal of Multilingual and Multicultural Development, 33*(2), 167–186.

Park, S. M., & Sarkar, M. (2007). Parents' attitudes toward heritage language maintenance for their children and their efforts to help their children maintain the heritage language: A case study of Korean-Canadian immigrants. *Language, Culture and Curriculum, 20*(3), 223–235.

Parlakian, R., & Seibel, N. (2002). *Building strong foundations: Practical guidance for promoting the social emotional development of infants and toddlers.* Washington, DC: Zero to Three.

Pianta, R. C. (1999). *Enhancing relationships: Between children and teachers.* Washington, DC: American Psychological Association.

Pianta, R. C., & Nimetz, S. (1991). Relationships between children and teachers: Associations with classroom and home behaviour. *Journal of Applied Developmental Psychology, 12*, 379–393.

Qi, R. (2011). The bilingual acquisition of English and Mandarin: Chinese children in Australia. New York: Cambria Press.

Slavin, R. E. (1996). Research on cooperative learning and achievement: What we know, what we need to know. *Contemporary Education Psychology, 21*, 43–69.

Tagoilelagi-LeotaGlynn, F. A., McNaughton, S., MacDonald, S., & Farry, S. (2005). Bilingual and biliteracy development over the transition to school. *International Journal of Bilingual Education and Bilingualism, 8*(5), 455–479.

Wu, H. P., Palmer, D. K., & Field, S. L. (2011). Understanding teachers' professional identity and beliefs in the Chinese heritage language school in the USA. *Language, Culture and Curriculum, 24*(1), 47–60.

Zeichner, K. (1999). The new scholarship in teacher education. *Educational Researcher, 28*(90), 4–15.

Chapter 9
Implementing Formative Assessment in Vietnamese Classrooms: Strategies to Navigate Cultural and Structural Obstacles

Thanh Pham and Lam H. Pham

Abstract Western-based pedagogical practices have become favourite pedagogies in Asian classrooms. However, the success of these Western-based pedagogies largely depends on how local teachers and students create transformed practices, so that they could navigate local cultural and structural barriers. This one-semester study aimed to uncover the complexities of the implementation process of formative assessment in a Vietnamese higher education classroom. The study used activity theory as the theoretical framework. Participants were a lecturer and 100 students of a class at a Vietnamese university. The results showed that there were various structural and cultural obstacles, especially existing rules and norms in Vietnamese classrooms, that hindered the implementation of formative assessment practices. However, the initiative was implemented successfully because the stakeholders involved in the implementation process knew how to cooperate and negotiate their roles effectively in a community.

Keywords Formative assessment · Vietnam · Asia · Pedagogies · Reform · Activity theory

9.1 Introduction

A large volume of research has reported positive effects of formative assessment on students' learning. For example, Etkina (2000) found that formative assessment helped students to reflect on their knowledge, to learn how to ask questions, and to

T. Pham
Monash University, Melbourne, Australia
e-mail: thanh.t.pham@monash.edu

L. H. Pham (✉)
Deakin University, Melbourne, Australia
e-mail: lam.pham@deakin.edu.au

© Springer Nature Singapore Pte Ltd. 2021   137
D. Bao, T. Pham (eds.), *Transforming Pedagogies Through Engagement with Learners, Teachers and Communities*, Education in the Asia-Pacific Region: Issues, Concerns and Prospects 57, https://doi.org/10.1007/978-981-16-0057-9_9

predict what questions their teacher is likely to ask. This study also found that formative assessment helped teachers identify difficulties their students experienced while learning new material, so that they could adjust their teaching to the students' needs and match the levels of difficulty of learning and testing. Carrillo-de-la-Peña, Baillès, Caseras, Àlvar Martínez, and Pérez (2009) reported that students who took part in formative assessment achieved higher marks in the final assessment than students who did not participate. Kay, Li, and Fekete (2007) and McDonald and Boud (2003) further revealed that formative assessment practices had a positive impact on students' performance and helped strengthen students' metacognitive skills, so that they became more aware of useful learning strategies—of learning how to learn. Recently, Weurlander, Söderberg, Scheja, Hult, and Wernerson (2012) found formative assessment motivated students to study, making them aware of what they had learned and where they needed to study more.

Formative assessment has a broad meaning, but Black, Harrison, Lee, Marshall, and Wiliam (2003) noted that there are three main aspects of formative assessment including oral and written feedback, peer assessment, and self-assessment. Self-evaluation is a common formative assessment practice that asks students to evaluate their own preparation and performance. Boud (1990, p. 109) argues that 'self-assessment is fundamental to all aspects of learning' because self-assessment provides the students with reflective skills and trains them to be able to evaluate their own merits and shortcomings and how to improve their weaknesses. Peer assessment requires students to provide verbal feedback to one another and then help them improve their test performance and skill performance (Topping, 1998). Finally, oral and written feedback is one of the main components of formative assessment because Price, Handley, and Millar (2011) claim feedback helps students reconstruct their ideas, avoid misconceptions, and expand their understanding.

During the last two decades, Asian governments have carried out what Sahlberg (2004) calls 'the Global Education Reform Movement'. Its purpose was to meet the demands of a globalised knowledge-based economy and to seek to improve their systems of education and maintain or improve their national performance in the Programme for International Student Assessment and other international comparisons of student achievement. Within two decades, Asian teachers and students have been bombarded by numerous reports that have called for a change in teaching and learning from the traditional teacher-centredness to student-centredness. Accordingly, formative assessment has become a favoured pedagogy in many Asian classrooms. For instance, the educational system in Indonesia has responded to the need of producing excellent graduates who are creative, confident, and able to compete in global competitions (Indonesian Higher Education Directorate, 2014). Therefore, the country strongly advocates for the deployment of pedagogical practices [like formative assessment] that could provide students with creative, independent, and confident skills (Tobias, Wales, Syamsulhakim, & Suharti, 2014). In China, the government has launched several reforms attributed to the requirement for a quality-oriented education model (Yan, 2015) in which students can develop a wide range of all-round abilities besides academic competence. These reforms focus on changing from the teacher-centred approach to a student-centred one and moving from 'assessment of learning' to 'assessment for learning' (Hu, 2013).

Sharing this trend, the Vietnamese government and Ministry of Education and Training have recently recognised that the conventional summative assessment that has mainly focused on the reproduction of factual and procedural knowledge is becoming ineffective to promote capacities and skills that are essential for success in today's diverse and data-driven globalised environments such as critical thinking, problem-solving, self-managed learning, and interpersonal and communicative skills (Duong, Nguyen, & Griffin, 2011; Moss, Girard, & Haniford, 2006). Therefore, local educators and policy-makers are calling for alternative formative assessment practices like portfolio, self-assessment, peer assessment, and weekly report (Duong et al., 2011). The quotation cited in 'Solutions for changing of teaching methodologies' (2004, p. 50), a conference proceedings issued by the Ministry of Education and Training of Vietnam, below shows how eagerly Vietnamese policymakers want to push the reform.

> . . . Changing methodologies is urgent. The urgency does not allow us to wait until all of the conditions are fulfilled. We have to do it right now!

Although formative assessment is desirable, various studies have found a wide range of barriers at both macro and micro levels that hindered the deployment of this practice in Asian classrooms. For example, formative assessment aims to improve both students' academic achievement as well as interpersonal skills like higher-order and critical thinking skills, in-depth conceptual understanding, real-world problem-solving abilities, and communication skills (Light & Cox, 2001). By contrast, assessment in Asian classrooms tends to use quantitative assessment to test textbook-based knowledge (Pham & Renshaw, 2015). Also, Asian children grow up with such Confucian teachings as 'To be modest', 'To learn self-efface', and 'Keep head down'. It is unacceptable and abnormal for Asian students to brag or stand out. Therefore, Asian students would find it culturally inappropriate when being asked to engage in self-assessment where they need to evaluate their performance. They are also very unlikely to support peer assessment practices because a large volume of literature has found that Asian students have a strong belief that teachers are the only ones who can give 'trustworthy' feedback and correct answers, thus peers' feedback and ideas are not highly evaluated (Yang, Badger, & Yu, 2006). Moreover, harmony is the essence of Confucian theories of social interaction (Chen, 2001). It is of paramount importance in Confucian culture to such a degree that it is viewed as the cardinal cultural value in Confucian societies (Chen & Starosta, 1997). In group work, Asian students tend to establish a harmonious relationship and try to avoid conflicts as much as they can. Therefore, Asian learners certainly do not want to assess their peers' work as a way to criticise peers' points of view.

Last but not least, for oral and written feedback and peer assessment to be implemented effectively, the class size needs to be small enough so that the teacher could monitor students' interactions and have sufficient time to give feedback. However, classes at Asian colleges are often large, certainly in comparison with many Western countries. For instance, Phuong-Mai (2008) claims that on average Vietnamese classes contain 50–70 students, in China 50–60, in Japan 45, and in

Korea 43. In such large classes, the teacher would not have enough time to examine and monitor each group to ensure they are working effectively.

Acknowledging these disparities, Brown, Kennedy, Fok, Chan, and Yu (2009) claim that bringing about change in assessment in Asian countries is not a simple technical issue of introducing different assessment tools, different timing of assessments or different feedback processes. Rather, it is a more fundamental issue concerned with deeply held cultural values. Reformers need to consider not only the rationale for reforming assessment practices but a range of cultural, institutional, and technical issues that will inevitably constrain or afford the effective change. Various researchers have found that teachers could only bring formative assessment into Asian classrooms if they are flexible and know how to work out transformed practices that are a combination of the initiatives and local heritages to make the reforms culturally and structurally appropriate to the local socio-cultural context (Hall & Burke, 2003; Pham & Renshaw, 2015). Researchers have argued that if reformers do not work on transformed practices, Western-based pedagogical practices cannot sustain in Asian classrooms (Pham, 2014; Pham & Renshaw, 2015).

As such, for formative assessment to be implemented successfully in Asian classrooms, there is a need for further research on how local teachers and students could develop transformed practices to navigate cultural and structural barriers. This chapter utilise activity theory as a theoretical framework to examine how Vietnamese teachers and students reacted to the requirements of genuine formative assessment principles and how they transformed formative assessment practices. Activity theory has been recognised as an effective tool that could enable researchers to examine disparities between various activity systems and how the implementers navigate disparities to bring about a successful reform (Pham & Renshaw, 2015).

9.2   Theoretical Framework: Activity Theory

Activity theory has evolved through three generations of research. The third-generation conceptualises multiple activity systems as its unit of analysis. Specifically, Engeström (1999) claims that when two activity systems which work with rules underpinned by different traditions and perspectives interact or are grafted onto each other, various contradictions and tensions are created in all six components of an activity system (as shown in Fig. 9.1). To deal with these contradictions and tensions, actors in the activity systems are required to understand multiple perspectives and develop solutions to solve the disparities between the two activity systems. Solutions in this situation often entail the generation of new hybrid activities or transformed practices that include elements from both activity systems (Konkola, 2001). Space where these hybrid and transformed practices are developed is called the 'third space' or a 'boundary zone', that, according to Engeström (1999), is characterised by alternative or competing discourses and points of view. Engeström also claims that the third space affords opportunities for the transformation of conflicts and tensions into rich zones of learning (Engeström, 2001).

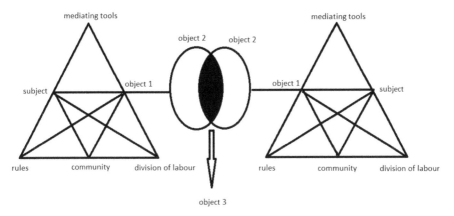

Fig. 9.1 Two interacting activity systems as a model for the third generation of activity theory (Engeström, 2001)

Engeström (2001) points out the following five principles that members in the activity systems need to take into consideration and go through if they want various systems to work with each other effectively.

1. Activity systems as the unit of analysis—the analysis needs to be interpreted in relation to other relevant activity systems to establish the background of the activity system.
2. The multi-voicedness of an activity—heterogeneous voices need to be heard as an activity will be different for each individual, revealing multiple layers and perspectives.
3. Historicity of an activity system—an activity system 'takes shape and gets transformed' over time with the analysis uncovering its history.
4. Contradictions as driving forces of change in activity—clashes between 'opposite starting points' not only can generate conflict but also reveal opportunities for change.
5. Expansive transformation in activity systems—new understandings of an activity arise from participants addressing contractions and questioning their actions, leading to new possibilities.

The present study examined how these five principles were applied in Vietnamese classrooms and how the application of these five principles enabled Vietnamese teachers and students to develop transformed formative assessment practices that could work with the local teaching and learning culture effectively.

The present research was guided by two questions:

1. What were the perceptions of Vietnamese teachers and students towards formative assessment?
2. What were transformed formative assessment practices that were developed to engage Vietnamese teachers and students in formative assessment?

9.3 Methodology

9.3.1 Participants

Participants were 1 teacher and 100 students taught by the teacher at a Vietnamese university. There was also a practitioner teacher who attended the class to observe and learn teaching experience. This practitioner teacher was the participating teacher's former student and she was about to start her teaching job in the following semester. The participating teacher volunteered to participate in the research because she would like to update her teaching practices. This has been a strong requirement at Vietnamese universities during the last decade.

9.3.2 Procedures

To achieve the aforementioned goal, mediating artefacts employed consisted of a range of tools, both formal and informal, including: (1) the questioning formulation strategy that required the students to form as many questions as they could after each reading; (2) self-assessment that required the students to evaluate their performance after each weekly assessment; (3) peer assessment that required the students to assess each other's oral and written performance; and (4) oral feedback that required the teacher and peers to be engaged in formal and informal classroom conversations to provide the students with feedback. These tools primarily aimed to help the students evaluate their merits and weaknesses and then to determine the most effective learning strategy for themselves in the future.

9.3.3 Data Collection

To examine changes in the mediating artefact and tools, the subjects, the rules, the members involved in the community and the division of labour, a combination of structured lesson observations, structured interviews, and informal discussions was used. The main data collection method was through individual interviews conducted twice during the semester, one at the middle of the semester and one at the end of the semester. In the interviews, the students were given a list of questions that aimed to investigate issues relating to the research objectives. Interview questions were open and flexible so that interviewees could respond with what was important to them and what met their interests. Interviewees could provide a detailed response and pursue topics not covered by the questions. The researcher asked for ten volunteers including five males and five females. Each interview lasted for 30 min and was audio recorded.

Observations were undertaken by the participating teacher and the two focus groups in each class. The teacher and the focus groups were observed once per week by the researcher and an assistant for 30 min. Two groups were chosen from each classroom for observations as Gillies (2006) has shown that it is possible to obtain a representative sample of the students' discourse across classes by sampling the discussions of two groups in a class.

9.3.4 Data Analysis

All interviews were conducted in Vietnamese because the participants were not confident in answering questions in English. Most of the interviews were conducted by a research assistant who was very experienced in conducting interviews. All data were transcribed by and translated into English by the research assistant who was very fluent in English. Because the researcher was fluent in both Vietnamese and English, he then double-checked the translation and discussed with the research assistant until they all agreed with the translation. Both the researcher and the research assistant participated in coding the data and continuously cross-checked the codes until the inter-rater agreement was 100%. A deductive approach was applied to analyse the data. The data were disentangled into segments (this can be a word, a single sentence or a paragraph) so that annotations and codes could be attached to categories. Any code that referred to the same categories was grouped into one. Afterwards, in each category, the researcher grouped any code that referred to the same phenomenon as a theme.

The observations aimed to count the number of different individuals contacted by the teacher during each 30 minutes and the language used by the teacher in speaking to those individuals.

9.4 Results

The third activity theory generation warns that when some activity or practice is brought in a new context or goes international, the implementation process often faces challenges created by cultural diversity, different traditions or perspectives (Engestrom & Sannino, 2010). To make the reform go smoothly, local implementers often have to take a wide range of influential factors at various levels (e.g., policies from the top, rules and norms of the existing system, traditions and perspectives of local implementers, and local institutional constraints) into consideration to subsequently develop new conceptual tools to understand multiple perspectives and design a new form of the practice to fit into the new socio-cultural context. Perrenoud (1998) emphasises this idea when arguing that on the reformative process there is a need for ongoing regulation and flexibility. These warnings were well reflected in the present study showing that when formative assessment practices were brought to

Vietnamese classrooms, many tensions and contradictions were emerging, leading to various changes in all factors in the reformative system including subjects, mediating artefact/tools, rules, members of the community, and division of labour. It was seen that all factors in the reformative system had close connections with each other and could pull and push each other. Change in one factor led to change in other factors too. Within the scope of this chapter, the researcher only attempted to report and discuss how existing rules and norms in Vietnamese classrooms impacted the choice of mediating artefact and tools and created changes in the division of labour.

9.4.1   The Choice of Appropriate Mediating Artefacts

During the implementation process, tensions were clearly identified between the subjects' experience and perceptions and recommended formative assessment practices. Consequently, there were many changes in the choice of mediating artefact. The teacher could not use some tools that had been recommended and discussed before the study. In return, they suggested and employed new tools that emerged as necessary and important mediations to enhance the students' learning. The process of changing the mediating artefacts was captured as follows:

9.4.2   The Teacher and Students' Responses
to the Questioning Formulation Strategy

When the questioning formulation strategy was introduced, the researcher's expectation was that the teachers and students would be able to implement it, and the teacher's expectation was that their students would be able to use this strategy. However, as the participants proceeded with the task, they realised that this strategy was not easy. Although the students could create questions, most of them aimed to test information in the text. Very few could formulate higher-order knowledge questions that aimed to test something beyond the text. Table 9.1 shows the number of the types of questions that the students in a focus group could formulate in a class.

Table 9.1 Number of types of questions a focus group formulated in a class

Types of questions	Number
From the text	8 (e.g., How was the traditional model applied in analysing the results? What features made the place different from other areas?)
Not in the text	2 (e.g., How did the principles of the traditional practice differ from the updated one?)

Table 9.2 Main problems faced by the students when practising the questioning formulation strategy

Reasons	Exemplar messages
Not familiar with the technique	'This is the first time we did this'
Do not have time to place with the text	'To make a difficult question, we need to read again and again and think about what the text refers to. This process takes time but we don't have much time actually'
Not prepare the readings beforehand	'It seems that my group mates do not prepare the readings before coming to group discussions. That is why we usually have to spend time reading first before we can create questions'

The interview conducted with five students after the first class revealed various problems facing the students when practising the questioning formulation strategy as shown in Table 9.2.

Surprisingly, the interview conducted with the teacher also showed that the teacher found this strategy not as easy as she had thought. The teacher said: 'It is not easy. We usually think we don't have to plan because we use it [making questions] every day. But if we want to move learning deeper we need to think about the kind of questions and why you are asking them'.

9.4.3 Emerging Mediating Artefacts

Experiencing the students' unproductive performance on the questioning formulation strategy, the teacher then asked the researcher whether there was any other technique that could push the students to be more engaged in the activity. The researcher then instructed the teacher and students to use the *guided reciprocal peer questioning* list originally developed by King (1997) with such sample questions as '*How would you use ... to ...? Explain why ...? What is the difference between ... and ...?*' to scaffold each other whenever they worked in teams. Gillies and Boyle (2005) found that when students were guided by complex questions or verbal interactions, they could model similar practices or even develop them to a more complex level. Consequently, from the third week, the students were provided with a list of scaffolding prompts to formulate questions when they worked on their readings.

From the students' side, they also looked for their method to overcome the problem. It was very interesting to see one group using yahoo.com forum as a tool to enable group members to discuss and practise reviewing and formulating questions before each class. The observations showed that this group was able to formulate more questions and better quality questions compared to the other group (Table 9.3).

Table 9.3 Number of types of questions two focus groups formulated before and after the use of an online forum

	Before using an online forum	After using an online forum
Group 1 (who used the online forum)	14	19
Group 2	13	14

9.4.4 Changes in the Actors' Roles

In addition to changes in the mediating artefacts, tensions between the rules and norms and the division of labour inevitably led to changes in the actors' roles. The researcher, the teacher and the practitioner teacher reconsidered their presumed roles and changed to their newly assigned roles as the semester proceeded.

Regarding the researcher's role, to enable the students to be more engaged in the formative assessment practices, the researcher gradually moved from observing to partially participating in the learning process. He changed from a non-participating role to a consultant because he gradually became involved in designing various teaching and learning activities. The employment of the *guided reciprocal peer questioning* list was an example of changes in the researcher's role. Also, since the students struggled to formulate quality questions, the researcher became a facilitator who moved around small group discussions to scaffold them in order to develop higher-order knowledge questions.

Regarding the roles of the teacher and the practitioner teacher, there were also significant changes in their performance tasks and responsibilities. Initially, the teacher explained that they worked as facilitators to help groups. However, during group discussions, many students tended to approach the teacher for urgent help when facing a problem. In return, the teacher seemed very willing to help the students find the answer. Consequently, the teacher changed her role from facilitating groups to supervising individuals. This subsequently led to the fact that the teacher did not have enough time to engage fully with the development of learning activities; thus she passed the development of weekly multiple-choice tests to the practitioner teacher. The teacher explained that the practitioner teacher was entirely capable of designing these tests because she studied this subject in her degree. Also, because she attended all classes, she understood what was covered in each class well enough to develop the tests. Since the practitioner was involved in developing the tests, she gradually became more engaged in the students' learning process. Towards the end of the semester, her role was not much different from the role of the main teacher.

9.5   Discussion

Barriers hindering the implementation of formative assessment in the present study were connected to some typical Asian cultural traits. First, the unproductive performance of the students on the questioning formulation strategy was consistent with the findings of some previous studies. For instance, Pham (2014) found that students in cultures and societies described as being hierarchical [like Asian students] often learned ineffectively without the teacher's detailed instruction. These students are also seen as often having difficulties in developing their higher-order knowledge if they are required to study entirely independently of the teacher or are not guided by scaffolding prompts. Nisbett (2003) further claimed that Asian learners do not know how to use 'why' and 'how' questions to scaffold each other's knowledge as well as their Western counterparts do.

Second, the change of the teacher's role from a facilitator to a supervisor in the present study evidenced that the teacher might find it difficult to accept the teacher-equal-student relationship—a cultural cardinal in Asian classrooms (Phuong-Mai, 2008). This might also be because the teacher's main concern would be focusing on completing the curriculum to prepare the students for exams. Therefore, she did not want the students to spend much time on in-class discussion. Pham and Renshaw (2015) revealed that in Asia's examination-oriented education system, teachers and students are constantly under intense pressure to achieve quantitative goals such as the amount of knowledge that should be disseminated within the scheduled time and the success rate at the end of a semester or school year but not the quality of in-class discussions.

These findings showed that both cultural and structural barriers prevented the implementation of formative assessment. However, this research showed how the local implementers including the researcher, the teacher, the students, and the practitioner teacher made efforts and used their creativity to navigate existing barriers. For instance, the students used their hard-working culture and outside-class working habit—two typical cultural cardinals of Asian students (Renshaw & Power, 2003) to create an online forum to practise the questioning formulating strategy. When the teacher was involved in too much supervision of individual students and did not have enough time to run the class, she did not simply give up other formative assessment activities but managed to involve the practitioner teacher in monitoring the class. To enable the students to be able to work on formative assessment activities effectively, both the researcher and the practitioner teacher were willing to increase their involvement in the teaching and learning process as the semester progressed.

Negotiations and changes in the roles of all actors in the present study reflected what Edwards (2009) warned about constant changes in actors' roles in an activity system. Specifically, Edwards claimed that for an activity system to operate smoothly the originally designated roles and pre-ordained views of the artefact had to be re-negotiated when the environment changed. Transposing roles and rules from one context to another can lead to tensions. Instead, the fluid environment generated the need for those involved to explore their 'relational agency' as a means to renegotiate a shared understanding of what they were doing, with whom, and why.

9.6   Conclusion

The analysis of the intersecting activity systems of formative assessment and the traditional teaching and learning in Vietnamese classrooms in the present study has provided an example to illustrate Engeström's (1987) argument that activity is a historically and culturally mediated phenomenon. Disparities between the two systems resulted in challenges facing actors in the system. The success of the initiative largely depends on how actors cooperate and negotiate their roles so that they can support each other to overcome barriers. Activity theory suggests one method to create such a collaborative culture, which is to see the implementation process as adaptation. Resistance and contradictions should be treated as an important dynamic force driving the continuous development of an activity system. People at the micro-level (i.e., teachers and students) should not be seen as implementers and simply receivers of the reform but also as negotiators of their interests during the reformative process (cf. Corbett & Wilson, 1995). Therefore, macro-level people should treat resistance at the micro-level as positive responses, so that they can find flexible solutions to work with the lower level. This is important because Ball (1990) argues that the response to policy direction always involves some kind of creative social action. When the micro-level reacts against the change, it could mean that they find something wrong or inappropriate inside the change. In this case, the macro level cannot rigidly insist on keeping the methods to enforce their policy. Rather, they should ask why implementers resist or what factors block the implementation process. By asking such questions, some revisions in their policy may be needed. This may lead to a change in the outcomes that the macro-level sets out to achieve depending on how the micro-level people respond to the reform. Besides, the materials used in reform should be treated as cultural tools to be appropriated. Western-based pedagogies have been strongly imported into Asian classrooms. Unfortunately, the literature has reported very little evidence showing how people at macro and micro levels supported each other to implement the reform. The present study suggests that the implementation process of any reform should be treated as a negotiation process in which the values of various systems and stakeholders should be taken into consideration.

References

Ball, S. J. (1990). *Politics and policymaking in education*. London: Routledge.
Black, P., Harrison, C., Lee, C., Marshall, B., & Wiliam, D. (2003). *Assessment for learning: putting it into practice*. Buckingham: Open University Press.

Boud, D. (1990). Assessment and the promotion of academic values. *Studies in Higher Education, 75*, 101–111.

Brown, T. L., Kennedy, G., Fok, K., Chan, K., & Yu, M. (2009). Assessment for student improvement: Understanding Hong Kong teachers' conceptions and practices of assessment. *Assessment in Education: Principles, Policy & Practices, 16*(3), 347–363.

Carrillo-de-la-Peña, M., Baillès, E., Caseras, X., Àlvar Martínez, G. O., & Pérez, J. (2009). Formative assessment and academic achievement in pre-graduate students of health sciences. *Advances in Health Sciences Education, 14*(1), 61–67.

Chen, G.-M. (2001). Toward transcultural understanding: A harmony theory of Chinese communication. In V. H. Milhouse, M. K. Asante, & P. O. Nwosu (Eds.), *Transcultural realities: Interdisciplinary perspectives on cross-cultural relations* (pp. 55–70). Thousand Oaks: Sage.

Chen, G.-M., & Starosta, J. W. (1997). A review of the concept of intercultural sensitivity. *Human Communication, 1*, 1–16.

Corbett, D., & Wilson, B. (1995). Make a difference with, not for, students: A plea to researchers and reformers. *Educational Researchers, 24*(5), 12–17.

Duong, M. T., Nguyen, T. K. C., & Griffin, P. (2011). Developing a framework to measure process-orientated writing competence: A case study of Vietnamese EFL students' formal portfolio assessment. *RELC Journal (Journal of Language Teaching and Research), 42*(2), 167.

Edwards, A. (2009). Agency and activity theory: From the system to the relational. In A. Sannino, H. Daniels, & K. Gutierrez (Eds.), *Learning and expand with activity theory* (pp. 197–211). Cambridge: Cambridge University Press.

Engeström, Y. (1987). *Learning by expanding*. Helsinki, Finland: Dept. of Education, University of Helsinki.

Engeström, Y. (1999). Activity theory and individual and social transformation. In Y. Engeström, R. Miettinen, & R. L. Punamaki (Eds.), *Perspectives on activity theory* (pp. 19–37). Cambridge: Cambridge University Press.

Engeström, Y. (2001). Expansive learning at work: Toward an activity theoretical reconceptualization. *Journal of Education and Work, 14*(1), 133–156.

Engestrom, Y., & Sannino, A. (2010). Studies of expansive learning: Foundation, findings and future challenges. *Educational Research Review, 5*(1), 1–24.

Etkina, E. (2000). Weekly reports: A two-way feedback tool. *Science Education, 84*, 594–605.

Gillies, R. (2006). Teachers' and students' verbal behaviours during cooperative and small-group learning. *British Journal of Educational Psychology, 76*(2), 271–287.

Gillies, R. M., & Boyle, M. (2005). Teachers' scaffolding behaviours during cooperative learning. *Asia-Pacific Journal of Teacher Education, 33*(3), 243–259.

Hall, K., & Burke, W. (2003). *Making formative assessment work: Effective practice in the primary classroom*. Buckingham: Open University Press.

Hu, G. (2013). English language teaching in China: Regional differences and contributing factors. *Journal of Multilingual and Multicultural Development, 24*(4), 290–318.

Indonesian Higher Education Directorate, Ministry of Education and Culture. (2014). *Buku Kurikulum Pendidikan Tinggi.*

Kay, J., Li, L., & Fekete, A. (2007*). Learner reflection in student self-assessment*. In: Proceedings of ninth Australasian computing education conference (ACE2007), Ballarat, Australia.

King, A. (1997). ASK to THINK TEL WHY: A model of transactive peer tutoring for scaffolding higher-level complex learning. *Educational Psychologist, 32*(4), 221–235.

Konkola, R. (2001). Harjoittelun kehittämisprosessi ammattikorkeakoulussa ja rajavyöhyketoiminta uudenlaisena toimintamallina [Developmental process of internship at polytechnic and boundary-zone activity as a new model for activity]. In T. Tuomi-Gröhn & Y. Engeström (Eds.), *Koulunja työn rajavyöhykkeellä: uusia työssä oppimisen mahdollisuuksia [At the boundary-zone between school and work: new possibilities of work-based learning]* (pp. 148–186). Helsinki: University Press.

Light, G., & Cox, R. (2001). *Lecturing: Large group teaching. In learning and teaching in higher education: The reflexive professional*. London: SAGE.

McDonald, B., & Boud, D. (2003). The impact of self-assessment on achievement: The effects of self-assessment training on performance in external examinations. *Assessment in Education, 10* (2), 209–220.

Moss, P. A., Girard, B. J., & Haniford, L. C. (2006). Validity in educational assessment. *Review of Research in Education, 30*, 109–162.

Nisbett, R. E. (2003). *The geography of thought: How Asians and Westerners think differently. . .And why*. New York: Free Press.

Perrenoud, P. (1998). From formative evaluation to a controlled regulation of learning process. Towards a wider conceptual field. *Assessment in Education, 5*, 85–102.

Pham, T. (2014). *Implementing cross-culture pedagogies: Cooperative learning at Confucian heritage cultures*. Singapore: Springer.

Pham, T., & Renshaw, P. D. (2015). Adapting evidence-based pedagogy to local cultural contexts: A design research study of policy borrowing in Vietnam. *Pedagogies: An International Journal, 10*(3), 256–274.

Phuong-Mai, N. (2008). *Culture and cooperation: Cooperative learning in Asian Confucian heritage cultures: The case of Viet Nam*. Netherlands: IVLOS Institute of Education of Utrecht University.

Price, M., Handley, K., & Millar, J. (2011). Feedback - focusing attention on engagement. *Studies in Higher Education, 36*(8), 879–896.

Renshaw, P., & Power, C. (2003). The process of learning. In J. L. Keeves & R. Watanabe (Eds.), *International handbook of educational research in the Asia-Pacific region* (pp. 351–363). Dordrecht: Kluwer Academic.

Sahlberg, P. (2004). Teaching and globalization. *International research Journal of Managing Global Transitions, 2*(1), 65–83.

Tobias, J., Wales, J., Syamsulhakim, E., & Suharti. (2014). *Towards better education quality. Indonesia promising path. A case study report*. London: Overseas Development Institute.

Topping, K. (1998). Peer assessment between students in colleges and universities. *Review of Educational Research, 68*(3), 249–276.

Weurlander, M., Söderberg, M., Scheja, M., Hult, H., & Wernerson, A. (2012). Exploring formative assessment as a tool for learning: Students' experiences of different methods of formative assessment. *Assessment & Evaluation in Higher Education, 37*(6), 747–760.

Yan, C. (2015). We can't change much unless the exams change: Teachers' dilemmas in the curriculum reform in China. *Improving Schools, 18*(1), 5–19.

Yang, M., Badger, R., & Yu, Z. (2006). A comparative study of peer and teacher feedback in a Chinese EFL writing class. *Journal of Second Language Writing, 15*, 179–200.

Chapter 10
Making Sense of Teacher Agency Within a Vocational-Academic Integration Program at a Chinese Vocational High School

Jing Shi and Venesser Fernandes

Abstract Four years after the Chinese Vocational Education Reform was initiated, research in this area has found unfavorable outcomes. The implementation of policy and the dedicated reform actions for promoting the status of vocational education has not effectively improved the equity issue with Chinese society. Previous studies have focused on investigating the perspectives of school leaders and on explaining the political and social factors that have hindered school-level policy implementation. These studies have neglected to focus on the role and involvement of teachers in this process and their voices are noticeably absent. According to Ball, Maguire, and Braun (How schools do policy: Policy enactments in secondary schools, Routledge, 2012), marginalizing the critical voice of teachers in policy activities of negotiating and conceptualizing school-level policies causes imminent failure in their implementation. It has been noted that there is an obvious absence in the research literature that identifies teachers as policy agents involved in transforming schools. This study addresses this gap by investigating teacher voice and agency within a vocational high school in Ningbo city, Zhejiang Province, China. Through an in-depth explorative organizational case study, this study focused on the experiences of five high school teachers. The findings revealed that at an institutional level there was disinterest in policy dialogue by vocational teachers. A major reason for this disinterest was a lack of participatory engagement by school leadership and teaching staff on policy matters.

Keywords Policy enactment · Vocational high school · Vocational education reforms · Vocational-academic integration program · Teacher agency · Chinese context

J. Shi (✉) · V. Fernandes
Monash University, Melbourne, Australia
e-mail: jing.shi@monash.edu

10.1 Introduction

This chapter focuses on making sense of teacher agency in the Vocational-Academic Integration program run in Chinese vocational high schools. Within this context, the policy titled—the *Guidance on the Experimental Program for Deepening the Vocational-Academic Integration Reform*—issued by the Ningbo Education Bureau (Ningbo Education Bureau, 2016) was used in framing this study. This policy is as an interpretation of the national-level policy document *Modern Vocational Education System Construction Plan (2014–2020)* (MOE, 2014). Earlier on this *Plan* was issued by the Ministry of Education, China (2014) to upgrade various sectors within its vocational education system to meet national developmental targets (Stewart, 2015). Ningbo's integration policy emphasizes on the senior secondary field of vocational education reform. It aims at guiding the experimental work of the pilot Vocational-Academic Integration program for high schools in the region.

To clarify the background, in China, vocational and academic secondary education are two distinct systems due to their differences in their educational objectives, curriculum, and assessment methods. Vocational senior secondary schools equip students with job-oriented and marketable skills, while academic schools prepare students for university education (Sun, 2010). Students enrolled in vocational schools have two future pathways after graduating, to join the workforce or to go further with their vocational higher education (Li & Zhao, 2014; Liu & Wang, 2015). This streaming however excludes them out of opting later for academic tertiary education and better job prospects in society (Li & Zhao, 2014; Sun, 2010). Additionally, the increasing emphasis on university credentials by employers has resulted in limited job opportunities for these vocational graduates in local, national, and international job markets (Jaeger, 2014; Koo, 2015; Wang, 2011). Furthermore, this selection of a single limited pathway is not chosen by the Chinese students themselves but done for them by the way the system has been designed. In other words, they do not choose to enroll either in the academic or vocational pathway, instead, they are scored by a standard examination at the end of Year 9 and stratified across the two pathways based solely on their test scores; students with scores higher than a particular set score can enrol into academic schools while the ones who have scores below a certain minimum can only join vocational schools (Ling, 2015; Shi, 2012). As a result, the public opinion holds vocational education at an inferior status as compared to academic education (Koo, 2015; Schmidtke & Chen, 2012; Shi, 2013; Xiong, 2011). In the last two decades, the Chinese government has recognized the significant impact of a strong vocational education system on its economic and social growth. Due to this, the government has made concerted efforts on improving the quality and status of vocational education and equality-related issues (Halliday, 2007; Jaeger, 2014; Stewart, 2015) by introducing several new measures such as the reforms to the *Vocational-Academic Integration* policy and its derived policy at the local level of Ningbo City in Zhejiang Province.

10.2   Research Significance

Four years after the *Modern Vocational Education System Construction Plan (2014–2020)* (MOE, 2014) and its derived local policies introduced in Ningbo City (Ningbo Education Bureau, 2016), research in the area has encountered some hurdles. The implementation of this policy and the dedicated reform actions for promoting the status of Vocational Education and Training (VET) has not been accepted widely within Chinese society. Recently, many Chinese studies (Huang, 2016; Liu & Liu, 2015; Xu & Shen, 2015; Zhou, 2017) have investigated school leaders' perspectives on the policy and its reforms. These studies have focused on explaining the political and social factors hindering school-level policy interpretations. A major limitation found has been the absence of the agentic voice of teachers. Ball, Maguire, and Braun (2012) suggest that marginalizing the critical voice of teachers in policy activities of negotiation and conceptualization at the school level is a significant cause of failure in policy implementation. Spillane (2004) discusses that disruptions in practice are often accounted for as teachers' interpretation and sense-making as well as responsiveness to policy initiatives. There is a lack of research literature within Chinese vocational education reform to provide deeper insight into the influence of teacher's voices on policy reforms.

The purpose of this research study was to address this gap by exploring the perspectives of teachers towards this policy reform within a vocational high school in Ningbo city. As a qualitative explorative research study, this chapter does not intend to generate conclusive solutions to the existing problem. It focuses on providing a deeper understanding of Chinese vocational teachers' sense-making on policy reforms and explores emerging themes within the area of Vocational-Academic Integration reforms in China.

The following main research question and subsidiary research questions addressed within this chapter are given below.

How do vocational high school teachers make sense of the Vocational-Academic Integration program in Ningbo City, Zhejiang Province, China?

(a) How does the Vocational-Academic Integration program influence the teaching and learning process?
(b) How does the Vocational-Academic Integration program address student learning and development?
(c) How does the Vocational-Academic Integration program position vocational high schools?

10.3   Theoretical Background

10.3.1   Teacher Agency in Policy Implementation and Practice

Regarding work in the contemporary education policy analysis, researchers (Ball et al., 2012; Honig, 2006) found that the implementation outcomes of a particular policy differ from school to school due to many contextual limitations such as teacher commitment and experience, school infrastructure, school history, and student demographics. Based on this complexity, studies on how policy has been implemented (or not) have covered everything from the design of the policy to the diverse responses of agents in implementation practice (Ball et al., 2012; Colebatch, 2006; Spillane, Reiser, & Gomez, 2006). Ball et al. (2012, p. 21) refer to these "responses" as the "interpretation" of policy, which is a sense-making of policy based on a school's specific and unique contextual background, recipients, and subject cultures.

In many of Spillane's studies (Spillane, 2004; Spillane et al., 2006; Spillane, Reiser, & Reimer, 2002), policy sense-making has been termed as the cognitive perspective of implementation agents. Spillane et al. (Spillane et al., 2002, p. 388) highlight that "what a policy means for implementation agents is constituted in the integration of their existing cognitive structures (knowledge, beliefs, and attitudes), their situation and their policy signals." In other words, individual policy actors, including school leaders and schoolteachers, make sense of, interpret, and enact policies based on their backgrounds and attitudes, as well as their circumstances concerning what they understand the policy to be. How school actors make sense of a policy to some extent determines their reactions and responses to their enactment.

Based on the cognitive perspective, many research studies of policy enactment have focused on investigating teachers' attitudes and perceptions towards education policies in various contexts (Ableser, 2003; Saborit, Fernández-Río, Cecchini Estrada, Méndez-Giménez, & Alonso, 2016; Steinbach & Stoeger, 2016; Trouilloud, Sarrazin, Bressoux, & Bois, 2006; Wagah, Indoshi, & Agak, 2009). These accounts suggest that the attitudes of teachers are crucial factors for the proper implementation of the policy. Wagah et al. (2009) discuss that personal or collective attitudes impel agent(s)' reaction, favorable or unfavorable, to propositions, objects, and situations. Factors that may influence teachers' attitudes towards policy enactment include school leaders' interpretation of policy as well as the prior knowledge, experiences, and beliefs of individual teachers (Haber, 2005; Wagah et al., 2009).

10.3.2   Vocational-Academic Integration

The concept of integration of vocational/academic education was posed and studied since the last century (Bodilly, Ramsey, Stasz, & Eden, 1993; Callahan, 1999;

Kincheloe, 1995; Young, 1993). Callahan (1999, p. 11) defines the notion of Vocational-Academic Integration as,

> A strategy that focuses on the blending of academic and vocational education, resulting in clear performance standards which involves interdisciplinary education, cross-curriculum planning, and applied academics ... it promotes strong problem-solving, communication, and teamwork skills necessary for success in the workplace... Work-related skills are also incorporated into the school curriculum to motivate students into choosing career interests.

In other words, integrating academic education (AE) and vocational education (VE) highlights a set of practical skills for students, emphasizing on applied academic knowledge in VE, and helps in producing challenging and meaningful curricula with clear performance standards. Callahan's definition of the integration of AE and VE (1999) represents the mainstream cognition of scholars in the 1990s (Bodilly et al., 1993; Kincheloe, 1995; Young, 1993) who have regarded the intention of integration as an answer to provide future workers with skills needed in a changing workplace.

In the context of China, the notion of Vocational-Academic Integration as links and communication between Academic Education (AE) and Vocational Education (VE) was first posed in 2002 and has been repeatedly mentioned in the ongoing development of vocational education (Li & Tang, 2016). However, it has not been concentrated closely until the recent decade (Guan, 2014; Li & Tang, 2016; Liu & Chen, 2013). In 2014, the *Modern Vocational Education System Construction Plan (2014–2020)* included Vocational-Academic Integration as one of its crucial concepts (MOE, 2014). Scholars regard integration as a key to address problems in the traditional education system, such as students' lack of motivation to use academic knowledge and poor employability (Sun, 2010). The integration is also a vital component to ensure the sustainable economic growth of the nation (Jaeger, 2014; Stewart, 2015) and a critical aspect is to address the equity issue within VET (Ling, 2015; Shi, 2012; Xiong, 2011).

Several Chinese research studies have emphasized on studying the implementation of the Vocational-Academic Integration policy (Huang, 2016; Ling, 2015; Liu & Liu, 2015; Xu & Shen, 2015; Zhang, 2014; Zhou, 2017). The major problem in this policy practice has been complete contrary attitudes towards the program and its implementation from academic high schools as compared to vocational high schools respectively, where vocational schools welcome the program while academic schools underrate the usefulness of this program (Ling, 2015; Liu & Liu, 2015; Xu & Shen, 2015; Zhou, 2017). Meanwhile, this problem has been influenced by school-level misinterpretations of the policy intention and a lack of motivation found among practitioners as well (Liu & Liu, 2015; Zhou, 2017).

10.3.3   Research into the Vocational-Academic Integration Program

Liu and Liu (2015) clarify that the Vocational-Academic Integration policy is a form of disruption to the deeply rooted social ideology of inferiority being associated with VET. Owing to unequal future developmental opportunities, most stakeholders including parents, students, and educators believe academic education is the only pathway through which children can change their social stratum and enhance their self-esteem in the future (Jaeger, 2014; Koo, 2015; Liu & Liu, 2015). These kinds of values and beliefs have led to a tense competition in the tracking of students into vocational or academic pathways. This has further resulted in a public perception that a high rate of acceptance of students into reputable schools at the higher level of education is the only standard to evaluate and appraise the educational quality of a school (Liu & Liu, 2015; Xu & Shen, 2015; Zhang, 2014). In such a climate, middle schools attach significant importance and success to the number of their students entering reputable academic high schools. Likewise, academic high schools focus on preparing their students to get high scores in the *National University Entrance Examination* (Liu & Liu, 2015; Sun, 2010). Due to this, it is not surprising that the promotion of Vocational-Academic Integration reforms with policy intentions aimed at facilitating VET is not yet fully accepted as an equivalent pathway within Chinese society. More work in disrupting these notions needs to be done at multiple levels before a change in perception and wider acceptance of VE takes place across China.

Another implementation issue that has surfaced is the lack of up-to-date and relevant assessment and evaluation mechanisms to support the Vocational-Academic Integration within the school curriculum processes (Liu & Liu, 2015; Liu & Wang, 2015; Zhang, 2014). As mentioned above, education in China has mainly been examination-oriented, and this feature has led students and school teachers to focus on narrowed and limited curriculum that is solely assessed in final examinations (Liu & Liu, 2015; Xu & Shen, 2015; Zhang, 2014). For example, some experimental academic schools have attempted to set up elective vocational subjects for students to build career interests (Liu & Wang, 2015; Zhou, 2017) in line with adhering to this integration policy. However, these vocational education classes in academic high schools have ended up becoming marginalized because they do not directly contribute towards preparing students for their final examinations, which remains the primary focus of education in the academic high schools. Liu and Liu (2015) therefore call for a corresponding reform in the *National University Entrance Examination* to ensure that a conducive environment that strengthens the implementation of the Vocational-Academic Integration policy reform can be developed.

Findings from the literature review for this research study also found that there is a significant gap in the research literature on the sense-making of teachers, in both academic and vocational high schools, concerning the utility and application of the Vocational-Academic Integration program (Liu & Liu, 2015; Zhou, 2017). Discussing the critical role of Chinese teacher agents in policy enactment processes, as discussed by Ball et al. (2012) and Spillane (2004), is useful in further understanding the issues and challenges being faced at the coalface by the teachers who are working with these students in their respective classrooms.

10.4 Research Methods

This qualitative exploratory case-study research was conducted in a vocational high school in Ningbo City, Zhejiang Province. The site was purposefully selected because of its uniqueness. Choosing Ningbo City as the location of the study was of geographical relevance. Zhejiang Province is one of the "pioneers" and "innovators" in Education Development in China, while Ningbo as its major city has benefited from taking the lead in piloting education policies and experimental activities over the years (MOE, 2017). Since 2013, the Vocational-Academic Integration program has been implemented in Zhejiang Province. The purpose of this study has been to investigate how this integration policy has had an impact on the teaching and learning processes in vocational high schools. It also investigates the extent to which this has influenced student learning and development as well. In making sense of teacher agency within this case study high school, this study has investigated the experiences of teachers who have been involved in this program and explored whether vocational high schools have found that their positional standing has improved after the implementation of this Vocational-Academic Integration policy.

10.4.1 The Bounded System

While conducting case-study research, it is essential to explore the bounded system of the unit, which provides researchers with evidence for the evaluation of the case (Creswell, 2014; Merriam, 1998; Yazan, 2015). In this study, this bounded system included the research investigations done as a part of this research study at the chosen case-study high school. Within this chapter, the *policy guidelines document—Guidance on the Experimental Program for Deepening the Vocational-Academic Integration Reform* (Education Bureau of Ningbo, 2016)—was used primarily in the exploration of the pilot program. It defines the notion of Vocational-Academic Integration as providing students with diverse opportunities for education pathways and improving education for students with different potentials. The *policy guidelines document* demonstrates five dimensions for activity within the program. These include: (1) transfer requirements, (2) recognition of credit, (3) elective courses, (4) integration of teacher resources, and (5) integration of education activities (see Table 10.1). Simultaneously, the *policy guidelines document* underlines the collaborative tasks for individual vocational and academic high schools to cooperate in pairs to negotiate and agree on a specific practical program.

Table 10.1 Guidance on vocational-academic integration program

Dimensions	Policy Guidelines Document
Student transferring requirements	– Students who attend the *Program* and meet the assessment requirements of both partner schools (one academic and one vocational high school) can submit their transfer applications at the end of the first and the second semester of year 10. – Secondary vocational school students transferred to academic high schools are eligible to undertake the National University Entrance Examination. They can be awarded the standard academic secondary education diploma after completing the credits required by the academic high school. – Academic school students can transfer to vocational schools where there is a vacancy by passing an examination in the first and the second semester of year Ten and Eleven. – Academic school students transferred to vocational schools should meet the graduation standards of vocational education before they can get a diploma and obtain the vocational qualification certificate.
Recognition of credit	Partner schools should: – Cooperate and work out a method for credit transition based on the curriculum of the individual schools and their education plan. – Establish mutual recognition of credit points to recognize credits obtained by students from previous schools.
Elective courses	– Academic schools offer courses of *"knowledge development and humanistic accomplishment"* (translated from Chinese) for vocational school students to enhance their academic course requirements. – Vocational schools help academic school students to strengthen their career-planning by improving student life skills and career awareness.
Integration of teacher resources	Partner schools should: – Establish a management system for the integration of class teachers. – Promote a mutual exchange of teaching ideas and learning resources among vocational and academic school teachers by improving the engagement and enthusiasm of teachers within the integration program.
Integration of education activities	Partner schools should maintain communication among teachers and carry out inter-school cooperation and mutual interaction in teaching and research work, subject competitions, research projects, skill competitions, and innovation and entrepreneurship.

Source: Guidance on the Experimental Program for Deepening the Vocational-Academic Integration Reform (Ningbo Education Bureau, 2016, pp. 1–2)

10.4.2 The School-Level Pilot Program

As a response to the *Guidance Document*, the Vocational-Academic Integration program has been experimentally implemented under the cooperation of F Vocational High School and X Academic High School. In September 2017, F school enrolled a cohort of 30 middle school graduates into the program. Throughout the first semester, the cohort of 30 Year Ten students and their teaching team were expected to completely follow the curriculum and assessment of X Academic High

Table 10.2 F Vocational High School Integration Program: the technique for assessment

Examination title	Examination time	Percentage of final grade	Note
September monthly exam	End of September	10%	
October monthly exam	Middle/end of October	10%	
Mid-term exam	Middle of November	20%	Using X academic high school examination paper
December monthly exam	Middle of December	10%	
Final exam	Middle of January	50%	Using X academic high school examination paper

*The subjects assessed include Chinese literacy, mathematics, English language, physics, chemistry, geography, history, politics, and information technology.

Source: School documents provided by research participants

School. At the end of the first semester, 4 out of these 30 students would have an opportunity to transfer to X Academic High School, and the other 26 students would remain in the vocational educational pathway that they were already enrolled in. There were two highlighted requirements for transferring to X school: first, the four students should be ranked the top in the final grading within the pilot cohort of students (Table 10.2 illustrates how the final grade was calculated), and second, the four students should also be ranked at 80% within a student group at X Academic High School. Four Year Ten students whose scores satisfied the two requirements could transfer to X school by the end of the first semester. It was interesting to note that the number was capped at four regardless of actual achievement of the group, so that, if more than four students were meeting both requirements, the four students scored at the top would be accepted. More interestingly, while these four students would be transferred into the Academic High School, they would remain enrolled as Vocational High School students.

10.4.3 Participants and Data Collection

This exploratory study involved a small sample ($N = 5$) of F Vocational High School teachers from a single case-study school. The five participants were all from F Vocational High School, and they were purposefully selected because of having rich experiences in engaging with the pilot program. In the study, two 60-min semi-structured individual interviews and one 50-min focus group interview with three teachers were conducted to collect first-hand data for addressing the research questions (Table 10.3). To triangulate the data, four sources of evidence were used. These included:

Table 10.3 Information of the five teacher participants in the case study

Participants (pseudonym)	Participated in	Years of teaching in VE	Position
Zhang	Individual interview	15 years	Department director, teacher of vocational courses (grades 11 & 12)
Yon	Individual interview	6 years	Chinese literacy (grade 11)
Wen	Focus group	11 years	Chinese literacy (grade 11)
Sue	Focus group	15 years	Vocational subjects (grade 11)
Hu	Focus group	21 years	Vocational subjects (grade 11)

Source: Research participants

1. related-policy documents at the national level
2. related-policy documents at the local level
3. school documents provided by the research participants
4. interviews and focus group discussions with the participants

10.5   Findings and Discussion

10.5.1   *Influence on the Teaching and Learning Process*

Participants in the interviews gave voice to their perspectives on the teaching and learning process. Within the program, teachers were required to teach the class according to the Year Ten curriculum at X Academic High School with the same progress rate and schedule, or an even faster pace to ensure their students succeeded in comparison with academic high school students. On account of the existing practice, teachers expressed significant concerns about their work. Firstly, teachers lost autonomy in their curriculum design and teaching plans. As Yon discussed,

> It has restricted our teaching. I am a Chinese Language teacher, and I used to teach literacy with interaction to the student's vocational major. . . it also helped students to understand and learn the prose better. However, it cannot be done for students in this program.

Yon had to change her teaching style to follow the curriculum plan of X Academic High School. For her, it was quite stressful to use the teaching materials of the Chinese literacy unit within the academic curriculum. Similarly, Wen stated that "We are merely the implementers of the particular teaching plan developed by the teaching team of X Academic High School, we are very passive in this collaborative process." The participants indicated that it was impossible to alter or innovate any part of the teaching plan due to certain restrictions, as Zhang determined that "the X Academic High School curriculum was all about textbooks and textbooks, and massive exercises to strengthen memory and rote learning of students under the 'baton' of the *National University Entrance Examination.*"

Another concern was raised by Hu, a vocational subject teacher. As mentioned before, within the program, the cohort of 30 students in the first semester of Year Ten was only taught the X Academic High School Curriculum. Except for four students who successfully passed the assessment, the other 26 students still needed to complete their senior secondary education at F Vocational High School. Therefore, the vocational subject teachers were then held accountable to teach the content of the entire academic year of Year Ten within the following semester to the remaining 26 students as they had spent the first semester learning from the curriculum plans of X Academic High School and preparing for the examination from that curriculum. Hu indicated that,

> We have been toiling in the second semester, both teachers and students... I always attempt to be innovative in teaching to expand students' knowledge further than their textbooks... However, this semester, I was obliged to forego any interesting curricular teaching focus due to insufficient time and energy.

As indicated, these findings suggest that vocational teachers who were involved in the Vocational-Academic Integration program at F Vocational High School lost autonomy to a significant extent in their teaching plan and curriculum design. The participants also demonstrated a lack of interest due to the current circumstances of teaching in the Vocational-Academic Integration program being implemented at their school. According to Wagah et al. (2009), the attitude of teachers is a key factor for the proper implementation of the policy. It was found that teachers who believed their work was negatively affected by the program had a higher probability of getting demotivated or being less active in their pedagogical practice. The findings from this small-scale study are similar to those found by Liu and Liu's (2015) study, which also suggested that there was a lack of motivation among practitioners for the Vocational-Academic Integration policy.

10.5.2 Influence on Student Learning and Development

To address the second research subsidiary question, participants Hu, Sue, Wen, and Yon discussed their doubts on what the program had contributed to students' learning and development. Within the focus group discussion, Hu first posed her concern about the current program with the related problem of students' learning of vocational subjects. In Hu's words,

> The fact is when students see the strict requirement for the academic learning... they easily lose confidence and give up at the very beginning of the semester.

From Hu's argument, it was understandable that Hu as a vocational course teacher had a deep concern for her students. As explained earlier, in the current Chinese education system, VE and AE are two distinct systems (Sun, 2010). Vocational high schools prepare students for the job market and the national higher vocational education examination (Li & Zhao, 2014; Liu & Wang, 2015). The 26 "unsuccessful" students from the Vocational-Academic Integration cohort, who had spent semester one on academic curriculum learning, would need to make an extensive effort to catch up on the regular learning over that semester that their peers had engaged in within regular vocational classes and also put in a substantial effort to succeed in the competitive final examination for vocational higher education. Sue, another vocational course teacher in the focus group discussion, agreed with Hu. Moreover, Sue elaborated on another sub-group of students within the cohort of 30, who indeed cherished this chance of being involved in the program, they worked hard and eagerly anticipated obtaining this opportunity yet failed to reach the criteria set for entry into X Academic High School. Sue was worried about the psychological state of these students and found that a number of these students, after having failed, faced high levels of disappointment, melancholy, and depression. On the other hand, Zhang held a relatively positive attitude towards student performance within the program. Zhang indicated that for some students within the cohort, through the strong pressure and extensive academic learning tasks, they were allowed to gain helpful skills and habits such as being more disciplined, more organized, and diligent. According to Zhang, these good learning habits facilitated and improved the performance of these students and found that it had positively assisted them in their learning habits and choices.

In addition to the concerns raised about the "unsuccessful" students, Yon and Wen also discussed their concerns about the four successful students who had continued their education in the academic pathway. Wen clarified that although the four students were selected through a rigorous assessment, their learning ability and knowledge basis were still incomparable with the average X Academic High School students who once were outstanding in middle school education. For them, it would be an enormous challenge as well as pressure to adjust to the tense way of exam-oriented learning at X Academic High School. Wen used the phrase "they may not understand the instructional style of the teachers within their new classroom." In addition to Wen's concern about studying, Yon considered various aspects of a student's personal development. She added that,

> The four students would also have trouble making new friends at X Academic High School, and these students may also be labelled as 'the vocational students'.

Yon referred to individual differences and abilities among students and explained how the uncertain influences of the program generated a higher level of anxiety for these students. Furthermore, both Wen and Yon suggested that follow-up investigations into the academic performance of the four students, personal development, and well-being after they joined classes at X Academic High School would be useful to ascertain the value-added component of this program. These findings indicated that the vocational teachers at F Vocational High School had a very different perspective on how the program affected students' learning and development. It was found that these issues raised by teachers within this study had also been raised by previous research studies (Liu & Liu, 2015; Xu & Shen, 2015; Zhou, 2017), and confirmed the significance of making sense of teachers as change-agents in everyday school practice.

10.5.3 The Position of Vocational High School Within the Pilot Program

As a teacher and a department director, Zhang had a more in-depth insight into the status and position of F Vocational High School and its partnership with X Academic High School for the implementation of the pilot program. In his words,

> The Vocational-Academic Integration policy suggests a mutual direction of integration... yet scarcely is it found that students from X Academic High School would want to transfer to the vocational pathway at F Vocational High School. Hence the flow of student-exchange is uni-directional with VE being considered less than AE.

As indicated through this excerpt, Zhang found that F Vocational High School held an unequal status as compared to X Academic High School in their partnership. Also, he pointed out that this inequity was a derivative of the existing equity issue discussed in the introduction section of this chapter. To explain this further, he explained that the current program did not reach a higher level of cross-program parity as stated by the *policy guidelines document* which offered an open opportunity for students to switch freely from both education pathways. The findings suggested that this was largely on account of the existing low reputation of vocational education in Chinese society. This finding was also aligned with Liu and Liu's (2015) argument that the deeply rooted social ideology of the inequivalent status of VE was one of the main obstacles which had hindered the chance of successful implementation of the Vocational-Academic Integration policy.

To further elaborate upon this, Zhang deeply reflected on the rationale behind this issue,

> There are two reasons. Firstly, X Academic High School only accepted to engage in this program due to the government (policy) mandate... So, we must follow X school's requirement of how the students in the program are taught and examined and how the program is operated.

In other words, the high market demand for an academic school education indirectly benefited F Vocational High School to some extent by improving its school branding. In other words, utilizing the slogan of "partnership with X Academic High School" as an advertisement for the program F Vocational High School was able to improve its reputation and attract good quality enrolments. Zhang used the word "gimmick" to describe this pilot program as it indicated the tokenistic vocational education improvement strategy that was being used.

According to Zhang, the administrators of F Vocational High School sought a cooperative partnership with X Academic High School at all costs solely for maintaining these associated benefits. However, the high cost of what these agreements included was that F Vocational High School had to agree to compromise on following its own unique educational learning processes as well as assessment strategies and learner growth and development pathways. It had to re-design itself according to X Academic High School. This caused a high level of stress for the teachers at Year Ten level without proper consultation with them on the policy reform enactment at their school. The unequal cooperative clauses regarding the design of the teaching and learning process as well as the assessment process only reinforced to further sustain the lower status occupied by F Vocational High School even after this collaborative relationship was established.

The findings from this case-study school indicated an inferior position of F Vocational High School within the pilot program. The account by Zhang, a middle-level teacher leader at the school, provided a realistic picture of how the pilot program was understood, interpreted, and made sense of by teacher agents in the school setting. His account strongly supported similar findings of unfavorable outcomes that have been discussed in previous research studies (Huang, 2016; Ling, 2015; Liu & Liu, 2015; Xu & Shen, 2015; Zhou, 2017).

In his report *Made in China: Challenge and Innovation in China's Vocational Education and Training System*, Stewart (2015) suggests that major policy reformation and focus needs to be paid towards the improvement within perceptions and status of VET education in China before these changes can take place within society. Stewart (2015, p. 32) suggests that,

> Education and training need to be conceived of as lifelong pursuits that enable individuals, enterprises, and nations to adapt to rapid change continually. Bridges and pathways should be built between VET and general/academic education and higher education. There are many different models for doing this, for example, creating applied universities as the capstone of the VET system or developing community college-like institutions that provide students both technical and academic options and flexible credits towards adult education. These could be tried out in different parts of China to see what works best. Whatever the model, the principle should be 'no dead ends' (p. 32).

In the case of F Vocational High School, these bridges and pathways were uni-directional and promoted more inequity between the two schools. In not taking into account the agentic voices of teachers, the integration of the Vocational-Academic Integration policy did not bring about the desired change that was envisaged but instead highlighted issues of inequity towards the cohort of 30 students enrolled in the program and their respective teachers at Year Ten. Concerns for student wellbeing for those that had transferred to the X Academic High School also brings up issues around student mental health and wellbeing within the program.

10.6   Conclusion

In this chapter, we have gone through the theories that explain the importance of making sense of teacher agency within policy practice (Ball et al., 2012; Colebatch, 2006; Honig, 2006; Spillane, 2004). We have identified the research gap, represented by the perspectives of teachers in the enactment of a policy introduced for bringing about transformation and reformation within Chinese vocational education schools. By an exploratory qualitative case study, we have explored the gap in research and discussed relevant findings. The teachers in the chosen vocational high school expressed high caution towards the practice of the pilot integration program as it was currently being offered at the time of this study. They found that through the program they had suffered a loss of autonomy in classroom teaching to adjust the pace of instruction; uncertain benefits for student learning and development; and a sense of professional inferiority while engaged in a partnership with teachers from their fellow academic high school. By exploring the sense-making of vocational high school teachers towards the Vocational-Academic Integration program, we provide a realistic picture, for audiences both within and out of the vocational education research field, on how the pilot program must be further reviewed by addressing the concerns of teachers around the program design and implementation. As a recommendation for future research directions, more research work needs to be done on how equitable integration of VE into AE and AE into VE can be made, leading to consideration of university pathways for students completing this program.

References

Ableser, J. (2003). Elementary teachers' attitudes, perceptions, and practices towards the implementation of a violence-prevention curriculum. *Journal of School Violence, 2*(4), 81–100.

Ball, S. J., Maguire, M., & Braun, A. (2012). *How schools do policy: Policy enactments in secondary schools*. London: Routledge.

Bodilly, S., Ramsey, K., Stasz, C., & Eden, R. (1993). *Integrating academic and vocational education: Lessons from eight early innovators*. Berkeley, CA: National Centre for Research in Vocational Education.

Callahan, K. (1999). *An action research study of the integration of academic and vocational education in a suburban high school and technology career centre* (Doctor of Education). Temple University.

Colebatch, H. K. (Ed.). (2006). *Beyond the policy cycle: The policy process in Australia*. Sydney: Allen & Unwin.

Creswell, J. W. (2014). *Educational research: Planning, conducting, and evaluating quantitative and qualitative research* (5th ed.). Sydney: Pearson.

Guan, J. (2014). The modernity of the modern vocational education system. *China Higher Education Research, 2014*(11), 25–28.

Haber, R. (2005). *An introduction to psychology*. New York: Holt. Rinehart and Winston.

Halliday, J. (2007). Chapter 11: Social justice and vocational education. In L. Clarke & C. Winch (Eds.), *Vocational education: International approaches, developments, and systems* (1st ed., pp. 149–159). London: Routledge.

Honig, M. (2006). *New directions in education policy implementation: Confronting complexity*. New York: State University of New York Press.

Huang, X. (2016). Integration of the general and vocational education in Chinese senior high schools. *Journal of Hebei Normal University Educational Science Edition, 18*(1), 57–61.

Jaeger, C. (2014). The choice for China: What role for vocational education in green growth? *China & World Economy, 22*(5), 55–75.

Kincheloe, J. (1995). *Toil and trouble. Good work, smart workers, and the integration of academic and vocational education. Counterpoints: studies in the postmodern theory of education* (1st ed., p. 7). New York: Peter Lang Publishing.

Koo, A. (2015). Expansion of vocational education in neoliberal China: Hope and despair among rural youth. *Journal of Education Policy, 31*(1), 46–59.

Li, D., & Tang, L. (2016). Research on basic factors of present vocational education system construction in China. *International Journal of Academic Research in Business and Social Sciences, 6*(3).

Li, L., & Zhao, W. (2014). Expansion of higher education, high school flow diversion, and educational opportunity inequality in China. *Journal of Xi'an Jiaotong University (Social Sciences), 34*(5).

Ling, M. (2015). "Bad students go to vocational schools!" education, social reproduction, and migrant youth in urban China. *The China Journal, 73*, 108–131.

Liu, J., & Chen, G. (2013). Reflections on developing secondary vocational education in high-poverty areas. *Chinese Education & Society, 46*(4), 68–74.

Liu, L., & Liu, J. (2015). An original analysis of difficulties of the integration of academics with vocational education in our high schools. *Journal of Educational Science of Hunan Normal University, 14*(2).

Liu, L., & Wang, J. (2015). Integration of general education and vocational education in Chinese high schools: Basic mode and development status. *Education Research Monthly, 2015*(9), 3–11.

Merriam, S. B. (1998). *Qualitative research and case study applications in education.* San Francisco, CA: Jossey-Bass.

Ministry of Education. (2014). *Modern vocational education system construction plan (2014–2020)* (pp. 1–36). Beijing: Ministry of Education.

Ministry of Education. (2017). *Promote the reform of secondary vocational education to build Ningbo vocational education brand (Chinese). Moe.gov.cn.* Retrieved from http://www.moe.gov.cn/jyb_xwfb/xw_zt/moe_357/jyzt_2017nztzl/2017_zt02/17zt02_mtbd/201705/t20170511_304387.html

Ningbo Education Bureau. (2016). *Guidance on the experimental program for deepening the vocational-academic integration reform (Chinese). Jyj.ningbo.gov.cn.* Retrieved from http://jyj.ningbo.gov.cn/zwgk/article/show_article.asp?ArticleID=50743

Saborit, J., Fernández-Río, J., Cecchini Estrada, J., Méndez-Giménez, A., & Alonso, D. (2016). Teachers' attitude and perception towards cooperative learning implementation: Influence of continuing training. *Teaching and Teacher Education, 59*, 438–445.

Schmidtke, C., & Chen, P. (2012). Philosophy of vocational education in China: A historical overview. *Journal of Philosophy of Education, 46*(3), 432–448.

Shi, W. (2012). Development of TVET in China: issues and challenges. In M. Pilz (Ed.), *The future of vocational education and training in a changing world* (1st ed., pp. 85–95). Germany: Wiesbaden, Springer.

Shi, W. (2013). Issues and problems in the current development of vocational education in China. *Chinese Education & Society, 46*(4), 12–21.

Spillane, J., Reiser, B., & Gomez, L. (2006). Policy implementation and cognition: the role of human, social, & distributed cognition in framing policy implementation. In M. Honig (Ed.), *New directions in educational policy implementation: confronting complexity.* New York: SUNY Press.

Spillane, J., Reiser, B., & Reimer, T. (2002). Policy implementation and cognition: Reframing and refocusing implementation research. *Review of Educational Research, 72*(3), 387–431.

Spillane, J. P. (2004). *Standards deviation: How schools misunderstand education policy.* Cambridge, Mass: Harvard University Press.

Steinbach, J., & Stoeger, H. (2016). How primary school teachers' attitudes towards self-regulated learning (SRL) influence instructional behaviour and training implementation in classrooms. *Teaching and Teacher Education, 60*, 256.

Stewart, V. (2015). *Made in China: Challenge and innovation in china's vocational education and training system* (pp. 1–33). Washington, DC: National Centre on Education and the Economy.

Sun, L. (2010). Enhance academic study in vocational education in China. *International Education Studies, 3*(3), 141–144.

Trouilloud, D., Sarrazin, P., Bressoux, P., & Bois, J. (2006). The relation between teachers' early expectations and students' later perceived competence in physical education classes:

Autonomy-supportive climate as a moderator. *Journal of Educational Psychology, 98*(1), 75–86.

Wagah, M., Indoshi, F., & Agak, J. (2009). Attitudes of teachers and students towards art and design curriculum: Implications for vocational education in Kenya. *Educational Research and Review, 4*(10), 448–456.

Wang, H. (2011). Access to higher education in China: Differences in opportunity. *Frontiers of Education in China, 6*(2), 227–247.

Xiong, J. (2011). Understanding higher vocational education in China: Vocationalism vs Confucianism. *Frontiers of Education in China, 6*(4), 495–520.

Xu, Y., & Shen, Y. (2015). Difficulties and solutions to vocational-academic integration under the modern vocational education system (Chinese). *Education and Vocation, 2015*(10), 9–13.

Yazan, B. (2015). Three approaches to case study methods in education: Yin, Merriam, and Stake. *The Qualitative Report, 20*(2), 134–152.

Young, M. (1993). A curriculum for the 21st century? Towards a new basis for overcoming academic/vocational divisions. *British Journal of Educational Studies, 41*(3), 203.

Zhang, S. (2014). Analysis of barriers to the construction of modern vocational education system (Chinese). *Zhijiao Luntan (Vocational Education Forum)., 2014*(1), 35–38.

Zhou, W. (2017). Practice and reflections on the implementation of "vocational-academic integration" in secondary vocational schools—Take the example of cooperation of Deqing vocational secondary school and ordinary middle school (Chinese). *Zhiye (Occupation), 24*(8), 45–46.

Chapter 11
Teacher Learning Through Dialogue: The Cases of Vietnamese Teachers

Thi Diem Hang Khong

Abstract Changing daily practices, especially from one based on one-way lecturing into a more dialogic one is a challenging task for many teachers. This is strongly applicable in the case of Vietnamese teachers across various subjects. This case study aims to investigate the experience of two young primary school teachers in Vietnam trying to adopt a more dialogic approach in daily Vietnamese reading lessons. The results show that despite the previous dominance of teachers' questions, classroom interactions became more dialogic with a significant increase in both students' questions and the quality of classroom talk during whole-class discussions. This happened when the teachers delegated the authority to the students to ask and choose their preferred questions and facilitated the discussions with more open questions. The changes in both teachers' daily practices suggest a shift in classroom power and identity—the students became co-generators of knowledge. Further, disappointment with current practices, rather than their efficacy, and the search for better ones motivated the two teachers to change their pedagogies.

Keywords Teacher learning · Professional development · Dialogic approach · Professional dialogue · Bakhtin · Vietnam

11.1 Introduction

There is a growing consensus that the quality of children's learning and education is conditioned by classroom dialogue (Littleton & Mercer, 2013). Yet, teachers can be unaware of teacher-student talk patterns and functions (Mercer, Dawes, & Staarman, 2009). Hence, what is uttered during lesson time may go unnoticed whether it positively contributes to student learning or even causes harmful effects. While there exists a strong need for educators to obtain a solid understanding of dialogic

T. D. H. Khong (✉)
Faculty of Education, Monash University, Melbourne, Australia
e-mail: hang.khong@monash.edu

© Springer Nature Singapore Pte Ltd. 2021
D. Bao, T. Pham (eds.), *Transforming Pedagogies Through Engagement with Learners, Teachers and Communities*, Education in the Asia-Pacific Region: Issues, Concerns and Prospects 57, https://doi.org/10.1007/978-981-16-0057-9_11

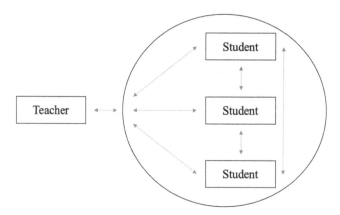

Fig. 11.1 Interactions among students and teachers in dialogical pedagogy

approaches and productive classroom interactions, investigations into how teachers learn to adopt these pedagogies in their daily practices are still limited and tend to focus on the impacts of pedagogies on instruction and student learning. Therefore, this study aimed to explore in-depth the professional learning experiences of individual teachers as they attempt to incorporate a dialogic approach in daily lessons.

11.2 Talk Pedagogy and Teacher Learning

Classroom talk plays a critical role in children's learning. There is ample evidence that certain types of talk and talk pedagogies can promote student learning and intellectual development in diverse educational contexts (Gillies, 2016; Mercer et al., 2009). Productive talk and talk pedagogies include exploratory talk, collaborative reasoning, accountable talk, dialogic teaching, and Philosophy for Children (P4C). This study focuses on the introduction in Vietnamese schools of dialogical pedagogy, a term coined by Skidmore (2006) to refer to a general framework for dialogic interactions among students and between students and teachers across disciplines (see Fig. 11.1).

Ultimately, dialogical pedagogy aims to open up space for dialogue in the classroom to provide intellectual stimulation and extend students' understanding, thinking, and learning (Fisher, 2007). It requires classroom members, including students as well as teachers, to respect and trust each other, to be open to new and different ideas, and be willing to change perspectives in the presence of sound evidence and reasons. In dialogical pedagogy, student talk becomes more substantial and interactions between teachers and students and among students greatly resemble those identified by Hennessy et al. (2016). Although productive classroom talk and talk pedagogies are strongly advocated, realising these dialogical approaches in daily practices poses enormous challenges for teachers (Davies, Kiemer, & Meissel, 2017) since they need to undergo fundamental changes in terms of practice, beliefs

(Sedova, Salamounova, & Svaricek, 2014), and identity (Davies et al., 2017). Yet little has been researched into what and how teachers learn to incorporate productive classroom dialogue or talk pedagogies in their practices.

A synthesis of research shows that teachers learn about dialogic approaches through workshops (Davies et al., 2017; Gillies, 2016), workshops in combination with in-class coaching/mentoring (Reznitskaya et al., 2009; Scholl, 2013), workshops, and video-based training (Sedova, Sedlacek, & Svaricek, 2016), and long-term onsite professional development (Webb & Treagust, 2006). Studies about classroom talk and talk pedagogies have been conducted mostly from the 1990s. While making significant contributions to the field, research in this field mainly focuses on the impact of talk and talk pedagogies on students' learning outcomes and, to some extent, teachers' pedagogical practices. Hence, it leaves many unanswered questions about the specifics of teacher learning: What meanings do they make out of their professional learning experiences with talk pedagogies? What supports teachers as they learn about them?

Based on these gaps in the literature, this study investigated teachers' learning experiences when they were engaged in a type of talk pedagogy called dialogical pedagogy in the context of Vietnam, an under-researched country whose problems and struggles in the education sector can be shared with many other Asian nations. It examined the what and how of teacher learning in their attempts to incorporate dialogical pedagogy in their daily practices. Employing a multiple case study research design, it sought to answer the following research questions:

1. What meanings do Vietnamese teachers make when they experience professional learning related to dialogical pedagogy, and as they seek to foster such pedagogy in their classrooms?
2. How does dialogue help them learn?

11.3 Theoretical Framework

11.3.1 Bakhtin's Dialogue

This study drew on the notion of dialogue and other related concepts proposed by Mikhail Bakhtin (1981, 1986). For Bakhtin, a dialogue has an extended meaning beyond the commonly held view (Renshaw, 2004), not only in terms of what it entails and what condition it requires but also whom it addresses. It has both epistemological and ontological implications. Dialogue, in Bakhtin's view, occurs when two voices representing different perspectives come into contact with each other. A dialogue requires speaker and listener or addresser and addressee. Bakhtin (1986) refers to the orientation to the other in one's speech as 'addressivity'. Nonetheless, different from the general sense of listeners in face-to-face dialogues, addressees in Bakhtin's works can be either physically present or absent. This becomes possible since dialogue 'simultaneously and perpetually operates on a vertical plane, as an internal dialogue-oriented within the self, and on a horizontal plane, as an external dialogue between subject and addressee' (Krasny, 2003, p. 29).

Further, differences in world views and perspectives between an insider and outsider (Wegerif, 2011) create a dialogic gap which, in turn, creates dialogic space. Yet, the use of the metaphor of space allows interlocutors to play with it for their purposes: they can either open, widen, deepen, or close it. Here the concepts of authoritative discourse and internally persuasive discourse seem very helpful. Bakhtin (1981) differentiates these two: While authoritative discourse[1] forces us to accept its ideas, internally persuasive discourse seeks to persuade us from inside. As such, whereas the former tends to close a dialogue, the latter tends to invite diverging ideas and thus open up dialogic space.

11.3.2   Teacher Learning Through Dialogue

This study conceptualised teacher learning as 'the co-construction (or reconstruction) of social meaning from within the parameters of emergent, socially negotiated, and discursive activity' (Hicks, 1996, p. 136). As such, teachers learn by engaging in dialogue with each other. Nsibande (2007) defines professional dialogue as 'a discussion between peers that allows the other to explicitly articulate, appreciate and extend their understanding of practice' (p. 4). Teachers may have conversations with colleagues and peers about professional matters which help them construct and negotiate meanings of practice, critically examine it, and identify their self through the experiences of colleagues and their own (Clark, 2001). Among the most researched form of teacher dialogue is the dialogic reflection (Rashid, 2018), pre-service or in-service teachers reflect upon observed lessons through conversations with colleagues. This post-lesson reflection can be oriented to generate actions or meanings of practices. Teacher dialogue enables 'the learning of new knowledge, questions and practices and, at the same time, the unlearning of some long-held and often difficult to uproot ideas, beliefs, and practices' (Cochran-Smith, 2003, p. 9). As such, it supports teachers to grow professionally (Corrigan & Loughran, 2008) not only in terms of knowledge accumulation but also identity and beliefs as well.

Apart from dialogic reflection together with colleagues, teachers are also engaged in conversations with self through self-reflection. It may take place during or after the lesson which Schon (1983) terms as reflection-in-action and reflection-on-action, respectively. In reflection-in-action, practitioners keep thinking in their heads to analyse classroom situations and make decisions moment-by-moment. Reflection-on-action, on the contrary, allows them to step back and have more time for contemplation not only about their actions but students' responses and learning as well. One of the most common ways for teachers to individually reflect on practices includes reflective writing in the forms of logs, diaries, journals, and narrative

---

[1]This is not to completely negate all forms of authoritative discourse. In certain disciplines such as science and medicine and in certain contexts, authoritative information is deemed necessary, particularly to save lives.

Fig. 11.2 Teacher learning through dialogue in professional contexts

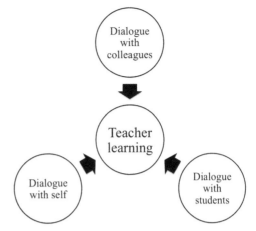

inquiry (Norris, 2009). Through dialogue with self and with others, teachers make meanings out of their own or colleagues' practices and thus understand their inner selves better. In so doing, they grow more professionally.

Although teachers' learning from other practitioners, and students' learning from peers through discussion, have been researched in the extant literature, the case of teacher learning through verbal exchanges with students receives only minimal attention. Yet, students can be resources for teacher learning (Scholl, 2013). Thus, it is argued that in professional contexts, teachers can learn through three channels of dialogue for teacher learning: dialogue with colleagues, dialogue with self, and dialogue with students (see Fig. 11.2). Although colleagues and students (the first and third channels, respectively) are both physically present in the dialogue, each audience group deserves one separate category itself. Firstly, each group represents important dialogue partners whom teachers can draw on for their professional growth in very different ways. Secondly, such categorisation together with dialogue with self will enable us to understand how teachers learn both during and after practice, both inside and outside the classroom door.

11.4 Methodology

This study examined the learning experiences of primary school teachers when they engaged in dialogical pedagogy, particularly what they learned and how they learned it through dialogue. In doing so, it investigated the questions of what and how of professional learning. To achieve these aims, it employed a multiple case study research design (Creswell, 2007; Merriam, 2009). Creswell (2007) defines a case study as 'a qualitative approach in which the investigator explores a bounded system (a case) or multiple bounded systems (cases) over time, through detailed, in-depth data collection involving multiple sources of information (e.g. observations, interviews, audio-visual material, and documents and reports), and reports a case description and case-based themes' (p. 73). Merriam (2009) gives various examples of a bounded system such as an individual, a group of individuals, an institute, a programme, a process, or a social unit. This study investigated two Vietnamese teachers with each of them being a bounded system—a case and also unit of analysis.

11.4.1 Country Context

The study was conducted in Vietnam, a country characterised by a centralised education system. Although the Ministry of Education and Training has attempted reforms, Vietnam education is still confronted with many issues. A strong emphasis on examinations, achievement focus, a rigid and theory-based curriculum as well as infrastructure constraints have led to teachers' one-sided lecturing style and passive learning among students. To cover all the required curriculum within limited class time, teachers tend to adopt a 'correct answer-seeking' method in daily lessons (Nguyen, 2014), leading to fast-paced lessons (Saito, Tsukui, & Tanaka, 2008).

Regarding the learning materials, during the data collection period, there were two sets of textbooks used in Vietnam at the primary school level: standard textbooks and Viet Nam Escuela Nueva (VNEN) ones. Despite following a similar curriculum, VNEN textbooks are designed as three-in-one self-instructional guides which tend to be less challenging, but causing rigidity and restricting teacher autonomy (Le, 2018). In this study, a teacher used a standard textbook while the other used a VNEN one.

11.4.2 Participants

This study focused on two teachers from two public primary schools (A and B) in Bac Giang province, Vietnam, and their learning related to Vietnamese lessons. Both of the teachers, Huong and Thanh (pseudonyms) were relatively young in their late 20s and had 5 and 8 years of experience respectively after completing a four-year university education. They were all homeroom teachers in charge of Grade 4. Whereas Ms. Thanh worked for a lower-achieving school in the capital city, Ms. Huong served for a leading school in a rural district about 15 km from the city. Detailed demographic information about the participating teachers is provided in Table 11.1.

Table 11.1 Demographic information about the focused teachers

Teacher	School	Grade	Class size	Gender	Years of experience	Qualification
Ms. Huong	A	4	32	F	5	BA
Ms. Thanh	B	4	26	F	8	BA

11.4.2.1 Ms. Huong

Ms. Huong, a young but recognised teacher at school A with 5 years' experience, served as a homeroom teacher of a Grade Four class with 32 students. She conducted her first reading lesson in a teacher-centred way, spending a lot of time on reading aloud and asking many questions of the students. Observing students' passive responses, she was not satisfied with her practice. Ms. Huong conceptually examined dialogical pedagogy after the first reading lesson, comparing it with her usual approach. In the researcher's absence, she tried out dialogical pedagogy, teaching her students how to make their questions about the texts after conducting reading lessons as usual. The students struggled at first since they had never done so but improved gradually. The second observed lesson showed a quick turnaround: both the teacher and students thoroughly enjoyed the whole-class discussion. Ms. Huong continued this approach even after the data collection period. However, she was not willing to share it with other colleagues who did not practise it for fear of misunderstanding and being unfavourably judged.

11.4.2.2 Ms. Thanh

A relatively young teacher with a Bachelor of Education degree, Ms. Thanh had 8 years of experience and was only in her second year at school B. She began to conduct lessons following the VNEN model after starting to work for the current school which was a completely new experience for her. In the first two reading lessons after the workshop on dialogical pedagogy, Ms. Thanh still followed all suggested steps in the VNEN textbook. Despite her dissatisfaction with reading lessons which, in her view, were boring for the students, she struggled to devise an alternative. She was then introduced in detail on how to conduct a reading lesson following dialogical pedagogy. She was convinced immediately and started to implement it in her third lesson in the researcher's presence. She spent significantly more time on the comprehension part and let the students generate their questions while reading in silence and before bringing them for whole-class discussion.

Further, Ms. Thanh would like to gather ideas from other colleagues about the new approach; thus, she decided to conduct a lesson for whole-school observation and reflection. She was criticised by some colleagues for allowing the students to freely ask questions and having no clear focus. She considered their points and continued to adjust her lessons after reflection with the researcher and school leaders. One of the leaders even demonstrated in the classroom how to support the students to differentiate question levels for better discussion quality. In the final observed lesson, the students demonstrated a significant change that surprised Ms. Thanh. They were much more engaged with asking questions and having discussions with each other.

11.4.3   Data Collection Methods

The two teachers participated in a half-day workshop about dialogical pedagogy which was delivered to all teachers in the two schools by myself—the researcher. Following the workshop, each case teacher was observed ten times as they conducted reading and mathematics lessons followed by ten reflection sessions. In this study, only reading lessons were reported. Data were collected from December 2016 to April 2017 from four sources, namely, (1) observations of daily reading lessons; (2) reflection sessions on those observed lessons; (3) teacher interviews; and (4) field notes and reflection notes. These methods were purposefully chosen based on their strengths to provide rich information about teachers' learning experiences related to dialogical pedagogy. Data were then analysed both deductively and inductively. Regarding the former approach, three provisional codes (Saldaña, 2009) were generated based on the proposed model of teacher learning through dialogue in professional contexts and the research questions prior to detailed data coding and analysis. In the inductive approach to analysing data, data were substantially coded using primary-cycle coding methods which answer the 'what' question of the data followed by secondary-cycle coding methods which focus on the 'how' and 'why' of the data (Saldaña, 2009; Tracy, 2012). MAXQDA 12 software was used to manage and code the data.

11.5   Findings

This section depicted the meanings made by the cases of teachers, Ms. Huong and Ms. Thanh, as they engaged in professional learning about dialogical pedagogy and attempted to implement it in their daily practices. Each teacher's learning was presented separately from three angles, namely, learning from dialogue with self, with the researcher and colleagues, and with students.

11.5.1   Ms. Huong

11.5.1.1   Learning from Dialogue with Self

Reading Lessons Should Be More Attractive to Students

Ms. Huong's first Vietnamese reading lesson was titled 'Hoa hoc tro' (Students' flower). It is a descriptive text which blends the description of flamboyant trees and flowers and a student's feelings. Although the students were very familiar with flamboyant trees, it was still challenging for them to become connected with the text as the lesson was conducted conventionally. The teacher led the whole-class discussion in which she asked more than ten questions. She reflected upon the lesson:

> ...after conducting the lesson 'Students' flowers', I felt unsettled because the children might be still able to answer the questions I raised. However, they did reply uneasily, their faces indicated. They did not feel relaxed, almost like they were forced to answer their teacher's questions.... (Interview, April 12, 2017)

Ms. Huong's dissatisfaction did not stop at this particular lesson but all reading lessons in her experience:

> Reading lessons are quiet and boring not like other subjects. [Students] keep reading and reading and being corrected [for their pronunciation]... Students have to repeatedly read aloud so they feel bored. (Interview, April 12, 2017)

In this remark, there seemed to be another self who judged her practices and this absent addressee (Bakhtin, 1986) set higher expectations for reading lessons: they should not be that boring but instead attractive to students. Ms. Huong's disappointment led her to consider an alternative approach.

Contemplation About and Experiment with Dialogical Pedagogy

Being introduced to dialogical pedagogy, Ms. Huong kept repeating or confirming each step to take to make reading lessons more dialogic and bring about more contribution from students: 'That means in the reading comprehension part, we will not [ask questions] but let students do it to see how it goes'. (Reflection, February 15, 2017). Her response to the introduction was not of immediate acceptance; rather, she conceptually examined it to understand what is involved and how it was different from the current practice:

> My point is reading lessons must include reading aloud and comprehension. These are two main components of lessons...For us, reading aloud tends to be a bit longer. And then comprehension, I mean the two are equal. In your way, comprehension is the main component which students focus the most... (Reflection, February 13, 2017)

In the quote above, Ms. Huong did not mean to address the researcher as she was not asked to compare the two approaches. In other words, she was deeply engaged in a conversation with self or a physically absent listener (Bakhtin, 1986) to understand her practice, the new pedagogy, and their meanings. Being aware of the difference is the first step toward change. For Ms. Huong, learning about a pedagogy was to experiment with it which resonates with existing literature about teacher learning (Feeney, 2016). She decided to try it in her own time: in two successive lessons, she taught her students how to generate their questions from the text at the end of usual reading lessons. She found it very difficult as the students did not know how to do it at first. Yet, they were eventually able to do so, though the question level was still basic. This was followed by a turnover in the second lesson observed by the researcher.

Fear of 'Going Against the Stream'

Even though Ms. Huong was committed to continuing the new approach in her class, she did not dare to share the practice with other colleagues from outside and even within the school:

> I do not dare [to conduct a lesson adopting dialogical pedagogy in front of the public]...it is unlikely that the observers would understand it. They need to observe several lessons with different approaches so that they may analyse and compare lessons. Now I do differently, it is like going against the stream. (Interview, April 12, 2017)

Ms. Huong was talking to herself, reflecting on her unique circumstance. On the one hand, she was convinced of the benefits of dialogical pedagogy. On the other hand, another self—an absent addressee (Bakhtin, 1986)—placed it in her current work context and practice community and weighed its benefits against the consequences. At the time of data collection, Ms. Huong as well as other participants were the only ones, at least in the whole province, who attempted to implement dialogical pedagogy. Thus, there was a possibility of being misunderstood and unfavourably judged as not following the necessary steps.

11.5.1.2   Learning from Dialogue with the Researcher

The Meaning of Reading

For many Vietnamese teachers, reading lessons mean students practise reading aloud and answer some questions provided in the textbook or given by teachers. Reading deeply in silence rarely took place in both schools under this study before the introduction of dialogical pedagogy. By engaging in reflective dialogue with the researcher, Ms. Huong attempted to incorporate this new practice into her reading lessons. She then started to question the practice of superficial reading and develop a new understanding of reading in silence:

> One must read in the real sense to come up with such questions and answer peers' questions. If they just read superficially, read aloud smoothly but do not comprehend the text's content, how can they answer peers' questions later on? I feel that (following your approach) students can share ideas more. In my approach, students practise reading aloud more. In your approach, students can also practise reading a lot; however, they do it by reading in silence. Only when reading in silence, one can concentrate; reading aloud is just to finish sentences. We understand better by reading in silence than reading aloud. (Interview, April 12, 2017)

Her words were not purely her own (Bakhtin, 1981) but blended with the researcher who suggested dialogical pedagogy and emphasised time for reading for oneself to the degree that they became an 'internally persuasive discourse' (Bakhtin, 1981). The new understanding of reading prompted Ms. Huong to change her reading practice, as evident in the following sections. Practitioners must keep questioning the meaning of routine practices and be exposed to new ideas. In other words, they can unlearn deep-rooted practices and learn new ones (Cochran-Smith, 2003), thereby growing more professionally.

How to Uplift Students' Questions and Their Learning

As Ms. Huong attempted to enact dialogical pedagogy in reading lessons, the students provided some questions about each text on which they were working. It does not necessarily mean that all the questions were on a par with each other due to the students' new experience of questioning and their various levels of understanding. Through reflective dialogue with the researcher after each lesson, Ms. Huong became more aware of the question level and which one to examine further for exploration of the lesson content:

> I like it very much when you [the researcher] stopped at those students with good questions from which we can further explore the lesson content. That is what I like most when you observed lessons and supported me. Normally there were many questions; however, the answers did not have a specific focus. Even though I myself is the teacher but hardly I knew which answer was of better quality. (Interview, April 12, 2017)

This learning was possible due to inherent different perspectives (Wegerif, 2011) held by Ms. Huong and the researcher—the observed and the observer, and the insider and outsider, respectively. In line with the literature, this quote shows that professional development which is situated in practice and includes observation as well as reflection supports teacher professional learning (Borko, Jacobs, & Koellner, 2010).

11.5.1.3   Learning from Dialogue with the Students

Improvising Questions

About 3 weeks after the first lesson, the researcher observed the second reading lesson by Ms. Huong, a story entitled 'Ga-vrot in the principal stockade'. Although the lesson objectives stated by the teacher were almost the same as in the previous reading lesson (reading aloud and comprehension), it was conducted in a very different manner. The students came up with their questions and started to discuss their questions in groups followed by many being eager to share theirs with the whole class. There was a series of why questions. Further, one student asked his peers to give another title for the story, which was followed by six different ideas.

Ms. Huong carefully listened to each child, pressed them to explain their thinking, and even challenged them with her questions. The following vignette clearly demonstrated how she followed the children's thinking:

T: Why do you think Ang-zon-ra and Cuoc-phe-rac did not go out to pick up the bullets but only Gavrot did so?
S: Me, me.

T: Why? Why do you think Ang-zon-ra and Cuoc-phe-rac did not go out but only Gavrot?

S: Me, me,

T: Let's think together, why?

S: Me.

T: QL, please.

S: Teacher, because Gavrot was small so he could hide himself in the thick smoke.

T: That's your idea. Who else? T Please.

S: Teacher, Gavrot did not have to shoot others while Ang-zon-ra and Cuo-phe-rac were shooting so they could not go out.

T: (laugh) That's is T's idea. H, please.

S: Teacher because Ang-zon-ra and Cuo-phe-rac were scared but Gavrot was calm and was not afraid.

T: In your opinion, were Ang-zon-ra and Cuo-phe-rac brave?

S: No.

T: They were not brave, why they could go to the principal stockade?

S: Me.

S: I think the other two were scared.

T: That means they were not as brave as Gavrot, were they? Well, thanks H. I think both Ang-zon-ra and Cuo-phe-rac were brave, weren't they? All the characters in the story "Gavrot in the principal stockade" were brave enough so that they could go to the principal stockade, is it right? I think Gavrot was small and quick so he was more quick-minded and he went out to pick up the bullets. Do you think like me?

Whole class: Yes. (Daily lesson, March 7, 2017)

Ms. Huong listened to the children; at the same time, she made sense of what they said and challenged them to critically reflect on their ideas (English, 2016). She challenged the children with the question 'Do you think Ang-zon-ra and Cuoc-phe-rac were brave?' after one student said that these two were afraid while only Gavrot was brave. Her ability to improvise questions was thanks to the dialogue she had with her students, revealing a dialogic gap (Wegerif, 2011) between the two. However, as the lesson concluded, Ms. Huong could not give them more time to think deeply about it.

Students' Capability

Ms. Huong felt so relaxed after the lesson that she could not help but share her feeling with a neighbouring colleague. She also reflected on the lesson, comparing this lesson to the previous one in terms of the teacher's role and students' role, the struggle, and enjoyment. She was most attracted by the students' questions in the reading comprehension part. By relinquishing the floor (Bakhtin, 1986) to the students, Ms. Huong could observe their responsive understanding reflected in the questions they raised about the text:

I felt relaxed because students themselves got the main content of the text without my instruction or provision of questions. I find that students are capable like what you [researcher] suggested which is to let students ask questions and raise questions. (Reflection, March 8, 2017)

Ms. Huong could recognise the children's growth in their participation in learning and agency (Hennessy, Dragovic, & Warwick, 2018). By trying out dialogical pedagogy and engaging in dialogue with the students, she not only learnt how her students could react differently to different approaches but also learnt to trust in their capacity (Bonner, 2006) if they were given opportunities. She continued to adopt dialogical pedagogy for her third observed lesson and even after the data collection period ended.

11.5.2 Ms. Thanh

11.5.2.1 Learning from Dialogue with Self

Current Reading Lessons are Not Attractive and Challenging Enough

Similar to the case of Ms. Huong, Ms. Thanh was not happy with reading lessons. Although she followed a predetermined teaching sequence and kept asking questions of students, deep inside her, a physically absent self (Bakhtin, 1986) set up higher expectations and judged the current practice as not attractive and challenging enough to the students:

I found that the students got bored with reading lessons. They were not interested in them. That's why I wanted to change the teaching approach, but I did not know how (Interview, April 13, 2017)

This dialogue with self is critical as dissatisfaction with classroom realities motivates teachers to learn professionally (Appova & Arbaugh, 2018) and thus improve their practice.

'I expect something from students' in each lesson

Adopting dialogical pedagogy, Ms. Thanh discovered the joy of conducting reading lessons which was in contrast to the boredom created by a conventional way of teaching:

I'm most interested in the part the students raise their questions because I was expecting but not knowing what kind of questions they ask and whether the questions are of good quality...Adopting this approach I find that not only the students become more interested [in the lessons] but also there is something in each reading lesson very different from the past ones. I'm also more excited, expecting something from them. (Interviews, April 13, 2017)

Even though responding to the researcher's question, she was conversing with an absent addressee (Bakhtin, 1986) who could understand her feeling—a sense of excitement for something yet to be known before each lesson.

11.5.2.2 Learning from Dialogue with the Researchers and Other Colleagues

The Meaning of Reading Comprehension

After the first lesson conducted in her usual way, Ms. Thanh reflected upon it together with the researcher and a vice-principal who was very supportive of innovative approaches and strongly emphasised quality of children learning. In the conversation, the meaning of reading and reading aloud was questioned first by the school leader:

Vice-principal: Ultimately, in one's whole life, one must be able to read. Reading comprehension plays an extremely important role, whether one is an ordinary citizen, a general, or a president. It is a tool for lifelong learning. Yet, at school, children do not learn to comprehend texts, just reading aloud has no meaning.
Ms. Thanh: Reading aloud well without comprehension is purposeless. (Reflection, December 22, 2016)

This episode provides an excellent example of 'internally persuasive discourse' (Bakhtin, 1981). What the vice-principal shared is not authoritative words; he was not forcing his ideas on Ms. Huong but pointed to the most critical point—the meaning of reading comprehension in life. Thus, Ms. Huong came to recognise it immediately. Probably this awareness functioned as the key for her to take further steps in the future.

Students Can Understand Better by Constructing Their Knowledge

After the first two observed lessons, Ms. Thanh attempted to adopt dialogical pedagogy from the third observed lesson onwards. After practising reading aloud, she let her students read in silence, write down their questions about the text, try to come up with their answers, and bring the questions to the whole-class discussion. Listening to them, having a dialogue with them, and observing their progress over time, Ms. Thanh discovered how students learn from a constructivist perspective. She compared VNEN approach and dialogical pedagogy:

First, with VNEN, students are supposed to self-study the knowledge available in the textbook; in other words, they are forced to do. The teacher does not show them the way; however, it is stated step-by-step in the textbook. It draws a way so students have to follow it. However, it is different from that approach [dialogical pedagogy]. Students self-study not in the way others show them but they need to find out their own. From concrete details, they generate their questions. (Interview, April 13, 2017)

Learning by Going Public and Adapting

After conducting several reading lessons following dialogical pedagogy, Ms. Thanh decided to share her practice with all the colleagues in her school so that she could get ideas from them and improve further:

> I find this approach [dialogical pedagogy] very interesting. Now I would like to conduct a lesson to see what kind of ideas they have because I think more heads will be better than one, isn't it? Each has his or her idea. For example, I'm doing this way but others may suggest a different direction. (Reflection, February 14, 2017)

Ms. Thanh was the only participant who went public. She did receive various ideas: while the vice-principal pointed out the strength of the approach as providing opportunities for students to learn by themselves, other colleagues criticised her practice as having no focus. She did not feel discouraged but took their points seriously and later adapted her practice. Differences between her view and other practitioners' one created a dialogic gap (Wegerif, 2011) through which she learnt more about her role as a teacher.

11.5.2.3   Learning from Dialogue with the Students

'I trust my students more'

When Ms. Thanh implemented dialogical pedagogy in reading lessons, the students' responses were very positive and the questions and discussion improved after each lesson. By providing opportunities for them to ask questions, she accepted that she had to let go of her role as a knowledge holder or expert. She did 'relinquish the floor to other [students] or to make room for the other's active responsive understanding' (Bakhtin, 1986, p. 71). Listening to them and having a dialogue with them, she recognised their great capacity. Thus, she developed her stronger trust in the learners.

> I have undergone many changes since I adopted this approach [dialogical pedagogy]. . .in previous lessons, there might be challenging questions but I did not dare to raise. However, now I trust my students more. . . .students will be able to solve it if they exchange ideas. (Interview, April 13, 2017)

This trust in students' capacity resonates well with the experience of Hispanic teachers participating in a professional development programme (Bonner, 2006). Such belief is deemed very necessary for educators to have high expectations for learners and to assign them intellectually stimulating tasks. This is particularly important in the context of Ms. Thanh's school which used to be a low performing one for many years.

11.6 Discussion

This study depicted the cases of two primary school teachers attempting to adopt
dialogical pedagogy in daily reading lessons in the context of Vietnam, a developing
country with a centralised education system and prevailing traditional ways of
teaching and learning. It provided strong evidence for the emerging theory of teacher
learning through dialogue in the Bakhtinian tradition with various partners including
colleagues, self, and students both during and outside lesson time. Throughout the
professional learning, the participating teachers engaged in a series of reflective
dialogue with the researcher and school leaders and thus were exposed to alternative
views and ways of thinking. In their study, Tan and Nashon (2013) also reported a
similar finding regarding collaboration among Singaporean teachers. Further, the
studied practitioners experienced conversing with the other self in them through self-
reflection. Finally, they also had a dialogue with students in daily lessons. The
difference in perspectives among dialogue partners created a dialogic space
(Wegerif, 2011) for the teachers to generate meanings out of their experience with
dialogical pedagogy.

Whereas research on teacher learning tends to emphasise colleagues as important
partners, it is contended that the self and students constitute other crucial sources for
teacher learning and growth. In this study, the case teachers could make meanings
not only about the pedagogy itself but also about the nature of reading, textbook
problems, children, themselves, and how to learn. Engaging in dialogue with self,
both Ms. Huong and Ms. Thanh became aware of their dissatisfaction with current
practices. Ms. Thanh learnt that she was excited about the unforeseeable contributions from students which she did not experience when adopting the previous
teacher-centred approach. Both of the teachers tried to make sense of dialogical
pedagogy using different strategies. The last two categories—learning about themselves and learning how to learn—would contribute to expanding teachers' knowledge base beyond what is advocated by Shulman (1987).

The cases of Ms. Huong and Ms. Thanh demonstrate that professional learning
through dialogue could lead to teacher change in cognitive, social, and ethical terms.
Cognitively, the teachers improved their understanding of dialogical pedagogy, the
nature and meaning of reading, the problems of current curriculum and textbooks,
how students learn, and how they could uplift student learning. Socially, they formed
a new relationship with students—one that is based on trust. This positive teacher–
student relationship is critical for students' psychological and cognitive development
(Douis, 2017). In ethical terms, the teachers underwent an identity shift from
curriculum followers to learning facilitators, from bureaucrats to professionals.

The new professional identity emerged as they interacted with various parties in
their work context (Beauchamp & Thomas, 2009). The process of intensive joint-
reflection and self-reflection helped the participating teachers examine themselves
and deeply think about the question 'Who am I?' (Korthagen, 2004). In dialogical
pedagogy, where knowledge is negotiated and co-constructed through discursive
activities, teachers no longer rely on predetermined teaching sequences. Instead,

they need to facilitate children learning and improvise questions as classroom discussion unfolds. In so doing, they gain autonomy as professional teachers who can make the best judgements about how lessons flow in a given moment based on fluid classroom situations.

The cognitive, social, and ethical changes of the participating teachers point to a central theme 'Who are lessons for?' In Ms. Huong and Ms. Thanh's previous approaches, lessons were to follow the authorities, textbooks, and teachers' guide. As the teachers attempted to experiment with dialogical pedagogy, they realised that reading lessons should be for children, their enjoyment, their comprehension, and their construction of knowledge. Children should be the main protagonists of lessons; thus, teachers need to make efforts to accommodate them and improvise along the way. Practitioners must keep this in mind in conducting every lesson.

11.7   Conclusion

The process of learning about and adopting dialogical pedagogy was not one without a struggle. In Vietnam where one-way lecturing and correct-answer seeking are commonly observed (Ngo, Meijer, Bulte, & Pilot, 2015; Nguyen, 2014), a pedagogy that promotes productive talk among classroom members represents a very new practice to many practitioners. The case teachers in the study either experienced or anticipated colleagues' criticism of the new pedagogy. While teachers may reflect on the criticism and improve the practice further, unconstructive and evaluative feedback can prevent them from being willing to open their classrooms to the public and share good practice. Researchers tend to advocate the coherence between professional development activities and local and national policies (Garet, Porter, Desimone, Birman, & Yoon, 2001). However, when policies do not promote changes or progressive reforms are yet to come, small-scale experiments with productive pedagogies such as dialogical pedagogy are deemed necessary initially to gradually inspire other teachers.

References

Appova, A., & Arbaugh, F. (2018). Teachers' motivation to learn: Implications for supporting professional growth. *Professional Development in Education, 44*(1), 5–21. https://doi.org/10.1080/19415257.2017.1280524.

Bakhtin, M. (1981). Discourse in the novel (M. Holquist & C. Emerson, Trans.). In M. Holquist (Ed.), *The dialogic imagination* (pp. 259–422). Austin: University of Texas Press.

Bakhtin, M. (1986). The problem of speech genres (V. McGee, Trans.). In C. Emerson & M. Holquist (Eds.), *Speech genres and other late essays* (pp. 60–102). Austin: University of Texas Press.

Beauchamp, C., & Thomas, L. (2009). Understanding teacher identity: An overview of issues in the literature and implications for teacher education. *Cambridge Journal of Education, 39*(2), 175–189. https://doi.org/10.1080/03057640902902252.

Bonner, P. J. (2006). Transformation of teacher attitude and approach to math instruction through collaborative action research. *Teacher Education Quarterly, 33*(3), 27–44.

Borko, H., Jacobs, J., & Koellner, K. (2010). Contemporary approaches to teacher professional development. In P. Peterson, E. Baker, & B. McGaw (Eds.), *International encyclopedia of education* (pp. 548–556). Oxford: Elsevier.

Clark, C. M. (2001). *Talking shop: Authentic conversation and teacher learning*. Williston, VT: Teachers College Press.

Cochran-Smith, M. (2003). Learning and unlearning: The education of teacher educators. *Teaching and Teacher Education, 19*(1), 5–28.

Corrigan, D., & Loughran, J. (2008). *Mentoring for the teaching profession: Snapshots of practice*. Paper presented at the British Educational Research Association annual conference, Heriot-Watt University, Edinburgh.

Creswell, J. W. (2007). *Qualitative inquiry & research design: Choosing among five approaches* (2nd ed.). Thousand Oaks, CA: Sage.

Davies, M., Kiemer, K., & Meissel, K. (2017). Quality talk and dialogic teaching—An examination of a professional development programme on secondary teachers' facilitation of student talk. *British Educational Research Journal, 43*(5), 968–987. https://doi.org/10.1002/berj.3293.

Douis, V. (2017). Developing positive teacher relationships with students. In K. Smith & J. Loughran (Eds.), *Quality learning: Teachers changing their practice* (Vol. 22, pp. 79–84). Rotterdam: Sense Publishers.

English, A. R. (2016). Dialogic teaching and moral learning: Self-critique, narrativity, community and 'blind spots'. *Journal of Philosophy of Education, 50*(2), 160–176. https://doi.org/10.1111/1467-9752.12198.

Feeney, E. J. (2016). How an orientation to learning influences the expansive–restrictive nature of teacher learning and change. *Teacher Development, 20*(4), 458–481. https://doi.org/10.1080/13664530.2016.1161659.

Fisher, R. (2007). Dialogic teaching: Developing thinking and metacognition through philosophical discussion. *Early Child Development and Care, 177*(6), 615–631. https://doi.org/10.1080/03004430701378985.

Garet, M. S., Porter, A. C., Desimone, L., Birman, B. F., & Yoon, K. S. (2001). What makes professional development effective? Results from a national sample of teachers. *American Educational Research Journal, 38*(4), 915–945.

Gillies, R. M. (2016). Dialogic interactions in the cooperative classroom. *International Journal of Educational Research, 76*, 178–189. https://doi.org/10.1016/j.ijer.2015.02.009.

Hennessy, S., Dragovic, T., & Warwick, P. (2018). A research-informed, school-based professional development workshop programme to promote dialogic teaching with interactive technologies. *Professional Development in Education, 44*(2), 145–168. https://doi.org/10.1080/19415257.2016.1258653.

Hennessy, S., Rojas-Drummond, S., Higham, R., Márquez, A. M., Maine, F., Ríos, R. M., et al. (2016). Developing a coding scheme for analysing classroom dialogue across educational contexts. *Learning, Culture and Social Interaction, 9*, 16–44. https://doi.org/10.1016/j.lcsi.2015.12.001.

Hicks, D. (1996). Contextual inquiries: A discourse-oriented study of classroom learning. In D. Hicks (Ed.), *Discourse, learning, and schooling* (pp. 104–141). New York: Cambridge University Press.

Korthagen, F. (2004). In search of the essence of a good teacher: Towards a more holistic approach in teacher education. *Teaching and Teacher Education, 20*(1), 77–97. https://doi.org/10.1016/j.tate.2003.10.002.

Krasny, K. A. (2003). *Dialogic spaces: Bakhtin's social theory of utterance in reader response (Order No. MQ79968)*. Available from ProQuest Dissertations & Theses Global. (305300190).

(Master). University of Manitoba Retrieved from https://search-proquest-com.ezproxy.library.uq.edu.au/docview/305300190?accountid=14723

Le, H. M. (2018). Another textbook project? The implementation of Escuela Nueva in Vietnam. *Educational Research for Policy and Practice, 17*(3), 223–239. https://doi.org/10.1007/s10671-018-9230-x.

Littleton, K., & Mercer, N. (2013). Educational dialogues. In T. C. K. Hall, B. Comber, & L. C. Moll (Eds.), *International handbook of research on children's literacy, learning, and culture* (pp. 291–303). Oxford: John Wiley & Sons, Ltd.

Mercer, N., Dawes, L., & Staarman, J. K. (2009). Dialogic teaching in the primary science classroom. *Language and Education, 23*(4), 353–369. https://doi.org/10.1080/09500780902954273.

Merriam, S. B. (2009). *Qualitative research: A guide to design and implementation*. San Francisco: Jossey-Bass.

Ngo, V. T. H., Meijer, M. R., Bulte, A. M. W., & Pilot, A. (2015). The implementation of a social constructivist approach in primary science education in Confucian heritage culture: The case of Vietnam. *Cultural Studies of Science Education, 10*(3), 665–693. https://doi.org/10.1007/s11422-014-9634-8.

Nguyen, V. K. (2014). Dạy học theo phương pháp "tìm kiếm câu trả lời đúng" tại các trường phổ thông ["Seeking correct answers" teaching approach in general schools]. Retrieved from https://sgd.bacgiang.gov.vn/chi-tiet-tin-tuc/-/asset_publisher/ygLgruflAjDS/content/day-hoc-theo-phuong-thuc-tim-kiem-cau-tra-loi-ungtrong-cac-truong-pho-thong-

Norris, K. S. (2009). *Making sense of teaching: A holistic approach to teacher reflection about practice*. Denton, TX: University of North Texas. (Doctoral dissertation).

Nsibande, R. (2007). *Using professional dialogue to facilitate meaningful reflection for higher education practitioners, enhancing higher education, theory and scholarship*. In: Proceedings of the 30th HERDSA annual conference, Adelaide, 8–11 July 2007.

Rashid, R. A. (2018). Dialogic reflection for professional development through conversations on a social networking site. *Reflective Practice, 19*(1), 105–117. https://doi.org/10.1080/14623943.2017.1379385.

Renshaw, P. D. (2004). Dialogic learning teaching and instruction: Theoretical roots and analytical frameworks. In J. v. d. Linden & P. D. Renshaw (Eds.), *Dialogic learning: Shifting perspectives to learning, instruction, and teaching* (pp. 1–15). Dordrecht: Kluwer Academic Publishers.

Reznitskaya, A., Kuo, L.-J., Clark, A.-M., Miller, B., Jadallah, M., Anderson, R. C., & Nguyen-Jahiel, K. (2009). Collaborative reasoning: A dialogic approach to group discussions. *Cambridge Journal of Education, 39*(1), 29–48. https://doi.org/10.1080/03057640802701952.

Saito, E., Tsukui, A., & Tanaka, Y. (2008). Problems on primary school-based in-service training in Vietnam: A case study of Bac Giang province. *International Journal of Educational Development, 28*(1), 89–103. https://doi.org/10.1016/j.ijedudev.2007.08.001.

Saldaña, J. (2009). *The coding manual for qualitative researchers*. London: Sage Publications.

Scholl, R. (2013). *Transforming pedagogy through philosophical inquiry*. Brisbane, QLD: The University of Queensland. (Unpublished doctoral thesis).

Schon, D. A. (1983). *The reflective practitioner: How professionals think in action*. London: Basic Books.

Sedova, K., Salamounova, Z., & Svaricek, R. (2014). Troubles with dialogic teaching. *Learning, Culture and Social Interaction, 3*(4), 274–285. https://doi.org/10.1016/j.lcsi.2014.04.001.

Sedova, K., Sedlacek, M., & Svaricek, R. (2016). Teacher professional development as a means of transforming student classroom talk. *Teaching and Teacher Education, 57*, 14–25. https://doi.org/10.1016/j.tate.2016.03.005.

Shulman, L. S. (1987). Knowledge and teaching - foundations of the new reform. *Harvard Educational Review, 57*(1), 1–22.

Skidmore, D. (2006). Pedagogy and dialogue. *Cambridge Journal of Education, 36*(4), 503–514. https://doi.org/10.1080/03057640601048407.

Tan, Y. S. M., & Nashon, S. M. (2013). Promoting teacher learning through learning study discourse: The case of science teachers in Singapore. *Journal of Science Teacher Education, 24*(5), 859–877. https://doi.org/10.1007/s10972-013-9340-5.

Tracy, S. J. (2012). *Qualitative research methods: Collecting evidence, crafting analysis, communicating impact.* Oxford: Wiley-Blackwell.

Webb, P., & Treagust, D. F. (2006). Using exploratory talk to enhance problem-solving and reasoning skills in grade-7 science classrooms. *Research in Science Education, 36*(4), 381–401. https://doi.org/10.1007/s11165-005-9011-4.

Wegerif, R. (2011). Towards a dialogic theory of how children learn to think. *Thinking Skills and Creativity, 6*(3), 179–190. https://doi.org/10.1016/j.tsc.2011.08.002.

Chapter 12
Teacher Change in Science Education: What Could Be Done to Make This Happen?

Lam H. Pham and Russell Tytler

Abstract Representations have been widely applied to teaching and learning in Western classrooms and recently in several Asian countries. More and more Asian schools are calling for the application of this approach in teaching science. However, little has been known about how the construction of representations could enable teachers to make changes in their pedagogical practices. This chapter discusses how to enable teachers to make changes in their pedagogical practices in science education, and how to understand the change process. Specifically, the chapter discusses various models and how each model supports teachers to change their practices. Among existing models of pathways of growth for individual teachers, the Interconnected Model of Teacher Professional Growth (IMTPG) has been widely utilised in evaluating how science teachers change their pedagogical practices when they are engaged in using representations. IMTPG has been largely supported by researchers in science education because it is a comprehensive model that fully explains how internal and external factors work together and influence each other to bring about changes in teachers' pedagogical practices. The key factor that makes the model advanced and different compared to other models is that it emphasises teachers as active learners who enact and reflect during their teaching.

Keywords Representations · Teacher change · Pedagogies · IMTPG · Science

12.1 Introduction

Representations constitute a multimodal language that includes a wide array of visual and spatial modes. Representations are used in teaching science to describe scientific phenomena and to assist students to solve scientific problems. Recently, more and more researchers have advocated student construction of representations in

L. H. Pham (✉) · R. Tytler
Deakin University, Melbourne, Australia
e-mail: lam.pham@deakin.edu.au

© Springer Nature Singapore Pte Ltd. 2021   189
D. Bao, T. Pham (eds.), *Transforming Pedagogies Through Engagement with Learners, Teachers and Communities*, Education in the Asia-Pacific Region: Issues, Concerns and Prospects 57, https://doi.org/10.1007/978-981-16-0057-9_12

teaching and learning science. This is because the practice has widely been reported to have positive effects on students' learning (Ainsworth, 2008; Wu, Krajcik, & Soloway, 2001). Various studies have evidenced that these learning gains are brought about because students are more motivated in learning science when representations are constructed (Kress, Jewitt, Ogborn, & Tsatsarelis, 2001); the application of multiple representations helps students enhance their knowledge because they need to know how to utilise various representations logically (Johnstone, 1991); and the development of representations requires a high level of reasoning, so students have a better chance to develop conceptual understanding and facilitate problem-solving in science effectively (Hubber, 2013).

Little has, however, been known about how the construction of representations could enable teachers to make changes in their pedagogical practices. This is an important aspect of teachers' professional development because how teachers teach is closely correlated to students' learning outcomes (Pham, 2014; Pham & Renshaw, 2015). It is therefore worthwhile to examine how a focus on representations could influence teachers to change their practices, subsequently leading to changes in students' learning outcomes. This chapter aims to discuss what could be involved in the journey that teachers take to change their pedagogical practices. This journey has been seen differently by various researchers. In this chapter, we will, therefore, discuss how various perspectives on teacher change are built on and compensate each other. Importantly, the chapter will discuss how the application of representations could drive teachers to make changes in their pedagogies. Bringing about changes in pedagogies so that teachers can adopt student-centred pedagogical practices has been a focal point in many Asian countries in the last two decades (Pham, 2016). Therefore, the critical discussion provided in this chapter would inform Asian teachers to consider useful and applicable practices if they want to apply representations in their science classrooms.

12.2   Teacher Change from Various Perspectives

The term 'teacher change' is expressed in various ways that amount to different interpretations (Clarke & Hollingsworth, 2002). For instance, Guskey (2002) claims that 'teacher change' could refer to 'teacher learning', while Clarke and Hollingsworth (2002) and Zwart, Wubbels, Bergen, and Bolhuis (2007) emphasise that this term also means 'teacher growth'. There have been a number of researchers studying the process of teacher change or teacher learning. Generally, this progress takes into account whether and how a teacher changes their knowledge, beliefs, and attitudes toward changes in their practices (Richardson & Placier, 2001; Wubbels, 1992). The process of teacher change is usually reported as models of teacher professional growth. There has been some debate about the progress of teacher change depicted by the different models.

An early model developed by Fullan (1982) emphasised changes in beliefs and attitudes of teachers toward new pedagogical strategies as the foundational steps of

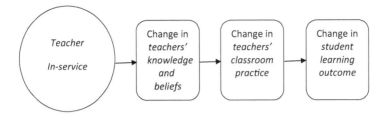

Fig. 12.1 Traditional model of the process of teacher changes

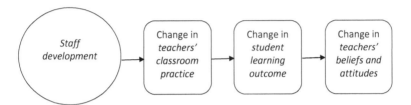

Fig. 12.2 Model of the process of teacher change (Guskey, 1986)

the teacher change progress. Fullan (1982) explains that the outcome of teacher change, such as a change in teaching practice, needs to be seen as the results of changing teacher knowledge, beliefs, and attitudes. It means that when teachers change their knowledge, beliefs, and attitudes toward new pedagogical strategies, their teaching practice will improve and as a result, student outcomes will be improved. This process is captured in Fig. 12.1 below.

In contrast, the nature of teacher changes is re-shaped by Guskey (1986) who suggests a model of teacher change in which the change of teachers' practice, obtained from professional development (PD) programmes, results in changes in students' learning outcomes, and subsequently leads to changes in teachers' knowledge, beliefs, and attitudes. The nature of teacher change in this model is a linear and reflective progress as captured in Fig. 12.2. However, Guskey (2000) acknowledges that due to the constraints in the learning and teaching context and environment, PD programmes may not effectively support the change of teachers' classroom practice.

In sum, the above models, and the associated professional development programmes, mainly target the change in teacher knowledge, belief, and attitude and do not focus on the teacher's initial knowledge, beliefs, and attitudes which may have a positive contribution to the professional development programmes. Furthermore, the school context is one of the important elements in professional development programmes but it has not been emphasised in the models above. Especially, the models above ignore the aspect of stimulating teacher learning (Ball & Cohen, 1999) and fail to take into account existing knowledge about how teachers learn (Ball & Cohen, 1999; Borko, 2004). As a result, the nature and process of teacher change is the subject of debate. Borko (2004), Clarke and Hollingsworth (2002), and

Fig. 12.3 Elements of a
professional development
system (Borko, 2004)

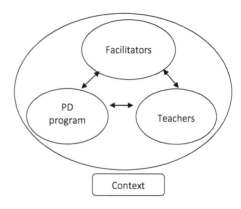

Desimone, Porter, Garet, Yoon, and Birman (2002) have argued that teacher change
is a non-linear process, which includes processes in which teachers are engaged in
active and meaningful learning.

The typical non-linear model designed by Borko (2004) explains the elements
constructing the professional development system. In this model, the professional
development programmes, the teachers, the facilitators, and the context where the
teacher works are the main elements of a professional development system as shown
in Fig. 12.3 below. Borko (2004) points out that the relationships among these
elements have been studied in various ways. However, the exact mechanism of how
these elements are correlated has not been explored. Therefore, the nature of teacher
change processes is still unclear in this model.

Generally, each of the models discussed above has some limitations that prevent
the full explanation of how teachers change their pedagogical practices. In 2002,
Clarke and Hollingsworth developed the Interconnected Model of Teacher Professional Growth (IMTPG) model which has been much cited as an effective model to
examine the process through which teachers make changes in their teaching practices. This model is seen as the most comprehensive model that offers an examination of a wide range of factors that could influence how teachers change. The model
is comprised of four domains which encompass the teacher's world: the personal
domain includes teachers' knowledge, beliefs, and attitudes; the domain of practice
emphasises professional experimentation; the domain of consequence contains
salient outcomes related to classroom practice; and the external domain includes
external sources of information or stimuli as seen in Fig. 12.4. These domains
involve both personal factors and the professional teaching context of the teacher.
For instance, the external domain is outside the individual world of the teacher while
the remaining three domains direct the teacher's professional actions as they construct the individual teacher's professional world of practice.

Importantly, as can be seen from Fig. 12.4, the mechanism of changes can be
identified by the mediating processes of reflection and enactment where the teacher's
learning process and the conditions that support teachers' professional development
are the core issues (Clarke & Hollingsworth, 2002). An 'enactment' illustrates the

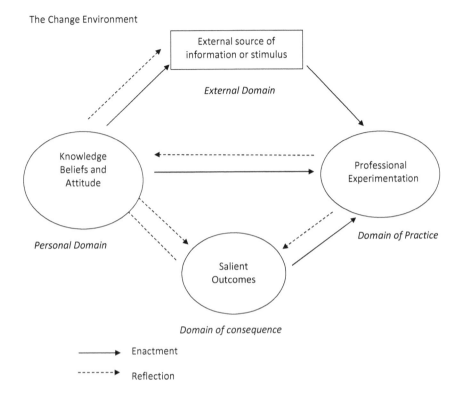

Fig. 12.4 Clarke and Hollingsworth's (2002) IMTPG model

translation of teacher's beliefs or knowledge of a pedagogical model into action in their practice, as a result of 'what the teacher knows, believes or has experienced'. The term 'reflection' refers to the 'active, persistent, and careful consideration' of teachers in reflecting on a classroom experiment (Clarke & Hollingsworth, 2002, p. 951). In other words, reflection involves the ability to call up an experience to create directions for future actions (Korthagen & Vasalos, 2009). Through the reflection and enactment process, change can take place, and change in one domain leads to change in another domain (Clarke & Hollingsworth, 2002). The emphasis on teachers' enactment and reflection as important factors that could enable teachers to make changes in their pedagogical practices has been widely advocated by researchers such as Loughran (2007) who claims that teachers need to be seen as active and constructivist learners.

12.3   IMTPG: An Applicable 'Teacher Change Framework' for Teaching Science Using Representations

In the literature, there is a growing consensus that there is a need for research tools to investigate and understand a teacher's change or a teacher's professional development (e.g. Beijaard, Verloop, Wubbels, & Feiman-Nemser, 2000; Eraut, 1994). In the context of research about teacher's change in coming to enact the representation construction approach, this demand is particularly high. This is because very little has been known about the connection between how teachers change their teaching practices as a result of their implementation of representations.

The IMTPG model has been utilised as an applicable model that can explore teacher changes through the implementation of the representation construction approach. So far, Hubber and Chittleborough (2014) were one of the very few researchers who used IMTPG as a framework to examine how teachers teaching Year 8 students changed their practices when using the representation construction approach. In Hubber and Chittleborough's research, the IMTPG model was the main analytical tool used to explore teachers' experience in preparation and application of the teaching sequence. These authors have recognised the IMTPG model as a useful instrument that can be flexible in identifying the experiences of teachers in different situations and in identifying issues for implementation of research developed pedagogy (Hubber & Chittleborough, 2014).

In very recent research, Wongsopawiro, Zwart, and van Driel (2017) also described a method of analysing teacher's change using the IMTPG model. In the context of a one-year professional development programme that was conducted with school science teachers in Illinois, USA, IMTPG appeared as a model that enables the capture of teacher changes, 'making it possible to describe the changes and uncover the processes for research purposes' (Wongsopawiro et al., 2017). In this study, the IMTPG model helped researchers explore changes in teachers' pedagogical content knowledge (PCK) by way of their processes of enactment and reflection. Particularly, the analysis through the IMTPG model revealed that teachers gained understanding about selecting and implementing instructional strategies to further promote their student learning when they analysed and reflected on student learning in classroom practices (Wongsopawiro et al., 2017). Among the domains of the IMTPG model, the consequence domain played a crucial role in the teacher's PCK development. As such, the interaction between this domain and other domains should be of concern (Wongsopawiro et al., 2017).

Hubber and Chittleborough (2014) and other researchers advocated the usefulness of using IMTPG as a framework to investigate how teachers change, for instance in enacting fundamental pedagogical change such as representation construction, due to four main reasons. First, the IMTPG model of teacher growth is mainly designed for describing the development of individual teachers and used to track teachers' changes in their classroom practices (Clarke & Hollingsworth, 2002). In accordance with Clarke and Hollingsworth's ideas, van Driel (2014) claimed that the IMTPG model can serve as a crucial tool to understand individual teacher's development in a detailed way via identifying relationships between the four domains (Van Driel, 2014). In other words, the IMTPG model allows the possibility of characterising teachers' knowledge development as an idiosyncratic process. Interestingly, this model also identified the emergence of differences in the development of distinct aspects of the knowledge of a given teacher (Van Driel, 2014).

Secondly, the IMTPG model could be used as a lens for designing professional learning approaches supporting teachers' adoption of the representation construction approach for specific topics to apply into classroom practices and to organise workshops, as part of a teacher training programme. This is because underpinning the IMTPG model, changes in teachers' knowledge are considered as a consequence of active and meaningful learning. In this concept, teachers' change becomes a development process in which the teachers build their own PCK via the knowledge and experience gained from the pedagogical development process and their classroom practices (Clarke & Hollingsworth, 2002). The process of teachers' knowledge construction obtained from their classroom practices and PD programme is crucial to create shifts in teachers' knowledge and practices. Third, the IMTPG model was usefully adopted to study the change of teachers through the enactment of the representation construction approach because it offers the opportunity to study different patterns of teacher change (Clarke & Hollingsworth, 2002, Hubber & Chittleborough, 2014). The model includes chains of elements that are responsible for changes in teachers' knowledge and practices as a process of growth or learning. These studies showed the power of the model in tracking these chains or sequences of enactment leading to growth, and its adaptability to fit different instances of the domain.

Last but not least, van Driel (2014) concluded that science teachers' professional learning of pedagogical content knowledge (PCK) may effectively be supported if they are exposed to the opportunities of experimenting with new teaching approaches in their practices and opportunities of reflecting on their experiences, both individually and collectively. On the other hand, the IMTPG model, especially the external domain or sources of information and stimuli implies the collegial interactions as argued above. The collegial interaction or teacher collaboration in a professional learning community would effectively help the teachers in reflecting on their experiences. As the matter of fact, inclusion of the IMPTG model in research about teacher change through the application of the representation construction approach would improve teachers' professional learning PCK. Furthermore, the IMPTG model has been proved to work as a powerful tool that can offer more insight into the processes involved in professional learning (Van Driel, 2014). In particular, this model makes explicit the tacit change pathway of teacher practices, so it makes it possible to indicate powerful elements within professional learning programmes (Van Driel, 2014).

However, although the IMPTG model potentially works as a fruitful tool to investigate teacher change through the application of the representation construction approach, the emerging question of how teacher's professional development programmes contribute to changes in teachers' professional knowledge and their practice, in a way that enhances student learning and appreciation of science, still needs more investigation (Desimone, 2009; Yoon, Duncan, Lee, Scarloss, & Shapley, 2007). To promote student learning outcomes as well as teachers' knowledge growth or to make the teacher change happen, the teacher's collegial cooperation is an important element. The section below further discusses the interpretation of the external domain as the collegial interactions in the school contexts.

12.4 Teacher Collaboration in a Professional Learning Community: A Key Factor in the External Domain of the IMTPG Model

In order to promote successful teacher professional learning, collegial cooperation or exchange among teachers or of teacher professional communities plays an important role (Borko, 2004; Putnam & Borko, 2000). Voogt et al. (2011) has demonstrated that the IMTPG model can be applied to research about teacher's collaborative curriculum design and implementation. In the IMTPG model of Clarke and Hollingsworth (2002), the external sources of information *are those* located 'outside of the teacher's personal world' and could be interpreted in various ways. For instance, professional publications and conversations with colleagues are both important external sources of new information and stimulus. Moreover, teacher interaction via network meetings to exchange knowledge and experiences is also taken into account as a key element of the external domain by Witterholt and her colleagues (Witterholt, Goedhart, Suhre, & van Streun, 2012).

To successfully apply the student representation construction approach into classroom practice, the participating teachers are required to stimulate the active and self-regulated learning of students during their teaching practice. To engage students to construct their own representations effectively, teachers should act as a stimulator in the students' learning process (Bolhuis & Voeten, 2004). This multimodal pedagogy may require teachers to adjust their teaching strategies as well as their perceptions toward the use of the representation construction approach in teaching chemistry. In order to deal with these challenges, many studies indicate the advantages of teachers collaborating with each other and with teacher educators to develop a professional learning community (Shulman & Gamoran Sherin, 2004) where they can learn, discuss, and exchange ideas and experience for the betterment of their professional practices. It has been evident that the collaborative learning community is a powerful environment for teachers' professional learning and development. Teacher professional learning is defined as 'the sharing of insights about teaching and learning between teachers in order to gain a sense of professional control and ownership over their learning' (Berry, Loughran, Smith, & Lindsay, 2009, p. 578). Skerrett (2010) re-defined teacher professional learning in the context of the learning community. Skerrett (2010) considered the teacher learning community as a group of teachers who continually inquire into their practice and, as a result, discover, create, and negotiate new meanings that improve their practice.

In terms of collaboration among teachers, teachers' culture of sharing and discussion of their practical experiences (external domain) is stressed as a supporting factor for the development of teacher learning communities (Stoll & Louis, 2007). Through such collaboration, teachers can negotiate and generate new materials as well as teaching strategies and receive feedback from the other teachers (Butler, Novak Lauscher, Jarvis-Selinger, & Beckingham, 2004; Putnam & Borko, 2000). In very recent research, Park and So (2014) conducted a project about a collaborative teacher learning community to investigate how teacher learning and growth is supported by collaborative professional learning. Park and So (2014) claimed that teachers' collaboration in a learning community effectively supports their learning and professional development. Through collaborative learning with colleagues, teachers experienced professional growth and learnt to self-reflect on their classes via the collaborative professional learning community (Park & So, 2014). Especially, in accordance with the teacher collaboration research above, Wongsopawiro et al., 2017 also emphasised the role of teacher collaboration in the pathway of teacher change. Underpinned by the IMTPG model, the teacher collaboration in a professional learning community happened when they learned about new instructional strategies and assessment methods through literature reviews and discussions with peers (Wongsopawiro et al., 2017).

On the other hand, the collaboration between teachers and university educators is also a crucial element in the external domains of the IMTPG model that contributes to teacher learning and development. This is because the cooperation of teachers and university educators can promote new forms of discourse about teaching and learning. These discourse communities are powerful contexts for improving the practices of all of the participants (Putnam & Borko, 2000). Likewise, Erickson and his co-workers (Erickson, Brandes, Mitchell, & Mitchel, 2005) reported that the collaboration between teachers and teacher educators improved the learning environment in classrooms for students and teachers; created models of professional development for school and teacher educators; and provided valid knowledge about learning and teaching issues in classroom settings. Teacher-teacher educator collaboration has resulted in opportunities for the professional development of all the collaborative participants (Erickson et al., 2005). Interestingly, Wongsopawiro et al., 2017 used the IMTPG model to analyse science education teacher change and confirmed the role of collaboration between teachers and university staff in teacher professional development. These authors found that university educators in the external domain 'triggered teachers' knowledge of instructional strategies'. Likewise, the IMTPG model was confirmed as a 'very useful analytical tool that used to investigate teachers' knowledge development'. Analysis of teacher change research data using the IMTPG model showed 'how changes in teachers' knowledge occur, why they occur, and sometimes under what circumstances they can occur' (Wongsopawiro et al., 2017).

12.5   Conclusion

This chapter has discussed how to enable teachers to make changes in their pedagogical practices in science education, and how to understand the change process.
The literature has reported various models that could serve as a framework guiding
the development of PD programmes as well as evaluating how teachers change their
practices. Each model has its own focus and proposes different journeys that teachers
would go through when they make changes. Among existing models of pathways of
growth for individual teachers, IMTPG has been widely utilised in evaluating how
science teachers change their pedagogical practices when they are engaged in using
representations. IMTPG has been largely supported by researchers in science education because it is a comprehensive model that fully explains how internal and
external factors work together and influence each other to bring about changes in
teachers' pedagogical practices. The key factor that makes the model advanced and
different compared to other models is that it emphasises teachers as active learners
who enact and reflect during their teaching. Therefore, teachers should be considered
as important stakeholders who should be involved in determining the development
of PD programmes. Importantly, within the external domain of the IMTPG, collaborations among teachers are an important 'external factor' that influences teachers to
make changes.

References

Ainsworth, S. (2008). The educational value of multiple representations when learning complex
    scientific concepts. In J. K. Gilbert, M. Reiner, & M. Nakhlel (Eds.), *Visualization: Theory and
    practice in science education* (pp. 191–208). New York: Springer.
Ball, D. M., & Cohen, D. (1999). Developing practice, developing practitioners: Toward a practice-
    based theory of professional development. In L. Darling-Hammond & G. Sykes (Eds.), *Teach-
    ing as the learning profession: Handbook of policy and practice* (pp. 3–32). San Francisco, CA:
    Jossey-Bass.
Beijaard, D., Verloop, N., Wubbels, T., & Feiman-Nemser, S. (2000). The professional develop-
    ment of teachers. In R. J. Simons, J. V. d. Linden, & T. Duffy (Eds.), *New learning*
    (pp. 261–274). Dordrecht: Kluwer Academic.
Berry, A., Loughran, J., Smith, K., & Lindsay, S. (2009). Capturing and enhancing science
    teachers' professional knowledge. *Research in Science Education, 39*, 575–594.
Bolhuis, S., & Voeten, M. J. M. (2004). Teachers' conceptions of student learning and own
    learning. *Teachers and Teaching: Theory and Practice, 10*(1), 77–98.
Borko, H. (2004). Professional development and teacher learning: Mapping the terrain. *Educational
    Researcher, 33*(8), 3–15.
Butler, D. L., Novak Lauscher, H., Jarvis-Selinger, S., & Beckingham, B. (2004). Collaboration and
    self-regulation in teachers' professional development. *Teaching and Teacher Education, 20*(2),
    435–455.
Clarke, D. J., & Hollingsworth, H. (2002). Elaborating a model of teacher professional growth.
    Teaching and Teacher Education, 18(8), 947–967.

Desimone, L. M. (2009). Improving impact studies of teachers' professional development: Toward better conceptualizations and measures. *Educational Researcher, 38*(2), 181–200. https://doi.org/10.3102/0013189X08331140.

Desimone, L. M., Porter, A. C., Garet, M., Yoon, K. S., & Birman, B. (2002). Does professional development change teachers' instruction? Results from a three-year study. *Educational Evaluation and Policy Analysis, 24*(2), 81–112.

Eraut, M. (1994). *Developing professional knowledge and competence.* London: Falmer Press.

Erickson, F., Brandes, M. G., Mitchell, I., & Mitchel, J. (2005). Collaborative teacher learning: Findings from two professional development projects. *Teaching and Teacher Education, 21*(3), 787–798.

Fullan, M. (1982). *The meaning of educational change.* New York: Teachers College Press.

Guskey, R. T. (1986). Staff development and the process of teacher change. *Educational Researcher, 15*(5), 5–12.

Guskey, R. T. (2000). *Evaluating professional development programs.* Thousand Oaks, CA: Corwin Press.

Guskey, R. T. (2002). Professional development and teacher change. *Teachers and Teaching: Theory and Practice, 8*(3/4), 381–391.

Hubber, P. (2013). Teacher perspectives of a representation construction approach to teaching science. In R. Tytler, V. Prain, P. Hubber, & B. Waldrip (Eds.), *Constructing representations to learn in science* (pp. 135–149). Rotterdam, Netherlands: Sense Publishers.

Hubber, P., & Chittleborough, G. (2014). *Teacher change in implementing research developed representation construction pedagogy.* Paper presented at the Groupe international de recherche sur l'Enseignement de la physique (GIREP) and the multimedia in physics teaching and learning (MPTL) international conference, University of Palermo, Italy.

Johnstone, A. H. (1991). Why is science difficult to learn? Things are seldom what they seem. *Journal of Computer Assisted Learning, 7*(1), 75–83.

Korthagen, F., & Vasalos, A. (2009). *From reflection to presence and mindfulness: 30 years of developments concerning the concept of reflection in teacher education.* Paper presented at the EARLI Conference, Amsterdam. An adaptation of this paper is published in Lyons, N. (ed.) Handbook of reflection and reflective inquiry: mapping a way of knowing for professional reflective inquiry. New York: Springer.

Kress, G., Jewitt, C., Ogborn, J., & Tsatsarelis, C. (2001). *Multimodal teaching and learning: The rhetorics of the science classroom.* London: Continuum.

Loughran, J. (2007). Science teacher as learner. In S. K. Abell & N. G. Lederman (Eds.), *Handbook of research on science education* (pp. 1043–1066). Mahwah: Lawrence Erlbaum.

Park, M., & So, K. (2014). Opportunities and challenges for teacher professional development: A case of collaborative learning community in South Korea. *International Education Studies, 7*(7), 96–108.

Pham, T. (2014). *Implementing cross-culture pedagogies: Cooperative learning at Confucian heritage cultures.* Singapore: Springer.

Pham, T. (2016). Student-centredness: Exploring the culturally appropriate pedagogical space in Vietnamese higher education classrooms using activity theory. *Australian Journal of Teacher Education, 41*(1), 1–21.

Pham, T., & Renshaw, P. D. (2015). Adapting evidence-based pedagogy to local cultural contexts: A design research study of policy borrowing in Vietnam. *Pedagogies: An International Journal, 10*(3), 256–274.

Putnam, R., & Borko, H. (2000). What do new views of knowledge and thinking have to say about research on teacher learning? *Educational Researcher, 29*(1), 4–15.

Richardson, V., & Placier, P. (2001). Teacher change. In V. Richardson (Ed.), *Handbook of research on teaching* (4th ed., pp. 905–947). Washington, DC: American Educational Research Association.

Shulman, L. S., & Gamoran Sherin, M. (2004). Fostering communities of teachers as learners: Disciplinary perspectives. *Journal of Curriculum Studies, 36*(2), 135–140.

Skerrett, A. (2010). There's going to be community. "There's going to be knowledge": Designs for learning in a standardized age. *Teaching and Teacher Education, 26*(2), 648–668.

Stoll, L., & Louis, K. S. (2007). *Professional learning communities-divergence, depth and dilemmas*. New York: Open University Press.

Van Driel, J. H. (2014). Professional learning of science teachers. In C. Bruguiere, A. Tiberghien, & P. Clement (Eds.), *Topics and trends in current science education* (pp. 139–156). Dordrecht: Springer.

Voogt, J., Westbroek, H., Handelzalts, A., Walraven, A., McKenney, S., Pieters, J., & de Vries, B. (2011). Teacher learning in collaborative curriculum design. *Teaching and Teacher Education, 27*(8), 1235–1244.

Witterholt, M., Goedhart, M., Suhre, C., & van Streun, A. (2012). The interconnected model of professional growth as a means to assess the development of a mathematics teacher. *Teaching and Teacher Education, 28*(5), 661–674.

Wongsopawiro, S. D., Zwart, C. R., & van Driel, H. J. (2017). Identifying pathways of teachers' PCK development. *Teachers and Teaching, 23*(2), 191–210. https://doi.org/10.1080/13540602. 2016.1204286.

Wu, H. K., Krajcik, S. J., & Soloway, E. (2001). Promoting an understanding of chemical representations: Students' use of a visualization tool in the classroom. *Journal of Research in Science Teaching, 38*(7), 821–842.

Wubbels, T. (1992). Taking account of student teachers' preconceptions. *Teaching and Teacher Education, 8*(2), 137–150.

Yoon, K. S., Duncan, T., Lee, S. W.-Y., Scarloss, B., & Shapley, K. (2007). *Reviewing the evidence on how teacher professional development affects student achievement (Issues & Answers Report, REL 2007-No. 033)*. Washington, DC: U.S. Department of Education, Institute of Education Sciences, National Center for Education Evaluation and Regional Assistance, Regional Educational Laboratory Southwest. Retrieved from http://ies.ed.gov/ncee/edlabs/regions/southwest/pdf/REL_2007033.pdf.

Zwart, R. C., Wubbels, T., Bergen, T. C., & Bolhuis, S. (2007). Experienced teacher learning within the context of reciprocal peer coaching. *Teachers and Teaching: Theory and Practice, 13*(2), 165–187.

Part III
Transforming Pedagogies Through Community Engagement

Chapter 13
Posting Your Thoughts: A Pedagogical Perspective of Blogging

Joseph A. Foley and Marilyn F. Deocampo

Abstract This chapter argues that "blogging" is a part of social networking that can provide a broader perspective on communication in general and education in particular. Communication becomes possible when blogging, not because this adheres to global or regional norms, but because bloggers are able to bring their communication into alignment by expressing agreement as well as disagreement with each other. Drawing on examples from blogs in Singapore and the Philippines, what is in focus is not so much shared codes in terms of English but more on interaction using language resources (translanguaging) available to the bloggers. What seems more important is this ability to adjust to the diversity of contemporary contexts of communication. Research into English still seems to focus more on differences between "inner," "outer," and "expanding" circle variants, rather than how English and other language resources are made use of and have become available for people in different geographic, ethnic, and socio-economic backgrounds. Providing people with the freedom to function beyond the conventions of their traditional boundaries has the potential to keep society more open-minded in discussing issues, both in the classroom and/or online so that participants not only develop their language skills but also their critical awareness of the world around them.

Keywords Blogging, · Communication · Translanguaging · Multilingualism · Singapore · Philippines

13.1 Introduction

The role of blogging in the "cyber-world" has the potential to make us rethink our channels of communication in what is a multilingual world. A number of researchers (Beres, 2015; Canagarajah, 2011; Garcia, 2009; Garcia & Sylvan, 2011; Garcia &

J. A. Foley (✉) · M. F. Deocampo
Assumption University, Bangkok, Thailand

© Springer Nature Singapore Pte Ltd. 2021
D. Bao, T. Pham (eds.), *Transforming Pedagogies Through Engagement with Learners, Teachers and Communities*, Education in the Asia-Pacific Region: Issues, Concerns and Prospects 57, https://doi.org/10.1007/978-981-16-0057-9_13

Wei, 2014; Garza & Langman, 2014) in examining the nature of language as a tool for communication and learning have used the term "translanguaging" (Williams, 2002). According to these studies, translanguaging is more than simply switching between codes or language mixing but rather it refers to the users' construction and use of original and complex interrelated discursive practices that cannot be easily assigned to one or another traditional definition of language. In other words, it is this process of "languaging" that makes up the users' complete language repertoire. Similarly, Baker (2006), Canagarajah (2011), and Creese and Blackledge (2010) have suggested that the concept of translanguaging in multilingual settings of the classroom is more of a fluid linguistic tool that is shaped according to the sociocultural and historical environment. More importantly, there is no fixed structure to translanguaging; it is not a unique and standard code-system as often presented when we teach languages as if they were simply parallel forms of communication.

13.2   Yahoo Singapore and Yahoo Philippines as Open-Source Platforms

Blogging sections on *Yahoo Singapore* and *Yahoo Philippines* are open-source platforms where people share their views on different topics and reactions to various events. Although the bloggers may come from different walks of life, age, gender, and geographical locations, they participate in discussions that can often create an acrimonious but continuous dialogue. Historically, a weblog or blog for short is recognized by its regularly updated, time, and date stamped posts, running down the computer screen in chronologically reverse order (i.e., the most recent post comes first). Crucially there is an "Add Comment" feature so that readers of posts can leave their opinions, questions, or thoughts. Finally, there is a writing style element: blogs are written by one individual who gives his/her thoughts generally in a spoken style (McIntosh, 2005, p. 2). Often, comments are posted anonymously to express appreciation or disagreement about something. For example, in Singapore, digital media as the new domain of collaborative discourse allows a certain degree of anonymity to the bloggers, thus giving people a voice, to realize the freedom of speech and empowerment that may not have been possible before. In the Philippines because of the range of languages used, the geographical spread, and the lack of resources compared to the island state of Singapore, there is a somewhat greater degree of freedom of expression in society as government control is more difficult to impose. Both countries have "English plus another language" bilingual education systems, although English is more dominant in Singapore. This is because English is considered the L1 while other languages are categorized as L2 (even an individual's mother tongue). In the Philippines, English and Tagalog play the dominant role in the bilingual education system, although there are many other languages used throughout the archipelago (Deocampo, 2014). One of the consequences of this digital communication as seen in *Yahoo.sg* and *Yahoo.ph*, besides the willingness to communicate, is that interactions have a number of distinct characteristics that help create "space" and "time" between the "addresser" and the "addressee." As a result, this changes the landscape of communication. Emotions play an important role and such emotions can be contagious and often hidden within the individual discourse. Writers and readers can bring their feelings and emotions together which produce the "we" factor and so that it became a collaborative affair as it creates a sense of intimacy between those who are involved as well as antipathy. What seems to inspire "bloggers" is a sense of togetherness or disagreement that the "tie that binds" that can make these groups of people become one (Harper, 2010).

13.3   The Theoretical Framework

The theoretical framework for translanguaging is based on the sociocultural theory of Vygotsky (1992) as well as Zentella's (1997) anthropolitical linguistics and the Community of Practice (CoP) approach (Lave & Wenger, 1991). Vygotsky gave a crucial importance to the sociocultural context when exploring the meaning that language conveys. Anthropolitical linguistics is important because it addresses the political aspects of the power of language used particularly in relation to marginalized groups. Finally, CoP is bounded by social acts performed within a circumscribed community. In this study of blogging in *Yahoo Philippines* and *Yahoo Singapore,* we can see that blogging, almost by its nature, involves socially and culturally contested environments as in anger leading often to racism where the participants engage drawing on the full range of functional and formal elements that comprise an individual's linguistic repertoire.

Blogging, it will be argued, is part of social networking and can provide a broader perspective on a central goal of language education. That is people who are resourceful users have both good access to a range of linguistic resources and are good at shifting between styles, discourse, registers, and genres. Communication in the electronic medium becomes possible not because we adhere to global or even regional norms, but because language users are able to bring their communication into alignment with each other. Drawing on examples from blogs in Singapore and the Philippine context, what is revealed is the need to focus less on a supposed shared code in terms of English and more on the interaction among language resources, activities, and spaces. In multilingual contexts, we need a more fluid yet "principled approach" (obviously "English classes" cannot be 25% in English and 75% in another language). What is more important is adjusting to the diversity of contemporary contexts of communication (Pennycook, 2014). For even after a great deal of research on English varieties, the focus still seems to remain on the differences between the "inner circle" varieties and their "outer" and "expanding" circle variants. Yet all varieties of English are in complex relations of power with other varieties. For example, it is clear that in the Philippines and Singapore the situation is far more complex than merely placing it in the "outer circle" as if that explained the many "Englishes" in use. What is important to see is not about how Philippine or

Singapore English differs from American or British English but how English and other language resources are spread and used and made available to people of different classes and ethnicities in these countries. Also, if we simply circumscribe these forms of English as a multilingual franca (Jenkins, 2015) then we have to see them as an emergent mix that is always in flux. Consequently, this "languaging" should not default to "English" or any other predefined language but instead be placed as processes of interaction rather than an assumption about the medium (Pennycook, 2014).

13.4   Research Methodology

The research focuses on language and power. Power in itself is complicated, as it depends on *who has it* and *how people understand* it and this is where ideology plays an integral part. According to Lukes (2005), power must be understood not only in terms of who participates but also in terms of who does not because power has "three faces," *the public, a hidden face*, and *an insidious face*. Gaventa (2007) called these "three forms of power": *visible form of power, hidden form of power*, and the *invisible form*. As Weedon (1997, p.21) explains, the power of language used as an instrument includes: "the place where actual and possible forms of social organization and their likely social and political consequences are defined and contested. Yet, it is also the place where our sense of ourselves, our subjectivity, is constructed." The medium used was exploring digital media or online journalism and the role it plays in people's personal views about different issues that otherwise would go unheard, at least publicly. *Yahoo.ph* and *yahoo.sg* are examples of a number of sites where the writer/reader is not only provided space (comment section) to freely give opinions about the news and certain issues but also each other's point of view. In other words, it gives access to "power" in so far as there is an opportunity for the writers/readers to express their concern about issues that print media may not provide.

The data of this study was composed of selected news articles in *yahoo.sg* and *yahoo.ph* over 7 months. The news coverage includes politics and governance, focusing on certain issues: "immigration," "housing," "education," "graft and corruption," and "religion." The reason for this selection was because these topics were headline news. The data was composed of **1990 conversational turns or comments** (original postings and replies to the postings) but only **a sample of the comments** have been selected to illustrate the flow of the interactions in the comments and the linguistic resources used. Because of the pedagogical aspect of this study, the variety of semiotic systems as well as the translanguaging used by the participants provided an indicator of the resources employed in communicating.

13.5   Bloggers as Participants

The information about the participants' name and age was ambiguous because of their partial anonymity. Although each participant has their aliases/pseudonym, the gender and the race such as Malay, Singaporean, Eurasian, Caucasian, or Filipino are not necessarily revealed in their profile. However, it is clear from the topics discussed that many of the participants are teachers, students, parents, and casual bloggers from the Philippines and Singapore interacting in the *yahoo.ph* and *yahoo.sg* online news comments section.

The Study Posed Two Questions

1. In what way are *translanguaging and other semiotic forms* used to communicate by bloggers in *Yahoo News* in Singapore and the Philippines?
2. What is the relevance of *translanguaging* in blogging for education, especially language teaching?

13.6   Examples of Data Collected

Note: *the examples shown are* **as** *written by the participants.*

Yahoo.ph
The article initiating the discussion from the Philippine Daily Inquirer 22 August 2011:
More than 26,000 foreigners are currently studying in various schools throughout the Philippines with South Koreans topping the list, according to the Bureau of Immigration...

Example 1
BUT LOOK AT THE REAL SITUATION:
Almost 40% of the children's population are not studying because of various reasons:
Money—Expense for Schooling (Although from public school, **still baon** *[pocket money]* **and other** things have expenses).
Shelter—(SELF-EXPLANATORY)
Food—Pangkain na nga lang minsan wla, ang magaral p kya??? *[There is no food sometimes, how much more for study?]*
GOVT—UNSUPPORTIVE GOVT.
BUT STILL MANY POOR PEOPLE CANT AFFORD SCHOOLING EVEN IF ITS PUBLIC SCHOOL...
TSK TSK, THIS GOVT TLGA MUKANG PERA! IMAGINE MAS INAASISST UNG MGA KULAPO NA YAN SAMANTALA UNG SARILI NILANG KABABAYAN NA MAHIHIRAP WALANG MAKAIN TPOS PAGAARAL P KYA??????? NASAAN ANG TAMA>?

Translation: [*This government is really money face. Imagine they assist those foreigners while their poor countrymen are without food, how much more in terms of schooling. Where is right?*]

Example 2

Aanhin mu ung [*what will you do with a*] **progressing quality of education** yet majority of the citizens here dont benefit with it???? **nagiicp ka???** [*Are you thinking?*]

Example 3

cnsbe ko lang po na progressing naman ang education, but it's true na may mga Pilipino na hindi nakakapag aral peo wala naman **kinalaman yan sa quality ng educ :)**

Translation: [*I'm just saying that our education is progressing. . . that there are many Filipinos who didn't go to school but it doesn't represent (the Philippines) education quality*]

Example 4

puros kayo reklamo, lublob mo sarili mo sa Marianas Trench, leche ka! **HA HA HA**!!!

Translation: [*You're all complaining, drown yourself in the Mariana Trench, you're ludicrous!*]

Example 5

Yes its a choice, ur ryt. . . . **Although my mga free schools tau for scholars**, still my **miscellaneous expenses din yan** My only point is regarding this article, dont focus on increasing numbers of foreign students but be proud if majority of the poor people are studying..... peace out people. Just an opinion........ R u people graduated already????

Translation: [*Although we have free books, still there are other miscellaneous expenses.*]

Example 6

wow PSHS, may **mga national highschool naman** po ang **mga town where less ang competition and true na nsa tao** na yn kung **gs2 nia ipursue..may mga state colleges din sa bwat town na parang PUP:))**

Translation: [*we have national high schools in other towns where the competition is less. And it's true, it depends on a person whether s/he wants to pursue [education]. There are state colleges in town like PUP (University of the Philippines)*]

Example 7

@dhong **may officemate ako before**. . .sa **public school** sa bulacan sya nag aral, hes father was a drunk and **labandera yung nanay nya** [*I had an officemate before, she studied in public school in Bulacan. Her father was a drunkard and her mother was a laundry woman*]. . . she told me she used to cry herself to sleep when she was a kid watching her mom being beaten up by her dad...**kasi ayaw ibigay nung mom nya yung kinita nya sa paglalaba sa dad nya para lang ibili ng alak** [*because she (mother) wouldn't want to give the money she earned to her husband to buy alcohol*]

...she said that was the turning point...she decided that she doesnt want that kind of life anymore...**nag aral sya ng mabuti**...graduated top of her class...**then nag phil-sci sya** [*she studied Phil-Sci*]...then she graduated magna cum-laude (stats) sa [*in*] UP on time. and now she and her family are living comfortably...**hanga ako sa babaeng yun** [*I am so impressed with that woman*]... **naiiyak sa lungkot pag tinatanong sya bat hindi sya mangibang bayan**...**passionate sa pilipanas**...**ayaw nyang umalis**...she believes **na theres** still hope for the philippines...i hope shes right....im just sayin...[*she cried of loneliness if you asked her why she didn't go overseas to work. She loves the Philippines. She wouldn't want to leave.*]

Example 8

@dhong **nag public school ka ba**? [*did you study in a public school?*] coz i did! elementary school in the province...the weird thing is....**mas maganda ang turo ng public schools kesa sa private school sa province** [*The teaching in public schools is better than private schools*]...**wala kaming sariling books. hinihiram lang namin yung books nag ginagamit naming** [*We didn't own books, we just borrowed all books we used*]...**may numbers yung book** [*books were numbered*]. 1 book is to 3 students...**so hintayan talaga lalo na pag reading yung subject** [*we had to wait especially if it was a reading subject*]...you need to be patient enough to wait for your other bookmates to finish before turning the page...**hindi ko tinitingnan na dehado ako nun compared to kids na may sariling mga libro....mas marami akong natutunan nun** [*I didn't think I was left out compared to those kids who own books. I learned more*]...learned to be patient, to share, and to be sensitive to others differences.....

Example 9

@singkit so as basis to ur statements the motivated girl did her output by herself. Not by her family, relatives or even govt**?????**

Example 10

Yes, di naman talga valid reason ang kahirapan. Others will say, **libre nga ang tuition eh paano ang ganto ang ganyan. Hindi na matapos paghahanap ng suliranin.** I was in public form elementary to college, never I had all those basic needs to support my education. **Pro ok lang. Pasok pa din kahit walang baon. Kasi alam ko ang 15 years ko of education na aking tyinatyaga kapalit ay mga dekada ng ginhawa. Marami kasi gusto pagbibigyan ng binhi ang gusto kinabukasan namumunga na. Kaya natin to. Filipino kaya tayo.**

Translation: [*Poverty is not really a valid reason. .... the tuition is free, how about other things. It's an unending hardship... But it's ok. I still attended although my pocket was empty. Because I know that the 15 years of sacrifices in education will be rewarded by decades of comfort. Majority want to share the fruit of others' labor. We can do it. We are Filipinos*]

Translanguaging and Other Semiotic Forms of Communication as Used in *yahoo.ph* Samples of Blogging

- Code-switching and mixing:

  - **Aanhin mu ung** [*what will you do with a*] **progressing quality of education** yet majority of the citizens here dont benefit with it???? **nagiicp ka???** [*Think*]
  - she told me she used to cry herself to sleep when she was a kid watching her mom being beaten up by her dad...**kasi ayaw ibigay nung mom nya yung kinita nya sa paglalaba sa dad nya para lang ibili ng alak** [*because she (mother) wouldn't want to give the money she earned to her husband to buy alcohol*]
  - you need to be patient enough to wait for your other bookmates to finish before turning the page...**hindi ko tinitingnan na dehado ako nun compared to kids na may sariling mga libro....mas marami akong natutunan nun** [*I didn't think I was left out compared to those kids who own books. I learned more*] ...learned to be patient, to share, and to be sensitive to others differences
  - 54 students in a class, **experienced a week na walang pasok cuz of bagyo and baha inside the classroom** [*I experienced that the school was closed for a week because the classroom was flooded*]

- Onomatopoeia

  - **TSK TSK,** THIS GOVT TLGA MUKANG PERA! ..[*This government is really money face*]
  - leche ka! **HA HA HA**!!!

- Emoticons

  - be positive:))))))))))
  - parang PUP :))

- CAPITALIZATION

  - IMAGINE MAS INAASISST UNG MGA KULAPO NA YAN SAMANTALA UNG SARILI NILANG KABABAYAN NA MAHIHIRAP WALANG MAKAIN ... NASAAN ANG TAMA>?
  - choose NOT TO BE VICTIMS ANYMORE

    Translation: [*Imagine they assist those foreigners while their poor countrymen are without food ... Where is right?*]

- Interjection and excessive use of punctuations as vocalization

  - PAGAARAL P KYA??????? [*how much more schooling?*]
  - relatives or even govt?????
  - R u people graduated already????

Yahoo.sg

The article initiating the discussion from Yahoo! Newsroom, 24 October 2011
   Singaporean students feel the heat from foreign counterparts
   Local university and junior college students are feeling the heat from foreign students for coveted spots at local universities. They were reacting to the news last

week that international students make up 18 per cent of the total undergraduate intake in Singapore's universities for the academic year 2011.

Example 1
why??? hahaha cause the ruling party trust them more than us thats why. . . .

Example 2
Wait long long lah, **we have an useless bunch of PAP MPs** & Ministers

Example 3
Bravo to William's comment. I fully agreed with you. They should pay the amount only rich foreigners can afford it. **Pay until they "lao sai"** [*diarrhea*]

Example 4
Walk around any campus, **you be SHOCK! PR and foreigners**. . . **I not suprised** if it surpass Singaporeans

Example 5
i was @ NUS couple weeks back and i thought i was at the university of delhi. the student canteen was **infested with india nationals jialat jialat!!!!**!!!

Example 6
NUS = No Undergraduate Singaporeans! LOL

Example 7
Dear Miws, **please open your ears BIG-BIG**, see your countrymen that are suffering. . . can you still seat are your golden throne and enjoy your millions with peace of mind**???** if you are still able to, there's nothing much to say to you anymore, the almighty is all-seeing, you will get your just deserts.

Example 8
why foreigner got so many 好康**?** [*grants*]why local pay full fees?

Example 9
Lolololols. Looks like you're gonna be the first one to run dear:) Stop hating. Just do what you are supposed to do as a local and don't mind the "foreigner trash." **You're too insecure lah! HAHA**

Example 10
Why study so hard lor? Do you think Singaporean with a Degree can find a job in Singapore, **you wait long long orredy**.........foreign talent with foreign education comes first, **our education system not working lah!** Better take your **$$$$** and start doing some **small biz** or go overseas to find work, u stand **better chance aboard** then at home!

Example 11
KOW PAY KOW BOO for what????????????? Me and many of my friends are overseas graduates, 100+ applications not a single reply, **why?????????????????**
Translanguaging and Other Semiotic Forms of Communication as Used in yahoo.sg Samples of Blogging

- why foreigner got so many 好康? [*grants*]
- infested with india nationals **jialat jialat!!!!**
- Pay until they **"lao sai"** [*diarrhea*]
- Mixing "standard" and colloquial forms of English.

  - **Wait long long lah**, we have an useless bunch
  - Walk around any campus, **you be SHOCK!** PR and foreigners... **I not suprised** if it surpass singaporeans.
  - find a job in Singapore, **you wait long long orredy**.
  - our education system **not working lah**
  - Such strangers **should go and fly kites instead**
  - **if my father sponsor me overseas, I will go already.**

- the use of acronyms

  - **NUS = No Undergraduate Singaporeans! LOL**

- Excessive punctuation and interjections as vocalizations

  - KOW PAY KOW BOO **for what?????????????**
  - not a single reply, **why?????????????????**
  - infested with india nationals jialat jialat!!!!!!!

- onomatopoeia

  - why??? **hahaha** cause the ruling party emoticons,

- Netspeak & emoticons

  - **Lolololols.** Looks like you're gonna be
  - Better take your **$$$$**

- CAPITALIZATION

  - **I HATE PAP TO DEEP INTO MY BONE!!!!!!**
  - they tell us **GOOD BYE SUCKER!**
  - they should **SHUD UP**[*shut up*]

- repetitions of words as intensifier

  - Wait **long long** lah
  - please open your ears **BIG-BIG**

13.7 Discussion

What is clear from this data is that discourse patterns in Singapore and the Philippines *Yahoo* blogging use a repertoire of languages and this is a natural part of the wider mobilization of their semiotic resources. "Languages start to be seen not so much in terms of systems as in terms of a series of practices, as something we do, not as an object in the curriculum but as an activity" (Pennycook, 2014, pp. 113–114). Communication through this form of translanguaging integrates the spoken and written form, as the form is not so important compared to the meaning. For example, there is the use of *interjections* to let the readers know in an almost physical way, what the feelings of the bloggers actually are at a given moment. CAPITALIZA-TION, excessive *punctuation marks,* and the *elongation* of words are common stylistic devices. These forms of discourse are developed and shaped according to the way different phenomena are perceived both in terms of the psychological and social makeup of the participants. Anthropological linguistics can also be seen as the bloggers employ their linguistic resources to express their opinions on education from what might well be marginalized points of view in terms of the political power structures. This is especially true as Singapore is a highly controlled society a hegemony of "calibrated coercion" (George, 2012, p. 5). However, there is also a desire "to connect with people" as this can be a manifestation of power by establishing different alliances and forming solidarity in a "community of practice." The social aspect of language where English is viewed as a *world language* and can be seen as a more fluid concept based on the idea that people's linguistic repertoires "reflect the polycentricity of the learning environment in which the speaker dwells" (Blommaert & Backus, 2013, p. 20).

13.7.1 Pedagogical Implication

The pedagogical implication leads to the concept of the *Common European Framework of Reference for Languages: Learning and assessment* (CEFR, 2001, 2018) that has been introduced in various forms in Southeast Asia (Foley, 2019). One of the purposes of CEFR is the promotion of the formulation of educational aims and outcomes at all levels. Its "can do" aspects of proficiency are intended to provide a shared pathway for learning and a more flexible instrument to gauge progress. The principle is based on the CEFR view of language as vehicle for opportunity and success in social, educational, and professional domains. This presents the language learner/user as a social agent, acting in the social world and exerting agency in the learning process (CEFR, 2018). The goal is a communication's perspective guided by what someone "can do" in terms of "language" rather than a deficiency perspective focusing on what the learners have not yet acquired.

The message from CEFR is that language learning should be directed towards enabling learners to act in real-life situations, expressing themselves and accomplishing tasks of different natures. The action-oriented approach puts the co-construction of meaning (through interaction) at the center of the learning and teaching process. The construction of meaning may take place across languages and draw upon learners/users' plurilingual and pluricultural repertoires (as illustrated in these examples of blogging). CEFR distinguishes between multilingualism (the co-existence of different languages at the social or individual level) and plurilingualism (the developing linguistic repertoire of an individual learner/user).

The fundamental point is that plurilinguals have a single, interrelated, repertoire that they combine with their general competencies to accomplish tasks. Such tasks might require moving from one language to another or giving an explanation in another language to make sense of what is said or written (CEFR, 2018; Foley, 2019). Translanguaging is an important tool in helping to address through blogging the issues of multicultural communities in the classroom, neighborhood, and nation. Teachers in particular can help learners/users employ different semiotic approaches available to them to convey meaning and promote learning. Such devices enhance language learning in both L1 and L2, as well as value each student's languages, social practices, and beliefs to promote a community of learners within the power structures of their society.

13.8   Conclusion

In a world in which interracial conflicts and tensions seem to have become an inevitable phenomenon of daily life, a greater awareness of how language is used as a powerful tool in blogging has opened up opportunities to use such developments in technology to create online communities where multilingual and multicultural education is crucial. Providing people with the freedom to function beyond their ethnic and cultural boundaries keeps societies more open-minded. Discussing issues whether it be directly in the classroom or online can help learners/users not only develop their language skills but also their critical awareness of the world around them. In this sense, multilingualism and multicultural education can be a factor in implementing intercultural exchange and help learners to gain democratic values and attitudes. CEFR (2001, 2018) was introduced as an attempt to move away from seeing the languages used in a multilingual setting as separate entities, recognizing that learners in such settings have a linguistic repertoire at their disposal. The logic of translanguaging for language teaching is that the multilingual teacher with equivalent qualifications should be the preferred teacher. That the use of other languages should be possible in the classroom to help the learners/users develop their language skills for effective communication. On the part of the teacher, multilingual teachers should feel proud of their skills and put them to use. Twenty-first-century technology allows learning to be at the finger-tips of every learner/user. It connects people to the world without changing location. It provides choices about the what, when, and where. This is an era where gaining access to things both local and global is possible. In other words, the ability to use translanguaging and other semiotic systems as part of the power structure of social networking should be seen as a major asset in the multilingual classroom.

References

Baker, C. (2006). *Foundations of bilingual education and bilingualism* (Bilingual Education and Bilingualism, 54) (4th ed.). Clevedon; Buffalo: Multilingual Matters.

Beres, A. M. (2015). An overview of translanguaging: 20 years of 'giving voice to those who do not speak'. *Translation and Translanguaging in Multilingual Contexts, 1*(1), 103–118.

Blommaert, J., & Backus, A. (2013). Super diverse repertoires and the individual. In *Multilingualism and multimodality* (pp. 9–32). Brill Sense.

Canagarajah, S. (2011). Codemeshing in academic writing: Identifying teachable strategies of translanguaging. *Modern Language Journal, 95*(3), 401–417.

Council of Europe. (2001). *Common European framework of reference for languages: Learning, teaching and assessment.* Council of Europe, Language Policy Unit: Strasbourg. Retrieved from www.coe.int/lang-cefr

Council of Europe. (2018). *Common European framework of reference for languages: Learning, teaching and assessment, Companion volume with new descriptors Council of Europe*, Language Policy Programme: Strasbourg. Retrieved from www.coe.int/lang-cefr

Creese, A., & Blackledge, A. (2010). Translanguaging in the bilingual classroom: A pedagogy for learning and teaching? *The Modern Language Journal, 94*(1), 103–115.

Deocampo, M.F. (2014). *A cyber-ethnographic study and a critical discourse analysis of yahoo.Ph and Yahoo.sg news pulse.* PhD. Dissertation. Assumption University. Bangkok, Thailand.

Foley, J. (2019). Issues on the initial impact of CEFR in Thailand and the region. *Indonesian Journal of Applied Linguistics, 9*(2), 359–370.

Garcia, O. (2009). *Bilingual education in the 21ˢᵗ century: A global perspective.* Malden, MA: Blackwell.

Garcia, O., & Sylvan, C. (2011). Pedagogies and practices in multilingual classrooms: Singularities and pluralities. *The Modern Language Journal, 95*(3), 385–400.

Garcia, O., & Wei, L. (2014). *Translanguaging: Language, bilingualism and education.* Basingstoke: Palgrave Macmillan.

Garza, A., & Langman, J. (2014). Translanguaging in a Latin@ bilingual community: Negotiations and mediations in a dual-language classroom. *Association of Mexican-American Educators (AMAE) Special Issue, 8*(1).

Gaventa, J. (2007). Levels, spaces, and forms of power: Analysing opportunities for change. In *Power politics.* London: Routledge.

George, C. (2012). *Freedom from the press: Journalism and state power in Singapore.* Singapore: National University of Singapore.

Harper, R. H. R. (2010). *Texture: Human expression in the age of communication overload.* Cambridge: Massachusetts Institute of Technology Press.

Jenkins, J. (2015). Repositioning English and multilingualism in English as a lingua franca. *English in Practice, 2/3*, 41–85. De Gruyter Open.

Lave, J., & Wenger, E. (1991). *Situated learning: Legitimate peripheral participation.* New York: Cambridge University Press.

Lukes, S. (2005). *Power: A radical view* (2nd ed.). New York: Palgrave Macmillan.

McIntosh, E. (2005). From learning logs to learning blogs. *Scottish Center for Information on Language Teaching and Research.* Retrieved from http://www.scilt.org.uk/Portals/24/Library/slr/issues/13/SLR13_McIntosh.pdf

Pennycook, A. (2014). Principled polycentrism and resourceful speakers. *The Journal of Asia TEFL, 11*(4), 1–19.

Vygotsky, L. (1992). *The Collected works of L.S. Vygotsy, vols 1–2.* New York: Plenum Press.

Weedon, C. (1997). *Feminist practice and poststructuralist theory.* Oxford: Basil Blackwell.

Williams, C. (2002). *Extending bilingualism in the education system. Education and lifelong learning committee report.* National Assembly for Wales. Retrieved from http://assemblywales.org

Zentella, A. C. (1997). Growing up bilingual: Puerto Rican children in New York. *Lingua, 1*(103), 59–74.

Chapter 14
Service Learning in a Suburban Community in Vietnam: Pre-Service EFL Teachers as Agents of Change

Nguyen Hoang Tuan and Dat Bao

Abstract This chapter discusses a case study based on six-week teacher placement in a bachelor program. The placement, which provides training to students who will become primary school teachers in the future, is treated at the same time as a research project in which data are collected from participants' reflective journals. The purpose of the study is to serve the improvement of the program as much as it serves student learning. A cohort of 28 student teachers volunteered to participate in an eight-week placement. Their major task is to teach basic English to disadvantaged primary-school-age children in Thu Dau Mot suburban areas. The disadvantaged children include orphans, members of low-income families, and children with disruption or absence of schooling. Findings from the study reveal participants' rich, hands-on experience with real-world challenges in bringing education to at-risk children, a deep understanding of multiple perspectives on the teaching profession, and insightful lessons from the everyday struggle to motivate children learning. Involving participants in the dual role of both teacher and researcher, the project demonstrates how a higher-education curriculum can be negotiated by the students themselves. The study also expands literacy practice by prioritizing new experience over current knowledge, by accepting student self-discovery over expert authority, and by constructing mutual support over the transfer of academic skills.

Keywords Service learning · Affect · Real-world experience · Mutual support · Multiple perspectives · Negotiated curriculum

N. H. Tuan (✉)
Thu Dau Mot University, Binh Duong, Vietnam
e-mail: tuannh2012@tdmu.edu.vn

D. Bao
Monash University, Melbourne, Australia

© Springer Nature Singapore Pte Ltd. 2021
D. Bao, T. Pham (eds.), *Transforming Pedagogies Through Engagement with Learners, Teachers and Communities*, Education in the Asia-Pacific Region: Issues, Concerns and Prospects 57, https://doi.org/10.1007/978-981-16-0057-9_14

14.1   Introduction

This chapter presents an empirical case study set in the context of a primary pre-service teacher placement program in Vietnam. Data are collected from participants' reflective journals and the focus of the study is to build insights for improving the program and to maximize the education quality at the primary level. The placement involves the practice of teaching English to disadvantaged primary-school-age children in Thu Dau Mot suburban areas. By our definition in context, disadvantaged children include orphans, members of low-income families, and children with disruption or absence of schooling.

14.2   Discourse on the Topic

14.2.1   The Need to Care About Affect in Education

The idea of educating the heart is not a novel endeavor. During ancient times, Aristotle already emphasized that educating the mind without engaging the heart would not deserve to be called education. Schmier (2005) also asserts that a worthwhile instructive cause must involve the development of character, values, and visions rather than "the hoarding of facts and honing of skills" (p. 151). Along this line of ideology, one important tradition that advocates such affective engagement is service learning, which emphasizes the need to connect the academic facility with personal and social development. Scholars in language education have appealed for a revision of the curriculum to include the development of empathy and other humane values (Barreneche, 2011; Calvin & Rider, 2004; Hertzler, 2012). Despite this concern, language teaching in Vietnam continues to focus mainly on the acquisition of knowledge and skills. Arguably, one needs a holistic approach and experiential learning that combines reflective thought and social action for learners' individual empowerment.

This chapter narrates a project designed to promote a heart-centered approach to language education through service-learning experiences. It is based on empirical research in which data include students' reflective writings and final reports by in-service teachers during their school placement. The whole intention of the study is to see how these teachers experienced the challenges of teaching English to disadvantaged children. As data speak for themselves, the participants not only enjoyed a sense of personal satisfaction that came from seeing the results of their investment in building relationships, but they also recognized the importance of service learning as a meaningful way to create value in the community.

14.2.2 Service Learning as a Global Practice

Service learning is not one pedagogy by itself but represents a blend of various instructional traditions put together. It is a form of experiential education that combines academic study with community service. Originating from the foundation of voluntary social work, this pedagogical philosophy has expanded its practice and implication in a variety of disciplines including business administration, communication, education, among others. Within education, service learning has connected with helpful theories from the work of Dewey (1938), Lewin (1946), Piaget (1953), and Schon (1987), who believe in the value of learning through action combined with reflection. Other scholars who contributed to the approach are Freire (1973) who advocates equity in educational reform, Vygotsky (1926/1997) who emphasizes learning through the construction of individualized meaning, and Bruner (1961) who believes in understanding abstract concepts through doing.

In 1979, Simon defines the approach in more concrete terms in which he identifies the voluntary and experiential nature of service learning, an insight that formed the foundation of characteristics for its practice until today. Historically, service learning has pervaded educational practices in various continents and nations over the past several decades. For example, in 1966, service learning entered into the American educational system. In 1996, it became a pioneering program in Canada. In 1967, the UK embraced the concept of community education with key elements of service learning. Other countries in Europe kept up at different times in adopting the approach, with more challenges in Eastern Europe due to mistrust in bureaucracies (Carla & Ferrara, 2017). Service learning entered South Africa in 1997 under community service programs in higher-education sectors and was introduced in other African countries nearly a decade later.

In East Asia, service learning has been a gradual presence over the past 20 years. It has been extremely popular in Japan ever since its first introduction in 1995 with pilot practice in Ojiya Primary School. By 2012 nearly 4000 schools across Japan have applied this learning system. Service learning grew popular in Australia since 1999 in a movement known as transformative pedagogy which combines community service with academic skills. It was promoted in Korea in 2000; and started in 2006 in Lingam, China with projects in sciences, business, and arts. The early 2000s continued to see similar pioneering projects happening in Hong Kong and Taiwan.

In Southeast Asia, it was during 2000–2005 that service learning was introduced to the region through the Singapore International Foundation. Service learning came to Thailand in 2004 as relating to an international response to the tsunami tragedy. In Vietnam, service learning was initially an imported practice, with international participation such as from Hometown Heroes Service-Learning Project in 2009, Glocal Literacy Foundation in 2011, among others. Thu Dau Mot University, in Binh Duong Province, was one of the first local institutes to launch its pioneering project as a domestic initiative. The rest of the chapter will now turn onto our empirical project as the main discussion.

A review of recent literature related to service learning and foreign language teaching supports the view that students should be challenged to think critically and act compassionately through service learning. Minor (2001) identifies two reasons for situating service learning into a foreign language program, namely the need to create meaningful contexts for language learners, and the need to cultivate humane values. Of the two reasons, the second one hasn't received much attention until recently. Indeed, it is through service learning that students can work through a social change perspective as in the case of Ryan Lambert, a student from Central Michigan University. Participating in a fund-raising activity to help fight malaria, Ryan recognized that he and his classmates learned many practical skills from management of real-life tasks. More importantly, through responding to these tasks, they learned the significance of serving others (Miller & Nendel, 2010). It is also through service learning that students are given the opportunity to reach their full potential. Reflecting on what was gained by helping those in need, Ryan was amazed at how much he grew holistically as an individual.

In addition to language proficiency development, many research studies also recorded students' personal transformation through service learning (Pellettieri & Varona, 2008). Wilson's analysis of students' reflective writing (2011) demonstrates that students who were involved in service learning are more likely to be empathetic towards others than students who were not. Closely related to service learning is the concept of social and emotional competence: "Social and emotional competence is the ability to understand, manage and express the social and emotional aspects of one's life in ways that enable the successful management of life tasks such as learning, forming relationships, solving everyday problems, and adapting to the complex demands of growth and development" (Elias, 1997, p. 2).

14.3   Scope of the Study

The study which is known by Thu Dau Mot University as the Service-Learning Experimental Project began in March 2016, when the university organized a six-week placement for students who were undertaking a bachelor's degree in English language education. For the first time, the placement program employed service learning as its core philosophy and practice. The project was developed with a contrastive design in mind: sending middle-class urban student teachers to a semi-rural area to work with underprivileged children from a low-income community. The aim of this experimental project is for in-service teachers to explore an unfamiliar environment with unknown challenges. We believe that such extended experience would expose our students to new learning opportunities and drive their potential towards a different perspective, somewhat removed from the regular urban education setting that they usually know well, stay comfortable with, and might take for granted.

14.4 Research Methodology

The project is a phenomenological qualitative case study of teacher experiences. It examines pre-service teachers' self-documented participation in a placement program in the real world where individuals were not only embarked on teaching practice in a challenging context (that is, working with disadvantaged children with minimal or no schooling background) but were also given the autonomy to negotiate their own practice (such as making decisions in problem-solving and decision-making). Participants then recorded their reflection on placement events in work-journal writing. Such documentation, which served as data for the project, was then employed to formulate this chapter in sub-themes, analysis, interpretation, and recommendations. The project is phenomenological in the sense that it concentrates on the understanding of participants' conscious understanding of their direct experience with instructional design and implementation.

The design, instead of focusing on mainstream education as many placement programs would do, is built upon less common target groups of disadvantaged school-age children. The teaching implementation, in the meanwhile, is not formal schooling practice but was less formal, contextualized instruction whereby teaching approaches would be adapted to suit its context and target students. As far as data are concerned, the first-person point of view is respected. We believe that when the scope of the study is peculiar rather than ordinary, new insights are likely to be drawn for a different kind of perspectives and, hopefully, a novel contribution in pre-service teacher placement dynamics.

14.4.1 The Choice of English as a Taught Subject

Language is closely connected with life and culture. Vietnam has witnessed the rise and fall of a number of dominant foreign languages over many centuries. In various parts of the country, foreign languages including Chinese, French, Russian, and English, respectively, had once enjoyed dominant status. Across the nation, after the Vietnamese government introduced the open-door policy in 1986, English has gradually taken over the significance of Russian, following the dissolution of the former Soviet Union which consequently reduced its influence over Vietnam. English is gaining increased popularity in the country, not only due to employment and educational opportunities but also due to the fact that English language education has entered into teacher training, resources, and curriculum in various subject areas.

At present, there is a tendency for English to be introduced to school children at an early age, based on the belief that the future of the nation requires an efficient connection with internationalized education and the global labor market. Along with this expectation, English has been strongly promoted with the government's recent ambitious language policy that has mobilized around $US2 billion from governmental and non-governmental sources to implement English language education at all levels starting at grade 3 by the year 2020.

14.4.2 Research Location and Student Profile

The teacher participants, however, are not obliged to take the challenge of joining this project. Instead, the project adopts a voluntary nature. As it turned out, 28 pre-service teachers volunteered to participate in an eight-week placement program. Their task is to teach basic English to disadvantaged primary-school-age children, aged between 7 and 15, in Thu Dau Mot suburban areas. Being disadvantaged in this context refers to children who are orphans, who come from low-income families, or who suffer from disruption or absence of schooling. The choice of the target group is inspired by the need to make education more accessible to less fortunate children in Vietnam, who due to financial and geographical reasons have not been able to attain an education which they deserve. In the meanwhile, many of the teacher participants already had teaching/tutoring experiences before they joined their university study program, thus some members of this group could also be in the category of in-service teachers. For the convenience of discussion and to reflect participant role in the university program, we will refer to all the participants as "pre-service teachers."

With the target group of this project being underprivileged children, a survey was conducted in the local communities in Thu Dau Mot city, Binh Duong province, to identify children of this category. As a result, we recruited 196 children in a suburban community in Thu Dau Mot city, including 10 vicinities, namely Phu Loi, Phu Hoa, Phu My, Phu Tho, Phu Tan, Tan An, Hiep Thanh, Chanh My, Dinh Hoa, and Hoa Phu. Twelve English classes were organized according to the traveling distance between the vicinities. Class size varied between 10 and 28 children. A team of two to three in-service teachers was assigned to share-teach each of these classes.

14.4.3 Preparations for Pre-Service Teachers Prior to Placement

To prepare student teachers for this intensive program, a practical five-day intensive training module was developed and provided. The main material for the placement is a textbook called *Super Kids* (2005), an enjoyable six-level English series for children, which are packed with playful characters and engaging storylines. During the discussion, everyone learned how to teach, manage a class, assist learning, solve classroom problems, and support children even after class should arise issues regarding their learning difficulty and social well-being. The most essential set of skills during this training program is not just knowledge, but more importantly, it is about developing sensitivity and sociocultural competence for working with disadvantaged children. Since many of these children never had a chance to go to school, entering into the classroom might be a whole new world for them that would require a sense of safety, acceptance, nurture, and trust, without which learning would not happen. The basic themes during the training included:

- Identifying key concepts and skills in service learning
- Building expectations and developing commitment through discussion
- Learning to use the textbook
- Learning about the target children and their context
- Anticipating problems and planning solutions

The tools being employed during both this training and the subsequent placement include knowledge and skills input, oral presentation, visualization of fieldwork incidents, classroom teaching, observation of children learning, peer communication, parental support, individual and team reflection, journal entries, and multimedia materials. Such multiple resources are, for example, PowerPoint presentations, printed materials, teacher-driven collages for students, recorded events on a computer, shared information via emails, and news reported through local media.

The focus of placement practice is on social and emotional learning that is achieved through reflection upon real-world teaching experience. Kolb's model of experiential learning (1984) is applied whereby the student teachers, first of all, enter into concrete experience. Next, they observe and reflect on it. Based on this, participants learn to conceptualize real phenomena, which they then proceed to test-apply in an improved action. At the beginning of the training, the student teachers are given a chance to warm up their capacity by visualizing and anticipating the forthcoming challenges. Some of the questions raised include:

- What are you looking forward to?
- What are you nervous about?
- What do you think you might learn from this project?

Participants were also given the opportunity to assess their thoughts and feelings as well as those of others, to handle emotions and empathize with others, to develop personal relationships, and to cooperate in solving life-related problems. The whole idea is to encourage students to engage with service learning in an in-depth, personalized manner. The above questions geared the students towards "a mission," as they called it, whereby it is necessary for participants to equip themselves with what it takes to enter the field. To lend further support to the student teachers, the trainer provided them a list of social interaction skills and asked them to reflect on a set of Can-Do statements, such as in the examples below:

I can attend to others both verbally and non-verbally to make them know that they
   have been understood. I can clearly express my thoughts and feelings both
   verbally and non-verbally. I can take turns and share in both pairs and group
   situations.
I can consider all perspectives involved in a conflict in order to resolve the conflict
   peacefully and to the satisfaction of all involved. I can make and follow through
   with clear "NO" statements, to avoid situations in which one might be pressured.
   And I can delay acting in pressure situations until adequately prepared.
I can identify the need for support and assistance, and I can access available and
   appropriate resources.

During both training and placement, reflective journal writing served as a scaffolding
tool to assist students in making meaning out of their experience. A set of guiding
questions are provided to help students reflect on their experience, although the
teachers do not have to answer all of them:

- Did the project help you perceive your strengths and weaknesses?
- What challenges did you experience during your teaching?
- How did you handle classroom situations?
- What kinds of social interaction skills have you gained or improved?
- What values have you developed in teaching disadvantaged children?

The student teachers were then encouraged to critically examine the impact of
their teaching experiences and communicate their feelings about the community in
their journals. They were also asked to submit a final report as a summary of their
overall experiences. Bringle and Hatcher (1999) highlighted the important role of
reflection activities "in their capacity to yield learning, support personal growth,
provide insight, develop skills, and promote civic responsibility" (p. 184).

14.5   Main Findings and Discussion

The findings below are based on the pre-service teachers' reflection writings and
final reports. Data are viewed through an interpretive qualitative lens and thematic
analysis is the approach employed to bring out meaningful patterns in participants'
experience. On this foundation, major areas of discovery are identified and presented
in this section, which are related to four key themes, namely perspectives, challenges, support, and social environment.

14.5.1   Stretching Ability and Changing Perspectives

Most teacher participants, to begin with, were used to a comfortable urban lifestyle.
Many cannot visualize themselves in circumstances where the standard of living

stays much below the basics. The placement has allowed them to experience such a world to learn through personal thinking, through taking photos to capture issues, and through discussing ways of supporting the children's learning. This process not only helps participants build new knowledge and develop relevant skills, but it also allows them to adopt an alternative angle of educational practices. Eventually, what became rewarding is the awareness of their role in making a difference. It is important to realize that these innocent children, who have suffered from poor living conditions, became passionate about learning new things. This generation deserves more thoughtful intellectual and emotional nurture because they are part of the nation's future.

In their final reports, one teacher shared a story of affective growth, which came through her own progress:

> "In the first week, the children's enthusiasm convinced that when I invested efforts, they will yield some sort of rewards. The second week taught me a bit more: one will work better when having a good team in which everyone gives their best. When the third week came, I realized the importance of a leader to manage our participation. My fourth week's experience allowed me to see how one must be flexible and pro-active in solving problems. As time went by, everyone builds their competence further in so many ways."

14.5.2   Teaching in Response to Challenges

Not every child exhibits the same behavior. Some seem to be pleasant, enthusiastic, and cooperative; while others, due to their own life circumstances, can be withdrawn, naughty, disagreeable, or even resentful at times. Because of this, sometimes the children could not get along. To be able to work with a wide range of positive or disruptive dispositions requires student teachers not only a good set of social and pedagogical skills but also a high level of commitment, love, and empathy. One teacher wrote in her reflective journal:

> "I feel excited and also worried about my new job. Excited because I can learn something new that challenges myself. I am uncertain if I can complete this job well or not. Perhaps I need to prepare everything very well, learning how to share information and communicating effectively. I need to know how to attract children's attention."

As data show, only up to the fourth week of the placement program, when rich experiences were built, did the teachers become competent in addressing problematic scenarios that made social learning difficult for the children. One participant, in her journal entry, narrates how she identified some children's learning behavior with her own childhood. It became a thought-provoking and emotional process when the teacher sensed that she was relearning every lesson through the internal eyes of less fortunate children. It was during such moments that participants adjusted their perspectives to understand the child's real issues, which could never have happened without personal hands-on exposure. As Rosado (1990) contends, the ability to walk in the shoes of others while working with them is an essential act in helping them remove their suffering.

14.5.3 Providing Support Without Judgement

In many school settings, students sometimes get misunderstood by teachers for not working hard enough. For the ordinary teacher, it seems uncommon practice to make personal efforts in gathering information about every individual student as a way of tailoring instruction towards specific needs. This is because that would require a great deal of time, energy, and dedication, especially when one has to teach a large number of students. In the current project, however, that was not the case. One teacher participant in the project gave himself the investigating task when one of his students skipped lessons and appeared reluctant in coming to the classroom. While it would be easy for any teacher to assume laziness in this case, the teacher participant took the liberty to find out the reason why and brought the student back to class. He noted in a journal entry:

> "As I eventually learned, the travel from home to school was a long distance and involved heavy traffic, which proved to be unsafe for the young child to walk alone. Although her father was willing to give her a ride, he was constantly drunk, which made the trip even more life risky. Her mother grew worried and did not know what to do except keeping the child at home. I came to learn about all this only after coming to see her mother. Based on our discussion, we eventually came up with a solution to help the child return to safely study with her classmates."

This incident demonstrates an exemplary lesson that is worth thinking about for educators who are committed to making a difference. As Weare and Gray (2003) indicate, the development of teachers' emotional and social competence requires a warm, caring, and empathic human being who can build sensible personal relationships with others. It is such a commitment to the project and concerns for the children that help develop rapport between teachers and students. As one teacher explained:

> "This week the children and I became closer than the past few weeks. We were no longer strangers to each other. It rained heavily, but most of the children came to class on time. I suddenly felt warm at that time although I was wet and cold too."

In addition to skills development, many teachers recognize the values they have created for their students. As one student teacher puts it:

> "I can see how difficult the children's life circumstances are and they need more ways to learn and improve such conditions. I believe one can change children's lives through English lessons. English is a means not only of communication but also of finding good jobs in the future."

14.5.4 Building an Environment of Care

Out of care and dedication for the children, the teachers made efforts to create extra resources for them beyond the textbook. In one example, a teacher printed a picture in a large size for the class to view better. To make sure everyone participated and enjoyed the lesson, he also cut a set of characters into individual flashcards and organized for the children to construct a story in teams. Other teachers prepared little gifts to motivate students' learning. Some teachers even collected money from members of the teaching team to purchase learning materials for the children. Sometimes the teachers visit their students' families to find out more about the children's day-to-day living conditions.

In return, many students expressed love and appreciation for their teachers by learning hard and behaving well. In one incident, a child came to class with a rose as an expression of thanks to her teacher. Together teachers and students created a culture of high morale and mutual mindfulness. It is through the everyday small deeds that one can see how social needs play a meaningful role in teaching and learning. As the placement came to a close, the children created a collective drawing on the board, with positive decorative images and everyone's names, to express gratitude and the best wishes for their teachers. Arguably, local wisdom took place when teachers and students self-initiated their own values and constructed ways of making the educational process most memorable.

14.6 Major Contribution in the Field

This research project has a strong significance in how higher-education curriculum is negotiated by the students themselves, especially when their major task is to conduct an academic investigation into their own placement. Such practice is of an unusual nature. Most of the time when placement is organized by a university, it is student teachers' performance that is assessed by university lecturers towards marks and grades. In the case of Thu Dau Mot University project, however, the focus is for student teachers to assess themselves without the lecturers' judgement. Most importantly, what the student teachers experienced plays the role of improving training and curriculum for the university. No student failed the placement. Instead, everybody passed for having contributed to the implementation and adaptation of a service-learning model to support learning in a semi-rural community. The fact that the children themselves were happy and, in their diary writing, expressed their love for learning and satisfaction with their teachers have spoken volumes about the success of the program.

The project also sends out a meaningful global implication as it expands literacy practice by prioritizing new experience over current knowledge, by accepting student self-discovery over expert authority, and by constructing mutual support over the transfer of academic skills. Readers might like to note that these teacher participants are not only new in their teaching career, but they are also unfamiliar with the community context and feel nervous about launching a new education model. Because of this, the university program would not increase stress by imposing an assessment on top of their anxious performance. As one teacher noted:

"For me, the hardest part of my job is how to communicate with young learners. I am self-conscious of my limited experiences in teaching English for children. I do not know whether children like me or not. I wonder how I am able to cope with if the children do not come to my class, and how I deal with them if my teaching method does not work."

Eventually, it is the freedom to struggle and learn for oneself that marks the beauty of this project, which gives it a distinctive feature not overly common in in-service teaching placement across other international contexts. In addition, since the children in the study had hardly experienced any previous schooling in their lives, for a committed team of teachers to come to them with open arms and inspire their learning interest is to create a well-localized approach to literacy transformation in the developing world.

14.7 Limitation of the Project

Despite its accomplishment, the project seems to be characterized by two minor limitations. First of all, embarking on an initial stage of the experiment, the study has a short-term nature and is yet to indicate a follow-up plan to promote educational sustainability for the community involved. Secondly, unlike most teaching placement practices around the world, the in-service teachers performed their tasks without collaborative mentorship happening between the visiting institute and the host community. Instead, most professional advice is derived one-sidedly from the university department, whereas guiding knowledge about the culture of the community had to be acquired by the student teachers themselves. While this drawback might leave a type of burden on the participants, it also plays the role of pushing them to the optimal learning efforts. In an ideal situation, a local cultural adviser if available would serve well as a source of information that might ease the teachers' knowledge-accumulating task to a certain degree.

One example of such a lack of sociocultural knowledge is the student teachers' struggle to understand the nature and the life circumstances of the children. Some of them, being physically and mentally disadvantaged, might be slower than students who are formally educated in a school setting. Others have to work as a street vendor, selling snacks or lottery tickets all day, and thus they often feel tired when coming to class. The student teachers admitted that their weakness is related to the wrong choice of words and lengthy explanations which made the children depressed, which might fail to create a friendly classroom atmosphere.

14.8 Implications

Based on the above findings and discussion, we would like to make specific recommendations for curriculum and research development. Besides lessons learned from the project, there are aspects of curriculum and research improvement that we would consider for the future, especially when service learning continues to be incorporated into in-service teachers' placement in the semesters to come. We would like to propose three recommendations:

First, there is a need to strengthen community-based research agenda. In this first experimental project, we have looked at issues such as teacher reflection, modified perspective, social relationships, among others. Over the time, it is important to prepare a list of research agenda, so that each time service-learning placement takes place, a new research design with new or revised activities is brought to improve student learning and teacher development.

Secondly, it is important to consider building a network of partnerships to ensure program quality. Some examples of partners could be social work organizations, public relations offices, community advisors, funding bodies, and research institutes. Due to the nature of service learning, it is advisable to work in collaboration rather than to remain one university independently conducting the whole program.

Thirdly, it would be helpful and interesting to consider disseminating program and research outcomes in seminars, conferences, and publications. Such interaction also allows for university curriculum to be revised, including a training handbook, a website or google drive for sharing strategies, and a module that provides systematic content in service learning. At the moment, Thu Dau Mot University has established a syllabus of this type as part of the English-department curriculum.

14.9   Conclusion

Our findings support the heart-centered approach to language education with a focus on the learners' social and emotional competence. Findings from the study reveal pre-service teachers' practical experience with real-world challenges in making education accessible to at-risk children. Through such experience, an enriched, multiple perspective on the teaching profession was developed, with insights into the everyday challenge to motivating children learning. Involving participants in the dual role of both teacher and researcher, the project demonstrates that pre-service teachers can take on the role of agency in negotiating higher-education curriculum content. The study expands literacy practice by prioritizing new experience over current knowledge, by accepting student self-discovery over expert authority, and by constructing mutual support over the transfer of academic skills.

We do not have evidence of the long-term impact of service learning on students' academic attainment since the project is still in its early stage. But our analysis of students' reflective writing confirms the view that service learning combined with reflection is a pedagogical tool to help language learners discover their personal power to make positive changes in their communities. Through this form of experiential learning, students better understand the feelings, needs, and perspectives of others as their level of responsibility and caring is enhanced.

It was a helpful practice to provide students with guided questions and other forms of scaffolding during the process to assist them in overcoming the difficult situations they are in. Timely and on-going support from the faculty was given to help pre-service teachers analyze their service learning experiences. It is recommended that students should be given opportunities to "live" with the language, rather than "learn" the language, through community-based projects as a way of being.

The experiment takes on both a local and global significance, which comes from three main reasons. First of all, the study employed international resources to improve a local educational context, such as an imported textbook and a worldwide learning philosophy. Secondly, it looks at educational practice from a different perspective, when the bilingual training is provided by an urban institute while the implementation is in a semi-rural setting. Thirdly, although the placement takes place locally, it actually resonates with the accomplishment of similar community programs that support learning around the world. With these, this project has contributed to the overall landscape of positive research outcomes from other service-learning projects that have been conducted in other contexts.

As is evident, plenty of studies in this area have pointed consistently to the enhancement of teachers' social skills, academic achievement, and civic engagement (see, for example, Billig, 2009; Conway, Amel, & Gerwien, 2009; White, 2001). Most teachers feel that with a commitment they can make a difference in the world's education and in the quality of community life. As far as learning is concerned, students have improved various aspects of their development such as self-worth, positive attitudes towards schooling, more commitment towards the community (Billig, Root, & Jesse, 2005). By and large, research findings regarding the above progress have been fairly consistent, which continues to indicate the optimistic values of service learning. It is interesting and helpful to see that many institutes that are serious about global learning, such as Thu Dau Mot University, have made service learning a graduation requirement and a life-long commitment to education.

References

Barreneche, G. (2011). Language learners as teachers: Integrating service learning and the advanced language course. *Hispania, 94*(1), 103–120.

Billig, S. H. (2009). Does quality really matter: Testing the new K–12 service-learning standards for quality practice. In B. E. Moely, S. H. Billig, & B. A. Holland (Eds.), *Advances in service-learning research: Vol. 9. Creating our identities in service-learning and community engagement* (pp. 131–158). Greenwich, CT: Information Age.

Billig, S. H., Root, S., & Jesse, D. (2005). The relationship between quality indicators of service-learning and student outcomes: Testing the professional wisdom. In S. Root, J. Callahan, & S. H. Billig (Eds.), *Advances in service-learning research: Vol. 5. Improving service-learning practice: Research on models that enhance impacts* (pp. 97–115). Greenwich, CT: Information Age.

Bringle, R., & Hatcher, J. (1999). Reflection in service learning: Making meaning of experience. *Educational Horizons.*, 179–185. Retrieved from https://www.american.edu/ocl/volunteer/upload/Bringle-Hatcher-Reflection.pdf.

Bruner, J. S. (1961). The act of discovery. *Harvard Educational Review, 31*, 21–32.

Calvin, L., & Rider, N. (2004). Not your parents' language class: Curriculum revision to support university language requirements. *Foreign Language Annals, 37*(1), 11–25.

Carla, R., & Ferrara, C. (2017). *Service-learning in Central and Eastern Europe. Handbook for engaged teachers and students.* Buenos Aires: CLAYSS. Disponibile in archivio digitale al sito www.clayss.orgVai.

Conway, J. M., Amel, E. L., & Gerwien, D. P. (2009). Teaching and learning in the social context: A meta-analysis of service learning's effects on academic, personal, social, and citizenship outcomes. *Teaching of Psychology, 36*, 233–245. https://doi.org/10.1080/00986280903172969.

Dewey, J. (1938). *Experience and education.* New York, NY: Kappa Delta Pi.

Elias, M. J. (1997). *Promoting social and emotional learning: Guidelines for educators.* Alexandria, Virginia: Association for Supervision and Curriculum Development. Retrieved from http://www.ascd.org/publications/books/197157e4/chapters/The-Need-for-Social-and-Emotional-Learning.aspx.

Freire, P. (1973). *Education for critical consciousness.* New York: Continuum.

Hertzler, M. (2012). *Service learning as a pedagogical tool for language teachers. Touch the world. Central states conference on the teaching of foreign languages report.* Retrieved from www.csctfl.org/documents/2012Report.pdf.

Kolb, D. (1984). *Experiential learning: Experience as the source of learning and development.* Englewood Cliffs, NJ: Prentice-Hall.

Lewin, K. (1946). Action research and minority problems. *Journal of Social Issues, 2*(4), 34–46.

Miller, M., & Nendel, J. (2010). *Service-learning in physical education and other related professions: A global perspective.* Burlington, MA: Jones & Bartlett Learning.

Minor, J. M. (2001). Using service-learning as part of an ESL program. *The Internet TESL Journal, 7*(4). Retrieved from http://iteslj.org/Techniques/Minor-ServiceLearning.html.

Pellettieri, J., & Varona, L. (2008). Refocusing second language education. *Academic Exchange Quarterly, 12*(3), 16–22.

Piaget, J. (1953). *The origin of intelligence in the child.* New Fetter Lane, NY: Routledge & Kegan Paul.

Rosado, C. (1990). *The concept of cultural relativism in a multicultural world.* Retrieved from http://www.rosado.net/articles-relativism.html.

Schmier, L. (2005). *Random thoughts III: Teaching with love.* Stillwater, OK: New Forum Press.

Schon, D. (1987). *Educating the reflective practitioner.* San Francisco: Jossey-Bass.

Vygotsky, L. S. (1926/1997). *Educational psychology.* Boca Raton, FL: CRC Press.

Weare, K. & Gray, G. (2003). *What works in developing children's emotional and social competence and wellbeing? Research report RR456.* Department for Education and skills. Retrieved from https://pdfs.semanticscholar.org/e0db/f579cf518046eebabed4815aab795e2119fc.pdf

White, A. (2001). *A meta-analysis of service-learning research in middle and high schools* (unpublished doctoral dissertation). University of North Texas, Denton.

Wilson, J. (2011). Service-learning and the development of empathy in US college students. *Education & Training, 53*(2), 207–217.

Chapter 15
Parents as Teaching Allies: Some Cases in Japanese Schools

Eisuke Saito

Abstract Parental involvement in their children's education has been investigated in various ways, mainly regarding governance, the support provided to the children at home, or relationships between teachers and parents. However, parents also might be supporters and/or resources for teaching practices, an aspect which has not been studied in depth. In Japan, there is an approach to school reform called lesson study for the learning community, underlining the importance of parental participation in pedagogical practices. This chapter categorises types of parental involvement using three published cases. Four participatory parental roles in pedagogical practices were identified: (1) learners, (2) resources, (3) endorsers, and (4) catalysts.

Keywords Parental participation · Pedagogical reform · Lesson study for learning community · Parental endorsement · Parents as a resource

15.1 Introduction

Parental participation in their children's education has been researched in various ways, and several issues have been noted. Regarding the types or extents of parental involvement, Morgan, Fraser, Dunn, and Cairns (1992) classified cases in the United Kingdom as (1) most parents are content to work in close two-way interactions with teachers on behalf of their children, (2) parents seek relationships with the school or part of the school with increasing involvement, and (3) parents are involved at the management level in school operations (Morgan et al., 1992). This classification corresponds to a study on South African minorities that found most parents actively participated in school activities and were aware of their educational rights and responsibilities (Mncube, 2010).

E. Saito (✉)
Monash University, Melbourne, Australia
e-mail: eisuke.saito@monash.edu

© Springer Nature Singapore Pte Ltd. 2021
D. Bao, T. Pham (eds.), *Transforming Pedagogies Through Engagement with Learners, Teachers and Communities*, Education in the Asia-Pacific Region: Issues, Concerns and Prospects 57, https://doi.org/10.1007/978-981-16-0057-9_15

Reasons for parental participation also have been investigated. Deslandes and Bertrand (2005) found that parents who believed their participation was one of their responsibilities (i.e., attending teacher conferences or calling the school to consult with teachers) were more likely than others to become more responsive to the schools. Then, if their children convey the teachers' requests to their parents for their opinions or information, parents were likely to increase their involvement (e.g., by meeting with teachers). In the Korean context, Zhao and Akiba (2009) found that principals were likely to consider parental involvement as important to decreasing pupils' problem behaviours. Moreover, parental involvement in school improvement activities and discussions tended to facilitate further parental involvement (Snell, Miguel, and East (2009). Similar to Deslandes and Bertrand (2005), LaRocque, Kleiman, and Darling (2011) found several factors that influenced parental partici-pation, such as comfort level, knowledge, self-confidence, motivation, and language skills. Park and Holloway (2013) claimed that schools' efforts to reach out to parents strongly predicted parental involvement at school. In Eastern Europe, parents who support schools' initiatives to interact with them were more likely to participate, and parents' openness to communication depended on their engagement with their children's education (Radu, 2013).

The impact of parental involvement at school also has been studied. Some scholars have argued that parental involvement does not predict much about chil-dren's outcomes, despite being advocated to do so (Lau, Li, & Rao, 2011). Parents also might not ask their adolescents' teachers about psychological needs and devel-opment, despite parents' opinions that parent-school collaborations are very impor-tant to their understanding of those things (Antonopoulou, Koutrouba, & Babalis, 2010). However, Park and Holloway (2013) found that parental involvement posi-tively influenced their children's academic outcomes, perhaps even more than parental involvement at home. Interestingly, Clinton and Hattie (2013) found that children who believe that their parents talk with their teachers and attend school meetings were relatively more likely to have low achievement because they interpreted their parents' involvement to mean that they were not doing well in school.

Some studies found that parental involvement tended to decrease as children progressed through the grades. Hornby and Witte (2010) indicated that parents perceived their involvement in school as less important as their children aged, and their emphasis on supervision and/or support at home tended to increase (Goodall & Montgomery, 2013; Park & Holloway, 2013). Some scholars have proposed that parental involvement is initially unpopular. For example, Korean-American parents tended to selectively participate in school activities, appropriating and transforming the situations and demands set by the schools (Lee, 2005). In a study on Greek schools, parents were unlikely to establish cooperative relationships with their children's schools, despite the schools' efforts to provide several opportunities for stronger ties and the parent's strong beliefs that family-school collaborations are crucial to academic and psychological development (Antonopoulou et al., 2010). In New Zealand, Hornby and Witte (2010) noted a historical lack of emphasis on parental involvement and further suggested that ethnic minority parents have difficulty being involved in their children's schools because of language barriers. Last, Lau et al. (2011) indicated that Chinese parents tended to prefer home-based to school-based involvement.

In addition to parents' apprehensions, teachers might be reluctant to involve parents in school matters. For example, in a sample of South African teachers (Lemmer & van Wyk, 2004), parents were considered a problem because they needed careful handling and sufficient time. Similarly, American teachers tended to be apprehensive about involving parents, even regarding pupils' problem behaviours, particularly when they believed that the pupils' problems originated at home (Zhao & Akiba, 2009). Teachers might not be adequately trained to effectively collaborate with parents at the pre-service or in-service levels, suggesting that training is needed to overcome the difficulties of developing partnerships with parents (Hornby & Witte, 2010).

15.2 Purpose of the Study

Despite the rigorous nature of the previous research, a huge gap exists regarding parental participation in pedagogical practices and the ways that participation influences teaching practices, teachers, children, and parents. To help fill this gap, this chapter reviews cases of parental participation in pedagogical practices in Japan. The cases were selected from published sources, namely books, about the Lesson Study for Learning Community (LSLC) approach to teaching (Saito et al., 2015; Saito & Atencio, 2015). In LSLC, parents and local residents are important protagonists who learn and grow by participating in classroom pedagogical practices.

The three cases used for this study concern schools implementing the LSLC reform. Before providing the details of each case, LSLC is briefly explained. Then, each case is described. Case 1 is about LSLC applied to social studies. The teacher, parents, and pupils focused on local agricultural produce, which led them to open a market at the school for one day. Case 2 is about reading poetry aloud; parents read poems aloud to the class. Case 3 is different from Cases 1 and 2 in that the mother did not intend to participate in the pedagogical practices. However, her presence in the classroom and her interactions with the teacher fundamentally changed the teacher's practices.

This chapter has the following sections. After this introduction, three cases are introduced, all of which were found in Japanese books on the framework of LSLC pedagogical practices. One case is part of the book by a teacher, Ms. Fukutani (Fukutani, 2003). A leading LSLC scholar, Manabu Sato, wrote the other two books (Sato, 2003, 2012a). Despite the numerous books and articles on it, most scholars of LSLC focused on pupils and teachers rather than parents. However, parental participation in their children's learning is an indispensable element of educational reform in the LSLC approach. Thus, this chapter aims to distinguish among three cases and discuss their meanings. After describing the cases, the chapter presents an analysis from which the cases' meanings are discussed. Lastly, conclusions are presented based on those meanings.

15.3 Lesson Study for Learning Community (LSLC)

Since the 1990s, poverty and socioeconomic inequality have been highlighted as serious problems in Japan (Kariya, 2001; Uzuki & Suetomi, 2015). A serious crisis in education started to emerge because of persistent long-term economic recessions, particularly manifested as waning interest in learning and increasing problem behaviours related to pupils' difficult life experiences (Kariya, 2001; Sato, 2012b). LSLC is an educational reform developed to reverse these trends, and it is widely practised in Japan (Saito et al., 2015; Saito & Sato, 2012). Many of the schools operating LSLC have large proportions of pupils with difficult lives, including single parents, poverty, and domestic violence (Sato, 2012a). The practitioners of and consultants to those schools have recognised that the children need to feel a sense of security to overcome their problems and concentrate on learning (Sato, 2012b). Thus, LSLC practitioners aim to develop school cultures in which the pupils and teachers mutually accept and appreciate each other, regardless of their backgrounds (Sato, 2012b).

However, LSLC is not merely a practical mechanism for school reform; it is a theory-based conceptual approach to school reform. The theoretical aspect is reflected in its vision, which has three dimensions: (1) to ensure high-quality opportunities for all pupils to learn, (2) to provide opportunities for all teachers to professionally grow, and (3) to provide opportunities for as many residents and parents as possible to participate in endorsing and supporting the reform to support the pupils. The LSLC philosophy is three-pronged: (1) publicness, (2) democracy, and (3) excellence. 'Publicness' means that all pedagogical practices should be transparent and open to colleagues, thereby making the classroom a public space. Moreover, anyone with any type of background should be appreciated as a protagonist of the school, which reflects a philosophy defined as 'democracy' as a type of community life (Dewey, 1916). Modern Japan is fiercely competitive from pressure under neoliberalism similar to the West (Harvey, 2005), and many pupils suffer from inequality due to the negative impacts of the increased economic gaps between haves and have-nots. LSLC aims to incorporate all pupils to improve their well-being. Lastly, excellence is underscored as a philosophical aspect of LSLC that defines learning as engagement in something of value, moving from the zone of proximal development today to the actual developmental level tomorrow (Vygotsky, 1978).

To realise its philosophy, LSLC comprises three activity components. Firstly, lessons should include 'collaborative learning', which is learning based on (1) children helping each other to understand class content so that every child participates in learning (Webb, 2013) and (2) courses with sufficient academic challenges and tasks to assure academic excellence and learning quality (Loughran, 2010). Secondly, schools must develop collegial and professional 'learning communities' among their teachers through teachers' observations of and reflections on each other's pedagogy (Sato, 2012b). As stated above, teachers should open their lessons to their colleagues at least once a year for observation and reflection, and about 50–100 observational sessions should occur throughout the academic year. The third component is 'local participation', which is defined as the engagement of as many parents and community residents as possible in the learning process as learners and/or resources (Sato, 2012b). Participation and appreciation by parents and residents foster community endorsement of LSLC for the school as an effective way to reform education and promote mutual trust and collaboration for nurturing pupils (Sato, 2012b).

Case 1 LSLC and Social Studies

Fukutani's chapter in *Changing a School* (2003) focuses on third-year pupils in her social studies course. The course included a unit named 'Shopping in the City', which was taught in three parts: (1) preparation of and cooking with curry, (2) planning a vegetable shop, and (3) operating a vegetable shop.

Preparation of and cooking with curry. In the first part of the unit, the pupils visited the local market and purchased the ingredients to make curry. The preparation began at home with their parents' help, such as daily checking the price of potatoes and learning how to cook with curry in their families' ways. The pupils went to the shops to buy the ingredients and some of the parents volunteered to go with them. On a different day, the pupils and their parents cooked the curry together (the parental participation rate exceeded 80%), and fathers, as well as mothers, participated in the cooking. Throughout the process, the parents who participated expressed a high degree of satisfaction with the experience.

After the cooking lesson, the pupils participated in a group reflection session in another class about their observations during shopping. One pupil, Mariko, reflected on her experience from the producers instead of the consumers' or sellers' perspective based on the series of lessons. Mariko's parents were farmers and she was familiar with her parents' work. Moreover, there were many farmers near the school. Therefore, Ms. Fukutani designed follow-up lessons to include the operation of a vegetable shop at the school for one day with the help of Mariko's family. Ms. Fukutani's goal was to allow the pupils to look again at their environments, such as the nearby paddies fields and plastic greenhouses that the pupils must have seen every day while commuting to school.

Planning the vegetable shop. When Ms. Fukutani proposed to open a vegetable shop with actual production and sales, the pupils were excited and embraced the idea. To develop the design and plan of their shop, the pupils revisited the shops they wanted to use as models. The parents participated in those visits as chaperones. Because of their previous parental participation experiences, the pupils and the parents smoothly communicated with each other.

However, opening and operating a shop also was a new experience for Ms. Fukutani. After revisiting the shops, the pupils sorted out their observations in discussions and the parent volunteers facilitated the process. Based on the results of the discussions, Ms. Fukutani consulted with Mariko's parents, who referred her to six farm families. Then, Ms. Fukutani divided the class into six groups, each of which would be in charge of a type of produce: roses, cherry tomatoes, scallions, spinach, colza (rapeseed), and tomatoes. Then, the pupils and parents negotiated with the farmers to set the purchase prices and the methods of transport.

The pupils developed various ideas for marketing the shop. They created professional-looking flyers that explained the benefits of the produce and had statements from the farmers. Based on their earlier observations, the pupils designed posters for display in front of the shop with messages from and pictures of the farmers that were similar to the ones in the supermarkets. The parents participated in the overall design of the shop and one grandparent proposed various ideas to support the preparation, stating, 'Since you are working so hard, I also thought hard about what I can do... Please, everyone, keep going working. Let's open a good shop' (Fukutani, 2003, p. 171).

Opening the shop. On that first day of the vegetable shop, Mariko's parents brought the produce by car, and the pupils worked hard to prepare for the opening. The pupils developed various strategies to sell their vegetables, by collaborating with each other. The shop was a success—all of the produce was sold—and the pupils strived to do so because they knew how much the farmers were dedicated to producing their products. The pupils reported to the farmers about their experiences selling the produce, and the farmers expressed their appreciation of the pupils' efforts. As a result, the children were more knowledgeable about prices and fresh produce, and their interest in the topic was stronger than before the experience.

Case 2 Reading Poetry

In *Challenges Undertaken by Teachers* (Sato, 2003), Ms. Naito taught a unit on reading poetry aloud to a group. Ms. Naito chose this unit to encourage parental participation in a lesson and because she was interested in and enjoyed reading poetry aloud. Ms. Naito began reading poetry 10 years earlier at a workshop of a self-learning group, and, since then, she had used what she had learned there to enjoy reading poetry with her pupils. These pedagogical practices were opened to the parents to include them and local residents in poetry appreciation.

The relatively small class of 20 pupils was divided into two groups to read different poems as outlined in the lesson. The mothers read aloud a poem entitled 'Festival'. This poem is based on the phrases used when carrying a portable shrine, and the mothers read the poem like a chorus. Their reading was overwhelming and vivid, and all of the pupils were excited to listen to it. Starting the next day, the pupils also began reading 'Festival' because they were very inspired by the mothers' reading of the poem. All of the parents participating in the lesson noted that it was fun to read poems aloud and that it was important to collaborate with other parents in the lessons (Sato, 2003).

The next year, parental participation further developed in a different unit on integrated studies that investigated local trash issues. For the fieldwork and discussions, volunteer parents participated with groups of pupils as assistant facilitators. Sato (2003) pointed out significant changes in the parents' attitudes towards participating in their children's education. At the beginning of the process, the parents were anxious about whether they would be accepted just being in the classroom.

They slowly understood the meaning of participation and increased their trust in the teacher, the pupils, and their learning abilities. Sato (2003) concluded that their participation would help the school to be more open and its educational processes to be based on democratic partnerships.

Case 3 Unintended Benefits of Parental Participation

Sato (2012b) shared a case of one teacher's growth in *Reforming a School*. The teacher, Ms. Fukuda, spent the first 5 years of her teaching career at one school, and Sato observed her early career struggles and development. Ms. Fukuda's turning point occurred during her third year. A pupil in her class strongly refused to communicate, agree with, or understand her. Ms. Fukuda found the child's behaviours extremely problematic and stressful, and she decided that the mother's stress overflowed or was imposed onto the child, which was causing the behavioural problems.

Ms. Fukuda became very angry at the mother because of her pressure on her child, but one day, when Ms. Fukuda met with the mother, the mother tearfully pleaded with Ms. Fukuda about her difficulties. Since then, Ms. Fukuda was able to unconditionally accept the mother. Then, Ms. Fukuda changed her teaching style in that she struggled less to understand the pupils and started to accept and receive each child, connect the ideas, emotions, or thoughts found in their murmurs and meaningfully organise their learning together.

Sato (2012b) observed Ms. Fukuda during her first 5 years of teaching and recognised this change as influential on her entire professional practice. When she learned how and accepted the mother, Ms. Fukuda was able to extend her empathy to embrace each child and understand their backgrounds and contexts that she observed reflected in the classroom. Thus, a mother of one pupil played a significant part in helping Ms. Fukuda recognise what it means to be a teacher.

15.4 Analysis

The following analysis focuses on comparisons of the three cases described above. The following four themes on parental participation and roles are discussed: (1) learners, (2) resources, (3) endorsers, and (4) catalysts.

15.4.1 Learners

Particularly in Cases 1 and 2, the parents participated in the learning process with the pupils. In Case 1, parents described their experiences as, according to Sato (2003), 'parents were also saying in the reflective notes, "we would like to participate in any other opportunities to learn together with the pupils"' Fukutani (2003, p. 166). In Case 2, a parent described the experience as, 'I would like to reiterate that a poem is wonderful!' (Sato, 2003, p. 148). They enjoyed the learning content, appreciated the poems and/or reflected on their lives in more detail from the pupils' fresh perspectives.

The time that they spent learning with their parents also influenced the pupils. The parental role tended to be supervisory when they studied at home, and parental participation at school was an opportunity for them to observe their parents learning and enjoying the processes. Their parents' participation impressed the pupils regarding their parents' maturity and it inspired them to learn more deeply about the content of the unit. This was particularly evident in Case 2 when the pupils were inspired by their mothers' poetry reading (Sato, 2003). Fukutani (2003) mentioned the parents' attitudes during the planning process because the parents were also thinking: usually, the parents tended to teach only but in the process, they were thinking hard together with the pupils as learners.

15.4.2   Resources

The parents were resources in the classroom. In Case 1, it is clear that Mariko's parents enriched the curriculum by providing information, materials, and further resources (other farmers). Their contributions deepened the authenticity of the experience by showing the ways that professionals work, which increased the depth of the pupils' learning experience (Darling-Hammond, 2008). Moreover, the other parents that participated in the unit guided the pupils' learning as resources. Their expertise and professionalism, along with their parental interactions, changed the pupils' and the teacher's perspectives.

For example, when they opened the shop, Mariko's parents supplied the vegetables, and the teacher noticed that they had put some water with them to keep them fresh, which she previously had not done. The pupils and the teacher learned that 'the producers pay attention to such details, which many customers would not notice' (Fukutani, 2003, p. 173). Besides, in the process of planning the shop, one student (Kenji) did not listen to other students' opinions and tried to promote his ideas. Kenji's mother immediately intervened to direct him to listen to others' ideas. Ms. Fukutani stated, 'this is a mother's real power. Her way of guiding children is great and this was a precious opportunity for me to learn from her' (Fukutani, 2003, pp. 168–169).

15.4.3   Endorsers

Being an 'endorser' means supporting, encouraging, and promoting the reform pedagogies that LSLC teachers aim to implement. Endorsing emerges out of the deeper understanding that develops through participation in the teaching and learning process, particularly demonstrated in Cases 1 and 2. In both cases, the parents began to expand their support for the LSLC pedagogy, which was expressed by a parent who participated in Case 2: 'In comparison with the ordinary parental lesson observations, we could have a much closer look at the children and it was really good' (Sato, 2003, p. 148).

Parents' endorsements might lead to new governance in their schools. In other words, although discussions on school governance have tended to be about who serves on school governing boards and what they do on the boards (Ehren, Honingh, Hooge, & O'Hara, 2015), a key mission of education is learning and learning orientation is an important issue. By experiencing the actual learning process as participants, and by endorsing the reform pedagogical orientation (LSLC), participating parents govern the most important part of the mission of their schools—learning. This relationship is beyond the 'server-client' educational models under the neo-liberal worldview because it is an equal partnership between parents and teachers to support the growth and development of the pupils in the best possible way (Sato, 2012b).

15.4.4 Catalysts

The parents who participated in the teaching and learning processes were catalysts that inspired changes in the perspectives of the teachers and pupils regarding the content and the relationships. The mother in Case 3 was a catalyst for Ms. Fukuda, and, in this sense, she participated in the pedagogical practices. This mother did not participate in learning, function as a resource, or endorse the practices. However, she played a significant part in Ms. Fukuda's reassessments of and changes to her teaching style. Even amid a struggle, parents can unintentionally help teachers to reflect, revisit, and change their teaching practices when the teachers are sincerely seeking or unexpectedly understanding the meaning of signals from parents that the teachers might not otherwise notice.

15.5 Discussion

This chapter investigates three cases of parental participation in pedagogical practices in Japan. Four parental roles regarding their participation were identified: (1) learners, (2) resources, (3) endorsers, and (4) catalysts. In these cases, the teachers had positive results from actively involving parents in their classrooms. This was particularly evident in Cases 1 and 2. In contrast, Ms. Fukuda, the teacher in Case 3, was apprehensive about interacting with the parent because she believed that the child's problems originated at home, especially at the initial stage of her relationships with the pupil and mother (Zhao & Akiba, 2009). Ms. Fukuda considered this parent to be the cause of the problems because of her exhaustion (Lemmer & van Wyk, 2004). However, Ms. Fukuda changed her attitude towards the mother when she understood the mother's situation, which suggests a possible way to educate teachers about collaborating with parents at the pre-service and in-service levels (Hornby & Witte, 2010).

The Japanese cases in this study on LSLC are different from studies conducted in other East Asian countries. Compared to the Chinese case (Lau et al., 2011), the parents in Cases 1 and 2 enjoyed participating in their schools. Different from the selective and appropriated participation of Korean parents in the USA (Lee, 2005), the parents in Cases 1 and 2 participated when they were invited and eventually increased their participation in the learning activities. The parents in Cases 1 and 2 participated on behalf of their children and for themselves rather than as a way to develop the academic and psychological aspects of their children as was the Greek case (Antonopoulou et al., 2010). In Japan, the parents in Cases 1 and 2 enjoyed the processes and learning.

Consequently, in the cases, academic achievement was not necessarily the benchmark used to measure the value of parental participation, contrary to the approach taken by Lau et al. (2011) and Park and Holloway (2013). Participation in Cases 1 and 2 helped the children to positively understand their parents' participation, which is a major difference from the previous studies' use of indicators of performance (Clinton & Hattie, 2013).

Further, LaRocque et al. (2011) found that several factors affected the parental participation in the cases above; initially, not all of the parents were completely comfortable, but the more they participated and learned together, the more comfortable and inspired they became. As Deslandes and Bertrand (2005) previously had pointed out, parents tended to feel more invited and responsible to the schools as they participated. Also, the teachers in the cases presented herein worked to reach out to the parents, which increased parental involvement (Park & Holloway, 2013). However, the parents learned new things and increased their understanding of their children and their educations, which might have encouraged further parental participation. In this sense, these three cases are similar to Radu's (2013) finding that parents' openness to communication depended on the extent of their engagement with their children's education, although they were not necessarily focused on their academic scores and, instead, emphasised the quality of learning.

15.6   Conclusion

The cases presented in this paper are from published sources about teaching and learning at the primary educational level. Further investigations are needed for parental participation at higher educational levels. There are some studies about parental supervisions at home for secondary students (Goodall & Montgomery, 2013; Park & Holloway, 2013). However, for investigations in secondary education, significantly more attention is being paid to the pedagogical practices inside the classrooms like the interactions between pupils and teachers. In LSLC, parental participation is an indispensable element (Sato, 2012b), and, hence, there should be more studies on this phenomenon at the secondary level.

References

Antonopoulou, K., Koutrouba, K., & Babalis, T. (2010). Parental involvement in secondary education schools: the views of parents in Greece. *Educational Studies, 37*(3), 333–344. https://doi.org/10.1080/03055698.2010.506332.

Clinton, J., & Hattie, J. (2013). New Zealand students' perceptions of parental involvement in learning and schooling. *Asia Pacific Journal of Education, 33*(3), 324–337. https://doi.org/10.1080/02188791.2013.786679.

Darling-Hammond, L. (2008). Creating schools that develop understanding. In L. Darling-Hammond (Ed.), *Powerful learning: what we know about teaching for understanding* (1st ed., pp. 193–211). San Francisco, CA: Jossey-Bass.

Deslandes, R., & Bertrand, R. (2005). Motivation of parent involvement in secondary-level schooling. *The Journal of Educational Research, 98*(3), 164–175. https://doi.org/10.3200/joer.98.3.164-175.

Dewey, J. (1916). *Democracy and education: An introduction to the philosophy of education.* New York: The Macmillan company.

Ehren, M. C. M., Honingh, M. E., Hooge, E. H., & O'Hara, J. (2015). Changing school board governance in primary education through school inspections. *Educational Management Administration & Leadership, 44*(2), 205–223. https://doi.org/10.1177/1741143214549969.

Fukutani, H. (2003). By doing lessons together with parents, children changed. In T. Ose & M. Sato (Eds.), *Changing a school* (pp. 164–177). Tokyo: Shogakkan.

Goodall, J., & Montgomery, C. (2013). Parental involvement to parental engagement: a continuum. *Educational Review, 66*(4), 399–410. https://doi.org/10.1080/00131911.2013.781576.

Harvey, D. (2005). *A brief history of neoliberalism.* Oxford: Oxford University Press.

Hornby, G., & Witte, C. (2010). A survey of parental involvement in middle schools in New Zealand. *Pastoral Care in Education, 28*(1), 59–69. https://doi.org/10.1080/02643940903540363.

Kariya, T. (2001). *Kaisoka nihon to kyoiku kiki [Stratified Japan and educational crisis].* Tokyo: Yushindo.

LaRocque, M., Kleiman, I., & Darling, S. M. (2011). Parental involvement: The missing link in school achievement. *Preventing School Failure: Alternative Education for Children and Youth, 55*(3), 115–122. https://doi.org/10.1080/10459880903472876.

Lau, E. Y. H., Li, H., & Rao, N. (2011). Parental involvement and children's readiness for school in China. *Educational Research, 53*(1), 95–113. https://doi.org/10.1080/00131881.2011.552243.

Lee, S. (2005). Selective parent participation: Structural and cultural factors that influence school participation among Korean parents. *Equity & Excellence in Education, 38*(4), 299–308. https://doi.org/10.1080/10665680500299734.

Lemmer, E., & van Wyk, N. (2004). Schools reaching out: Comprehensive parent involvement in south African primary schools. *Africa Education Review, 1*(2), 259–278. https://doi.org/10.1080/18146620408566284.

Loughran, J. (2010). *What expert teachers do: enhancing professional knowledge for classroom practice.* London & New York: Routledge.

Mncube, V. (2010). Parental involvement in school activities in South Africa to the mutual benefit of the school and the community. *Education as Change, 14*(2), 233–246. https://doi.org/10.1080/16823206.2010.522061.

Morgan, V., Fraser, G., Dunn, S., & Cairns, E. (1992). Parental involvement in education: How do parents want to become involved? *Educational Studies, 18*(1), 11–20. https://doi.org/10.1080/0305569920180102.

Park, S., & Holloway, S. D. (2013). No parent left behind: Predicting parental involvement in adolescents' education within a sociodemographically diverse population. *The Journal of Educational Research, 106*(2), 105–119. https://doi.org/10.1080/00220671.2012.667012.

Radu, R. (2013). School-based parental involvement: A comparative assessment of predictors of satisfaction in south-east Europe. *Educational Studies, 39*(2), 167–182. https://doi.org/10.1080/03055698.2012.702891.

Saito, E., & Atencio, M. (2015). Lesson study for learning community (LSLC): Conceptualising teachers' practices within a social justice perspective. *Discourse: Studies in the Cultural Politics of Education, 36*(6), 795–807. https://doi.org/10.1080/01596306.2014.968095.

Saito, E., & Sato, M. (2012). Lesson study as an instrument for school reform. *Management in Education, 26*(4), 181–186. https://doi.org/10.1177/0892020612445101.

Saito, E., Watanabe, M., Gillies, R., Someya, I., Nagashima, T., Sato, M., & Murase, M. (2015). School reform for positive behaviour support through collaborative learning: Utilising lesson study for a learning community. *Cambridge Journal of Education, 45*(4), 489–518. https://doi.org/10.1080/0305764x.2014.988684.

Sato, M. (2003). *Kyoshitachi no chosen [Challenges taken up by the teachers]*. Tokyo: Shogakkan.

Sato, M. (2012a). *Gakko kenbunroku [School visit records]*. Tokyo: Shogakkan.

Sato, M. (2012b). *Gakko wo kaikaku suru (Reforming a school)*. Tokyo: Iwanami Shoten.

Snell, P., Miguel, N., & East, J. (2009). Changing directions: Participatory action research as a parent involvement strategy. *Educational Action Research, 17*(2), 239–258. https://doi.org/10.1080/09650790902914225.

Uzuki, Y., & Suetomi, K. (2015). The effects of childhood poverty on academic achievement and study habits. *Bulletin of National Institute of Education Policy, 144*, 125–140.

Vygotsky, L. S. (1978). *Mind in society: The development of higher psychological processes (V. M. Cole, John-Steiner, S. Scribner, & E. Souberman, Trans.)*. Cambridge, MA: Harvard University Press.

Webb, N. M. (2013). Information processing approaches to collaborative learning. In C. E. Hmelo-Silver, C. A. Chinn, C. K. K. Chan, & A. O'Donnell (Eds.), *The international handbook of collaborative learning* (pp. 19–40). New York, NY: Routledge.

Zhao, H., & Akiba, M. (2009). School expectations for parental involvement and student mathematics achievement: A comparative study of middle schools in the US and South Korea. *Compare: A Journal of Comparative and International Education, 39*(3), 411–428. https://doi.org/10.1080/03057920701603347.

Chapter 16
Educational Neoliberalism and the Annexation of Literacy: A Cautionary Tale in the Asia-Pacific Context

Niranjan Casinader and Ayub Sheik

Abstract One of the key facets of educational globalisation has been the increasing diffusion of learning programmes based on 'Western' principles, whether this is in the context of school curriculum frameworks, educational policy, or standalone 'international education programmes' (Casinader, Culture, transnational education and thinking: Case studies in global schooling, 2014). This has included the adoption of Euro-American concepts of literacy, ostensibly preparing people to participate in and receive the benefits of the globalised economy.

Within this transition, the regard for existing local systems of education has been limited; principles of 'Western' education have been promoted as inevitably intellectually superior and dominant. Whilst the promotion of global literacy through organisations such as the United Nations recognises the multiplicities of literacy (Parr and Campbell, International Review of Education, 58(4), 557–574, 2012) that exist, this process has also seen the constriction of notions of literacy (Bartlett, International Journal of Educational Development, 28(6), 737–753, 2008) into a Euro-American framework. This chapter seeks to critique the ways in which 'Western' notions of capitalism and rationalism have influenced the direction and intentions of global literacy initiatives, arguing that, instead of liberating people from socio-economic captivity, they contribute to a loss of the cultural identity embedded in local forms of knowledge and literacy.

Keywords Literacy · Asia-Pacific · Neoliberal education · Globalisation · United Nations Conventions · Multiple literacies

N. Casinader (✉)
Monash University, Melbourne, Australia
e-mail: niranjan.casinader@monash.edu

A. Sheik
University of Kwazulu-Natal, Durban, South Africa

© Springer Nature Singapore Pte Ltd. 2021
D. Bao, T. Pham (eds.), *Transforming Pedagogies Through Engagement with Learners, Teachers and Communities*, Education in the Asia-Pacific Region: Issues, Concerns and Prospects 57, https://doi.org/10.1007/978-981-16-0057-9_16

16.1 Introduction

Over the last two decades, there has been growing agreement amongst the international community that the empowerment of people on the margins of socio-economic opportunity depends ultimately on their level of literacy. As a result, assisted by the imprimatur of the United Nations Literacy Decade in 2003–2012, and UNESCO's Literacy for Education (LIFE) Programme, which targets the 35 countries with 85% of the world's illiterate people, there has been a salient improvement in patterns of global literacy. Between 2002 and 2011, multilateral aid expended on global education increased by more than 75%. In the period 1990–2011, the percentage of adult literacy improved from 75.87 to 84.1%, with women's literacy increasing from 69.4 to 79.9% (UNESCO Institute of Statistics, 2013).

Within the Asia-Pacific, however, the position has been more dichotomous. Although Central Asia, East Asia, and the Pacific were all recording literacy rates well above 90%, the regions of South and West Asia remained at the opposite end of the spectrum, with average illiteracy rates of over 50% (UNESCO Institute of Statistics, 2013). Such a mixed set of achievements highlights a duality in the impact of contemporary globalisation on matters of global literacy. On the one hand, the process has facilitated the formation of a global drive to raise the individual and collective power of individuals and communities, as they attempt to gain some control over their lives. However, the processes of educational globalisation have also constricted the dimensions of this worldwide engagement with illiteracy, guiding the movement into a unidimensional reality that has been framed by the neo-liberalisation of global outlooks. As such, the question as to the type of literacy that needs to be developed in the modern global context remains one of warranted contention.

At the commencement of the United Nations Literacy Decade, the view of literacy presented by UNESCO through its focus on the Education for All initiative (UNESCO, 2006), as an agent of change, appeared to be inclusive of the more dynamic and broader interpretation of the concept that had emerged. Rather than being restricted to the more traditional notion of it being an autonomous entity, or a set of skills to be acquired as a universal set (Bartlett, 2008; Papen, 2005), an understanding of literacy as being a more comprehensive and nuanced entity appeared to prevail. The concept was seen through four differing perspectives: as being autonomous; as applied situated learning, guided by its functional application; as text; and, more significantly in the context of this chapter, as an ideological concept that took into account the socio-cultural environment in which it was practised (Bartlett, 2008; UNESCO, 2006). From this last perspective, literacy was, and is, a reflection of a truly democratic form of education (Dei & Shahjahan, 2008), one that respects and utilises the lives of people in varying contexts.

In contrast, however, globalisation, as exemplified by the part that it has played in the neo-liberalisation of global education, has promoted a vision and actuality of literacy that is starkly at odds with the empowerment of the individual. Although globalisation is now accepted to be a multi-faceted phenomenon (Alexander, 2001; Appadurai, 1996; Giddens, 2003), the power of its economic face has directed a progressively narrowed global conception of human development. Over the last quarter-century, countries from outside the Euro-American sphere, such as China, Singapore, India, Brazil, and Korea, have increasingly adopted the 'Western' conception of industrialised development as the path to national prosperity. Even though some have made a conscious effort to retain some sense of local cultural identity in that process, such as Singapore (Kumar, 2013), Korea (Republic of Korea, 2013), and Malaysia (Ministry of Education Malaysia, 2012), the need to frame education and literacy programmes in a form that supports modernisation in alignment with the 'Western' philosophical contour has inevitably led to a contraction of the notion of global literacy as a socio-cultural construction. It has been placed into a Euro-American framework that aims to prepare people for active participation in a global community that, more and more, promotes 'Western' notions of democracy and socio-economic development as the only path to success.

This is not to say that global literacy programmes should ignore the skills of empowerment required to make the most of the socio-economic opportunities that can be provided by globalisation. The growing power of English as the language of global commerce has been reflected in the decision by some states such as Malaysia (Ministry of Education Malaysia, 2012) and South Africa (Department of Basic Education South Africa, 1997) to develop multi-lingual policies of language education, with a focus on English as a desirable global economic competency. These have been designed to provide its citizens with the capacity for global communication and participation whilst, at the same time, retaining the significance of local language(s), and therefore, cultural identities. However, the depth of this tapering of global literacy programmes in practice has been significant, if not always clearly observable. The utilitarian concept of literacy in the 'Western' idiom has been reinforced also by the increasing global acceptance of the relevance of international testing and comparison testing programmes such as PISA (Programme for International Student Assessment) and TIMSS (Trends in International Mathematics and Science Study), which, despite stated principles of cultural neutrality, are framed essentially around Euro-American conceptions of thinking and education (Casinader, 2013, 2014). The underpinning trope of these 'objective' international comparisons is based on the assumption that 'literacy' is a universal concept that is independent of culture and therefore measured by the same principles, regardless of location. However, as Bartlett (2008, p. 739) points out, the very common definition of literacy in quantitative development studies as being able to 'read and write' not only assumes a Euro-American concept of a functional society but is also rarely accompanied by any reference to the language being used in the comparison, with the underlying implication that the vehicle of communication has to be English if literacy is to have any international currency in its data comparability.

16.2 Discourse on the Topic

Since the last two decades of the twentieth century, the pace of social change and the transformation of national, regional, and global economies has accelerated without precedent. This transformation can be attributed to the formation of growing inter-connections and capitalistic relationships amongst peoples and nations of the world, and is a distinctive feature of globalisation, amidst a multitude of signifiers. The phenomenon of globalisation has seen the rise of an increasingly dominant social imaginary that casts the world as a single, interdependent market, one that facilitates the free flow of capital and resources (Giddens, 2003).

As such, globalisation is characterised by a deep ambivalence and contestation, which sees it both as a driver of cultural and economic disenfranchisement and as a catalyst for global movements such as transnational social activism, emancipation, and ecological sensitivity. For instance, amongst others, Korten (2001) has not only reinforced the view of globalisation possessing discernible political and economic traits that are intrinsically bound to 'Western' cultural imperialism, but that it is advanced by an alliance between the world's largest corporations and the most powerful governments. This coalition is fuelled by global patterns of financial capital flows (Appadurai, 2006), its defining project being to integrate the world's national economies into a borderless global system that, in the ultimate acknowledgement of Euro-American principles, prizes the optimisation of profit and a guarantee of assets and investments above all else. This study contributes to the growing body of literature that serves as a counter-discourse to global capital and neoliberal imper-atives that project dependence as independence, vulnerability as autonomy, manip-ulation as emancipation, and how these are tied to English language hegemony and literacy. This gap, therefore, constitutes a warrant for this study.

16.3 Methodology

This study owes a factual and interpretive debt to Arshadn-Ayers, Harvey, Apperdurai, and Round amongst others. Its argument is premised against neoliberal assumptions of literacy and the debilitating effect of global capital. This is elaborated by a neo-Marxist consideration of the machinations of global capital and its con-comitant effect on literacies situated at the periphery of economic concentration and power.

The rationale that motivates this study derives from the notion that 'Western' capitalism and rationalism embedded in globalisation have unduly prejudiced the direction and intentions of global literacy initiatives in favour of its insular interests. Instead of liberating people from socio-economic bondage, they have contributed to a loss of cultural identity embedded in local forms of knowledge and education by restricting global literacy to initiatives in basic education of a pre-determined type. To elucidate this claim, this chapter looks at globalisation and the capitalistic overreach that economically, culturally, and educationally, paradoxically impoverishes the very communities it purports to help by perpetuating literacies that sustain economic subjugation and intellectual disenfranchisement. This is achieved by a critique of liberal education and globalisation and a rebuttal of neoliberal forms of literacies cloaked as opportunity and empowerment.

16.4 Main Discussion

The resultant reconstitution of space and time, and its concomitant de-territorialisation of the nation-state (Appadurai, 1996; Papastergiadis, 2000), has seen the enactment of universal policies and practices that not only subsume regional ways of being but also exacerbate inequalities that are tied to disproportionate access to technology and capital. Consequently, the relationships between nation-states have been affected by the increasing influence of transnational corporations, as well as the contractual obligations that have arisen from debt repayment management and other agendas of national development. The master narrative that feeds this process is that of neoliberal economics, for it is an intellectual, social, and political perspective that shifts State imperatives from an ostensible pursuit towards the public good towards a set of contractual norms organised around the procurement of profit and the expansion of market share. Resistance to these entrepreneurial overtures by local communities that have felt that their way of life and interests to be threatened has been ameliorated through frequent co-option of the local political elite, as well as members of the groups previously excluded from participation into that community, into a new hegemonic bloc that 'represents' the face of the people. Such a distinctive *modus operandi* has been evident in various parts of the Global 'South', particularly on the African continent. In East Asia, one of the more extreme global examples can be seen in North Korea (the Democratic People's Republic of Korea). In such cases, the nation-state, with its monopoly on the assumption of legality through control of military and political force, has been a guarantor of the power relations and financial discipline expected of States and people located at the periphery.

The quest for capitalistic accumulation has been also accompanied by political and ideological globalisation to consolidate this form of neo-imperialism. A prime driver of political and ideological globalisation is the worldwide utility of, and access to, information, a process made possible by the ongoing electronic revolution. The logic of self-referencing modernity is carried to all parts of the planet by new information and communication technologies, and is implicated in what may be termed 'cultural modernism'. The subsequent cosmopolitan spaces that are created can be seen as the expression of 'Western' cultural hegemony, wherein a growing consumer base valorises Euro-American capitalistic conventions at the expense of their cultural heritage, knowledge systems, and ways of being. The pressure to conform to the universally promoted convention is relentless, so persistently in play that even some Asian nation-states that have attempted to maintain local cultural integrity in the face of a 'westernised' platform have been forced to reassess. Such has been the case with Malaysia, where the efforts to establish Bahasa Malay as the language of education since Independence have had to be modified in the face of the reality that participation in the globalised economy requires a more inclusive approach to the learning of English (Ministry of Education Malaysia, 2012). It was a choice borne out of practicability, not one of freely chosen cultural imperative.

It can be argued that the credo of neoliberal globalism, which puts forward the inevitability that everyone will be advantaged by an embracement of its philosophies and practices, can be seen largely as a contradiction in terms. The reality of globalisation is that there are an increasing polarisation and inequities in the social, economic, and political circumstances of peoples' lives (Alexander, 2001; Round, 2010); assumptions of the 'trickle-down' effect have been exaggerated. What it has achieved, however, is an exacerbation of existing socio-economic inequality by producing a crisis of chronic capital over-accumulation, thereby feeding the impulses to absorb surplus by imperialistic expansion, or face the consequences of crisis and deflation (Harvey, 2005, p. 97). It is pertinent that a former director of the World Trade Organisation (WTO) explained the organisation's agenda thus:

'More than ever before, trade and the rules of trade intersect with a broad array of other policies and issues—from investment and competition policy to environmental, development, health and labour standards. . . if we want real coherence in global policymaking and a comprehensive international agenda, then coordination has to come from the top, and it must be driven by elected leaders. . . progress in resolving the challenge of the new century will hinge on our ability not just to build a coherent architecture, but to build a political constituency for globalization. . . without the WTO, we will go back to a world of national barriers, protectionism, economic nationalism, and conflict' (Ruggerio, 2000, p. xv).

Unfortunately, this architecture, based on the principles of supposed economic efficiencies, and unregulated control in commodity production, has also become the regulatory framework for literacy in educational programmes. According to Arshad-Ayaz (2008), the neoliberal economic rationality embodied by globalisation has framed the restructuring of education in such a manner that its function has changed, moving from the production of knowledge and skills to the management and maintenance of wealth. Thus, public education is being increasingly influenced by corporate and market forces, a decentralised industrial relations agenda, and heightened levels of managerial control.

This commodification of education has encouraged the utilisation of an institutionally sanctioned form of literacy that consciously marginalises indigenous languages and literacy practices in favour of global imperatives, notwithstanding the fact that, at its most basic level, functional literacy skills in an individual's own language are the gateway to the empowerment of global citizenry. Amongst others, Street (2001) has drawn attention to the causal links made between literacy and economic development that are prominent in relevant national and international discourses. However, it is questionable to what degree literacy programmes are liberating people from socio-economic disadvantage (Freire et al., 1998) if they merely replicate the principles and values of the society that created their positional reality in the first place. Instead, literacy and other areas of education 'must be [an] instrument[s] of transforming action, a political praxis at the service of permanent human liberation. This, let us repeat, does not happen only in the consciousness of people, but presupposes a radical change of structures, in which process consciousness will itself be transformed' (Freire, 1985, p.140).

Under the UN Convention of Human Rights and UN Convention on the Rights of the Child, literacy is defined as a 'human right', critical to the social emancipation of peoples of the world. One gains perspective from the fact that globally, one in five adults cannot read nor write. Approximately 776 million people are illiterate, and two-thirds of these are women (Swiniarksi & Breitborde, 2003), highlighting the extreme nature of global gender-based polarisations. Whilst the situation in Asia is, by and large, much better than these global averages, with many countries possessing 95% + adult literacy rates, such generalisations hide some of the extreme exceptions that exist; for example, Pakistan, with only 54% literacy rates (42% for women), and Timor Leste with 58.3% adult literacy compared with 53% for women (Asian Development Bank, 2014, p. 158). However, literacy approaches that promote a 'human rights' culture can meet resistance when it is viewed as running counter to the educational agendas of governments and multinational corporations (Papen, 2005), which frequently label human rights advocates as 'subversive' or 'leftist' (Brabeck and Rogers, 2000). Thus, it becomes clear that dominant notions of what it means to be 'literate' serve to shape and marginalise identities through the grand narratives of capitalistic globalisation.

Another example of this constriction in the conception of literacy can be seen in the area of critical thinking and problem-solving skills, capacities that are now viewed by some as being encompassed within literacy education. The disconnect has been accentuated by the tendency to regard these dimensions of literacy from a Euro-American perspective, based on the long-established tendency in the literature to see critical thinking and problem-solving skills as uniquely 'Western' constructs of civilisation (for example, Dahl, 2010; Lipman, 2003). Within this highly skewed framework, the capacity to problem solve is very much associated with the individualistic and linear roots of Euro-American society, and yet, it is often treated as being culturally universal, despite emerging evidence that how problem-solving and other thinking skills are conceived and enacted does vary with cultural outlook (Casinader, 2014; Nisbett, 2003; Singh, 2013). Consequently, instead of emphasising the breadth of empowerment that would be generated by a more culturally comprehensive approach to literacy education, literacy initiatives are more focused on the thinking approaches that are deemed to be central to the needs of the modern globalised economy, at the expense of the inclusion and harnessing of the strengths inherent in local, more holistic forms of analysis and problem-solving. The development of Euro-American forms of thinking within literacy programmes has been promoted at the expense of local idioms.

16.5   Implications

In aiming to buttress this focus on the needs of a globalised workforce, the deeply contextual and cultural character of literacy is, more often than not, relegated to a status of incidental importance. Instead, what has emerged is a preoccupation with 'outcomes', predicated on concerns with quality, cost-benefit analyses, efficiency, and the advent of line managers to oversee educators, as well as the learning programmes that they implement and administer. When market mechanisms are preferred over democratic structures in education, plans for access, equity, and transformation are inhibited to ensure compliance with a global economic agenda that frowns on incompatibilities.

Attendant to this is the fact that, whilst knowledge transfer from the Global 'North' into the Global 'South' is intended to improve the skills and capabilities of its recipients, it also inadvertently shapes the outlook, value, and behaviour of those involved. The consequence is that, whilst globalisation has led to the expansion of the skills, understandings, and attributes that constitute literacy (Parr & Campbell, 2012), policymakers and dominant societal discourses have continued, paradoxically, to emphasise a narrow conception of literacy, as a commodity tied to economic interest on the global level.

16.6   Conclusion

The seemingly unfettered proliferation of capitalism has led to globalisation becoming a dominant force in the twenty-first century. Given the inherent neoliberal quest for surplus-value, the idea of the 'free market' has permeated most aspects of social life, including the construction of citizens as human capital (Tarc, 2012, p.12). Such a phenomenon has been impossible to resist, for neoliberalism has the capacity to nullify anything that attempts to resist the logic of the 'pure market'. As an ideology and reality, it is difficult to combat, for it represents the coordinated actions of all the forces that hold prevailing positions (Bourdieu, 1998, cited in Stromquist, 2002, p. 6). This innate trait presents itself also in functional literacy programmes that are predicated on outcomes centred on the facilitation of individual efficiency and the ability to carry out '. . .obligations more effectively. . .' (Oxenham, 200, p. 7), in which programmes are focused upon '. . .the process and content of learning to read and write for the preparation for work and vocational training, as well as a means of increasing the productivity of the individual. . .' (Rassool, 1999, p. 7).

As part of this process, international funding agencies, such as the International Monetary Fund, the World Bank, and less so, the United Nations Educational and Cultural Organisation (UNESCO), have been able to steer the implementation of international policies in respect of literacy programmes through the utilisation of such measures as stipulations placed on loans and grants to emphasise standardisation, efficiency, and measures of productivity (Wickens & Sanlin,

2007, p. 288). In consequence, national governments, including the growing economies of the Asia-Pacific, most notably China and India, have felt divested of effective influence, the power for which now lies within the international agencies themselves. This perceived lack of regional agency from outside the Euro-American sphere was one of the driving forces behind in the creation in June 2015 of the China-led Asia Infrastructure Investment Bank (AIIB), established principally because the needs of low- and middle-income states in Asia were not being met by the old guard of global financial organisational managers such as the IMF. Arguably, it is these same organisations that de-emphasise social welfare programmes, including literacy, in the drive to extract the efficiencies that consolidate a neoliberal agenda. In essence, literacy education at the global scale is being seen as a fundamental political tool, with educational programmes being employed as a form of ongoing social governance, fostering deficit perspectives that perpetuate a particular form of oppression (Lankshear & Knobel, 2006; Luke, 2003a, 2003b). Whether the AIIB will provide a new fulcrum upon which to redress that imbalance remains to be seen, but the opportunity now exists for a revision of the global direction upon which past literacy efforts have been conceived.

One way in which this longstanding intellectual subjugation of more localised understandings of literacy has been manifested overtly can be observed in the manner in which official discourses on literacy have come to be colonised by the language of economics, taking its idioms and arguments from the language of management schools, business consultants, and financial journals (Collini, 2011). This view is corroborated by Street's notion of 'multiple literacies' (2001), which sees them as social practices that are essentially contested and framed in competing relations of power. It is moot, then, just whose literacies are dominant, and who are marginalised. The end result is that the potential of literacy as a medium of holistic education, one that is premised on a democratic value system and critical thinking, is diminished. Current literacy policies and practices are reducing people at the periphery to the roles of client and consumer, actors in a knowledge economy that is designed to overlook the development of the whole person in favour of making people 'better' in a neoliberal fashion, as economically 'efficient' and 'productive' workers. Disappointingly, the establishment of the AIIB does little to raise hopes for the future, as its notions of infrastructure priorities fall into the same mantras of conventional, 'westernised' industrialised growth as existing programmes, with a stated focus on '. . .energy and power, transportation and telecommunications, rural infrastructure and agriculture development, water supply and sanitation, environmental protection, urban development and logistics' (The Asian Infrastructure Development Bank, 2015). Such a reality is depressingly remote from literacy education processes that might promote lifelong learning and recognise cultural variation, enabling people and societies to be fully liberated, with genuinely democratic life possibilities.

References

Alexander, R. (2001). *Culture and pedagogy: International comparisons in primary education.* Oxford: Blackwell Publishers.

Appadurai, A. (1996). *Modernity at large: Cultural dimensions of globalization.* Minneapolis: University of Minnesota Press.

Appadurai, A. (2006). *Fear of small numbers: Am an essay on the geography of anger.* Durham: Duke University Press.

Arshad-Ayaz, A. (2008). From producing citizens to producing managers: Education in a global-ized world. In R. K. Hopson, C. Camp Yeakey, & F. Musa Boakari (Eds.), *Power, voice and the public good: Schooling and education in global societies* (*Advances in education in diverse communities*) (Vol. 6, pp. 479–506). Bingley: Emerald Group Publishing Limited. https://doi.org/10.1016/S1479-358X(08)06018-X

Asian Development Bank. (2014). *Key indicators for Asia and the Pacific 2014* (45th ed.). Mandaluyong City, Philippines: Asian Development Bank.

Bartlett, L. (2008). Literacy's verb: Exploring what literacy is and what literacy does. *International Journal of Educational Development, 28*(6), 737–753. https://doi.org/10.1016/j.ijedudev.2007.09.002.

Bourdieu, P. (1998). The essence of neoliberalism, *Le Monde Diplomatique* (Jeremy J. Shapiro, Trans.). https://mondediplo.com/1998/12/08bourdieu

Brabeck, M. M., & Rogers, L. (2000). Human rights as a moral issue: Lessons for moral educators from human rights work. *Journal of Moral Education, 29*(2), 167–182. https://doi.org/10.1080/713679341

Casinader, N. (2013). *Cultural dispositions of thinking: Some implications for teaching and learning.* Paper presented at the XVI ICPIC conference: Critical thinking, enquiry-based learning and philosophical enquiry in education, Cape Town, South Africa.

Casinader, N. (2014). *Culture, transnational education and thinking: Case studies in global schooling.* Milton Park, Abingdon: Routledge.

Collini, S. (2011). From Robbins to McKinsey. *London Review of Books, 33*(16), 9–14.

Dahl, M. (2010). *Failure to thrive in constructivism: A cross-cultural malady.* Rotterdam: Sense.

Dei, G. J. S., & Shahjahan, R. (2008). Equity and democratic education in Ghana: Towards a pedagogy of difference. In J. Zajda, L. Davies, & S. Majhanovich (Eds.), *Comparative and global pedagogies: Equity, access and democracy in education* (pp. 49–69). Dordrecht: Springer.

Department of Basic Education South Africa. (1997). *Language and education policy.* Pretoria: Republic of South Africa. Retrieved from http://www.education.gov.za/DocumentsLibrary/Policies/tabid/390/Default.aspx.

Freire, P. (1985). *Teachers as cultural workers: Letters to those who dare teach.* South Hadley: Westview Press.

Freire, P., Araújo, F. A. M., Macedo, D. P., Freire, A. M. A., & Macedo, D. (1998). *The Paulo Freire reader.* Continuum.

Giddens, A. (2003). *Runaway world.* New York: Routledge.

Harvey, D. (2005). *A brief history of neoliberalism.* Oxford: OUP.

Korten, D. (2001). *When corporations rule the world.* Bloomfield, CT: Berrett-Koehler Publishers/Kumarian Press.

Kumar, P. (2013). Bridging east and west educational divides in Singapore. *Comparative Education, 49*(1), 72–87. https://doi.org/10.1080/03050068.2012.740221.

Lankshear, C., & Knobel, M. (2006). Digital literacy and digital literacies: Policy, pedagogy and research considerations for education. *Digital Kompetanse, 1*(1), 12–24.

Lipman, M. (2003). *Thinking in education* (2nd ed.). New York: Cambridge University Press.

Luke, A. (2003a). Making literacy policy and practice with a difference. *Australian Journal of Language and Literacy, 26*(3), 58–82.

Luke, A. (2003b). Literacy and the other: A sociological approach to literacy research and policy in multilingual societies. *Reading Research Quarterly, 38*(1), 132–141.

Ministry of Education Malaysia. (2012). *Malaysia education blueprint 2013–25: Preliminary report*. Kuala Lumpur: Ministry of Educafion.

Nisbett, R. (2003). *The geography of thought: How Asians and westerners think differently...And why*. New York: The Free Press.

Papastergiadis, N. (2000). *The turbulence of migration: Globalization, deterritorialization and hybridity*. Cambridge: Polity Press.

Papen, U. (2005). Literacy and development: What works for whom? Or, how relevant is the social practices view of literacy for literacy education in developing countries? *International Journal of Educational Development, 25*(1), 5–17. https://doi.org/10.1016/j.ijedudev.2004.05.001.

Parr, M., & Campbell, T. A. (2012). Understanding literacy as our WORLD inheritance: Re-visioning literacy discourse and its implications for teaching practice. *International Review of Education, 58*(4), 557–574. https://doi.org/10.1007/s11159-012-9297-1.

Rassool, N. (1999). Literacy for sustainable development in the age of information (Ser. The language and education library, 14). Multilingual Matters.

Republic of Korea, Ministry of Education. (2013). *Education system: Overview*. Retrieved August 2, 2012, 2013, from http://english.moe.go.kr/web/1692/site/contents/en/en_0203.jsp

Round, J. I. (2010). Globalization, growth, inequality, and poverty in Africa: A macroeconomic perspective. In M. Nissanke & E. Thorbecke (Eds.), *The Poor under globalization in Asia, Latin America, and Africa*. Oxford Scholarship Online. https://doi.org/10.1093/acprof:oso/9780199584758.001.0001.

Ruggerio, R. (2000). Reflections from Seattle. In J. J. Schott (Ed.), *The WTO after Seattle* (pp. xiii–xvii). Washington, DC: Institute for International Economics.

Singh, M. (2013). Educational practice in India and its foundations in Indian heritage: A synthesis of the east and west? *Comparative Education, 49*(1), 88–106. https://doi.org/10.1080/03050068.2012.740222.

Street, B. V. (Ed.). (2001). *Literacy and development: Ethnographic perspectives*. London: Routledge.

Stromquist, N. P. (2002). *Education in a globalized world: The connectivity of economic power, technology, and knowledge*. Lanham: Rowan & Littlefield.

Swiniarksi, L. B., & Breitborde, M.-L. (2003). *Educating the global village: Including the young children in the world* (2nd ed.). Upper Saddle River, NJ: Merrill Prentice Hall.

Tarc, P. (2012). The uses of globalization in the (shifting) landscape of educational studies. *Canadian Journal of Education/Revue canadienne de l'éducation, 35*(3), 4–29.

The Asian Infrastructure Development Bank. (2015). *About us*. Retrieved July 6, 2015, From http://www.aiibank.org/html/aboutus/AIIB/

UNESCO. (2006). *Education for all: Literacy for life education for all monitoring report*. Paris: UNESCO.

UNESCO Institute of Statistics. (2013). *Adult and youth literacy: National, regional and global trends, 1985–2015 UIS Information Paper*. Montreal: UNESCO.

Wickens, C. M., & Sanlin, J. A. (2007). Literacy for what? Literacy for whom? The politics of literacy, education and neocolonialism in UNESCO and World Bank-sponsored literacy programs. *Adult Educational Quarterly, 57*(4), 275–292.